To Bill Pa_____

Birthday June 200_

From Charles A. Parnell, Jr.

Ernest Vandiver

GOVERNOR OF GEORGIA

Ernest
Vandiver

Governor of Georgia

HAROLD PAULK HENDERSON

THE UNIVERSITY OF GEORGIA PRESS
ATHENS AND LONDON

© 2000 by the University of Georgia Press
Athens, Georgia 30602
All rights reserved
Designed by Erin Kirk New
Set in 10 on 13 New Caledonia by G&S Typesetters
Printed and bound by Thomson-Shore
The paper in this book meets the guidelines for
permanence and durability of the Committee on
Production Guidelines for Book Longevity of the
Council on Library Resources.

Printed in the United States of America
04   03   02   01   00   C   5   4   3   2   1

Library of Congress Cataloging-in-Publication Data
Henderson, Harold Paulk, 1942–
      Ernest Vandiver, governor of Georgia / Harold Paulk Henderson.
          p. cm.
      Includes bibliographical references and index.
      ISBN 0-8203-2223-7 (alk. paper)
          1. Vandiver, S. Ernest (Samuel Ernest), 1918–   2. Governors—
Georgia—Biography.   3. Georgia—Politics and government—1951–
4. School integration—Georgia—History—20th century.   5. Georgia—
Race relations.   I. Title.
      F291.3.V36 H46 2000
      975.8′043′092—dc21
      [B]   00-036420

British Library Cataloging-in-Publication Data available

CONTENTS

PREFACE

Samuel Ernest Vandiver Jr. served as governor in turbulent times during which the state coped with its greatest crisis since the Civil War. During his administration, the state's effort to avoid school desegregation finally ended with the federal judiciary's ordering the admission of two black students to the University of Georgia. A staunch defender of segregation, gubernatorial candidate Vandiver had promised to close the state's public schools before allowing their desegregation. Despite his commitment to the racial status quo, however, the governor could not bring himself to carry out his promise and prevailed upon the legislature to repeal the state's massive-resistance legislation. As a result, black students peaceably desegregated formerly all-white schools in Atlanta. To his credit, Vandiver refused to defy the federal courts' desegregation mandates for the university and the Atlanta schools. While believing that his open-schools decision would end his political career, Vandiver nevertheless concluded that the state's educational facilities must remain open for the well-being of its young people, its citizens, and the state. He succeeded in his efforts to resolve the desegregation issue peaceably and without the intervention of federal troops. The governor also succeeded in correcting the abuses and cleaning up the corruption that had plagued state government during the tainted administration of his predecessor. As a careful overseer of state expenditures, he even expanded state services without raising taxes. However, his efforts to save the malapportioned county-unit system of nominating state officials proved to be futile. Vandiver was the last governor nominated under the state's county-unit system. But more important, his administration marked the beginning of a transition from a state that was segregated and was dominated by rural and small-town voters to a state in which the legal facade of racial discrimination was dismantled and urban voters were the largest portion of its electorate.

Ernie Vandiver began his political career as a member of the Talmadge faction in state politics. He actively supported Eugene and Herman Talmadge, both of whom were staunch defenders of the rurally dominated political system and the segregated social order. Vandiver served as aide, campaign manager, and adjutant general for Governor Herman Talmadge. He later held the offices of lieutenant governor and governor. Vandiver attempted to return to the governor's office four years later in a race in which he was the acknowledged front-runner until health problems forced him to withdraw. Although the Franklin County native succeeded in achieving his political goals of serving as lieutenant governor and governor, he failed to fulfill his ultimate political ambition of serving in the U.S. Senate.

After the publication of my Arnall biography, Governor Vandiver asked if I would be interested in writing his biography. I agreed to do so with the same understanding that I had with Governor Arnall: the biography would be a scholarly endeavor with the author having final authority over content and interpretation. Governor Vandiver agreed and has graciously abided by that ground rule. I have interviewed Governor Vandiver extensively for this biography. I interviewed him earlier for my dissertation and Arnall biography. "Betty" Vandiver provided valuable information about her husband, the Russell family, and Georgia politics. Their children—Samuel Ernest "Chip" Vandiver III, Vanna Elizabeth "Beth" Vandiver, and Jane Brevard Kidd—graciously granted me interviews that allowed me insight into the personal side of Governor Vandiver.

Charlotte S. Pfeiffer, professor of English at Abraham Baldwin Agricultural College, has continually rescued me from the pitfalls of incorrect use of the English language. My wife, Teena Ann, typed the rough draft of the manuscript. My sister-in-law and husband, Betsy and Ben Williams, graciously allowed me to stay with them while researching at the University of Georgia. Gary L. Roberts, professor of history at Abraham Baldwin College, and Caroline S. Helms, professor of history and chairman of the college's Social Science Division, have been most supportive of this endeavor.

This biography could not have been written without the capable assistance and cooperation of the staff at the following libraries: Clark-Atlanta University, Georgia Department of Archives and History, Emory University, University of Georgia, Georgia State University, John F. Kennedy Library, Lyndon B. Johnson Library, South Georgia College, Valdosta State University, and the State University of West Georgia. Visual materials archivist Gail Miller DeLoach at the Georgia Department of Archives and History and Mary Civille, print librarian at the *Atlanta Journal-Constitution*, have been most helpful. Director Brenda J.

Sellers and the staff of the library at Abraham Baldwin Agricultural College have been most cooperative in this undertaking. I am also appreciative of the assistance of department head Sheryl B. Vogt and the staff at the Richard B. Russell Library for Political Research and Studies at the University of Georgia. Unlike Governor Arnall, who burned his papers at the end of his administration, Governor Vandiver thankfully did not. Instead he gave his papers to the Russell Library. The S. Ernest Vandiver Papers include office files, personal papers, correspondence, speeches, press releases, official reports, and newspaper articles and editorials. The professional manner in which Ms. Vogt and her staff assisted me in my research in the Vandiver Papers made my task much easier. The staff of the Russell Library has also transcribed the numerous interviews that I did for this project, which will be available after the publication of the Vandiver biography. I have also given the Russell Library tapes of numerous interviews done earlier for my dissertation and for the Arnall biography. These interviews will also be transcribed by the staff of the Russell Library and made available to the public. I owe special thanks to Sally C. Askew, reference–public service librarian at the Lumpkin School of Law Library at the University of Georgia, for her assistance. I am also grateful for the assistance of the staff (especially Keith Nash's) of the Special Collections Department of the Robert W. Woodruff Library at Emory University. Clifford M. Kunn, assistant professor of history and director of the Georgia Government Documentation Project at Georgia State University, has been most helpful in this endeavor. Appreciation is also extended to Melvin T. Steely, professor of history and director of the Georgia Political Heritage Series at the State University of West Georgia; Theodore B. Fitz-Simons, associate professor emeritus of history at West Georgia; attorney John R. Reinhardt of Tifton; Kristine M. Blakeslee, project editor at the University of Georgia Press; and copy editor Grace Buonocore for their assistance.

Many of Vandiver's political associates and friends are still alive, and I had the opportunity to interview many of them. I am most appreciative to the following individuals for granting me interviews: Louise D. Akin, William D. Ballard, Griffin B. Bell, William H. Bonner, William R. Bowdoin, George D. Busbee, Garland T. Byrd, James A. Dunlap, Glenn W. Ellard, Douglas Embry, Peter Zack Geer Jr., Robert A. Griffin, Robert H. Hall, David C. Jones, William L. Lanier Sr., E. Freeman Leverett, Henry G. Neal, Robert C. Norman, James C. Owen Jr., Homer M. Rankin, Carl E. Sanders, George T. Smith, DeNean Stafford Jr., Robert G. Stephens, and Herman E. Talmadge. In addition, I have made use of numerous other interviews done by others of Vandiver and major political figures during the time of his political career, all of which are cited in the bibliography. The author is indebted to scholars, politicians, and others for their writings on Georgia politics and politicians. I have made extensive use of the Atlanta newspapers' coverage of Vandiver's political career as well as Roy Harris's commentary on Vandiver in his *Augusta Courier,* a weekly political newspaper. Former governor Marvin Griffin's columns in his *Bainbridge Post-Searchlight* provided interesting observations on his major political foe. Roy F. Chalker Sr., chairman of the state highway board in the Griffin administration, published a weekly political newspaper, the *Georgia Recorder,* that provided critical analysis of the activities of Vandiver and his administration. The *Lavonia Times* was useful in understanding Vandiver, his parents, and his life in that community. Numerous other weekly and daily newspapers were examined.

Finally, a special word of appreciation goes to my wife, Teena Ann, and to my children, Hank and Mara Dare, for their patience, understanding, and moral support.

Ernest Vandiver

GOVERNOR OF GEORGIA

ONE

Franklin County Roots

Franklin County, which lies in the Piedmont region of Georgia about one hundred miles to the northeast of Atlanta, has the distinction of being one of the state's original counties. At one time, according to the *Lavonia Times,* the county had as much land area as the entire state of Rhode Island. The legislature created the county in 1784, naming it after Benjamin Franklin. In typical Georgia legislative practice, the state's lawmakers eventually carved it up with twelve counties either in part or in whole being created from Franklin County. Among the most prominent and respected families of the county were the Vandivers.[1]

The Vandivers' family association with Franklin County can be traced back to the early years of the nineteenth century. The first Van Der Veeres had migrated to the New World in the 1600s from Holland. One group of Van Der Veeres, whose name was anglicized to Vandiver, settled in the northeastern section of the United States and had gradually migrated down the East Coast. One of these Vandivers, Edward, lived in Maryland and fought in the Revolutionary War. After the war, he moved to South Carolina, where he farmed and fathered twenty children. One of his grandsons, Benjamin Pinkney Vandiver, established the northeast Georgia branch of the Vandiver family by moving to Franklin County in the 1820s. Benjamin fathered several children, one of whom, William I. Pinkney, was born in Franklin County in 1848. Although neither W. I. P. Vandiver nor his father owned slaves, they fought for the Confederacy in the Civil War to defend the principle of states' rights. The younger Vandiver's effort to enlist in Franklin County was unsuccessful because he was only thirteen. Determined to fight for the Confederacy, he journeyed to the other side of the state, where he found a more receptive recruiter in Floyd County. After the war, he married Mary E. Vaughters, whose family lived on the farm next to his father's. Following in his father's footsteps, W. I. P. Vandiver became a farmer in Franklin County.[2]

His marriage resulted in eight children; his first son, Samuel Ernest Pinkney Vandiver, was born on May 2, 1876. His parents named him Samuel after an uncle and Pinkney after his father and grandfather. The "Ernest" supposedly came from an aunt who, upon viewing the infant shortly after his birth, proclaimed that he looked "so earnest." While growing up on his father's farm, Ernest concluded that farming was not his calling in life. Instead, he chose teaching as an occupation and graduated from a teachers' training institution, the State Normal College, in nearby Athens. Vandiver taught for ten years in various locations throughout the state. Although he enjoyed teaching, he chose a more lucrative occupation and became a salesman for the Travelers Life Insurance Company.[3]

Since this job required a good deal of travel, Vandiver looked for a more stationary occupation after ten years. He returned to farming and became a successful and well-to-do farmer in Franklin County. By the time of his death in 1951, he owned more than thirty-five hundred acres of land and was one of the largest landowners and farmers in the county. He engaged in other business activities including the establishment of a successful cotton-seed mail-order business in Lavonia, a small town in Franklin County. Vandiver's Georgia Seed Company sold cotton seed throughout the South and boasted that one of his varieties of seed, Heavy Fruiter 5, produced the "best cotton" ever grown.[4]

As it had for decades, cotton still dominated the economy of Georgia and Franklin County. In 1930, farmers in the county grew about forty thousand acres of cotton; Vandiver himself had nearly fourteen hundred acres in cotton production. In the 1930s, Lavonia had several cotton gins, one of which was owned by Vandiver. He claimed that his gin in Lavonia was "one of the best gin outfits in the South." Periodically, Vandiver solicited customers by running ads in the local paper urging farmers "to come to the gin owned and operated by a real farmer." In one advertisement, Vandiver tried to relate to the farmers by claiming that he knew their problems because he himself was a farmer. Vandiver also assured potential customers that their cotton would be ginned "cheaper" at his gin because he did not have "high salaried men" in his company. The entrepreneur at one time even operated a lumber company and also had a feed mill at his gin where farmers could have crops ground into dry food for their livestock. On one occasion, Vandiver even advertised one of his donkeys "for service" in the local paper, urging his readers to raise "a few $300 mules and be independent for life."[5]

The forty-year-old Vandiver had been so busy with teaching, selling insurance, farming, selling seed, and pursuing other business enterprises that he had never found time to marry. By chance, one of his friends in Lavonia told Vandiver of a lovely widow whose home he was painting in the nearby town of Canon. An interested Vandiver prevailed upon his friend to introduce him to Vanna Bowers Osborne. They fell in love, and after a courtship of about a year they were married on May 2, 1916. Vanna Vandiver, who had two children by her previous marriage, was thirty-five years old. Her new husband celebrated his fortieth birthday on their wedding day.[6]

The Bowers, like the Vandivers, had deep roots in Franklin County. Vanna's great-great-grandfather, Job Bowers, had been born in Virginia in 1755. He migrated to Franklin County in the late eighteenth century and fought in the Revolutionary War. While he was on furlough to see his newborn son, Tories murdered him. His only child, William, later married Polly Cox and fathered thirteen children. Their oldest son, Job, married Elizabeth Ballinger and likewise fathered thirteen children. Their first son, William F. "Billy," strongly opposed secession even though his father owned slaves. According to family tradition, Billy cast a write-in vote for Abraham Lincoln in the 1860 presidential election. Nevertheless, Franklin County voters later sent Bowers to the state Senate for one term in the late 1860s. Billy's brother, John M. Bowers, had at one time been a Baptist minister. However, he had become dissatisfied with some of the church's beliefs and had become a member of and later a minister in the Universalist faith. John Bowers played a major role in the establishment of the Universalist Church in Canon, a small town in Franklin County. In addition to preaching, Bowers at one time owned and published the *Universalist Herald* and the *Canon Echo*. He enjoyed the reputation of being an independent thinker and even went against the prevailing Solid South mentality by voting Republican in presidential elections. His marriage to Mary Duncan resulted in seven children; Vanna was one of four daughters. She was born on July 3, 1881. Upon his death in 1911, the *Lavonia Times* praised Bowers as "a man of considerable means" who owned a six-hundred-acre farm and left an estate valued between $50,000 and $60,000.[7]

Ernest and Vanna Vandiver decided to live in her home in Canon, which had been built prior to her second marriage. Their marriage resulted in only one child, Samuel Ernest Pinkney Vandiver Jr., who was born on his mother's birthday, July 3, 1918, in Canon. Although both father and son had been named Pinkney, neither ever used the name. Ernest Jr., for all practical purposes, grew up as an only child, since his half brother and half sister were older and had left home while he was still a young boy. Vandiver's half brother, Henry P. "H. P." Osborne, had already turned eighteen when he was born. H. P. left for the Georgia Institute of Technology soon after Vandiver's birth and, after graduation from college, went into the construction business in the north Georgia area. H.P.'s younger sister, Berthine, was twelve at the time of Vandiver's birth. Following her graduation from high school, she left home to attend Wesleyan College. Berthine taught for several years before her marriage to Hiram Whitehead of Comer, a small town in nearby Madison County. Despite their age difference, Vandiver had a deep love and affection for both of his half siblings and "always felt like [his] half brother and half sister were just as close as if they had been full-blooded."[8]

The Vandivers lived in Canon for four years with Ernest Sr., commuting daily by horseback to Lavonia, eight miles away. They finally moved to Lavonia in 1922 to be nearer his business endeavors and farming activities. Both parents played a major role in the life of small-town Lavonia. Louise D. Akin, fourth-grade teacher of Ernest Jr., remembered his parents as being "a fine, fine couple." Dr. William H. Bonner, who grew up in Lavonia with Ernest Jr., remembered that the Vandivers "were unquestionable community leaders and among the more well-to-do people in town." Bonner remembered Ernest Sr. as someone who was very busy and never did a great deal of socializing. Sybil Elizabeth "Betty" Vandiver, wife of Ernest Jr., remembered her father-in-law as someone who "didn't have time for a lot of hanging around the corner talking or visiting at the filling station. He was out working." The older Vandiver had a sign on the side of his car that summed up his attitude, "Talk Business." Although Ernest Sr. never joined a church, Ernest Jr. viewed his father as someone who "always treated people fairly and honestly, and he was known as a man who, if he told you something, you didn't have to get it in writing." In addition to his numerous business endeavors, Ernest Sr. found time to serve on Lavonia's school board and on the board of directors of a local bank as well as being a Mason, a Shriner, and a member of the local Lion's Club.[9]

Bonner remembers Vanna Vandiver as being "very pleasant, a real Southern lady" who was more sociable than her husband. She participated in community affairs in a number of ways, including serving as president of the Lavonia Women's Club, Franklin County's Federation of Women's Clubs, and the local chapter of the United Daughters of the Confederacy in addition to being chairman of the board of trustees of the local library. She even prevailed upon her husband to donate land for Lavonia's city park. While retaining membership in her father's church in Canon, she played an active role in the activities of Lavonia's First Baptist Church. She also was a member of the Susannah Wesley Bible Class of Lavonia's Methodist church. Vandiver remembered his mother as being "a beautiful person and greatly beloved by everyone who knew her." When she died at the age of fifty-nine in 1941, a female Universalist minister conducted her funeral service at the First Baptist Church. The *Lavonia Times* commented that she had been "active in relieving suffering, promoting health, and in promoting the civic interests of the city and county."[10]

Ernest Jr. thoroughly enjoyed growing up in Lavonia, which had all the attributes of a small town and where "everyone knew everybody's else's business." Lavonia came into existence in 1878 as a depot town for the Elberton Air Line Railroad Company. The town had been named after Lavonia Jones, the wife of the president of the railroad company. By the time the community was incorporated in 1880, Lavonia had grown to 72 residents; Franklin County's population numbered 11,453. Fifty years later, the county had grown to 15,902 residents, with 1,511 claiming Lavonia as home. Whites constituted 83 percent of the population of Franklin County and 79 percent of Lavonia's population in 1930. Agriculture continued to dominate the county's economy, and cotton was still the major cash crop. In 1930, the U.S. Bureau of the Census classified the county as a rural county with 79 percent of those residents of the county ten years or older engaged in gainful employment working in agriculture.[11]

Vandiver attended grammar school in Lavonia and graduated from Lavonia High School in 1935. An average student and athlete, he played end and fullback on the high school football team. Vandiver attributed the reason for his making the team to the small number of boys going out rather than to his athletic abilities. The young Vandiver also made the basketball team. He enjoyed hunting, playing tennis, and going to the movie theater. Vandiver, an above-average tennis player, made it to the semifinal round of the Lavonia Tennis Tournament in 1933. A popular student, he had the lead role in his high school's class play, in which he played the role of "Bootes Benbow, a popular Senior." Bonner recalled that Ernest Jr., while growing up, "was a very pleasant, very outgoing, energetic, smart young man, and always popular." Akin remembered him as "an all-around fine person even, as a little boy."[12]

When he was twelve, Vandiver joined the First Baptist Church in Lavonia, the church his mother attended. He played an active role in the church, including participating in Baptist Young People's Union activities on Sunday nights. During the summers, his parents sent him to Camp Dixie for Boys, a private camp in nearby Rabun County. He attended the camp for five summers and received the Honor Camper Award his last summer. He liked the camp so much that he returned for two additional summers as a counselor. The camp attracted about two hundred boys each summer from well-to-do southern families. He considered his time at Camp Dixie a "tremendous experience" because it allowed him to make friends with boys from throughout the state and South. Some of his Georgia friends at the camp later became major supporters in his political campaigns.[13]

In addition to sending their son to camp during the summers, the Vandivers took their son out of school each year to travel to different locations throughout the country, such as Washington, D.C., and New York City. The two-week trips always started on his parents' wedding anniversary. On one of these excursions, they traveled to New York City and returned to Georgia via cruise ship to Savannah. His parents looked upon these trips as a learning experience for their son. Each night of the trip Ernest Sr. usually had his son write down what he had seen during the day that had impressed him. Ernest Jr. recalled: "My parents wanted me to learn; they wanted me to travel; they wanted me to know the history of our country." [14]

When Vandiver was about six years of age, his father hired a tutor to teach his son public speaking, then called expression. He received this instruction for four years and attributed it to his father's desire for him to be a good speaker and to prepare him for a political career. While in high school, Vandiver won the Tenth Congressional District's Declamation Contest, in which he recited Franklin D. Roosevelt's first inaugural address. Vandiver considered the winning of this contest and his Camp Dixie's Honor Camper Award as the two happiest memories of his childhood. Vandiver, in reflecting upon his growing up in Lavonia, concluded that he "had had a good childhood." [15]

His parents sought to instill a strong work ethic in their son by assigning him chores and responsibilities. During the depression years, the Vandivers, like most families in Lavonia, had a milk cow, and Ernest Jr. had the responsibility of milking it twice a day. Sometimes if football practice was too strenuous, he prevailed upon Laura Bowers, an older black woman who lived behind the Vandiver home, to do the milking for him. In return, he read the Bible to her. When Ernest Jr. turned six years old, his father gave him a two-acre plot of land on which to grow cotton. He had the task of keeping the crop free of weeds and of picking the cotton, a task he did until going off to school. As he grew older, Ernest Jr. helped his father with numerous farm chores. Ernest Sr. wanted his son "to know how to work." In reflecting on his childhood, Ernest Jr. concluded, "I was raised . . . to work." [16]

His parents loved him, and he in turn deeply loved them and was devoted to them. In a letter written from Camp Dixie, he boasted to his father, "You are the best daddy and mamma is the best mama that a boy ever had." He signed his correspondence to his parents with "Your loving boy" or "Always your devoted son." Laura Bowers, who was the daughter of a slave owned by the Bowers family, helped Vanna Vandiver with her household responsibilities including helping to raise Ernest Jr. Vandiver thought highly of this older black woman, whom he affectionately called Aunt Laura, admitting that he "loved her almost as much" as he did his parents. Vandiver enjoyed a normal childhood; smoking was the worst vice he acquired as he grew to adulthood. Both parents believed in disciplining when their son transgressed the acceptable limits of conduct. Ernest Sr. did most of the disciplining—usually with a peach tree switch carefully selected by Ernest Jr. from an orchard conveniently located behind the Vandiver home. Vandiver recalls his first whipping when, at a relatively young age, he turned a water hose on a group of his mother's friends on the Vandivers' front porch and thoroughly soaked them. Vandiver also recalled, "I got a whipping for running away nearly every day when I was small." While in high school, Vandiver "discovered girls," and his socializing with members of the opposite sex along with the many hours spent at football practice had a negative impact on his grades. Vandiver distinctly remembered his father telling him in a "very firm" manner that education had a higher priority than girls or even football. His social activities got him in trouble with his parents at least on one occasion. His parents were out of town, and he borrowed his mother's car without her permission to ride over to Royston, a neighboring town, for a date. The enterprising teenager, in order to cover up this transgression, disconnected the odometer in his mother's car. He had an enjoyable night on the town until his frantic efforts to reconnect the odometer proved unsuccessful, much to his regret.[17]

Vanna Vandiver had no interest in politics, but her husband did, even though he never ran for public office. Vandiver concluded that his father never sought political office because he was busy with his numerous business endeavors. Nevertheless, Ernest Sr. clearly wanted his son to enter the political arena and supposedly boasted upon his son's birth that a future governor of Georgia had just been born. On several occasions, Ernest Sr. made reference to his young son as a future chief executive of the state. Dr. Bonner recalled that it was common knowledge in Lavonia that Ernest Jr. was going to be involved in politics. Vandiver took his young son with him to numerous political rallies to hear political speeches. One speech in particular impressed the young boy. In 1930 Ernest Sr. and his twelve-year-old son went to hear gubernatorial candidate Richard Brevard "Dick" Russell Jr. of nearby Barrow County give a campaign speech. After hearing Russell's speech, Ernest Jr. recalled that he was "entranced with politics" and "first really considered entering the field of politics."[18]

Ernest Sr. supported Dick Russell in his campaigns for governor in 1930 and U.S. senator in 1932, but he was also drawn to another rising figure in Georgia politics—Eugene Talmadge. Ernest Sr. became a dedicated Talmadge supporter when the latter ran for state agriculture commissioner in 1926. In that campaign, the two opponents, Talmadge and Agriculture Commissioner John J. Brown, held a debate in Elberton. Ernest Sr. returned from that debate a confirmed Talmadge supporter and went to work on Talmadge's behalf in Franklin and surrounding counties. Ernest Sr. continued to support him in his political battles until Talmadge's death in 1946. Eugene Talmadge's son, Herman Eugene Talmadge, considered Ernest Sr. one of his father's principal supporters in the northeastern section of Georgia. Herman Talmadge viewed the support of Ernest Sr. as significant because he was a well-known businessman who had "substantial influence" in Franklin and surrounding counties. The efforts of Ernest Sr. paid off when Gene Talmadge overwhelmingly carried Franklin County in 1932 in his first gubernatorial race. In appreciation for his support, Governor-elect Talmadge appointed Vandiver a lieutenant colonel on his staff. The *Lavonia Times* called the appointment a climax to Vandiver's support of Talmadge. Later, Governor Talmadge invited Ernest and Vanna Vandiver to ride on the train carrying the Georgia delegation to Washington to participate in the inauguration of President-elect Franklin D. Roosevelt in March 1933. In a newspaper ad for his cotton gin, Vandiver expressed his continued support of Talmadge as governor. He told his readers: "We have a real dirt farmer for our Governor. Eugene Talmadge is the greatest Governor Georgia has ever had. Talking with the Governor the other day, he said to me: 'Vandiver, I will make some mistakes, but I am doing the best I can.' Boys, Gene Talmadge has a heart in him as big as a mule and he is 100 per cent for the wool hat and overall fellow."[19]

At first, the leading Talmadgite in Franklin County supported Franklin D. Roosevelt. In a cotton gin ad, the senior Vandiver expressed his belief, "A BETTER DAY IS AHEAD! We have a great President who is trying to make things better." The conservative Vandiver, however, became disenchanted with the New Deal as the president moved to the left politically. Governor Talmadge's increasing hostility to the New Deal probably strengthened Vandiver's opposition to the New Deal as well. In the U.S. Senate race in 1936, Ernest Sr. found himself in the difficult position of having to choose between two politicians he had supported in the past—Gene Talmadge and Dick Russell. Senator Russell ran as a Roosevelt supporter, and Talmadge, prohibited from seeking a third term as governor by the Georgia Constitution, opposed Russell in a reelection bid. That race split the Vandiver household, with Ernest Sr. supporting Talmadge and his wife remaining loyal to Senator Russell. Despite the senior Vandiver's efforts, Senator Russell carried Franklin County by 842 votes and won reelection.[20]

In that election, Ernest Jr. went along with his father and supported Talmadge. Ernest Jr. gave his first speech in a political campaign when he introduced Gene Talmadge at a campaign rally in Franklin County in 1936. The speech by Vandiver, then only eighteen years of age, so impressed Governor Talmadge, whose oratorical skills were well known, that he asked him to introduce him the following weekend at a rally in Dalton. Unfortunately for the young speaker, Governor Talmadge had earlier called out the National Guard in Dalton in support of the textile mills' management in a labor dispute, and many of the mill workers opposed the governor because of his intervention against them. Some of the more disgruntled showed up at the Dalton rally to express their displeasure with the governor, and the mood of the event turned hostile. As a result, Governor Talmadge asked Ernest Jr. to shorten his introduction, and he substantially abbreviated his own remarks. Talmadge lost the 1936 senate race against Russell but nevertheless challenged the state's senior U.S. senator, Walter F. George, two years later. This time Talmadge carried Franklin County, with the Vandivers' staunch assistance, even though Senator George won reelection.[21]

Talmadge finally won another election, this time for the governorship in 1940. Vanna Vandiver, who had been in poor health, died the following year. Shortly after her funeral, Governor Talmadge nominated Ernest Sr. to a position on the important three-man state highway board. Ernest Jr. viewed the nomination as a kindly act on the part of Talmadge to help his father get over the loss of his wife. The Lavonia Times called the appointment totally unexpected even though Ernest Sr. had been one of Talmadge's loyal supporters in his campaigns. Since no one from Franklin County had ever served on the highway board, this appointment further solidified the political and personal loyalty of Ernest Sr. and Ernest Jr. to Eugene Talmadge.[22]

Both parents stressed the importance of a college education to their son. Vanna Vandiver had insisted that her first two children attend college, which they did. She likewise insisted on the same for her youngest son. However, her husband doubted whether his son's educational experiences at Lavonia High School had sufficiently prepared him for college, since the local high school had only eleven grades and the graduating class of Ernest Jr. had only sixteen students. With his parents' encouragement, Ernest Jr. decided to enroll at Darlington School, a private boarding school in Rome, Georgia, which had an enrollment of 190 students in 1936. He enrolled for one year there, taking courses in English, French, math, and modern history. Vandiver learned how to study and complained, after once studying so much for a math exam, "I nearly put my eyes out."[23]

Vandiver considered his favorite teacher at Darlington to have been Roland B. Parker, who taught history. He remembered Parker as a fine person and a great teacher who made his classes so much fun that "you wanted to go to them." Ernest Jr. proudly boasted to his parents of his winning a trip to the circus for having written the best theme in Professor Parker's class. While at Darlington, he played on the tennis and junior varsity basketball teams. Even though he did not make the football squad, he was successful in getting on the debate team. The school held the J. M. Proctor Debate annually in front of the entire student body on Honors Day. Vandiver won the debate, arguing the affirmative side of whether the United States should have socialized medicine. He completed his year at Darlington with a B average and believed that he was now ready for college.[24]

While still in high school, Vandiver had decided on law as a profession, even though no one in his family had ever been a lawyer. In September 1936, he enrolled at the University of Georgia in a joint program that allowed him to complete an undergraduate degree in history and a degree in law in six years. Before Vandiver enrolled at the university, his father had him compile a list of goals to accomplish at the university and in later life. These included serving as president of the Pan-Hellenic Council and Phi Delta Theta social fraternity as well as maintaining a B average. His father asked him to update his goals in 1940, which now included election to Sphinx, the highest nonacademic honor society at the university; making a B average in law school; passing the bar exam; winning the governorship; moving up to the U.S. Senate; and becoming the "best lawyer in Georgia." Vandiver diligently went about trying to accomplish his long list of goals. He achieved an outstanding record of leadership during his years at the university, serving as president of Phi Delta Theta twice as well as serving as president of the Blue Key Leadership fraternity, the Phi Kappa Literary Society, his freshman law class, and the Pan-Hellenic Council. He also won election to the Sphinx Honor Society and held membership in Omicron Delta Kappa, the Gridiron Society, the Pelican Club, and Phi Delta Phi legal fraternity. Vandiver succinctly summed up his university experience: "My grades were not all that great, but I was active in campus politics."[25]

Classmates and fraternity brothers remembered Vandiver for his pleasing personality. A fraternity brother and close personal friend at the university, James C. "Jim" Owen Jr., recalled that Vandiver had a pleasant personality and "a warm, cordial approach to anybody; whether it was a stranger or whether it was a life-long friend." Another classmate at the university and co-recipient of the Camp Dixie Honor Camper Award with Vandiver, Robert C. "Bob" Norman, remembered Vandiver at Athens as an individual who was well rounded, friendly, and well liked. "He was not the back-slapping type of person," Norman recalled, "but he made good friends, and he kept his friends." Another classmate at the university, James A. "Jim" Dunlap, agreed that Vandiver was someone who had "a real knack of handling people well" because he was "extremely friendly, nice, fun-loving, attractive" and who was a natural leader. All three saw their classmate as someone who had political ambitions beyond the campus of the University of Georgia.[26]

In addition to campus politics, Vandiver also became interested in flying and enrolled in several training courses to learn to fly. After his graduation from the university with an undergraduate degree in history and a law degree in 1942, he enlisted as a pilot in the army air force. Even though he ruptured his left ear-drum during pilot basic training, Vandiver completed his pilot training and received a second-lieutenant commission in the army air force in March 1944. Recurring problems with his ruptured eardrum led to a medical evaluation board's taking him off flight status. Lieutenant Vandiver then received an assignment as defense counsel in court-martial cases at a military instillation at Yuma, Arizona. As a result of his success in representing several defendants, his superior reassigned him to advising airmen with legal problems. In 1945, Vandiver completed his military obligation with the rank of captain and returned to civilian life. He came home to Lavonia and became involved with his father's varied economic interests.[27]

Vandiver also became active in community affairs by heading up the newly organized Lavonia Chamber of Commerce. Politics also beckoned to him, and when Lavonia's mayor decided not to seek reelection, Vandiver announced his candidacy in October 1945. The twenty-seven-year-old Vandiver won his first bid for public office with no opposition and assumed his one-year term of office in January 1946. The mayor, the youngest in Georgia at that time, implemented a progressive program for improving Lavonia, including the construction of a recreation center as well as the extension and improvements of the city's water and sewerage lines. Mayor Vandiver also had fines for traffic violations increased and a traffic light installed at a busy intersection. His duties as mayor of Lavonia included presiding over city court for those charged with violating city ordinances. On one occasion, the mayor pro tempore held court in the absence of the mayor, who was out of town. The mayor pro tempore, who was not a lawyer or well versed in city court procedure, heard a rape case even though his court lacked jurisdiction. The mayor pro tempore found the accused guilty and fined the defendant ten dollars. The husband of the alleged rape victim, upset over the light punishment for the violation of his wife, took justice in his own hands and murdered the alleged rapist. As a result of this tragedy, Mayor Vandiver vowed never to miss another court session. Vandiver, receiving fifty dollars for his one-year tenure, viewed his mayorship as "quite an experience." He recalled, "If somebody's dog got in somebody else's yard, the first thing they did was to call the mayor and say, 'Get that dog out of my yard.'" He also vividly remembers his constituents calling him day or night seeking resolution of their problems.[28]

In addition to his mayoral duties, Vandiver took some refresher courses at the law school in Athens in order to prepare for the bar exam. He successfully passed the exam in December 1946 and began to consider where to practice. His father had a friend, Joseph D. Quillian, who had been practicing in Winder in Barrow County for thirty years. Quillian offered Vandiver a partnership in his firm, which was located in Winder, a city of more than four thousand residents, twice the size of Lavonia. Vandiver accepted the offer and the law firm of Quillian and Vandiver came into existence in May 1947.[29]

Actually, Vandiver's association with Quillian had begun several years earlier. He had spent several months in Quillian's law office prior to entering the service in 1943 to get the "feel of the law practice." During that time, he had met Sybil Elizabeth "Betty" Russell. However, since he was twenty-four and she was only sixteen, Vandiver had never asked her for a date, fearing her father "would shoot" him if he had asked her because of the age difference. Vandiver left Winder for military service in 1943, which was the same year Betty Russell graduated from Winder-Barrow High School. The petite, extroverted, and gregarious Miss Russell came from one of the most prominent political families in the state. Her uncle, Dick Russell, had risen rapidly through the political ranks, holding the positions of state representative, Speaker of the state's House of Representatives, governor, and finally, U.S. senator. Her father, Robert Lee "Bob" Russell Sr., was a federal district court judge and later would be appointed to the Fifth Circuit Court of Appeals. Behind the scenes, Bob Russell played an influential role in the numerous campaigns of his brother Senator Russell.[30]

The patriarch of the Russell family, Richard B. Russell Sr., had achieved a distinguished record as a businessman, lawyer, and judge. Known to his family as "Papa," Russell had served as chief justice of the Georgia Supreme Court for sixteen years prior to his death in 1938. Before his election to the state's highest court, Judge Russell had been a state legislator, superior court prosecutor, superior court judge, and member of the Georgia Court of Appeals. Papa Russell, despite his success in the judicial arena, however, had failed in efforts to win the governor's office and a seat in the U.S. Senate. His marriage in 1894 to Blandina "Ina" Dillard resulted in a large family of fifteen children, two of whom died in infancy. Papa Russell moved his rapidly expanding family from Athens to Winder in 1897. Five years later the Russells had moved again to a location about two and a half miles from Winder and chartered a new town, appropriately called Russell, which by 1940 numbered 126 residents.[31]

The Russells' second son, Bob Russell, was born on August 19, 1900, and married Sybil Nannette Millsaps, also of Barrow County, in 1923. She had been born on September 18, 1901. Their marriage resulted in four children: Robert L. "Bobby" Jr., Betty, Richard Brevard III, and Mary Ina. Betty Vandiver fondly remembered her mother as a remarkable woman because "she never talked about anybody; she loved you for what you were, and she didn't try to change you." Her mother worshiped her father, and while Sybil deeply loved her children, her life revolved around Bob Russell, who was "her guiding star." Betty remembered her father as "a very solemn, serious man" who carefully analyzed the pros and cons of every decision, a process that usually lasted several days.

The Bob Russells lived in a home next to Papa Russell. Betty enjoyed growing up in Russell and nearby Winder and being a member of the Russell family, a very close family in which "all the uncles and aunts felt like every child was theirs." Betty Russell felt "very loved all the time [she] was growing up." In particular, Senator Russell, who never married, took great interest in the activities of his numerous nephews and nieces. On one occasion, the senator wrote "Lady Betty," a nickname he had given her, to suggest that she "find a lipstick shade more attractive" than the one she had on when he last saw her. He enclosed $1.50 for that purchase.[32]

After the death of Papa Russell in 1938, Betty usually spent weeknights with Grandmother Russell to keep her company and Friday and Saturday nights with her maternal grandparents, Green S. and Bettie O. Millsaps, who lived in Winder. In those days, few boys had cars to drive anywhere, much less to Russell to date Betty. So she temporarily resided in Winder on the weekends to have a more active social life. Betty remembered Winder as an ideal little town to grow up in because "you didn't have to worry about anything." She tried out for the basketball team, only to be turned down because of her height of four feet, eleven inches. Instead, she was a cheerleader for four years. To her father's great consternation, his eldest daughter served as secretary and treasurer of numerous clubs in high school, and her handling of other people's money worried her father.[33]

Despite the love and affection of her parents and extended family, Betty decided to go to college out of state in an effort to make it on her own. She selected a small two-year liberal-arts institution, Sullins College, in Bristol, Virginia, where she majored in sociology and minored in psychology. But even at Sullins, Betty could not escape the Russell family's influence because the dean of the college had gone to school with none other than her Uncle Dick. While at Sullins, she joined the Science Club, sang in the glee club, and served as vice president of the Georgia Club. After two years, she transferred to the University of Georgia, from which she graduated in 1947 with a degree in sociology. Henry W. Grady Memorial Hospital in Atlanta hired her as a social worker with her job beginning in September 1947.[34]

While still in college, Betty Russell crossed paths with Ernest Jr. again. Betty attended summer school at the university in 1946. She and her roommate had decided on that particular night to spend a quiet evening in the dorm. However, two former male students, one of whom was Vandiver, dropped by to visit their former dorm mother and to inquire if she knew of any "nice girls" who wanted to go the Varsity, a nearby fast-food restaurant. The dorm mother prevailed upon Betty and her roommate to go out with these "nice boys." Politics dominated the conversation at the Varsity, since there was a bitter gubernatorial election going on that summer with Gene Talmadge seeking the governorship. Vandiver had been busy working in Talmadge's campaign headquarters in Atlanta. Betty—staunchly anti-Talmadge—had never forgiven Gene Talmadge for running against her Uncle Dick in the 1936 senatorial election. She reminded Vandiver that Talmadge had accused her Uncle Dick of paving the sidewalks of Russell with government funds and how he had erected a big sign offering a one-hundred-dollar reward for anyone finding a sidewalk in Russell. After this date between political opposites, Betty and Ernest went their separate ways, with Betty never anticipating seeing Vandiver again.[35]

The following summer, Betty Russell returned home from the university, passing time until her job at Grady began in September. Vandiver had returned to Winder to begin the practice of law. Perhaps remembering Betty from the Varsity encounter the previous summer, he called and asked her out for dinner. Betty accepted, and her brothers thought that it was "a hoot that this man was going to take [her]out and feed [her]." They started dating, and soon they were seeing each other almost on a daily basis. After a whirlwind courtship of six weeks, Vandiver asked Betty to marry him. She accepted, but they both agreed that he had to ask her father for his permission.[36]

Judge Russell had been out of the state on court business for several weeks prior to Vandiver's return to Winder and had missed the whirlwind courtship. When he returned home, his wife informed him of Betty's plans to get married. A concerned father asked, "To whom?" Shortly thereafter, Vandiver went to the Russell home to seek permission from the judge to marry Betty. The conversation took place on the screened porch of the Russell home. Betty's bedroom was located over the porch, and she confessed, "I was hanging out the window trying to hear what Daddy and Ernie were talking about." During the discussion, Judge Russell expressed the hope that the young couple would not do anything "precipitously." Although a University of Georgia graduate, Betty had no idea what that word meant; she quickly consulted her dictionary. In the meantime, Judge Russell gave his approval to the marriage to a delighted Vandiver.[37]

The other members of the Russell family also approved of Betty's choice, with the possible exception of one aunt who supposedly questioned why a Russell woman would want to marry a Talmadge man. The wife of Betty's uncle, Fielding D. Russell, expressed her approval, calling Vandiver "a lucky guy." Uncle Dick assured "Lady Betty," "If he suits you all right, you may be sure that I will be pleased with him." Another uncle, Dr. Henry E. Russell, wrote Betty, "[Vandiver] had better be a fine fellow for he is certainly getting one of the finest girls in the world." The marriage also had the approval of Vandiver's father. In a very touching letter to the Bob Russells, he promised to love Betty as his own and admitted:

Ernest, Jr. has his faults. He is a bit stubborn and self-willed and likes to solve things in his own way but he will listen to reason. Being my only son, I may have been too lenient with him in finances but since he is on his own he will be more conservative.

If he has any bad habits, except smoking, I do not know of them. He makes and holds friends easily. He likes people and they like him. He is honest and above board in his dealings. He may disagree with you but he will never deceive you. He loves law and politics and is a hard worker. He has been a grand son to Mother and me and I'm proud of my boy.[38]

The wedding took place September 3, 1947, in the First Baptist Church of Winder. Betty's uncle, Dr. Henry Russell, officiated. Jim Owen of Griffin, a classmate of Vandiver's at the university, served as best man, and groomsmen included Herman Talmadge, Bobby Russell, and Jim Dunlap. Miss Jerrye Griffeth served as maid of honor and Mrs. James D. Moore as matron of honor. The bride wore a traditional wedding dress of white duchess satin. She carried the wedding handkerchief of her grandmother Russell and wore a strand of pearls that was a gift of the groom. The *Winder News* account of the wedding described the bride as "lovely" and "vivacious." After a reception at the Winder Women's Clubhouse, the couple left for a honeymoon to Florida and New Orleans. When they returned to Winder, Vandiver resumed his practice of law.[39]

Vandiver's parents had given their son a solid foundation for success in life by instilling the virtues of honesty and hard work in him. They had deeply loved and cared for him and provided a family environment that had allowed their son to experience a happy and secure childhood. The Vandivers also had had the financial resources to provide their son with opportunities—travel, camp, speech lessons, prep school, a college education—that few boys growing up in the depression years in Georgia experienced. Vandiver could have easily remained in Franklin County and followed in his father's footsteps of being a landowner, a farmer, and a businessman, but he wanted more. Like his father, he loved politics. Unlike his father, however, he had the driving ambition to seek political office. This political drive would eventually take Ernest and Betty Vandiver to the Governor's Mansion in Atlanta.

Georgia at Midcentury

In the 1940s and 1950s, Georgia was in the process of evolving into an urban state with a diversified economy. Urban residents continued their demands for a more equitable political system, and black citizens increased their calls for the demise of legalized segregation and the unhampered right to vote. Although defenders of the old order fought to preserve the rural dominance of state politics and a segregated way of life, their efforts ultimately failed, resulting in a transformation of the social and political systems of the state. At midcentury, Georgia was undergoing significant change that would continue into the decade of the 1960s. Samuel Ernest Vandiver Jr. held positions of responsibility in the government of Georgia during these critical times—first as adjutant general, then as lieutenant governor, and finally as governor. He entered state politics as a staunch defender of the old order. But as governor, he reluctantly accepted the inevitable—the old order had to give way to the new.

Ernest Vandiver exercised political power in a state that could claim many distinctions—one of the original colonies, fourth state to ratify the Constitution, fifth state to secede from the Union, and first state to charter a state university. It also had the distinction of being the largest state east of the Mississippi. The Empire State of the South's population in 1950 of 3,444,578 made it the thirteenth most populous state in the Union. Among the southern states, only Texas and North Carolina had larger populations. However, even though Georgia had gained more than 320,000 new residents in the 1940s, the state's percentage of increase remained below the national average. Georgia still remained a rural state, with 54.7 percent of its population so classified by the 1950 census. However, the state had experienced a steady decline in its rural population since 1900, when 84 percent of Georgians were designated as rural residents.[1]

The rural nonfarm population of the state actually increased 60.3 percent in the 1940s to almost 923,000; during the same period, however, the rural farm population declined almost 30 percent to 962,453. Ninety-eight of the state's 159 counties experienced a decline in population in the 1940s. Of the state's sixty-four counties that had a population of 10,000 or less, fifty-five lost population. In contrast, the urban population of the state increased 28.7 percent in the 1940s. All the twenty-four counties that had cities of more than 10,000 residents experienced growth. Of the cities having a population of 2,500 or more, 96 percent gained population. The five largest cities in the state in 1950— Atlanta, Augusta, Columbus, Macon, and Savannah—had a combined population of 672,323, an increase of almost 98,000 since the previous census. The state's five Standard Metropolitan Areas saw their population increase an average of 31 percent. As a result in the growth of urban Georgia, one-fifth of the state's population resided in its five largest cities and one-third in its five Standard Metropolitan Areas. In 1950, urban residents made up 45.3 percent of the state's population. The 1950 census would be the last in which there would be more rural than urban Georgians. In the 1960 census, 55.3 percent of the state's population was classified as urban.[2]

Like other Deep South states, Georgia had a large black population. Only three other southern states—Mississippi, South Carolina, and Alabama—had a larger percentage of blacks than Georgia's 30.9 percent in 1950. Nevertheless, Georgia had experienced a decline in black population since the 1940 census, when blacks constituted 34.7 percent of the state's citizenry. Georgia's black residents in 1950 were poorer than the state's white citizens. Almost 85 percent of the black families in the state had annual incomes of less than two thousand dollars compared with 46.5 percent of the white families. Twenty-seven percent of employed blacks worked in agricultural jobs, and 16 percent found employment in manufacturing. In contrast, 26 percent of employed whites were in manufacturing and only 18 percent in agriculture.[3]

Not only were Georgia blacks poorer than white Georgians, but they also suffered from the effects of discrimination that had been imposed upon them by their state and local governments. Racial segregation in the public school system had been mandated by the state constitution and law since Reconstruction. Although the state and local governments had made few attempts to mandate segregation by law in other areas of society prior to the 1890s, segregation had evolved after Reconstruction mainly by custom. In the 1890s, however, the legislature and local governments began passing legislation relegating blacks to a separate and inferior legal status. "By the World War II years," one historian observed, "Georgia's segregated social system had hardened into a rigid caste structure accepted by virtually all whites and a substantial number of blacks." While the overwhelming majority of whites supported segregation in 1950, there were increasing indications of growing hostility to Jim Crowism among the blacks. Segregationists watched with apprehension as the issue of race relations gained increasing attention from the federal judiciary.[4]

Agriculture continued to be important to the Georgia economy. In 1950, the value of farm crops produced on Georgia's 198,000 farms was almost $419 million. Cotton was the most valuable farm crop produced in the state with a value of $114,485,000, followed by corn ($82,899,000), peanuts ($73,958,000), and tobacco ($50,664,000). The gross income from farming, including truck crops, livestock, and livestock products, totaled approximately $687 million. During the 1940s, the percentage of farm population declined from 43.8 percent of the state's population to 27.9 percent. The percentage of farms operated by tenants declined from 60.1 percent in 1940 to 42.8 percent in 1950. For the first time in the state's history, agriculture dropped from the largest to the second-largest employer, with only 21.2 percent of the workforce, a decline of more than 13 percent since 1940.[5]

Of the more than 1,254,000 employed Georgians , the largest number, 23 percent, were in manufacturing, a 4.3 percent increase since 1940. In 1950, Georgia had approximately 5,900 manufacturing plants, which employed more than 296,000 employees. The industry with both the largest number of employees and greatest volume of business was textiles. The lumber industry had the second-largest workforce and the largest number of plants. The average weekly earning of a Georgian employed in manufacturing was $43.52, which was $15.81 below the national average. The hourly wage of a Georgian employed in manufacturing was $1.08, thirty-nine cents below the national average. Women constituted 30 percent of the workforce in 1950, with 22.1 percent of the women employees in manufacturing jobs and 25.4 percent in personnel services. The total sales or receipts from manufacturing in the state in 1950 were $3,308,000,000 — almost five times the gross income of agriculture.[6]

Georgia was a poor state and its citizenry poorly educated. Indicative of the state's poverty was its rank among the states with reference to per capita income, which was $969 in 1950, considerably lower than the national average of $1,436. In fact, Georgia ranked forty-first out of forty-eight states in per capita income. Nor did the state fare much better in the area of educational achievement. The national median school year completed by persons twenty-five years or older in 1950 was 9.3. Georgia ranked forty-seventh in the nation, with a 7.8 median school year. The median school year of white Georgians twenty-five years or older was 8.8 years, that of black Georgians 4.9. The state ranked only forty-third

in the nation in expenditures per student attending public elementary and secondary school, whereas the salaries of public school personnel stood at two-
thirds of the national average.[7]

In addition to shortcomings in its educational system, Georgia had some major problems in its political system in 1950. These included a malapportioned
state legislature, a one-party political system, a malapportioned system of nominating state political officers, and the disfranchisement of most black citizens.
In 1950, white rural voters dominated the state's political system. The malapportioned state legislature and the county-unit system of nominating state officeholders concentrated political power in the hands of the white rural voters — the
most conservative voters in the state. More progressive white voters in the urban areas of Georgia had their political influence minimized by the county-unit
system. Blacks, the most liberal Georgians on race and economic policies, had
long been disfranchised and removed as a major threat to the state's political
and racial status quo. The state also had a one-party political system that had
come into existence after the Civil War. Thus, instead of organized political parties competing for control of the state capitol and public policy, factions within
the Democratic Party struggled for political power in Atlanta.[8]

Rural voters, despite the decline in numbers, still dominated the state legislature in 1950 because neither house had population-based representation. The
state Senate consisted of fifty-four senators chosen from the same number of
districts. Each district consisted of one to five counties with the overwhelming
majority of the districts consisting of three counties. Only Fulton, the most populous county in the state, had its own separate district. However, the 16,237 residents of the Thirty-second Senatorial District had the same senatorial representation as the 473,572 residents of Fulton County's district. The influence of
urban citizens in the upper house was further diminished by the constitutional
provision that required that senators from each district be rotated among the
counties in a district every two years. As a consequence, Muscogee County,
with 118,028 residents, elected a senator every six years. In the two intervening
elections, voters in either Marion County, with 6,521 residents, or Chattahoo-
chee County, with 12,149 residents, elected the senator. Bibb County residents
elected their senator every eight years, even though their county's population
was approximately four times that of the other three counties in the district.[9]

Nor could residents of populous counties find fairer representation in the
205-member state House of Representatives. Georgia had more counties than
any other state with the exception of Texas, which was four times as large. Under
the Georgia Constitution, the eight most populous counties had three representatives each, and the next thirty most populous had two each. The state's remaining 121 counties had one representative each in the lower house. Fulton County

with a population of more than 473,000 residents had only three representatives, while the least populated county in the state, Echols, had one representative to look after the interests of its 2,494 residents. The three least populated counties in the state, with a combined population of 9,755, had as much representation in the lower house as Fulton County. Even though the eight largest counties had 36.5 percent of the state's population in 1950, they had only 12 percent of the representation in the lower house. Conversely, the 121 least populated counties, which had only 37.5 percent of the state's population, had 59 percent of the representation in the House of Representatives.[10]

Georgia had been classified as a one-party state for so long that a contemporary observer might have assumed that such a condition had always existed. However, for several decades prior to the Civil War, Georgia had had a two-party system in which white Georgians divided along Whig or Democratic Party lines over economic, social, and political issues. The state emerged from the aftermath of the Civil War as a one-party state with former Whigs and Democrats forgetting their past differences to unite in the Democratic Party in opposition to Radical Reconstruction. As a result, the Democratic Party had become the dominant political party in Georgia and throughout the South. Democratic politicians had argued that economic, social, and political differences among whites had to be suppressed in order to maintain a united front against internal and external threats to white supremacy.[11]

Georgia entered the ranks of one-party states with the election of 1874. In that election, the last Republican to represent Georgia in the U.S. House of Representative in the nineteenth century suffered defeat. Not until the election of Howard H. "Bo" Callaway in 1964, ninety-two years later, did a Republican represent the state in the U.S. House of Representatives. The only Republican senator in the nineteenth century from Georgia completed his term in 1872. Not until 1980, 108 years later, was a Republican elected to represent Georgia in the U.S. Senate. Nor did the Republicans fare any better on the state and local levels. The last Republican to hold the office of governor ended his term in 1872. Not until ninety years later in 1962 did a Republican make a serious effort toward seeking the governorship, and not until the election of 1966 did a Republican pose a serious threat to Democratic control of that office. The overwhelming majority of state legislators and local officials had been and still were members of the Democratic Party in 1950.[12]

The Republican Party had not fared much better in presidential politics in the state. Prior to the 1964 presidential election, Georgia had never cast any electoral votes for a Republican presidential candidate. Since 1852 Georgians had faithfully given their electoral votes to Democratic presidential candidates. Louis M. Seagull, in his study of southern Republicanism, contended that "of all the deep South states, Georgia evidenced the greatest historic loyalty to the Democratic Party." The Georgia Republican Party in the nineteenth century had too many liabilities to make it a viable alternative to the Democratic Party. White Georgians associated it with Radical Reconstruction, the cause of the blacks, and the corrupt administration of Georgia's first Republican governor, Rufus B. Bullock.[13]

While those in control of the Georgia Democratic Party in the latter half of the nineteenth century had little to fear from a weak Republican Party, they had to contend with disgruntled white members of their own party. Conservative business interests, better known as Bourbons, dominated the post- Civil War Democratic Party. In protest against the policies of the business interests, agrarian malcontents supported the Independent movement of the 1870s and 1880s and then the Populist revolt of the 1890s. The Democrats resorted to various means including fraud, violence, black votes, and racism to turn back these challenges from the white malcontents. Not until the 1960s would the dominance of the Georgia Democratic Party be challenged again and then from the Republican Party. Thus, the politics of the state prior to the 1960s took place entirely within the confines of the Georgia Democratic Party.[14]

The politics of the Democratic Party since the early 1930s had consisted primarily of a struggle between the Talmadge faction and the anti-Talmadge faction. Eugene Talmadge's entry into gubernatorial politics in 1932 had changed the nature of Georgia's political system, which had been multifactional in the 1920s. As his biographer noted, Talmadge, who was elected state agriculture commissioner three times and governor four, "either dominated or haunted the political structure as few men have done in any state's history." V. O. Key Jr. contended that Talmadge's "personality and the vividness of his race and class appeals divided the Georgia electorate into two camps, whose struggles created a strong tendency toward bifactionalism." All contested primary elections between 1936 and 1954 in Georgia for U.S. senator or for governor featured Eugene Talmadge, his son Herman Eugene Talmadge, or a candidate of the Talmadge faction pitted against a candidate of the anti-Talmadge faction.[15]

The conflict between the two factions took place not only within the confines of the Democratic Party but also within a political system that maximized the influence of rural voters. Key referred to Georgia politics as the "Rule of the Rustics," and Charles B. Pyles maintained that prior to the reapportionment revolution of the 1960s rural interests dominated Georgia politics to a greater extent than in any other state. Certainly, Georgia's county-unit system maximized the influence of rural voters. The county-unit system, which had been party practice for several decades prior to its enactment into state law in 1917, applied to nominations for U.S. senator, governor, state House officers, justices of the supreme court, and judges of the state court of appeals. Representation in the malapportioned state House of Representatives determined voting strength in the county-unit system. Each county had two county-unit votes for each representative in the state House. The eight most populous counties received three representatives and thus six county-unit votes each. The next thirty most populous counties received two representatives and four unit votes each. The remaining 121 counties had one representative and two county-unit votes each. The total county-unit vote for the state consisted of 410 votes, and all nominations except those for U.S. senator and governor required a plurality of these votes. Senatorial and gubernatorial nomination required a majority, or 206, of the votes. In 1950, the state's eight most populated counties, which contained 36.5 percent of the state's population, had only 12 percent of the county-unit votes. In contrast, the 121 two-unit counties, with 37.5 percent of the population, had 59 percent of the unit vote.[16]

In short, the county-unit system significantly diminished the influence of the most populous counties and maximized the influence of the sparsely populated counties. It rewarded those candidates running for statewide offices who appealed to the rural voters, such as Eugene Talmadge. As Joseph L. Bernd observed, "Talmadge couched his appeal for votes in the rural idiom and he championed the farmers. His scorning of the few city counties was a profitable campaigning technique because a few votes in the county far outweighed the ballots in the city." Talmadge preached the values of the rural life—rugged individualism, hard work, frugality, and white supremacy. As one observer noted, "Old Gene often boasted that he did not want to carry a county with a streetcar, and he once pastured a cow on the lawn of the governor's mansion because Mrs. Talmadge was dissatisfied with the milk being delivered to her door in big slick Atlanta." Talmadge even had a barn and a hen house built on the grounds of the executive mansion, which was located in one of the finer neighborhoods of Atlanta. More respectable members of Georgia society expressed shock at such antics, but his rural supporters delighted in such actions of "Ole Gene"— whom his enemies called the "Wild Man from Sugar Creek." His biographer observed that to Talmadge's hard-core constituency of rural voters, "Gene Talmadge was almost a deity." Herman Talmadge quipped that one-third of the voters would follow his father to hell while another third wanted him in hell.[17]

While calling himself friend of the little man (whites only!), Eugene Talmadge advocated individual initiative, governmental economy, segregation, the negative state, and balanced budgets—all of which provided little economic assistance for those at the bottom of the state's socioeconomic ladder. In fact, Talmadge vigorously resisted the efforts of Franklin D. Roosevelt to assist the have-nots in Georgia. Talmadge's conservative economic and political philosophy—low taxes, economy in government, balanced budgets, and negative government—endeared him to the financial interests of Georgia. Key concluded that Talmadge's "strength was drawn from the upper and lower reaches of the economic scale. Industrialists, bankers, corporation executives provided funding. Poor farmers provided votes." One historian concluded that the Talmadge faction "consistently offered the most conservative—more correctly in many cases the most reactionary—social, ideological, and economic programs and policies available to Georgia voters." [18]

The core of the anti-Talmadge faction consisted of organized labor, blacks, the urban press, and middle- and upper-class urban residents. While the Talmadge faction remained loyal either to a Talmadge or to a Talmadge-backed candidate, a constant struggle occurred in the anti-Talmadge faction over leadership. Eurith D. "Ed" Rivers, a former Talmadgite, emerged as the first leader of the anti-Talmadge faction with his election as governor in 1936. Although Rivers obtained passage of a progressive agenda, the financial difficulties of his administration and his confrontations with other state officials damaged his governorship. State attorney general Ellis G. Arnall, also a former Talmadge supporter, assumed the leadership of the anti-Talmadge faction in 1942 upon his election as chief executive of the state. Arnall provided competent and progressive leadership as governor but was prohibited by the state constitution from seeking a second term. In the 1946 Democratic gubernatorial primary, the anti-Talmadge faction was divided between Rivers and James V. "Jimmy" Carmichael. Even though Carmichael won a plurality of sixteen thousand popular votes in the Democratic primary, Talmadge won the nomination—thanks to the county-unit system. [19]

However, Talmadge died before assuming office. During the 1946 primary, some Talmadge leaders had been concerned about his failing health. A provision in the Georgia Constitution stated that the General Assembly would choose a governor provided a candidate failed to receive a majority vote in the general election. Consequently, 675 Talmadge supporters wrote in Herman Talmadge's name in order to qualify him for eligibility by the state legislature in case anything happened to Eugene Talmadge. Amid a great deal of controversy, the legislature elected Herman Talmadge governor, and he served sixty-three days before the Georgia Supreme Court invalidated his election. The court held that Lieutenant Governor Melvin E. "M. E." Thompson should hold the governorship until the next general election, which was in 1948. [20]

As expected, Talmadge ran in 1948 against Acting Governor Thompson. He successfully portrayed Thompson as weak in maintaining the southern way of life, ran a well-organized campaign, proved to be an effective campaigner, and lacked the animosity his father generated. He won 52 percent of the popular vote and overwhelmed Thompson by winning 76 percent of the county-unit vote. Herman Talmadge proved to be a strong governor who was committed to bringing about an improvement of the quality of life of the citizens of the state. Departing from his father's Jeffersonian philosophy of government, Talmadge favored a major expansion of state services. He realized that the state's existing revenue sources—which consisted primarily of property, highway use, excise, and income taxes—could not provide sufficient revenue to fund the major expansion of state services he advocated. Georgia lagged behind the other states in the Southeast in spending for state services. Whereas the rate of expenditures for state services in the Southeast increased 134 percent between 1944 and 1949, Georgia's rate of expenditure had increased 97 percent, with only Mississippi having a lower rate of increase in the region. Of the eight southeastern states, Georgia ranked fifth in amount of taxes collected. The state lacked a general sales tax, even though twenty-seven states, including six in the Southeast, had levied such a tax by 1949. Sales tax revenue in the six southeastern states made up 22.3 percent of their total tax revenue. Certainly Georgians could not legitimately claim overtaxation by their state government, since no other state in the Southeast had a lower per capita tax burden than Georgia. At the same time, Georgia ranked second in the Southeast in per capita spendable income.[21]

Talmadge realized the political liabilities of raising taxes and had promised as a candidate in 1948 not to raise taxes without the approval of the voters in a referendum. The legislature authorized such a referendum to take place in April 1949 to allow the people to express their views on a state tax increase. Even though the voters overwhelmingly rejected an increase in state taxes, Talmadge, faced with a financial crisis, called the legislature into special session to increase the state's excise taxes on such items as gasoline, cigarettes, and liquor. The legislature approved the Talmadge stopgap measure to maintain the existing level of state services. However, additional revenue would have to be found to fund Talmadge's proposed expansion of governmental services. But first he had to be reelected. In the 1950 session of the legislature, Talmadge opposed increasing state taxes and successfully led an effort to defeat the passage of a state sales tax.[22]

Talmadge avoided the issue of taxes in 1950, while Thompson, who again opposed Talmadge, favored a state sales tax. Thompson accused Talmadge of violating his 1948 pledge of promising never to raise taxes without a referendum. Even though the tax increase in the special session had damaged his popularity, Talmadge still managed to defeat Thompson—but with less than 50 percent of the popular vote. However, as in the 1948 race, he achieved an overwhelming victory in the county-unit vote. Early in the 1951 legislative session, Talmadge supported a 3 percent state sales tax. The legislature passed the sales tax measure, which gave Georgia the necessary revenue to finance a major expansion of state services. The tax went into effect in April 1951, and in 1952 it brought in $96 million, or more than 30 percent of the total state revenue.[23]

As a result of this additional revenue, the state embarked upon a major expansion of state services. State appropriations for public education increased threefold, state allocations for teacher salaries more than doubled, state appropriations for vocational education were increased, and university system funding was raised substantially. In addition, the state undertook a massive program of building new schools and purchasing additional school buses. By the end of the Talmadge administration, the state had spent more money on education than all previous administrations had done in the history of the state. Spending in other areas of state services also increased. State spending for public welfare had grown substantially by the time Talmadge left office. The state increased the size of the Medical College of Georgia, undertook a substantial program of hospital construction, and doubled expenditures for the state's mental health facilities. The Talmadge administration undertook one of the largest highway construction programs in the state's history. Talmadge's support of economic development was demonstrated by the fact that the state led the South in industrial development for five of the six years that he served as governor. His industrial recruitment and development efforts resulted in more than fifteen thousand new jobs for the state and more than $50 million in new plant construction. Talmadge also played a major role in developing one of Georgia's basic industries— the forest resources industry.[24]

Although Herman Talmadge proved to be a capable and strong governor, whose leadership contributed to the state's expansion of services and to its economic development, he resisted efforts to modernize the state's political and social systems. Like his father, he opposed black participation in the state's political process. He also condemned and urged resistance to the U.S. Supreme Court's decision in 1954 that held segregated schools to be unconstitutional. He staunchly defended the rural-dominated county-unit system, even though it discriminated against a growing urban population in the state. On two separate occasions, Talmadge supported unsuccessful efforts to extend the county-unit system to general elections. Despite such shortcomings, Jack Bass and Walter De Vries praised Talmadge for his "modernizing influence as governor." Roger J. Pajari considered Talmadge a successful governor for "putting in place a large number of extremely important domestic programs to enhance the general welfare of the people of Georgia." Numan V. Bartley deemed the increased funding of Georgia's public school system "among the most important of the 'modernizing' reforms of the era." Another historian, James F. Cook, praised Talmadge's governorship for "noteworthy improvements" in state government. Prohibited by the constitution from seeking a consecutive term, Talmadge left the governorship in 1955 as one of the state's most popular chief executives. The following year, voters elected him to the United States Senate, an honor that had been twice denied his father.[25]

Although Georgia made substantial progress under the leadership of Herman Talmadge, black citizens still continued to face obstacles to voting in their state. In fact, most blacks in Georgia lacked the opportunity to vote. Blacks had originally gained suffrage in Georgia during Reconstruction and had first voted in the state in 1867 in elections for delegates to the 1868 Constitutional Convention. In those elections, 95,214 white and 93,457 black Georgians registered to vote. However, following the redemption of Georgia by the Bourbon Democrats in the 1870s, black voter participation declined even though blacks still legally retained the suffrage. Fraud, violence, and intimidation as well as a cumulative poll tax in the constitution of 1877 substantially reduced the number of black voters. Nevertheless, blacks still made up a sizable portion of the state's electorate.[26]

The most serious challenge to Democratic control in Georgia came from the Populists in the 1890s. In order to retain political power, the white Democrats resorted to violence and fraud as well as the black vote to turn back the efforts of the white Populists. In the aftermath of that struggle, the leadership of both the Populist and the Democratic parties agreed that the black vote should be eliminated to protect white supremacy in the state. The Populist Party soon faded from the political scene. The state Democratic Party excluded blacks from its primaries in 1900, and by 1904 only 28 percent of the blacks were registered to vote, compared with 67 percent of the whites. With the Republican Party virtually nonexistent and the Populist Party dead, blacks who still remained on the voting rolls lacked a political organization through which they could effectively participate in state politics. Nevertheless, fear by many whites of the possibility of blacks holding the balance of power in future electoral battles led to efforts to reduce black electoral participation further. A constitutional amendment adopted in 1908 provided for literacy tests and property qualifications for voting. As a result, only 4.3 percent of the blacks were registered to vote in the state by 1910. The blacks who survived the disfranchisement efforts voted only in state general elections or in a few local elections. By 1940, black voters had declined to somewhere between 10,000 and 20,000.[27]

The white primary had served as the major legal means of limiting black voting in Georgia in the first half of the twentieth century. However, legal challenges threatened the continuation of this means of disfranchisement. The white primary had first come under legal attack in Texas in the 1920s. The U.S. Supreme Court at first upheld the exclusion of blacks from the Democratic Party primaries in Texas by ruling that the party was a private association and that its primaries were neither a state activity nor an integral part of the state's electoral process. The court reversed its decision in 1944 by holding that state regulation of primaries constituted sufficient state action to invalidate white primaries. In the same year, a black resident of Columbus, Georgia, the Reverend Primus King, attempted to vote in the Georgia Democratic primary. Denied the right to do so, he filed suit in federal district court seeking to invalidate the state's white primary. To the shock of white segregationists in Georgia, the Fifth Circuit Court of Appeals held the state's white primary to be unconstitutional in 1946.[28]

Supporters of the white primary, led by Eugene Talmadge, called for a special legislative session to repeal all state laws regulating primaries, hoping such action would save Georgia's white primary. Although he was under intense pressure to do so, Governor Ellis Arnall refused to call such a session and threatened to veto any repeal legislation passed if the legislature convened itself. Arnall warned that the county-unit system could be discarded and that fraud would run rampant if the state repealed laws regulating primaries. As a result of Arnall's decision, blacks voted in a Democratic Party primary in Georgia in 1946 for the first time since 1900. At the close of voter registration in 1946, 118,387 blacks, or approximately 20 percent of the eligible black population, were registered to vote in Georgia. Since the state had earlier, at Arnall's insistence, abolished the state's poll tax, Georgia stood as the only Black Belt state that had neither a poll tax nor legal means to circumvent the federal courts' invalidation of the white primary. Georgia's black voter registration of 150,000 in 1946 greatly surpassed that of Mississippi's 5,000 or Alabama's 10,000. Of the southern states, only Texas had more blacks registered to vote.[29]

The Talmadges strongly opposed Arnall's decision to allow blacks to vote in Democratic primaries for good reasons. Blacks constituted the most solidly anti-Talmadge voters in the Georgia electorate. More than 90 percent of the black vote in 1946 primary was for the leading anti-Talmadge candidate, Jimmy Carmichael. Shortly before the 1946 primary, a widespread campaign led by Eugene Talmadge was launched to challenge and disqualify black voters. More than 16,000 black voters were purged from the voting rolls prior to the election. Joseph Bernd, in his analysis of the counties where the purges occurred, contended that Eugene Talmadge would have been defeated in the 1946 primary without the purge effort. In the 1948 Democratic primary, estimates of black participation ranged from 60,000 to 65,000, a substantial decline from the 1946 primary. Several factors attributed to the decline, including a lack of black enthusiasm for the anti-Talmadge candidate, M. E. Thompson; intimidation by the Ku Klux Klan and others opposed to black voting; voter purges; and election officials' hostility to black voters. By 1950, the participation of blacks had continued to decline, with approximately 43,000 voting in the 1950 gubernatorial primary.[30]

Despite the efforts of the Talmadges, restoration of the white primary in Georgia failed. Eugene Talmadge, as a gubernatorial candidate in 1946, had promised to restore the white primary. He had proposed to bypass intervention by the federal judiciary by removing primaries from state regulation. Herman Talmadge, following his legislative election as governor, obtained the passage of legislation divorcing primaries from state control. However, the state attorney general invalidated legislation signed by Governor Talmadge following the state's highest court's ruling against Talmadge's election. Acting Governor Thompson then vetoed Talmadge's white primary bill. Talmadge's effort to revive the white primary suffered an additional setback when in 1947 the U.S. Supreme Court ruled against South Carolina's efforts to continue the white primary as a private association activity. Instead of promising to preserve the white primary, Talmadge pledged in his successful 1948 campaign to make the primary as white as possible. In an effort to do so, he obtained the passage of the Voters Registration Act of 1949, which provided for the reregistration of the state's 1.2 million voters including the 150,000 black voters. The law required voters to reregister every two years and either to pass a literacy test or to answer ten of thirty factual questions. Difficulties in implementing the law led the legislature to abandon its efforts to reregister all voters. Nevertheless, despite the failure to revive the white primary, most black citizens still remained disfranchised in Georgia at the halfway mark of the twentieth century.[31]

As the decade of the 1950s began, segregationists in Georgia, including Ernest Vandiver, still clung to the desire to maintain the southern "way of life" in their state. Most white Georgians still believed it was possible to continue the disfranchisement of black citizens. Although aware of their declining numbers, rural Georgians still hoped to retain their control of state politics with the assistance of the county-unit system and a malapportioned state legislature. Unfortunately for the defenders of the old order, change in the 1950s and 1960s dramatically transformed Georgia's political and social systems. Those Georgians who hoped to maintain segregation, black disfranchisement, and malapportionment proved to be no more successful than their forefathers had been in preserving slavery.

THREE

Vandiver and State Politics, 1946–1955

In the decade following World War II, Georgians witnessed some of the most exciting political battles in the state's history involving some of its most interesting politicans occupying the office of governor—Herman Eugene Talmadge, Ellis Gibbs Arnall, Melvin Ernest "M. E." Thompson, and Samuel Marvin Griffin Sr. During this decade, Georgians witnessed a controversial legislative election of a governor, a Georgia Supreme Court decision invalidating that election, the restoration of a Talmadge to political power, the demise of the anti-Talmadge faction, and a U.S. Supreme Court decision that called for the dismantling of the state's segregated public school system.

Like his father, Vandiver actively supported the Talmadges in the state's bifactional political battles. His support of the Talmadges began as early as Gene's unsuccessful senatorial campaign in 1936. Vandiver, then only eighteen years of age, quickly became close friends with Gene's son, Herman Talmadge, who was five years older than Vandiver. In 1938, Gene opposed Senator Walter F. George in his reelection bid. Herman Talmadge served as his father's campaign manager while Vandiver worked as an unpaid volunteer in the unsuccessful campaign. Vandiver did not play an active role in Talmadge's gubernatorial campaigns in either 1940 or 1942 because he was a full-time student at the University of Georgia. But after returning from military service, Vandiver actively participated in Gene Talmadge's 1946 gubernatorial campaign. He traveled extensively throughout the state on behalf of Talmadge and worked closely with Herman Talmadge, who was again serving as his father's campaign manager. Talmadge won the Democratic gubernatorial nomination in 1946 and asked Ernest Jr. to be his chief aide in the upcoming administration. This selection offered Vandiver the opportunity to work directly for a governor. At the same time, another opportunity was presented to Vandiver. He received an offer from a prominent Atlanta lawyer, E. Smythe Gambrell, to join his Atlanta law firm. After seriously considering the offer with his wife, Vandiver decided to decline because, as Betty Vandiver recalled, neither one of them really cared about living in Atlanta for the rest of their lives.[1]

After turning down the Gambrell offer, Vandiver anxiously awaited the beginning of his new position in the upcoming Talmadge administration. The twenty-nine-year-old aide-to-be had risen quickly in politics, from being the youngest mayor in the state to being on the verge of becoming the incoming governor's chief aide. Unfortunately for Vandiver and the tranquillity of the state, Eugene Talmadge died before assuming the governorship. Talmadge had been hospitalized and had not been able to attend the state Democratic Party's convention in October 1946. In his place, Herman Talmadge had given his father's acceptance speech. The following month, the ailing Talmadge was officially elected governor by voters in the general election. However, the sick governor-elect suffered a relapse in November 1946 and had to be hospitalized again. His condition steadily declined, and on December 21, 1946, the sixty-two-year-old governor-elect died, a passing that resulted in the most bizarre political battle in the state's history.[2]

The constitution of 1945 failed to specify what action was to be taken when a governor-elect died. Article V, section 1, furnished three possible interpretations as to who Arnall's successor should be. One paragraph provided that the incumbent governor should hold office for four years "and until his successor shall be chosen and qualified." Another paragraph stipulated that the lieutenant governor would exercise the executive power in case of the death, resignation, or disability of the governor. A third paragraph provided that the person receiving the majority vote in the general election should be governor and further stipulated that the legislature would choose a governor from the two living candidates having the highest number of votes if a candidate failed to receive a majority of the votes in the general election.

Shortly after Talmadge's funeral, Lieutenant Governor–elect M. E. Thompson declared that the people had elected him to succeed to the governorship in the event of the death, disability, or resignation of the governor. As a result of Talmadge's death, Thompson insisted that the people wanted him to assume the executive power of the state. Outgoing governor Ellis Arnall, while maintaining his right to continue in office for another four years, nevertheless insisted that he would not do so. He concurred with Thompson's claim to the governorship and insisted that it was his constitutional duty to remain in office until Thompson assumed the executive power.[3]

Herman Talmadge also laid claim to the governorship from the basis of write-in votes cast in the general election. In that election, several individuals had received write-in votes for governor, and the press reported that the majority of these votes went to three persons: Herman Talmadge with 675 votes, James V. "Jimmy" Carmichael with 669 votes, and D. Talmadge Bowers with 637. Talmadge argued that the legislature had the responsibility of electing the next governor from the two living candidates with the highest number of votes in the general election—himself and Carmichael. Talmadge credited Gibson G. Ezell, a Talmadge supporter, with the idea of a write-in campaign. According to Talmadge, Ezell had been bothered by the question of what would happen if Eugene Talmadge died before his inauguration. Ezell found that the constitution did not specifically deal with that issue. However, it provided that the General Assembly could elect a governor from the two living persons having the highest number of votes if a candidate failed to receive a majority of the vote in the general election. Talmadge concurred with Ezell's argument and "passed the word to a few reliable friends" to arrange some write-in votes for himself. "You might call it an insurance policy. If I couldn't keep Papa from dying, at least I could keep him from dying in vain." Vandiver played no role in the write-in campaign, admitting that he "didn't know anything about that, until after it was done."[4]

When the General Assembly convened on January 13, 1947, the most important issue on its agenda was the resolution of the gubernatorial issue. As Georgians anxiously waited, both sides engaged in intensive lobbying on behalf of the gubernatorial candidates. Vandiver actively solicited the support of legislators on behalf of Talmadge's candidacy. One hundred and sixty-one legislators elected Talmadge governor while eighty-seven members voted "present" in the early morning hours of January 15, 1947. Talmadge's actual physical occupation of the governor's office in the capitol was temporarily stymied, however, by Governor Arnall, who refused to recognize Talmadge's election or to turn the governor's suite of offices in the capitol over to the newly elected governor. Governor Talmadge finally managed to gain physical control of the governor's office. While Arnall removed himself as an active participant in the fracas, Lieutenant Governor M. E. Thompson assumed the burden of challenging the legitimacy of Talmadge's election by insisting that he, not Talmadge, should be governor. In the midst of the furor, Governor Talmadge offered Vandiver the same position—chief aide—that his father had offered him. Vandiver readily accepted the offer and, as chief aide, took care of responsibilities such as answering correspondence, meeting with constituents, giving speeches, and performing other services as directed by the governor. One of his first responsibilities occurred several hours after Talmadge's election when the governor asked him to give a breakfast speech in his place to the Tomato Growers' Association. A tired and weary Vandiver complied.[5]

The legislative election of Talmadge was challenged in state courts, and the Georgia Supreme Court finally resolved the issue. On March 19, 1947, the state's highest court invalidated Talmadge's election and held that Thompson should serve as acting governor until the 1948 general election, at which time voters would choose someone to complete the remaining two years of Eugene Talmadge's fourth term. A disappointed Talmadge bowed to the court's decision, promising to take the issue to the court of last resort—the voters.[6]

Talmadge asked Vandiver to be his campaign manager for the upcoming campaign in 1948. As Vandiver considered the offer, he sought the counsel of his father, who advised him that accepting the position could mean much to his political career. "If you made good [it] would put you close to Talmadge . . . possibly as executive secretary to him." Vandiver accepted the offer, knowing that Talmadge had a great deal of confidence in him: "He knew that I would work hard and do the kind of job that needed to be done." Talmadge gave several reasons for his choice of Vandiver as his campaign manager: "He was new on the scene, not one of the old politicians. He was young. He was a war veteran, and he was connected to the Russell family." In addition, Talmadge expressed confidence in Vandiver's character, ability, and integrity.[7]

Vandiver looked upon his position as "a full time job." He was on the phone constantly talking to politicians and Talmadge leaders surveying the political climate and the support for Talmadge in their counties. Vandiver had the responsibility of scheduling speeches, procuring introducers, organizing political barbecues, and ensuring good attendance at Talmadge's speeches as well as issuing press releases. On one occasion during the campaigning, Vandiver introduced Governor Talmadge over a statewide radio network. "By electing him Governor," Vandiver claimed in his introduction, "we can show the rest of the nation that we do not propose to knuckle under to this effort to destroy our Southern institutions and traditions." On another occasion, Vandiver introduced Talmadge as the only candidate who could "be depended upon by the people to preserve, protect, and defend the County Unit System." Other Talmadge leaders, including Roy V. Harris, Charles D. Redwine, Hughes Spalding Sr., and James L. "Jim" Gillis Sr., assisted Vandiver and played major roles in the campaign. Talmadge won the 1948 primary, carrying 130 counties, although he led Thompson by only 45,000 popular votes out of approximately 700,000 cast.[8]

As Vandiver anxiously awaited the outcome of the election, another pending event competed for his attention. The Vandivers were awaiting the birth of their first child. Samuel Ernest "Chip" Vandiver arrived one week ahead of Talmadge's victory. While the Vandiver family was still rejoicing over Talmadge's election and Chip's birth, tragedy struck. Vandiver's seventy-two-year-old father suffered a near fatal stroke, remaining hospitalized in critical condition for more than two months.[9]

During this difficult time, Governor-Elect Talmadge contacted Vandiver to inquire if he would like a position in the Talmadge administration. Vandiver, after consulting with his brother-in-law Robert L. "Bobby" Russell Jr., decided on the position of adjutant general, the highest-ranking military officer in the Georgia National Guard. Prior to making his decision, Vandiver had checked with other states to inquire if any adjutant generals had used their positions as an advancement to the governor's office. He found that only in Georgia had an adjutant general become a state's chief executive: Marvin Griffin had served as adjutant general in both the Ellis Arnall and Herman Talmadge administrations prior to seeking the lieutenant governorship. Vandiver concluded that the position of adjutant general would be an excellent stepping-stone to higher office in Georgia.[10]

Serving as head of the Georgia National Guard certainly offered the young aspiring politician the opportunity to advance his political interests, since it consisted of about ten thousand men in more than 120 units scattered throughout Georgia. "It was an opportunity," Vandiver reasoned, "to get to know a lot of people over the entire state." As adjutant general, Vandiver occupied a highly visible position in leading and promoting the National Guard throughout the state. The National Guard also distributed a monthly publication to guardsmen, the *Georgia Guardsman*, which always contained comments by the adjutant general on the front page. As adjutant general, Vandiver also served as director of the Civil Defense Division of the state Department of Defense. This agency also published a monthly publication, the *Georgia Alert*, in which the director usually had a front-page article accompanied by his photograph. The agency even posted signs indicating evacuation routes to be used in an emergency or nuclear attacks with the director's name prominently displayed on them. In addition to these responsibilities, Vandiver served as director of the state's selective service system, which had an office in each county in the state.[11]

Under Vandiver's direction, the state and local governments embarked upon the largest National Guard armory construction program in the state's history. Armories were constructed with 75 percent federal funding and the remainder of the expense equally divided between the state and local governments. More than one hundred armories were built during Vandiver's tenure as adjutant general. The dedication of an armory usually included a speech of dedication by the adjutant general in the local community. The ceremony always drew a large crowd including most of the local politicians. In addition to a highly successful building program, the Georgia National Guard increased its membership to record levels during Vandiver's tenure as adjutant general.[12]

Only thirty years old at the time, Vandiver was the youngest adjutant general in the nation. He carried the rank of major general and was considerably younger than the adjutant generals in other states, who were in their fifties or sixties. He enjoyed working with them and served on the Legislative Committee of the National Guard Association of the United States and on the Executive Council of the Adjutant Generals' Association of the United States. Adjutant General Vandiver was named one of the five young Men of the Year in Georgia by the State Junior Chamber of Commerce in 1952 and received the Distinguished Service Award by the Georgia Chamber of Commerce in the same year. The following year, Vandiver was elected president of the National Association of Civil Defense Directors. As adjutant general, Vandiver considered his relationship with Governor Talmadge as "primarily military" rather than political. Nevertheless, he and Betty, at Governor Talmadge's request, attended the national governors' and the southern governors' conferences with the Talmadges. These opportunities allowed him to meet other southern political leaders as well as prominent state politicians from other parts of the country.[13]

When Talmadge ran for reelection in 1950, Vandiver offered to resign as adjutant general in order to assist the governor actively in his campaign. Talmadge turned down the offer because, as Vandiver explained, he "felt that he had the thing won." Although Vandiver did not resign or play an active role in the 1950 campaign, he did raise some money as a private citizen on behalf of Talmadge's campaign. In 1952 Vandiver played an active role on behalf of Senator Richard B. "Dick" Russell Jr.'s unsuccessful effort to gain the Democratic presidential nomination. He did so at Senator Russell's request and with Governor Talmadge's approval. Vandiver took a leave of absence as adjutant general and spent the summer months prior to the 1952 Democratic National Convention soliciting western state delegates on behalf of Russell. He also attended the 1952 convention as a Georgia delegate.[14]

During his service as adjutant general, Vandiver and his family lived in Atlanta, residing in an apartment until 1950, when they purchased a home in the city for thirteen thousand dollars. Two additional children were born during Vandiver's tenure as adjutant general: Vanna Elizabeth "Beth" on October 22, 1950, and Jane Brevard on February 12, 1953. A happily married man with three small children, Vandiver enjoyed directing the activities of the National Guard. Douglas Embry, who served as assistant information officer in the state Department of Defense under Vandiver, remembered Vandiver as someone who was well liked and respected and was a "natural leader." According to Embry, Adjutant General Vandiver was a good family man, a Christian, and an honest person.[15]

Although Vandiver enjoyed being adjutant general, he had long-held aspirations for higher public service. He publicly hinted as early as 1954 that he might enter the upcoming gubernatorial election. On February 26, 1954, he re-signed his position as state director of selective service in order to comply with a federal law that prohibited selective service directors from active involvement in politics. However, Governor Talmadge discouraged Vandiver—then only thirty-six—from seeking the governorship in 1954 and urged him to run for lieutenant governor instead. Vandiver agreed and on March 7, 1954, announced his candidacy for the second-highest elective office in Georgia. In his announce-ment, Vandiver promised to preside over the state Senate in an impartial and fair manner and to maintain "independence of thought and judgment." He promised cooperation with the next governor in promoting the "people's inter-ests" as well as supporting efforts to defend the county-unit system and segre-gation in the public schools. Vandiver resigned his position as adjutant general in June 1954. In doing so, he proudly emphasized his accomplishments in that position, which included increasing the Georgia National Guard to its largest size in the state's history, undertaking the largest armory building program in Georgia's history, and developing one of the best civil defense programs in the nation. Brigadier General Charles R. Fox, adjutant general of the Adjutant Gen-erals' Association of the United States, praised Vandiver's tenure as adjutant gen-eral as bringing "great credit" to his state, to the Georgia National Guard, and to himself by his serious approach to his "duties and gentlemanly conduct and wisdom." Colonel Bernard M. Davey, commander of the Georgia Air National Guard, commended Vandiver for leadership with which he inspired the guards-men with whom he had been associated.[16]

Vandiver had served his state well as adjutant general and now looked forward to a higher level of public service. Three other candidates—John W. Greer, William K. "Billy" Barrett, and William T. "Bill" Dean—also entered the lieu-tenant governor's race in 1954. Each presented a formidable alternative to Van-diver. State representative Greer's involvement in state politics began with his clerkship of the House of Representatives in 1939. He later served in Governor Eurith D. "Ed" Rivers Sr.'s administration as the governor's executive secre-tary and as a purchasing agent in the state Highway Department. Since World War II, he had represented Lanier County in the state's lower house. Greer, a progressive in state politics, had long been a major leader in the anti-Talmadge faction. He had managed Thompson's unsuccessful campaign against Talmadge in 1950. Greer had also vigorously fought Governor Talmadge's efforts to cre-ate private schools in Georgia in an effort to maintain segregation and had battled Talmadge's unsuccessful efforts to extend the county-unit system to gen-eral elections. Greer had led the opposition to Talmadge's efforts to save the white primary in the 1947 legislative session. He entered the lieutenant gover-nor's race with some liabilities, having been accused of engaging in illegal con-duct during the Rivers administration. In fact, a federal grand jury had indicted him with codefendant Hirman W. Evans for violating federal mail statutes and for engaging in a conspiracy to violate federal antitrust laws. Although Evans pleaded nolo contendere and received a fine of fifteen thousand dollars, Greer was never prosecuted even though he had been indicted. A Fulton County grand jury had also indicted Greer for attempting to defraud the state by circumventing state laws regarding competitive bidding for highway construction suppliers. Again, he was never brought to trial.[17]

Another candidate in the race, Billy Barrett, had been Talmadge's director of the state Department of Veterans Service since 1949. Barrett had represented Richmond County in the House of Representatives for two terms prior to World War II. Although Barrett strongly supported the Talmadges, he clashed frequently with fellow Richmond County politician and avid Talmadge supporter Roy Harris. Like Vandiver, Barrett headed a state agency with local offices scattered throughout the state. The other candidate for lieutenant governor—Bill Dean, a lawyer from Conyers—had the longest legislative career of the candidates. He had served in the House from 1935 to 1943 and had been in the Senate since 1943. Dean, as president pro tempore of the Senate, had presided over that body during the turbulent 1947 legislative session. A member of the anti-Talmadge faction in state politics, he actively campaigned on Thompson's behalf in the 1948 election.[18]

Vandiver officially began his campaign for the lieutenant governorship at the city park in Lavonia. More than three thousand supporters gathered to eat barbecue and to hear Vandiver's opening speech, in which he assured his audience that the farmer would "have a friend and a voice" within the structure of state government. He promised to protect the county-unit system and to support any action necessary to maintain segregation. Vandiver entered the campaign, according to the *Macon News,* as the leading candidate. He conducted a vigorous personal campaign for the lieutenant governorship and campaigned, along with Betty, in each of the state's 159 counties. "Betty and I got in an old Pontiac," Vandiver recalled, "which didn't have any air conditioning back then, and we went into every county in Georgia, and went to the courthouse and shook hands." Because of the oppressive heat of Georgia summers, the Vandivers usually drove to campaigning sites at night and politicked during the day. Betty described their campaign tactic: "[Her husband would] go up one side [of the street] and I'd go up the other and then we'd crisscross, and . . . meet to talk with people on the streets always urging voters to support Vandiver for lieutenant governor." The campaign duo passed out pamphlets entitled "This Is Your Life," which contained a summary of Vandiver's political career and several photographs of Vandiver and his family. James C. "Jim" Owen Jr., a personal friend and former University of Georgia classmate of Vandiver's, described the

Vandivers' style of personal campaigning: "They went to every little store, and Betty would be on one side of the street, he'd be on the other, and then they'd cross and swap awhile. That was very effective, very effective."[19]

Betty Vandiver proved to be a valuable asset to Vandiver's campaign. After all, she had grown up in one of the most political families in Georgia and had been around politics all her life. She was a natural campaigner who possessed an enthusiastic and extroverted personality and genuinely liked people and liked to talk with people. "I thought I had a good product to try to sell," Betty reminisced, "and I was doing my job and doing the best I could to sell him." Vandiver considered his wife to be an effective politician and conceded, "She got more votes than I did." Former state representative William D. Ballard viewed her as "one hell of an asset" to Vandiver's political career. Another close friend, Henry G. Neal, viewed Betty as "probably a better politician" than Vandiver, and David C. Jones, a former state representative from Sylvester, remembers Betty Vandiver as "a good street campaigner." He recalled her campaigning in Sylvester with the comment, "Folks just couldn't believe that Senator Russell's niece could get down with the people like that." Although Vandiver was certainly not an introvert, his wife was the more extroverted, talkative, and outgoing of the two.[20]

Vandiver's closest adviser in the campaign was his brother-in-law Bobby Russell. Vandiver and Russell had become close personal friends, and Vandiver considered him "as close, closer than any brother [he] could have had." Russell, like Vandiver, had attended Darlington and received a law degree from the University of Georgia. He was representing Barrow County in the state House of Representatives. Another member of the House and close personal friend of Bobby Russell's, Peter Zach Geer Jr., also helped in the campaign. C. Dixon Oxford of Dawson, who had been placed on the state highway board by Governor Herman Talmadge, also assisted with the campaign; his primary responsibility was in the important area of raising money. On their own, a group of Vandiver's friends and former college classmates organized to assist the Vandiver candidacy. This group included James A. "Jim" Dunlap of Gainesville, William P. "Bill" Trotter of LaGrange, Howell Hollis of Columbus, Griffin B. Bell of Atlanta, Robert C. "Bob" Norman of Augusta, John Miller of Savannah, and Jim Owen of Griffin. This group of about a dozen individuals gathered on a regular basis at the Capitol City Club in downtown Atlanta. Bob Norman recalled:

> There was a group of us who were his friends in college days who organized and met in Atlanta monthly, and organized, and contributed, and rallied up the state, and assumed responsibility for . . . raising money, making contacts, with former friends at the University of Georgia, making contacts with friends that we'd known ourselves, and in meeting in Atlanta. As the campaign grew on we met more often

in Atlanta. I suppose as the time came we sort of chose up the state and worked not only through the University of Georgia names but through names in different parts of the state where we came from and where we had contacts. We made up lists and so forth, and we went to Atlanta and met regularly, and wrote letters, and wrote cards, and did everything we could.[21]

Vandiver estimated that his state campaign cost approximately fifty thousand dollars, with his personal contribution constituting about half of that amount. Expenses incurred in the campaign included those for printing signs, hiring workers to put them up throughout the state, operating a state headquarters at the Henry Grady Hotel, printing "This Is Your Life" pamphlets, printing campaign postcards, paying for campaign expenses for the Vandivers' personal campaign trips to every county, and paying for several statewide radio broadcasts. Some of Vandiver's friends assisted his campaign by spending their own money to promote his candidacy in their counties. Vandiver's campaign had postcards printed that had his photograph on the front and a statement urging the reader to vote for him for lieutenant governor on the back. Betty recalled that her mother and her aunts sent the cards to everyone they knew in Georgia. These cards were distributed to Vandiver supporters throughout the state, who sent them to their friends and neighbors. One such supporter, Jim Owen, recalled that he obtained the roster of all the civic clubs in his hometown of Griffin and sent cards to every member of those organizations. He sent cards to all of his and his parents' friends and neighbors as well.[22]

In addition to his vigorous campaigning, Vandiver benefited from the support of Herman Talmadge, who was leaving office as one of the state's most popular governors. Although Talmadge did not openly endorse Vandiver or campaign with him, the governor conceded, "I passed the word throughout the state to my political friends and supporters to support Ernie Vandiver." Thus Vandiver campaigned with the support of the powerful Talmadge political organization. While Senator Russell continued his tradition of not endorsing political candidates, Vandiver commented, "Probably Senator Russell, when he could, would tell his friends to help me." Betty Vandiver conceded, "Uncle Dick was not the person to tell somebody how to vote, and I doubt if he actively got into it, but I supposed by innuendo, and there were enough people he could talk to that he did what he could for Ernie." However, Representative William L. "Bill" Lanier Sr. noted that Senator Russell did not have to endorse Vandiver because "every time Ernie was introduced he was introduced as having married Senator Russell's niece, so he didn't have to come out for him."[23]

At Talmadge's suggestion, Vandiver actively sought the endorsement of the state's newspapers and in particular the Atlanta papers. His efforts paid off. A

Sunday edition of the *Atlanta Journal-Constitution* praised Vandiver's "extraordinary fine quality of administrative ability" while he was mayor of Lavonia and adjutant general. The *Griffin Daily News* endorsed Vandiver because of his maturity and experience, and the *Camilla Enterprise* likewise praised him for his experience and ability as well as "his calm and deliberate manner of speech." Another paper, the *Bulloch Herald*, believed that Vandiver "would fill the lieutenant governorship with honesty and understanding," and the *Augusta Chronicle* praised him for "his leadership, enthusiasm, and aggressiveness." Not surprisingly, the *Winder News*, Betty Vandiver's hometown paper, called Vandiver "the ideal man for the second spot" in the state government. Vandiver's efforts to obtain newspaper backing succeeded, as he was endorsed by most of the newspapers in the state. "I went to them," he recalled, "and asked them to support me, and most of them did."[24]

The candidates in the lieutenant governor's election realized that the major race in 1954 was for the governorship. Interestingly, for the first time since 1926, a Talmadge did not run for either the governorship or a seat in the U.S. Senate. Lieutenant Governor Marvin Griffin entered the race as a candidate closely associated with the Talmadge faction and hoped to run as the Talmadge candidate. However, the leadership of the Talmadge faction split over Griffin's candidacy. Eventually, two other Talmadge supporters—House Speaker Frederick B. "Fred" Hand Sr. and Commissioner of Agriculture Thomas M. "Tom" Linder—entered the gubernatorial race. Two candidates emerged from the anti-Talmadge faction—former governor M. E. Thompson and state representative Charles L. Gowen. Four other minor candidates also threw their hat in the ring. Despite some formidable opposition, Griffin entered the 1954 governor's race favored to win. The lieutenant gubernatorial candidates failed to attract the crowds drawn by the gubernatorial candidates, and Vandiver decided to "pretty well follow the speakers in the gubernatorial election." As a result, he did a great deal of campaigning among the crowds that gather to listen to gubernatorial candidates. Vandiver saw "personality and footwork" rather than issues as being the dominant factor in the lieutenant governorship race.[25]

However, one issue—maintaining segregation in the public schools—overshadowed all others in both races in 1954. On May 17, 1954, the U.S. Supreme Court unanimously struck down segregation in public education, a decision that segregationists had been both fearing and expecting. In anticipation of such a decision, the state legislature had earlier undertaken action to minimize the impact of such a decision. In the 1951 session of the General Assembly, the lawmakers wrote into the general appropriations bill a prohibition for the expenditure of public funds for desegregated schools. The state's solons also debated but took no action on a constitutional amendment allowing the state to abolish its public school system in order to avoid desegregation. In 1953, the legislature approved the "private school" amendment, which authorized the use of state funds to provide tuition grants to allow students to attend private schools in order to avoid desegregation. The amendment further allowed the state to abandon its public school system. Voters were given the opportunity to determine the fate of this amendment in the 1954 general election. Governor Talmadge, a strong proponent of the amendment, contended that such a voucher system was the only way to avoid "strife and conflict" if desegregated schools were mandated by the federal courts. Talmadge vigorously denounced the court's decision in the Brown case and contended that Georgians would not accept this political decree, which reduced their constitution "to a mere scrap of paper." Senator Dick Russell, along with the other members of the state's congressional delegation, criticized the Supreme Court for its "flagrant abuse of judicial power." Governor Talmadge assured the citizens of Georgia, "We will not have mixed schools in Georgia as long as I am governor of the state."[26]

All the candidates for lieutenant governor supported the preservation of segregated schools in Georgia. Vandiver endorsed the proposed "private school" amendment and called for its ratification by the voters in the 1954 general election. Vandiver also favored the state's closing of any public school in which segregation was legally challenged. He favored the creation of a private school system in those counties threatened with desegregation. "If segregation breaks down," Vandiver stated, "I would favor a private school plan." On another occasion, he assured the voters that if elected, he would "never approve a budget supplying money to mixed schools or colleges."[27]

Governor Talmadge had earlier urged voters to adopt a constitutional amendment extending the county-unit system to general elections. The fate of proposed constitutional amendments was determined by the voters in general elections, which were held on a popular vote rather than on a county-unit basis. Despite the best efforts of Governor Talmadge, voters rejected the proposed amendments in 1950 and 1952. Whereas both Barrett and Vandiver had supported Talmadge's efforts, Greer and Dean had opposed the governor on this issue.[28]

As the campaign progressed, Vandiver exchanged numerous charges with Dean and Barrett. Interestingly, he ignored Greer, considering him the "nicest opponent" a politician could have. Nevertheless, while campaigning throughout the state, Vandiver did carry with him materials and newspaper clippings pertaining to Greer's earlier indictments. "I didn't want to use [the material], wasn't going to use it," Vandiver recalled, "unless he really attacked me, and he never did." Vandiver criticized Barrett for calling himself a farmer, charging,

"Mr. Barrett was raised in the city of Augusta and has never done one day of farm labor and does not own a farm." Vandiver also criticized Barrett for appointing a campaign manager who was a native of Ohio and who had never voted in Georgia. Vandiver reminded voters of a resolution introduced to expel Barrett from the House of Representative "because he materially changed a bill after its passage and sent it to the Senate." Vandiver also charged that Barrett, while serving as director of the State Veterans Services, had forced his employees to contribute to his campaign treasury and had had Veteran Service officers to tack up their boss's campaign posters all over the state. Barrett responded to Vandiver's attacks by charging that Roy Harris was directing Vandiver's campaign and that Vandiver, while adjutant general, had even written to national guardsmen asking each of them to contact twenty-five voters on behalf of his candidacy. Vandiver did not remember writing such a letter, but he conceded that his "headquarters" might have done so. Vandiver did receive strong support from the national guardsmen throughout the state. In fact, he concluded, "I think every one of them was supporting me." George L. Smith II, a member of the House of Representatives, later told Vandiver, "My captain of the National Guard unit down in Swainsboro told me if I didn't help you he wasn't going to vote for me!"[29]

Dean attacked Vandiver by charging that, as director of the state's Civil Defense program, Vandiver had used state funds to send the Civil Defense publication with its prominent display of Vandiver's name and picture "to every courthouse at a time when he was planning to run for governor or lieutenant governor." Dean further criticized Vandiver for gaining valuable publicity for his race by having his name prominently displayed on Civil Defense highway signs located throughout the state and for using state funds to advance his political career. Vigorously denying that he had done anything improper or illegal, Vandiver conceded that the Civil Defense agency did mail an "information publication to 35,000 Georgians but there was not one word of politics in the publication."[30]

On September 8, 1954, Georgia voters gave Vandiver an overwhelming victory in which he received 289,112 votes, or 48 percent of the popular votes cast, in the lieutenant governor's race. Vandiver carried 121 counties and received 77 percent of the county-unit votes. He won 7 of the 8 six-unit-vote counties, 23 of the 30 four-unit-vote counties, and 91 of the 121 two-vote counties. Greer came in a distant second with 22 percent of the popular vote and only 34 unit votes. Barrett received 20 percent of the popular vote and only 56 county-unit votes, and Dean finished a distant fourth with only 4 county-unit votes. Vandiver attributed his election to his University of Georgia classmates, his National Guard associations, and his many friends throughout the state. Other factors in-

cluded the support of Herman Talmadge and the powerful Talmadge organization, his vigorous personal campaign in every county, sufficient financial resources, widespread endorsements from Georgia newspapers, Betty Vandiver's
efforts, and his connection to the Russell family.[31]

Shortly after the election, more than two thousand supporters gathered for
an old-fashioned picnic in Lavonia to honor the town's native son. In his remarks,
a proud but tired Vandiver thanked his wife and brother-in-law and the work
of many friends throughout the state for his overwhelming victory. James L.
"Jimmy" Bentley Jr., executive secretary to Governor Talmadge, representing
the governor, commended Vandiver for his election. Senator Russell sent a congratulatory telegram, and Franklin County's state senator predicted another victory celebration in 1958 after Vandiver won the governor's race. Asked by a
member of the audience if he planned to seek the governorship, Vandiver responded, "The only thing I feel like running for now is a bed." Samuel Ernest
Vandiver Jr., then only thirty-six years old, had reached an important milestone
in his march to the governor's office. For now, though, he looked with anticipation to serving as lieutenant governor in the administration of Marvin Griffin.
Those four years would prove to be both challenging and interesting.[32]

FOUR

The Griffin Years

Samuel Ernest Vandiver Jr. stressed during his race for the lieutenant governorship that he was not endorsing or supporting any of the gubernatorial candidates. He promised to support whomever the voters elected governor when he thought the governor was right, but not when he thought the governor was wrong. "I will be an independent thinker, and I'll do what I think is right." Since the constitution prohibited a governor from succeeding himself, the lieutenant governor's office provided an excellent opportunity for advancement to the state's highest office. Although S. Marvin Griffin Sr. and Vandiver were influential leaders in the Talmadge faction, they were not close personal friends, and their relationship deteriorated during the four years that they served together as the state's two highest elected politicians.[1]

In October 1954 delegates attending the Democratic Party's convention in Macon officially nominated Griffin for governor and Vandiver for lieutenant governor. Following custom, the delegates adopted Griffin's platform, which called for the preservation of segregation, endorsed the private school amendment, urged the creation of a rural roads authority, and opposed tax increases. At the same time, the platform called for increased spending in such areas as public education, old-age pensions, and health facilities. The *Atlanta Constitution* editorialized that although the platform would "be received kindly," the incoming administration would face financial difficulties. State auditor Barton E. "B. E." Thrasher Jr. estimated that $60 million in new revenue would be needed in the upcoming fiscal year just to finance the normal expansion of state services and warned that state services would have to be reduced unless the state had additional revenue. Both Lieutenant Governor–Elect Vandiver and Marvin E. Moate Sr., who had been picked by Griffin to be Speaker of the House of Representatives, predicted that state finances would be the major issue before the 1955 session of the legislature. Vandiver, who had promised no tax increases in his campaign, called for the state to live within its present level of income. Griffin, who had also promised no new taxes in his campaign, now remained silent on the issue of raising taxes.[2]

Unlike Griffin, who had served in the General Assembly prior to becoming lieutenant governor, Vandiver had never been a member of the legislature. He had, however, dealt with lawmakers in his roles as aide to Governor Talmadge and as adjutant general. In addition, Robert H. "Bob" Jordan, a close personal friend and a state senator, helped Vandiver understand the parliamentary maze of lawmaking in the Senate. Vandiver's brother-in-law and close personal friend, Robert L. "Bobby" Russell, who had represented Barrow County in the House of Representatives since 1951, also helped Vandiver master the legislative process. Representative Moate, who had eight years of legislative experience, replaced Frederick B. "Fred" Hand, who had been Speaker since 1947 but who had left the House to run for governor in 1954. The two presiding officers were not close personal friends or political allies, but, as Vandiver explained, they "sort of got along" because they had to as concurrent presiding officers in the General Assembly. Although lacking the legislative experience of Speaker Moate, Vandiver, while presiding over the upper house, faithfully followed the advice that Senator Richard B. "Dick" Russell Jr., who had served as Speaker of the state House of Representatives, had given him: "No matter how you rule, always rule with vigor." Vandiver found the suggestion helpful, observing, "When you rule vigorously, they don't challenge you quite as much as they do when you are timid about it."[3]

Although only thirty-seven years old when assuming the position of presiding over the upper house, Vandiver never considered his age as being detrimental to his responsibilities in the Senate even though most senators were old enough to be his father. He became president of a malapportioned legislative body that consisted of fifty-four members—all white and all male. With the exception of the Fulton County senatorial district, senatorial districts consisted of several counties, with the Senate seats rotating among the counties every two years. The incoming lieutenant governor replaced one of the state's most flamboyant politicians as presiding officer of the Senate. One reporter described Griffin, who was well known for his gregarious nature and storytelling abilities, as "unquestionably one of the flashiest and most entertaining presiders that Georgia's legislative halls [had] seen in recent years." Herman Talmadge observed that if Griffin "hadn't gone into politics, Marvin could have made it as a professional comedian." Certainly the more reserved Vandiver was not as gregarious or as flamboyant as Marvin Griffin, but there were few politicians in Georgia who were.[4]

On January 11, 1955, Griffin and Vandiver took their oath of office as the state's two highest elected officials. Outgoing governor Herman Talmadge told more than ten thousand Georgians gathered on the grounds of the state capitol that he had left the incoming governor with a surplus of $12 million while achieving a record of "unparalleled progress." Governor Griffin assured the audience that his administration would continue the progress of the Talmadge administration and pledged to implement fully the Democratic Party's platform of expanded state services within the state's income and available resources. Conspicuously absent from his inaugural address was any reference to his campaign promise of no tax increases. Instead he called for the creation of a rural roads authority to undertake a major road improvement program, the improvement of the state's public school system, and the expansion of other state services. Griffin did remind his audience of one campaign promise—that there would be "no mixing of the races in the classrooms" of Georgia's schools and colleges during his administration.[5]

In his inaugural address, Lieutenant Governor Vandiver praised Talmadge for having "one of the most progressive administrations" in the state's history. However, he reminded his audience that the Talmadge administration had to dip into the state's surplus in its last two years to finance the increased demands for state services. Vandiver foresaw two major problems confronting Georgia in the immediate future. The most "pressing problem" he saw was maintaining segregated schools. He warned that the Supreme Court's effort to dismantle segregated public schools in Georgia would be "met by a wave of anger and fury, the like of which [had] not been evident [there] since the days of secession." Vandiver called for "calm heads and an intelligent plan of action" to resist the Court rather than resorting to mob rule. The other pressing problem facing the state, according to Vandiver, was Georgia's "vigorous appetite for ever increasing services" and the state's lack of adequate revenue to fund these services. On the question of whether Georgians favored higher taxes to pay for increased services, Vandiver concluded that "their answer would be 'not now.'" Instead of additional taxes, the lieutenant governor called for tightening the state's budgetary belt to cope with the existing financial problems.[6]

On January 20, 1955, the new governor spoke to the legislature and spelled out his legislative agenda. Legislators listened attentively to his remarks about the condition of the state's finances. Governor Griffin stressed that the state's growing population and expanding private sector required the state to expand its services. He gave several examples of the need for additional public services, including the projected increases in the public school population by thirty thousand pupils a year, an underfunded university system, and a projected increase in needy welfare recipients. He observed that the present state spending of $235 million exceeded state income by $10 million. Although Griffin promised to continue the existing level of state services by using the state surplus, he warned that such action would deplete that source of revenue by the end of the year. The lawmakers faced, he pointed out, a "very serious situation" of providing the present level of needed services with an insufficient revenue source.[7]

Under the state constitution, the General Assembly could extend the last appropriations act, which had been adopted in 1953, if it failed to pass a new one. The legislature readily agreed to extend the old appropriations act, which provided for an expenditure of $230 million plus an additional $27 million in spending if funding was obtained. The governor also called for the creation of a committee to consist of lawmakers and private citizens to examine state programs to determine which were essential, to recommend funding needed to operate essential agencies, and to recommend the means of obtaining adequate revenue to fund these programs over the next four years. He called for the committee to make its report no later than June 15, 1955. The legislature agreed and created the State Programs Study Committee. The membership consisted of the governor, the lieutenant governor, the state auditor, the attorney general, the state revenue commissioner, and the chairmen of the two legislative appropriations committees as well as representatives from local governments and the private sector. The committee elected Governor Griffin its chairman and Lieutenant Governor Vandiver its vice chairman. The question of raising taxes or reducing services by the legislature had temporarily been postponed until a later date.[8]

The first major test of political influence of the governor occurred over his call for a reorganization of the state highway board—a board that oversaw one of the most important agencies in state government. The board consisted of three members who were elected to staggered six-year terms by the legislature. Prior to the opening of the 1955 session, Governor Griffin called for the board's reorganization so that members would have terms concurrent with an incoming governor. Griffin gave this bill his highest priority in the upcoming legislative session. Specifically, the governor wanted the board reorganized in order to remove James L. "Jim" Gillis Sr. from his position as board chairman. Gillis, who had been serving as chairman since 1950, had two years of his term remaining; he had, however, backed Thomas M. "Tom" Linder against Griffin in the 1954 gubernatorial primary. Robert A. "Cheney" Griffin, the governor's brother, observed, "Mr. Jim was a fine fellow but he had backed somebody else for governor." Vandiver saw the effort as politics in that the governor "wanted somebody in there that he could control, and he couldn't control Jim Gillis." The Griffin administration wanted its own people on the board, Vandiver reasoned, "so that they could handle giving out the roads to whomever they wanted to and use it politically."[9]

Even though Jim Gillis had been a long time supporter of the Talmadges, Griffin still wanted him out. At first, Gillis refused to step down prior to the expiration of his term. However, any hope that Gillis may have had of Talmadge entering the controversy on his side ended when the former governor publicly stated that he was not going to become actively involved in this fight. Lieutenant Governor Vandiver likewise stated his neutrality on the reorganization bill. With both Talmadge and Vandiver taking a hands-off posture in the controversy, Gillis concluded that he did not have the votes in the legislature to sustain his position and reluctantly resigned from the board. Governor Griffin then withdrew his reorganization bill and urged the legislature to elect Dr. Walter A. Blasingame to replace Gillis on the board, which it unanimously did. Thus, Governor Griffin had prevailed in his first test of political strength in the legislature.[10]

The legislature also unanimously passed a bill backed by the governor creating a rural roads authority and authorizing it to issue up to $100 million in bonds to pave sixteen thousand miles of the most traveled and unpaved rural roads in the state. Other administration bills, such as those abolishing the Georgia Turnpike Authority, permitting the sale of automobile license plates at county courthouses, increasing workmen's compensation benefits, proposing an amendment increasing the state's bounty for the first successful oil well, and prohibiting the expenditure of state or local school funds for "mixed schools," easily passed the legislature. Charles Pou, a reporter for the *Atlanta Journal-Constitution*, wrote that the Griffin administration obtained "nearly everything" it requested in the 1955 session. The *Macon Telegraph* called the recently completed session "one of the easiest, quietest, most non-controversial" in the state's history, which it attributed to the governor's failure to submit a "far-reaching program."[11]

Vandiver assumed the leadership position in the Senate in 1955 believing that the upper house had too many standing committees. Early in the session, he appointed a study committee to make recommendations for improving the Senate's committee structure. At the beginning of the 1956 session, the committee made its recommendations, all of which were unanimously adopted by the Senate. These reforms included reducing the number of standing committees from thirty-eight to sixteen, limiting the number of standing committees a senator could serve on, and limiting the number of committee and subcommittee chairmanships that senators could hold. Margaret Shannon, a reporter for the *Atlanta Journal*, called the reforms "drastic and maybe historic." The *Macon Telegraph*, calling the changes "the most sweeping reform" in the state Senate in the past twenty-five years, attributed most of the credit for this "Efficiency Victory" to the lieutenant governor.[12]

The legislature gladly postponed serious consideration of state finances until after the State Programs Study Committee made its report. Shortly after the 1955 legislative session ended, the *Atlanta Constitution* warned, "The days of reckoning will come in the final months of 1955 when the state will have to cut back services or operate in the red." One administration spokesman, House Speaker pro tempore Harold S. Willingham Jr., expressed his opinion that Georgians were willing to pay additional taxes in order to finance expanded services and even predicted a special session in the summer to raise taxes. Governor Griffin, however, distanced himself from such sentiments by publicly stating that there were no plans to call a special session. The chairmen of both the House Ways and Means Committee and the Senate Finance Committee as well as Lieutenant Governor Vandiver endorsed the governor's statement. Vandiver expressed his opposition to "new taxes except as a last resort to prevent curtailment of necessary state services." He called for the wielding of an "economy ax" to eliminate unnecessary services before any consideration was given to raising taxes.[13]

Nevertheless, the governor's floor leader of the House, Denmark Groover, expressed his belief that additional revenue had to be raised to pay for the public's demands for increased state services. Senator W. Herschel Lovett, who also served on the state board of education, considered a tax increase as the only salvation for Georgia's schools. The *Atlanta Constitution* reminded its readers that the state ranked near the bottom in the South and in the nation in financial support of public education. "We're still falling behind," the *Constitution* concluded, "and the deficiencies are piling up on top of each other." The demand for increased taxes gained an important ally when state auditor Thrasher warned that almost four thousand teachers would not have their contracts renewed for the upcoming school year unless the state came up with additional revenue.[14]

On May 12, 1955, the governor hinted for the first time that a special session might be necessary. Two weeks later the State Programs Study Committee released its report. Vandiver conceded that he "didn't have much to do with that committee." The committee report noted that the various state agencies had requested a total of more than $100 million in additional revenue for the next fiscal year. The committee reduced that number to $65 million for the 1955–56 fiscal year to be increased to $73 million by the last fiscal year of the Griffin administration with the stipulation that two-thirds of the additional revenue would go to public education. The committee called for increases in taxes on cigarettes, alcoholic beverages, motor vehicle licenses, motor fuel, and insurance premiums and the elimination of federal tax deductions by state tax payers. The greatest source of new revenue was the committee's extension of the state's sales tax to services, which would bring in an estimated $21 million.[15]

After the release of the committee's report, Griffin conceded that his position of opposing tax increases had changed since his campaign promise of the previous summer. He stressed that the state could not continue its progress under the existing inadequate revenue system. Noting that more than thirty thousand new students would enroll in the state's public school system in the fall, the governor stated, "Believe me, I ain't gonna turn my back on the children, I don't care what I said last summer." On June 2, 1955, the governor issued a call for a special session to raise $65 million in new revenue. In his address to the special session, the governor proclaimed, "I shall not turn my back on progress, I shall not desert our children in their hour of need, I shall not shirk my responsibilities . . . in the task of developing fully our God-given human and natural resources." He urged the legislature to adopt the study committee's recommendation of increasing state taxes by $65 million. Lieutenant Governor Vandiver, unmoved by Governor Griffin's eloquence, disagreed with the governor on the extension of sales taxes to services. Noting that the state already raised more than $100 million annually from the sales tax, Vandiver contended that the increase would hurt those citizens who could least afford it. The lieutenant governor, conceding that additional money had to be raised or services cut, suggested that the state could save money by placing all state purchasing on a competitive basis—a policy that the *Atlanta Constitution* endorsed. The press generally opposed the special session and in particular the possibility of raising taxes. Several local chambers of commerce adopted resolutions in opposition, and one irate citizen in a letter to the editor of the *Atlanta Constitution* even called for Griffin's impeachment for calling the session.[16]

The House Ways and Means Committee unanimously voted down the extension of the sales tax to services despite the governor's support of the extension. Eventually the legislature raised taxes by more than $40 million, but only after it specified where the additional revenue would be spent and adopted a resolution creating a joint legislative committee to make a study of state government to recommend ways to eliminate waste in its operation. This committee, the Joint Legislative Economy Committee, was charged with submitting a report to the legislature prior to the 1956 session.[17]

In addition to coping with the problem of insufficient revenue in its first year, the Griffin administration had to deal with adverse publicity pertaining to its management of state government. Several months after Gillis's removal as chairman of the highway board, the members of the State School Building Authority voted to remove Fred Hand, who had opposed Griffin in the 1954 gubernatorial primary, as its chairman. Fred Hand, like Jim Gillis, had close political ties to former governor Herman Talmadge. In fact, Hand had served as chairman of the State School Building Authority as well as Speaker of the lower house of the legislature during the Herman Talmadge administration. The authority replaced Hand as its chairman with George P. Whitman Jr. The authority member who nominated Whitman publicly acknowledged that the members of the authority, all of whom had been appointed by the governor, were carrying out the wishes of Griffin in ousting Whitman as chairman. A displeased Hand, accusing the other members of the authority of secretly plotting with the governor to remove him from the chairmanship, attributed the maneuver to politics. Shortly after Hand's ouster, the chairman of the State Ports Authority, William R. "Bill" Bowdoin, was also voted out of his position. Bowdoin, a prominent and well-respected Atlanta banker, had also been placed on the board during the Talmadge administration. Bowdoin, accusing Governor Griffin of injecting politics into the operation of the ports authority, promptly resigned from the authority.[18]

In addition to these personnel matters, press reports appeared pertaining to administration officials allegedly selling merchandise and equipment to the state. These individuals included Senator George Whitman, chairman of the State School Building Authority and the state board of education; Robert Frankenfield, who had replaced Bowdoin as chairman of the State Ports Authority; Senator Daniel B. Blalock, chairman of the Jekyll Island State Park Authority; and James D. Pippen, a member of the State Oil and Gas Commission. Lieutenant Governor Vandiver called for the Economy Committee to investigate allegations of state officials' profiting by doing business with the state. "There must be," he declared, "no hint of scandal in the expenditure of your tax money." The *Atlanta Constitution* agreed that an investigation suggested by the lieutenant governor would clear up the "unhealthy atmosphere of improper use of state connections." Shortly after Vandiver's statement, the governor said that he would request legislation in 1956 prohibiting elected and appointed state officials from doing business with the state. The lieutenant governor commended the governor for his proposal and urged the legislature to give it favorable consideration. Governor Griffin also joined with the lieutenant governor in urging the Economy Committee to make a thorough investigation of "all the state's transactions in all fields." He promised prompt action against any state official engaging in wrongdoing. Finally, he issued an executive order that prohibited state officials from selling to the state unless they were businessmen, well established in the private sector.[19]

In September 1956 a Fulton County grand jury revealed that it had been investigating the State Purchasing Department because of numerous allegations of irregularities in the conduct of that agency's operations. Although the grand jury failed to uncover any violations of state law, it concluded that the state's purchasing system failed to assure taxpayers of the lowest and best prices for purchases. The grand jury's presentments quoted state supervisor of purchases Lawton Shaw, who "stated that the friends and supporters of the administration were favored whenever possible, provided prices or services were in line." The grand jury contended that the existing system allowed for the submission of bids by only a few interested bidders. It called for a system of competitive bidding open to all interested parties to replace the existing system, which afforded "unlimited opportunity for waste and illegal and unethical practices." The *Atlanta Constitution* concluded that the grand jury's presentments should "shock the public conscience." Although expressing satisfaction that the grand jury found no illegal practices or irregularities in the conduct of state business, Governor Griffin concurred with the broad objectives expressed in the grand jury's presentments.[20]

Shortly after the grand jury's revelations, members of the Economy Committee criticized operations of the Jekyll Island Authority. In particular, members criticized the authority's being unable to account for 650 gallons of paint and a purchase order for $8,000 worth of paint that was issued three months after its delivery. Other criticized activities included the awarding of a contract to an air-conditioning firm prior to the opening of the bidding process and a purchasing procedure in which telephone bids were solicited, which prevented verification of bids. State auditor Thrasher also noted that the chairman of the Jekyll Island Authority had interest in a firm that sold the authority $44,308 in new machinery or machinery parts during the past fiscal year. Two firms owned by the chairman of the authority sold the authority more than $101,000 of the $121,000 worth of heavy machinery purchased by the authority. Thrasher also pointed out that there was no competitive bidding when the authority negotiated a $207,893 paving contract with a company owned by a state senator. The *Macon Telegraph* condemned the authority's operations as being conducted in a "thoroughly unbusinesslike and incompetent manner." The Economy Committee recommended the abolishment of the Jekyll Island State Park Authority and a transfer of its functions to the State Parks Authority.[21]

Other alleged improprieties in the conduct of state business continued to surface. In October 1955 newspapers reported that state highway board chairman Blasingame had been involved in the selling of sand to the Highway Department. Thrasher charged Chairman Blasingame with performing an illegal act by authorizing the payment of state funds for the sand to a bank in which he was both a director and stockholder. Senator G. Evertt Millican, a member of the Economy Committee, charged that the state was paying two to three times more for highway paint than South Carolina and questioned the purchasing system used by the state Purchasing Department. Several months later, another Fulton County grand jury revealed that it, too, had investigated state purchasing as a result of accusations of gross misuse of the taxpayers' money. The grand jury recommended open competitive bidding in which all bidders represented established and bona fide business firms. Even though Governor Griffin charged that the jury's condemnation was based on "pure speculation," he nevertheless stated that he welcomed constructive criticism and would prosecute any state employees accused of wrongdoing.[22]

The Economy Committee made two reports prior to the opening of the 1956 session. The reports contained more than fifty recommendations for legislative action and considerably more that could be implemented by state agencies on their own. The committee, chaired by House floor leader Denmark Groover, limited its activities to its legislative charge of investigating state operations and recommending ways of making state agencies operate more efficiently. The committee, emphasizing that it did not "stray afield into the broader questions of ethics," estimated that $5 million a year could be saved if its recommendations were implemented. Concluding that most departments were operating in a businesslike manner, the Economy Committee nevertheless "found some matters being handled not conductive to good business." The committee did not attribute this situation entirely to the Griffin administration but rather concluded, "In most cases, this has been something that has been allowed to grow up over a period of time." The committee made twenty-seven specific recommendations concerning the state's purchasing system that could be implemented immediately. In particular, it urged the state purchasing agent to regain control of purchasing for all departments and called for all state purchases to be made on an annual bid basis "whenever feasible."[23]

The press strongly encouraged the 1956 session to enact the committee's recommendations, with the *Atlanta Constitution* suggesting that the elimination of wasteful practices should be "the primary concern" of the upcoming session. Lieutenant Governor Vandiver praised the work of the committee and called its creation the most important accomplishment of the 1955 special session. Vandiver had been advocating making the committee into a permanent body for several months, but Speaker Moate saw no reason to do so. Instead of a permanent committee, Representative Groover called for each standing legislative committee to "tighten up its own inspection of the various state agencies." Vandiver disagreed with Groover, arguing that only by having a permanent committee would the taxpayers know that they were "getting a dollar's worth in return for every dollar spent."[24]

Governor Griffin, although not calling for the creation of a permanent economy committee, nevertheless endorsed "the objectives of practically every one" of the committee's fifty legislative recommendations. Legislation introduced in the House by Representative Bobby Russell, Vandiver's brother-in-law, to create a permanent economy committee never got out of committee. Although the lieutenant governor suggested that the Senate create its own economy committee, a bill to do so received only one vote in committee. The *Atlanta Journal* bitterly accused the Griffin administration of orchestrating the defeat of the bills because an economy committee kept asking questions that were difficult to answer satisfactorily.[25]

Not only did the legislature fail to create a permanent economy committee, but it also failed to pass most of the legislative recommendations of the Economy Committee. The General Assembly did approve a resolution mandating that state agencies implement committee recommendations that did not require legislative action. State agencies were instructed to report to the 1957 session of the legislature on their progress toward implementation. The *Macon Telegraph* attributed the legislature's failure to pass the economy bills to the Griffin administration. Another paper, the *Rome News-Tribune*, called "the Legislature's failure to seek to bring about economy in our state government" the greatest disappointment of the 1956 session.[26]

However, Governor Griffin considered maintaining segregated schools rather than economy in government to be the major issue before the legislature in 1956. In fact, he described the issue as the "most vital question" the General Assembly would cope with since the creation of the state. Griffin endorsed six bills that had been proposed by the Georgia Commission on Education, an agency that had been created by the legislature in 1953. The bills allowed the governor to close public schools to avoid integration, provided state grants for students to attend private schools, authorized school boards to lease school property to private schools, empowered the attorney general to enjoin local public schools from desegregating, and permitted private school teachers to join the state teachers' retirement system. The legislature not only passed five of these bills but also adopted an interposition resolution declaring the Supreme Court decision of *Brown v. Board of Education* to be null and void, adopting legislation designed to preserve segregation in public parks and waiting rooms in interstate travel as well as authorizing the State Patrol and Bureau of Investigation to enforce segregation. "The legislature has moved decisively to let the whole nation know," Governor Griffin proudly told the lawmakers, "that Georgia stands steadfast in the fight to preserve segregation and to see that her institutions remain inviolate, come hell or high water."[27]

The legislature, at the strong urging of the governor, also enacted a law that permitted a newspaper to be sued in any county in which it had more than fifty subscribers. Previously, state law had limited libel suits to the home county of the newspaper. The new law applied only to newspapers published by corporations and not to those published by individuals. As a result, the law applied to only 11 of the state's 227 newspapers that were dailies in the state's largest urban areas and critics of the Griffin administration. Opponents of the legislation attacked it as unconstitutional, punitive, and retaliatory in purpose. Despite strong criticism, the legislature easily passed the legislation. It did so, however, without the support of the lieutenant governor. He opposed the bill, contending that Governor Griffin went "too far" on it. "I felt that it was wrong to have a law that was that strong."[28]

The press generally condemned the session as one in which the governor completely dominated the proceedings. The *Brantly Enterprise* agreed that the Georgia legislature had "developed rapidly into a first class rubber stamp" for everything the governor wanted. The *Rome News-Tribune* joined the criticism, noting that the past session "was noteworthy for its subservience to the governor." The *Macon Telegraph* editorialized that the session would be remembered because "Governor Marvin Griffin exercised virtually unlimited, almost dictatorial control." The *Waycross Journal-Herald* warned, "The legislature has virtually relinquished its place as an equal branch of the government." Lieutenant Governor Vandiver also joined in the criticism of the dominance of the executive in the state's political system. Declaring that the Georgia governorship had acquired the strongest concentration of executive powers of any state chief executive in the United States, he called for a restoration of a proper balance of power between the state's legislative and executive branches. Both the *Atlanta Constitution* and the *Atlanta Journal* commended Vandiver for raising the issue of the excessive power in the governor's office.[29]

In the aftermath of the 1956 session, Lieutenant Governor Vandiver looked forward to attending the Democratic National Convention in Chicago as a delegate. The lieutenant governor warned that many Georgians would "find the fishing good on election day" unless the Democrats nominated a presidential candidate who respected southern traditions. Prior to the opening of the convention, Illinois governor Adlai E. Stevenson, the leading contender for the Democratic presidential nomination, called for a plank in the party's platform in support of *Brown v. Board of Education.* John S. Bell, chairman of the Georgia Democratic Committee and a delegate to the convention, bitterly criticized Stevenson's action and stated that he would not vote for Stevenson's nomination. Vandiver, who had previously indicated that Stevenson was his first choice, now stated that he wanted to talk with Stevenson and find out "his real attitude toward the segregation question." The Georgia delegates, bound by the unit rule, decided to vote to support fellow Georgian Congressman James C. "Jim" Davis as a favorite-son candidate. Even though Stevenson gained the nomination on the first ballot, he did so without the support of the Georgia delegation. Interestingly, Senator Russell disagreed with the delegation's favorite-son strategy.

He favored solid southern support behind Senator Lyndon B. Johnson of Texas as a means of getting an acceptable civil rights plank for the South in the Democratic platform. However, Lieutenant Governor Vandiver, in a rare public disagreement with Senator Russell, saw the favorite-son strategy as "the only means to get Georgia's message across to the American public and to the convention."[30]

After obtaining the presidential nomination, Stevenson broke with tradition and allowed the convention to select the vice presidential candidate. The leading contenders included two U.S. senators from Tennessee—C. Estes Kefauver and Albert A. Gore Sr.—as well as Hubert H. Humphrey Jr. of Minnesota, John F. Kennedy of Massachusetts, and New York City mayor Robert F. Wagner. Estes Kefauver was considered the front-runner even though southern conservatives opposed him because of his liberalism. Kennedy appealed to the conservative southern delegates, who saw him as more moderate than the other contenders. Kennedy also had an important political ally—Robert B. "Bobby" Troutman Jr.—who worked diligently on his behalf among the Georgia delegation. Troutman had been classmates with Joseph P. Kennedy Jr. at Harvard Law School and had become a close friend of the Kennedy family. Even though the Georgia delegation supported Kennedy for the vice presidential nomination, Vandiver attributed that support more to a dislike for Kefauver rather than enthusiasm for Kennedy. The lieutenant governor considered Kefauver to be "anathema" to the Georgia delegation because of his liberalism. Vandiver, who had never met Kennedy prior to the convention, had the opportunity to visit with him on two occasions in 1957. Troutman invited Kennedy, who was intent on seeking the Democratic presidential nomination in 1960, to Georgia to meet several hundred prominent Georgia Democrats at receptions in Atlanta and at the Talmadge home in Lovejoy. Lieutenant Governor Vandiver attended both affairs and received a letter from Kennedy thanking him for his "very kind hospitality." Vandiver responded in a letter in which he stated that he appreciated the opportunity to get to know Kennedy better.[31]

Prior to the convening of the 1957 session, Governor Griffin called on the legislators to resist both increasing and reducing taxes. Lieutenant Governor Vandiver reiterated his opposition to raising state taxes and suggested the creation of an advisory budget commission to assist the governor in the preparation of the state budget. According to Vandiver, this body would consist of key legislative leaders who would meet with department heads to hear their requests for funding. "Then the commission," Vandiver contended, "would be in a position where it could advise the governor concerning money matters." The *Atlanta Constitution,* which in the past had been very supportive of the lieutenant governor's suggestions, editorialized that such a budget commission would be "meaningless in effect." Senator Fred D. Bentley proposed the addition of fifteen legislators to the Budget Bureau to assist the governor in preparing the appropriations bill. Under existing law, the governor was the sole member of the Budget Bureau. Governor Griffin warned legislators of his opposition to "all attempts to weaken or to shackle" his power as governor. Under pressure from Griffin, Senator Bentley modified his bill and made his proposed budget agency an advisory body to the governor. The revised bill passed the Senate but never reached the House floor for a vote. The challenge to the governor's budgetary powers had been turned back by Governor Griffin. The governor remained, in the opinion of the *Augusta Chronicle,* one of the most powerful chief executives in the country because he had "virtual control of the purse strings." [32]

In his State of the State address in January 1957, Governor Griffin called for no tax increases and pointed out that his administration had substantially expanded and improved government services. Boasting that more than $718 million worth of state projects either had been completed, had been approved, or would be let for contract in his administration, he called such an expenditure "unequaled for a comparable four-year period of time in the State's history." The governor further boasted of his administration's substantial progress in recruiting new industry for the state, increasing educational expenditures, increasing welfare assistance benefits, building roads, and improving health services. The *Atlanta Journal* concluded, "Measured by buildings built and dollars spent on education and other institutions operated by the state, these years have been record breakers." Even the *Atlanta Constitution,* a frequent critic of the governor, conceded that the Griffin administration's accomplishments were impressive. [33]

The administration continued to experience success in persuading the legislature to pass its legislation. William M. Bates, a political reporter for the *Atlanta Constitution,* considered the 1957 session as "pretty much of a success" for the governor. The *Macon Telegraph* agreed, although it noted that the governor had more difficulties during the 1957 session than during previous sessions. In fact, the *Telegraph* observed that the administration had to amend many of its bills to ensure passage and that even then the administration failed to obtain passage of all it requested. Nevertheless, the governor successfully defeated efforts to reduce state taxes, obtained the passage of several segregation bills, and obtained the passage of a resolution calling for the impeachment of several Supreme Court justices. The resolution had the strong support of the lieutenant governor, who also supported a resolution calling on Congress to declare the Fourteenth and Fifteenth Amendments null and void. [34]

Following the 1957 session, Vandiver and state revenue commissioner Truman V. "Red" Williams Sr., who were considered potential rivals in the upcoming gubernatorial election in 1958, clashed over two separate issues. Williams disclosed in April 1957 that $116,000 in voluntary contributions had been made to a special fund designed to supplement the Revenue Department's antimoonshine activities, which included paying informers and providing money for personnel to buy moonshine in order to obtain evidence. Williams refused to disclose the names of the contributors or the name of the recipients of these funds. Representative Wilson Brooks of Fulton County charged that liquor dealers in his county were "being shaken down by somebody" in order to obtain funds— an allegation that Williams denied. Governor Griffin praised Williams's efforts to combat moonshine activity but suggested abolishing the fund if it became "a bone of contention." After Williams publicly called for the continuation of the fund, Griffin appointed a six-member legislative committee to investigate the fund and to recommend whether it should continue to exist.[35]

Lieutenant Governor Vandiver charged that it was "wrong fundamentally" for any public official to "exact tribute" from persons or businesses over which the officials had power—in this case power to grant or deny liquor licenses. "It is my deep conviction," the lieutenant governor declared, "that subsidization and control of public law enforcement by any private group is a dangerous practice wholly foreign to our American concept of justice and impartial law enforcement." Williams, while conceding that most of the contributions came from legitimate liquor businesspeople, assured the committee that contributions were completely voluntary and that no force or intimidation had been used by his department to obtain contributions. Although not finding any abuses in the administration of the fund, the legislative committee expressed concern over the possibility of improprieties in the future. The governor, in compliance with the unanimous recommendation of the committee, issued an executive order abolishing the fund.[36]

The lieutenant governor and Truman V. Williams Jr., Red Williams's son, clashed over the issue of wiretapping. The younger Williams served as executive secretary of the Georgia Commission on Education—an agency created during the Herman Talmadge administration to draft legislation designed to maintain segregation in the state's public schools. Williams requested the purchase of some electronic equipment for use by the commission. The requested material included some equipment that could be used for wiretapping purposes. Lieutenant Governor Vandiver, who served on the commission, questioned the need for such equipment and observed that such a purchase had not been authorized by the commission itself. "I do not believe," Vandiver asserted, "that members of the Commission wish it to be turned into a State Gestapo where intrigue and dangerous tactics are substituted for sincerity, sound thinking and legal processes." Governor Griffin vigorously denied that the requested equipment would be used for wiretapping and requested the lieutenant governor to inform him of any Gestapo tactics used by commission employees.[37]

A lukewarm relationship between the governor and lieutenant governor had seriously deteriorated. Governor Griffin, contending that he had always been "very friendly" to the lieutenant governor, conceded however, "I don't think we saw eye to eye about everything, naturally." Their disagreements began early in the Griffin administration when Vandiver publicly disagreed with the governor over the extension of the sales tax to include services. To the further consternation of the governor, the lieutenant governor had called for investigation of the alleged improprieties in the conduct of state business, and the two had differed over whether the Economy Committee should be converted into an ongoing investigative body. Lieutenant Governor Vandiver had complained of the office of governor having too much power and had even suggested the creation of an advisory commission to assist the governor in preparing the state's budget. Griffin, prohibited from seeking reelection by the state constitution, hoped to find a more congenial candidate than Vandiver to seek the governor's office. But both Griffin and Vandiver had one more legislative session to cope with, and that session would have important consequences for the race for the governorship in 1958.[38]

FIVE

The 1958 Legislative Session

Although Ernest Vandiver's pursuit of the governorship began long before he became lieutenant governor, the intensity of that endeavor increased significantly during the Griffin years. These efforts were recognized by former House Speaker Roy V. Harris in a November 1956 issue of his newspaper, the *Augusta Courier*. According to Harris, Vandiver was "out in front and [had] the inside track" in the upcoming gubernatorial election. Harris attributed Vandiver's commanding lead to a vigorous personal campaign, a large network of friends and supporters throughout the state, his close political association with Senator Herman E. Talmadge, and his connection to the Russell family. In an article written in January 1957, William M. Bates, political editor of the *Atlanta Constitution*, agreed that Vandiver was "the leading contender" for governor. Bates's counterpart at the *Atlanta Journal*, Charles Pou, wrote in March 1957 that many politicians had already picked Vandiver as the "next governor, possibly without much of a struggle." The *Moultrie Observer* concluded that political pundits throughout the state by 1957 considered Vandiver "a shoo-in for governor to succeed Griffin."[1]

Reg Murphy, a political reporter for the *Macon News*, reminded his readers that since 1954 Vandiver had been conducting a vigorous personal campaign for governor that had carried him to every county in the state. In addition, he had conducted an extensive letter-writing campaign on behalf of his candidacy. Indicative of such a campaign was a letter Vandiver wrote to a supporter in April 1957 soliciting a mailing list of residents in his county and information he might have about "any funerals, illnesses, etc." As Vandiver spoke to various groups throughout the state in 1957, he was usually introduced as the state's next governor.[2]

Perhaps as a result of Vandiver's commanding lead in the upcoming election, the Association of County Commissioners invited him to speak at its annual convention in April 1957. His speech was the first a lieutenant governor had been asked to give to the group, which consisted of the state's most powerful politicians on the local level. John S. Bell, chief counsel for the association, introduced Vandiver, reminding the commissioners of the lieutenant governor's close association with Senators Russell and Talmadge and assuring them of Vandiver's dependability on segregation and the county-unit system. Vandiver's address, which was well received, stressed his support for preserving segregation in the public schools, maintaining the county-unit system, opposing tax increases, and supporting the need for increased efficiency in state government. In a direct slap at the governor, Vandiver stressed that there should be "no hint of fraud, graft, or corruption" in state government operations—a line that was applauded by the commissioners.[3]

Vandiver's uneasy relationship with Governor S. Marvin Griffin Sr. continued to deteriorate, perhaps because of Vandiver's active pursuit of the governorship. In July 1957, the governor fired Adjutant General George J. Hearn, Colonel Charles T. White, and Assistant Adjutant General Homer Flynn—all of whom were staunch Vandiver supporters. The governor justified his actions on the basis of their violation of his ban against politicking by state employees. The lieutenant governor angrily criticized the governor's "highhanded and dictatorial abuse of gubernatorial authority." He attributed their dismissal to their friendship with him and Senator Talmadge. Shortly after this flare-up, the Griffin administration terminated state agencies' contracts with a public relations firm headed by Sid Williams, who accused the governor of taking the action because of his support of Vandiver's gubernatorial candidacy. About the same time, a recently dismissed employee of the state Revenue Department attributed his firing to his telling a supervisor that Vandiver would carry his county in the upcoming gubernatorial election.[4]

In July 1957 the state's two highest politicians clashed again—this time over the dedication of a National Guard Armory at Toccoa. The lieutenant governor had earlier agreed to be the principal speaker at the dedication. However, Governor Griffin decided that he wanted to give the dedicatory address. On learning of the governor's request, the lieutenant governor withdrew from the ceremony in order not to create a controversy and embarrass his friends in Toccoa. Governor Griffin, the state's commander in chief, angrily retorted, "I would like to borrow the army back if he is through with it."[5]

In the midst of these disagreements, several other individuals were mentioned in the press in 1957 as possible gubernatorial candidates. They included state revenue commissioner Truman V. "Red" Williams Sr., state representative Denmark Groover Jr., state insurance commissioner Zachary D. "Zach" Cravey Sr., Congressman John J. Flynt Jr., state representative Charles L. Gowen, Atlanta businessman Ivan Allen Jr., and Roger H. Lawson Sr., who had replaced Dr. Walter A. Blasingame as chairman of the state highway board. Governor Griffin publicly insisted that he was not encouraging anyone to enter the race and that he did not intend to endorse a gubernatorial candidate. Vandiver, however, disputed the governor's claim, contending, "[Griffin] decided that I was not his friend and that he was going to pick a candidate to defeat me." The governor, in Vandiver's opinion, had picked Lawson as his candidate because Lawson with his "influence on the highway board could carry a lot of counties by promising roads and that sort of thing." [6]

Despite Vandiver's belief that Lawson would be his major opponent, Red Williams announced in March 1957 that he was a "potential" candidate. Williams had previously served one term in the state House of Representatives and had been an assistant attorney general in the Herman Talmadge administration. He had been appointed state revenue commissioner by Governor Griffin—a position he had held from the beginning of the Griffin administration. Vandiver, who strongly disliked Williams, believed that Williams's appointment was one of the worst mistakes the governor had made because "Red was not honest. Red was a crook." Williams, attempting to undercut Vandiver's lead in the governor's race, sought to portray Vandiver as someone who was "weak on segregation." Vandiver challenged Williams's claim of being a staunch defender of segregation, commenting, "I had heard of no previous statement or speeches from him indicating where he stood." Vandiver pointed out that he had "for many years been publicly fighting night and day for segregation, constitutional government, and the Georgia way of life." [7]

Shortly after Williams's announcement of his possible entry into the governor's race, a newspaper account of a Vandiver speech gave Williams grounds to question Vandiver's support of segregation. The lieutenant governor spoke to a civic club, and the *Atlanta Journal's* coverage of the event presented Vandiver as a moderate on the race issue. In the speech, he had called for resistance to the Brown decision while rejecting "the extremist position on both sides" of the race issue. The headline of the *Journal* article read, "Vandiver Takes Middle Road on Segregation." Vandiver quickly moved to challenge the headline by writing a letter to the editor of the *Journal* in which he called the headline inaccurate because nothing in his address "or in the body of the news story itself could have justified the use of such a headline or the conclusion stated by it." Vandiver emphasized in his letter that his stand on segregation was "the

same as that of responsible Southern leadership . . . as exemplified by Sen. Richard B. Russell, Sen. Herman Talmadge, Sen. Harry F. Byrd, Gov. Marvin Griffin,
Gov. George Bell Timmerman, and other such men" whose views were well
known. "There can be no 'middle road' on this issue. I favor utilizing to the
fullest extent, with no ifs, ands, or buts, all of the strength and resources of the
state government in the fight to protect our sacred institutions and our cher-
ished way of life."[8]

In June 1957 state highway board chairman Lawson finally entered the governor's race and resigned his position on the highway board as required by state
law. Lawson, who had been solicitor general of the Oconee judicial circuit for
six years, had been on the state highway board since mid-1955 and had been
chairman of the body since 1956. He had also been a member of the Rural Roads
Authority since 1955. With Lawson's entry into the race, Williams ended his potential candidacy, realizing that his candidacy would divide the pro-Griffin vote.
Lawson contended that the next governor must stand for integrity in public
office, maintain segregation, protect the county-unit system, and continue the
economic progress of Georgia—positions that the lieutenant governor had long
endorsed. Lawson, borrowing from Williams's strategy, accused Vandiver of
favoring a "middle of the road policy [on segregation] and gradual racial integration." Vandiver quickly retorted that Lawson's allegation was "so obviously
ridiculous that it [did] not deserve the dignity of a reply." Staunch segregationist
Roy Harris agreed with Vandiver and attacked those "Johnnies come lately" for
spreading rumors that Vandiver was soft on the most important issue in the state.
Harris reminded Georgians of Vandiver's association with the Talmadges—who
were well known for their segregationist views—and Vandiver's consistently
strong support of segregation over the years. Harris assured Georgians that Vandiver would "stand like the Rock of Gibraltar in the defense of the Georgia way
of life."[9]

Another possible candidate, Ivan Allen, a prominent Atlanta businessman and
president of the Atlanta Chamber of Commerce, also expressed interest in running. However, Allen's residence in Atlanta presented a major obstacle to his
gaining his party's gubernatorial nomination in the rurally dominated county-
unit system. Realizing that he faced an uphill battle to gain the nomination, Allen
undertook a five-month tour of the state in order to determine his popularity
with the voters. After completing a tour that carried him to more than one hundred counties, Allen, concluding that he could not win under the county-unit
system, announced his decision not to enter the race and endorsed Vandiver.[10]

Another possibility, state comptroller-general Zach Cravey, announced in
August 1957 that he, too, was considering entering the race because the state
needed in the governor's office "a man of wide experience and past accomplish-

ments." Cravey had had a long political association with the Talmadges. He had been appointed to the State Game and Fish Commission by Governor Eugene Talmadge and had been state comptroller-general since 1947. However, early in January 1958, Cravey announced his decision to seek reelection as comptroller-general. Thus, Lawson remained the only announced opponent to Vandiver.[11]

With the gubernatorial election still several months away, the state's attention turned to the upcoming legislative session. Early in January 1958 Lieutenant Governor Vandiver predicted a harmonious session because he saw "nothing controversial" coming before the legislature. Unfortunately for him, an issue emerged that proved to be most controversial—rural roads. The Griffin administration had easily obtained the creation of the Rural Roads Authority in the 1955 session, and that agency had been authorized to sell $100 million in bonds to construct roads in the rural areas of the state. While he had been chairman of the Rural Roads Authority and the state highway board, Lawson had urged the paving of more rural roads. Reports circulated in the press early in January 1958 that the governor intended to ask the legislators to increase the bonding authority of the Rural Roads Authority. Charles Pou concluded that such a request would be a "sure sign" of Griffin's backing of Lawson's gubernatorial campaign. Vandiver agreed and came out in strong opposition to any such request. The lieutenant governor emphasized his commitment to the necessity of rural roads, explaining, "I am a farmer and have lived in a small, rural county, practically all my life on a dirt road." However, he objected to the high cost of financing rural roads by the selling of bonds and warned that the state would either have to raise taxes or have to reduce state services in order to underwrite the bonds.[12]

Governor Griffin presented his State of the State address to the legislature on January 14, 1958. As Lieutenant Governor Vandiver looked on, the governor urged the legislature to increase the bonding capacity of the Rural Roads Authority by $50 million. Key Griffin legislative supporters, including House Speaker Moate, quickly announced their support of the governor's request while the lieutenant governor reiterated his opposition. Vandiver had conferred with various political leaders including Senator Talmadge as to what his course of action should be if the governor proposed to build additional rural roads. Senator Talmadge had urged Vandiver to oppose the governor, contending that it would be a political effort to try to trade roads for votes to defeat him in the gubernatorial election. According to Peter Zach Geer Jr., Senator Talmadge's advice to Vandiver was clear, "Don't let it pass, Ernie. This is the damn governor's race." The lieutenant governor agreed and concluded that the Griffin administration would have "traded roads for votes all over the state." Geer further pointed out, "You have to remember that we were still under the county-unit system." Senator Bobby L. Cook, expressing the views of Vandiver supporters, called the proposal "a political gesture on the part of the administration calculated to raise funds for the gubernatorial candidate of Governor Griffin." [13]

Shortly after the governor's address, Willis N. Harden, a member of the Rural Roads Authority since its creation, wrote the governor a lengthy letter in which he stated his opposition to the request for more money because it was politically motivated. Like Vandiver, he expressed concern over the cost of financing rural road construction by selling bonds. He further questioned whether an additional $50 million in bonds was "wise and necessary," since $35 million worth of bonds of the original $100 million authorized had not been sold. Furthermore, he noted that the authority had $33 million in projects that were to be let or that were being built. Harden questioned why the governor wanted to borrow more money for rural road construction when he already had more money than he could "use wisely" within the time he remained in office as governor. Harden concluded his letter by expressing his friendship with the governor and informing him of his resignation from the authority.[14]

Lieutenant Governor Vandiver responded to Harden's resignation by describing the governor's proposal an attempt to create a "political slush fund" with "millions of dollars in borrowed money to be used in road trading" in the upcoming governor's race. James L. "Jim" Gillis Sr., who had been removed as chairman of the state highway board by the governor in 1955, criticized the Griffin plan, calling it an "unbusiness-like proposal." Gillis, who had served as chairman of the highway board in the Herman Talmadge administration, noted that Governor Talmadge had built three times as many rural roads as Governor Griffin and had done so at considerably less cost. Griffin's proposal also came under intense criticism from many of the state's newspapers. The *Austell Enterprise* opposed the governor's plan because it smacked "plainly of an attempt to play politics pure and simple." Another paper, the *Thomaston Free Press,* opposed the governor's plan "to support the campaign of a gubernatorial candidate," and the *Albany Herald* saw Griffin as attempting "to authorize funds with which to influence the gubernatorial campaign outcome." It was, in the opinion of the *Walker County Messenger,* "a matter of playing politics." The *Augusta Chronicle* dismissed the request as "fiscal irresponsibility simply aimed at buying political support with the people's money." [15]

The *Macon News* referred to the fight between Vandiver and Griffin over the rural roads issue as the "Second Battle of Atlanta." The governor's brother, Robert A. "Cheney" Griffin, saw the disagreement as "one of the toughest fights" of Griffin's entire term as governor. Griffin B. Bell called the conflict "one of the most colorful things that ever happened in Georgia politics," and the *Atlanta Constitution* deemed it "one of the bitterest—and closest—political scraps a Georgia Legislature [had] seen in a decade." George D. Busbee, then a state representative, described the lobbying as "pretty intensive." [16]

Certainly the governor's request resulted in some of the most vigorous lobbying in the history of the General Assembly, with the governor and lieutenant governor playing major roles. Peter Zach Geer Jr. called Vandiver, who personally directed the opposition, "the commander of the forces" against the rural roads issue. The lieutenant governor, according to Geer, told the lawmakers that he was going to be the next governor and would have his own road program. According to Vandiver, "[Most legislators] figured that I was going to be governor, and they'd rather deal with me because I was going to be [around] longer than Marvin was." Cheney Griffin recalled that the lieutenant governor "went all out" to defeat the governor on this issue and conceded that Vandiver had an advantage in that many of the lawmakers were "looking down the road" to the fact that a new governor would take office in January 1959. William M. Bates, a reporter for the *Atlanta Constitution*, wrote that the lieutenant governor marshaled "every weapon and resource available." Vandiver's efforts included giving at least one television address, lobbying representatives, and encouraging county commissioners to contact their representatives to urge them to oppose the governor on this issue. Key supporters assisting Vandiver in this fight included Gillis, Geer, Senator C. Dixon Oxford, former House Speaker Harris, and Representatives Robert L. "Bobby" Russell Jr., Frank S. Twitty, George L. Smith II, and George T. Bagby. Although Senator Herman Talmadge publicly remained neutral, it was well known by lawmakers that he and most of his political organization supported Vandiver's position.[17]

Governor Griffin led the fight for his bond request. Bates wrote that the governor threw "the full weight of his administration plus all the personal influence at his command into the drive to pass the road bill." Vandiver complained of the "threats, the unbridled intimidation and the arrogant and high-handed pressures" employed by the governor. Vandiver told of legislators coming by his office "with tears in their eyes" because road projects, school projects, and jobs of state employees had been threatened by the administration "unless they knuckled under." Several representatives publicly complained of administration pressure. Representative George L. Jackson accused the state Highway Department of canceling a road project in his county because of his opposition to the governor's request. Representative Robert C. Matthews accused a member of the state highway board of threatening to cancel road projects in his county unless he supported the governor. Representative William D. Ballard made similar charges, and Representative Joe Hall Love accused Cheney Griffin of threatening to stop road construction projects in his county unless he supported the governor.[18]

The governor wrote county commissioners urging their support and requesting them to lobby their legislators on behalf of his bill. Key Griffin supporters actively lobbying for the proposal included Cheney Griffin; Lawson; Roy F.

Chalker Sr., who had replaced Lawson as chairman of the state highway board; House Speaker Moate; and revenue commissioner Williams. In particular, Cheney Griffin played a major role on behalf of the governor in lobbying activities. Former state representative David Jones remembered Cheney Griffin's having a simple message to the lawmakers: "If you don't go with us, we're going to punish you. If you go with us, we are going to reward you." One representative, an employee of the state Highway Department when the legislature was not in session, even claimed that the governor offered him a monthly raise of twenty-five dollars in return for his vote. Governor Griffin engaged in the traditional practice of governors of calling legislators to his office to lobby them personally on behalf of his request. Former representative David Jones remembered such an occasion well. In the midst of the controversy, the highway from Jones's hometown of Sylvester to Moultrie was being repaved by the state. According to Jones, "Griffin called me to the governor's office and told me he was going to cancel that road if I didn't help him." [19]

Governor Griffin's request, HB 694, was introduced into the House of Representatives on January 20, 1958, and referred to the State of the Republic Committee—a committee overwhelmingly pro-administration in composition. Without holding public hearings, the committee quickly approved the bill by an overwhelming vote of 22 to 4. The lieutenant governor expressed regret that no public hearings were held, but the governor praised the committee's vote. Vandiver and his major supporters quickly began lobbying to persuade representatives to send the bill back to committee for the purpose of holding hearings while the Griffin forces lobbied for a quick vote on the bill in the House. The House debated a motion to return the bill to committee for almost an hour before its adoption by a vote of 101 to 87. The *Macon Telegraph* called the vote a "tremendous victory" for the lieutenant governor, which occurred, according to the *Atlanta Constitution*, in spite of "overwhelming pressure from the governor's office." [20]

The State of the Republic Committee scheduled a hearing on the bill on January 27. Governor Griffin announced his intentions to attend and urged all Georgians who wanted to continue "a sound, economical and equitable rural roads program" to do likewise. An anti-Griffin senator, Dixon Oxford, accused the Griffin supporters of planning to pack the hearing by urging state employees to attend in order to "whoop it up" for the bill. Governor Griffin wrote county commissioners throughout the state to urge them to attend the hearing to lobby for the rural roads program. More than one thousand spectators attended the hearing, which was held in the chambers of the House of Representatives in order to accommodate the large crowd. Celestine Sibley, writing in the *Atlanta Constitution*, called the "jeering, cheering throng" the largest gathering in the House chambers since the legislative election of Herman Talmadge as governor in 1947. The hearing lasted more than four hours, with eloquent spokesmen on both sides urging the lawmakers to vote with them.[21]

The major advocate of HB 694 before the committee was the governor himself—well known for his oratorical ability. In fact, one historian concluded that the governor had few peers when it came to giving a political speech, and another called him "the master of the old-time stump speech." Both his critics and supporters agreed that Griffin excelled in political oratory. The governor lived up to his reputation in remarks supporting the bill that lasted more than forty-five minutes. Cries of "You tell 'em Marvin!" and "Tell them about them Yankee newspapers, Marvin!" along with cheers and applause punctuated the governor's enthusiastic speech. The governor accused the Atlanta newspapers and "certain politicians seeking personal gain" of attempting to destroy his rural roads program. He vehemently denied the charge that roads built by the Rural Roads Authority were more expensive than nonauthority roads. During his speech, he told the crowd of spectators that his administration had "not exerted any pressure" on legislators to vote for HB 694—a remark that evoked sustained laughter from the audience. The governor conceded that politics had been a factor in the construction of roads under previous bond issues; nevertheless, he claimed that it had been "good politics because everybody got some of it [road building]." But now Griffin insisted that a desire to help the rural areas rather than politics motivated his request. He accused the lieutenant governor and the Atlanta newspapers of bringing politics into the fight. They were willing, according to the governor, "to sacrifice the welfare of rural Georgia for their own selfish interest." As he finished, one elderly legislator commented on the governor's speech, "You don't hear that sort of thing much any more these days. It brings back memories."[22]

A politician who had heard his share of political oratory, former House Speaker Harris, followed the governor to the rostrum. Harris chose not to attack the governor directly, even expressing personal friendship with Griffin, and commended him for his strong stand in support of segregation. Harris chose instead to attack HB 694, alleging that it was concocted by the governor's "palace guard" as a "secret weapon to destroy Ernest Vandiver." Harris denounced the bill as a "damnable scheme" that would be, if passed, an "invitation to the greatest campaign of road trading . . . ever heard of." The question before the House, Harris emphasized, was not whether to build rural roads but whether to finance them with borrowed money or on a pay-as-you-go basis.[23]

Other speakers included Representatives William C. Hawkins, Porter W. Carswell, Frank Twitty, and George T. Bagby. Representative Hawkins ripped into the lieutenant governor's allegation that HB 694 was a "slush fund," contending, "The only slush in this bill is the slush of snow in north Georgia and the slush of mud in south Georgia." Representative Carswell urged passage of the bill, stating, "Marvin Griffin has gotten us out of the mud." Representative Twitty contended that he and other opponents of the bill were in favor of rural roads just as all of them were "for motherhood and against sin" but opposed increasing taxes to pay for them. As far as Griffin's denial of exerting pressure, Representative Twitty stated, "I have seen grown men in the past few days with tears streaming from their eyes. Don't tell me pressure hasn't been applied." Representative Bagby attacked the lobbying activities of the governor's brother and revealed that Cheney had threatened Bagby's brother's state job if he did not vote with the governor. Bagby told the House, "You tell me there's been no intimidation . . . Sho'ly they's a nigger in the woodpile somewhere." Following the debate, the committee recommended approval of the bill by a vote of twenty-one to five.[24]

The governor, pleased with the vote in the committee, returned to the House chambers that night to give his budget address. He proposed no new taxes, noting a surplus of $31 million in the state treasury, and urged a hold-the-line policy on governmental services. Lieutenant Governor Vandiver attacked the governor's request to increase the bonding capacity of the Rural Roads Authority as being inconsistent with a hold-the-line policy on taxes and services.[25]

The following day, January 28, 1958, the House brought up HB 694 for its consideration. In an effort to enhance the possibility of the passage of the bill, supporters amended it to increase the membership of the Rural Roads Authority. These new members included the presidents of the Georgia Farm Bureau, the Association of County Commissioners, and the County Agents Association. Despite this effort and the intensive lobbying by the administration, the bill received only 95 affirmative votes; 106 representatives voted against the bill—a stunning defeat for the governor. The defeat was the first that the governor had suffered on any important bill in his administration. "I lost the fight for the rural folks of Georgia," the governor lamented as he blamed the Atlanta newspapers for the defeat. Griffin promised to speak throughout the state to let rural Georgians "know who sold them out." Lieutenant Governor Vandiver hailed the vote as a "tremendous victory for the people" and commended the legislators "for their integrity, courage, and sincerity."[26]

The *Macon Telegraph and News* editorialized that the vote meant that Vandiver would be Georgia's next governor. William Bates concluded that the House vote left Vandiver "way out front in the race to be Georgia's next governor." The *Savannah Morning News* predicted that Vandiver would be the state's next governor unless a political miracle occurred before the general election. Another paper, the *Columbus Enquirer,* predicted that the lieutenant governor would not even have an opponent in the upcoming gubernatorial election. In the opinion of the *Rome News-Tribune,* the vote on HB 694 had clearly enhanced the lieutenant governor's opportunity to win the state's highest elective office. The *Albany Herald* saw Griffin's defeat as damaging to Lawson's campaign and possibly "politically fatal." It was. On March 18, 1958, Lawson withdrew from the governor's race, claiming that he was not "sufficiently known"—even though he had campaigned extensively over the state in the past eight months and had held highly visible and important positions in the Griffin administration.[27]

In addition to this humiliating rural roads defeat in the House and the withdrawal of Lawson, the Griffin administration suffered from a barrage of revelations of mismanagement and corruption in the months prior to the 1958 gubernatorial primary. Shortly after the rural roads vote, the Senate created a special committee to investigate the Rural Roads Authority. Lieutenant Governor Vandiver, as presiding officer of the Senate, appointed the committee. The following month the committee, chaired by Carl E. Sanders, made its report, which criticized the authority's excessive cost of construction, its indiscriminate location of projects, the poor quality of many of its roads, and its lack of maintenance of completed roads. The report recommended that the legislature abolish the authority and institute a pay-as-you-go method of financing future rural road construction. The committee further recommended a system that allocated funding for roads based on county size, population, and mileage. Whereas the governor attacked the report for its "untruths," the lieutenant governor praised the committee's efforts.[28]

The Senate had also created a committee to investigate the state port at the governor's hometown of Bainbridge. In testimony before the committee, state board of education chairman George P. Whitman Jr. revealed that his insurance agency insured the State Ports Authority's facilities. He informed the committee that he had split $20,239 in commission fees on this policy over the past three years with Harry Shore, the brother-in-law of the chairman of the authority, Robert E. Frankenfield. Whitman testified that he had done so at the direction of the governor. Shore, who had managed Griffin's gubernatorial campaign in Chatham County, testified that he had never owned an insurance agency and had even allowed his insurance agent license to expire. The personnel director of the state docks in Savannah testified that her personal car had been painted during work hours by authority employees. Authority chairman Frankenfield testified that a shipping company had been created with the governor, Cheney Griffin, state purchasing agent Lawton Shaw, and himself as major stockholders. Frankenfield admitted to having taken the authority's maintenance chief to Jacksonville, Florida, during regular work hours to inspect a vessel the shipping company had eventually bought. The chairman further revealed that bids on a portion of the Bainbridge port had been deliberately destroyed at his direction after a Bainbridge construction firm had been awarded the job, an action he defended as appropriate.[29]

In February 1958 the committee released its report. It called for the replacement of the existing five-member authority, all of whom were appointed by the governor, with a seven-member body consisting of three members appointed by the governor and four members who were state constitutional officeholders. The committee criticized Whitman and Shore's fee splitting, the alteration of authority purchase orders, the lack of competitive bidding for authority purchases, and the improper use of authority employees. The committee also criticized the general manager's use of authority secretaries and offices for private purposes. The committee further complained of a general "laxness" in the operations of the authority and called for rules and regulations to improve the conduct of authority business.[30]

Cheney Griffin, who served as his brother's executive aide and played an influential role in his brother's administration, also received some unfavorable publicity in the months prior to the Democratic primary. In April 1958 Cheney Griffin and J. M. Dunn, the mayor of Baxley, were indicted by a Fulton County grand jury on charges of cheating, swindling, and taking money to influence the governor. According to the indictment, a group of Appling County citizens had paid Cheney Griffin to get a resolution passed in the 1957 session that permitted them to purchase some state-owned land. According to the indictment, Mayor Dunn had told the group that the money was required to pay "necessary expenses" in order to get the resolution passed. After the governor signed the resolution, the leader of the group contended that he paid Cheney Griffin fifteen hundred dollars in cash for his influence. Both Griffins vehemently denied the allegations, and Cheney called them "part of a scheme of political persecution" against his brother's administration. In May 1958 a Fulton County superior court judge dismissed the indictments against Griffin and Dunn, ruling that cheating and swindling had not occurred because the resolution in question had been signed.[31]

Following the 1958 legislative session, the Griffin administration decided to remove several state employees on the grounds of economy. Critics attacked the dismissals as an effort to fire friends of the lieutenant governor or employees who opposed the governor on the rural roads issue. John Bagby, the brother of Representative George Bagby, who had been a leader in the fight against HB 694, was fired from his job with the Georgia State Patrol. Representative Bagby charged the governor with retaliation for his negative vote on the rural roads issue. The State Patrol officer assigned to drive the lieutenant governor was told to return to patrol duty or resign, and he promptly resigned. Four members of the House, who voted against the governor on HB 694 and who held state jobs when the legislature was not in session, also lost their jobs. In contrast, two state representatives who voted with the governor on this issue continued their state employment. By the first week of March, sixteen state employees had been terminated by the Griffin administration. Lieutenant governor Vandiver attacked the firings as indicative of "a complete breakdown in all merit principles." He called the firings "a childish move of desperation conceived in anger and panic by a government of cronies."[32]

The two departments in state government that came under greatest criticism during this period were the Revenue and Highway Departments. In March 1958 deputy sales tax director Jason Weems was fired by revenue commissioner Williams. An angry Weems went public and charged that employees of the sales tax unit had been pressured into contributing toward the financing of a television speech by Governor Griffin during the recent rural roads fight. Commissioner Williams also fired deputy revenue commissioner W. Vaughn Rice, who then accused Williams of allowing liquor sales in dry counties in return for contributions of one dollar per case of tax-paid liquor to the department's fund used to combat the making of moonshine. Rice also charged that Williams had withheld issuing liquor licenses until retailers and wholesalers contributed to the fund. A Fulton County grand jury in May 1958 condemned the delaying of issuing liquor licenses and urged the immediate discontinuance of its practice.[33]

The Revenue Department also came under criticism from business owners who complained of improper conduct by department employees. A Jesup grocer complained that he was told to pay $900 in cash to settle a $1,744 sales tax case. The grocer claimed the sales tax agent at the Douglas tax office refused to give him a receipt. A Douglas businessman alleged that he was told to pay $1,165 in cash to the manager of the Douglas office to settle a $2,200 sales tax case. Again no receipt was given. In May 1958 Williams fired the director of the sales tax unit, the sales tax consultant in the Atlanta office, and the regional manager in the Douglas sales tax office for mishandling tax records and money.[34]

The Revenue Department also had problems with the state's merit system. The *Atlanta Constitution* charged that more than one-third of the department's employees had not been employed or worked in compliance with merit system's rules and regulations. In one situation, the State Personnel Board had no record of one employee's being appointed to his position even though he had been on the state payroll since August 1955. The employee also worked as a bookkeeper for a lumber company that was owned by the chairman of the State Personnel Board. As a result of such revelations, both the governor and the State Personnel Board directed Commissioner Williams to comply with all merit system requirements. The director of the merit system complained that it took one of his employees working full-time just to keep up with the discrepancies with merit system requirements in the Revenue Department. A Fulton County grand jury observed that all the departments and agencies of state government had made a diligent effort to comply with merit system rules and regulations with the exception of the Revenue Department. After Williams promised to bring his department into compliance with merit system requirements, the grand jury declined to indict him for alleged violations of system regulations. The grand jury did charge the department with "flagrant violation of the letter and spirit" of the merit system.[35]

The Highway Department presented even greater headaches for the administration. In March 1958, the *Atlanta Constitution* reported on a Highway Department scandal that, in the opinion of one longtime department employee, surpassed the Highway Department's scandals that took place during the administration of Eurdith D. "Ed" Rivers Sr. In this case, the state had paid for street paving in the city of Baxley that had never occurred. Since 1955, the city had awarded state paving contracts totaling more than $240,000. The mayor of Baxley, J. M. Dunn, a member of the governor's honorary staff and close friend of Cheney Griffin's, handled the city contracts and awarded his construction company $125,000 of the contracts. Following the *Constitution's* revelation, state highway board chairman Roy Chalker directed the department's chief construction engineer, Charlie Leftwich, to investigate the allegations. Leftwich reported that only $213,792 of the contracted work had been actually done, with the city of Baxley receiving an overpayment of $28,190. However, he also claimed that $41,777 of additional work not contracted for had been done, so that the state had actually received $13,587 more paving than it had contracted for. Chairman Chalker conceded that the state paving contracts in Baxley were "very loosely handled" and called it a "miracle" that the state ended up with more paving than it had paid for. The *Atlanta Constitution*, in rejecting the miracle argument, labeled Leftwich's report a whitewash. Although confessing that the situation at Baxley was "embarrassing to everybody," Chalker called the irregularities an "isolated instance." In the aftermath, the two state highway engineers and an asphalt foreman who were in charge of the projects in Baxley lost their jobs. In a follow-up investigation, state highway engineer M. L. Shadburn reported that the Highway Department had paid the city more than $143,000 during the past three years for work that was never done.[36]

Other revelations pertaining to the Highway Department proved just as embarrassing to the Griffin administration. A member of the state highway board ordered the paving of a street in the city of Stone Mountain at a cost of almost twenty-eight thousand dollars despite the lack of a contract, a practice that the governor conceded violated state law. Another press report involved a state highway maintenance foreman using highway equipment and personnel in the operations of his sand business. Another revelation showed the use of state highway equipment and material in violation of state law on a private parking area under lease to a member of the Rural Roads Authority. In May 1958 newspaper accounts revealed that the state had paved residential streets in a newly developed subdivision in a city in the governor's home county—a violation of state law. Two of the developers, one of whom was the city's mayor, were on the governor's staff.[37]

Not only was Cheney Griffin his brother's aide in the governor's office, but he also held the position of mayor of Bainbridge and excelled in obtaining state highway funds for his city. In fact, by July 1958 only one of his paving requests—paving the city's tennis courts—had been turned down. The state paved such Bainbridge projects as landings at a boat club, streets in an industrial complex, and a city parking lot. The governor's home county also fared well with state highway funds. Decatur County had received more than $4,650,000 in state highway funds since the department's creation in 1919, with most of the funding occurring in the Griffin administration. Only twenty-four counties had surpassed the $4 million mark in paving contracts since the department was created in 1919. State highway board chairman Chalker's hometown of Waynesboro, population of five thousand, also did well with state road money—receiving almost $300,000 in the first three years of the Griffin administration.[38]

If such revelations were not sufficient to cause the governor concern, the *Atlanta Journal* reported in April 1958 that convict labor in violation of state law had been used on private property in Decatur County owned by the governor, Cheney Griffin, and Raleigh Rollins, a Griffin-appointed member of the State Board of Corrections. According to the *Journal*, convicts dressed in civilian clothes had erected a fence around sixty-five acres of land owned by the governor, cleared lots in a subdivision in Bainbridge owned by Cheney Griffin and Rollins, and built a boathouse for the governor's son. Governor Griffin contended the convicts were used without his knowledge or approval and attributed the revelations to disgruntled state employees, political enemies, and "a personal smear campaign" against him by the Atlanta papers. Rollins admitted to ordering the work done for the governor as a "neighborly gesture." In a report to the State Board of Corrections, the director of the agency, John M. Forrester, disclosed that no evidence could be found indicating that the governor had requested the use of convict labor on his property nor could evidence be found that convict labor constructed a houseboat for the governor's son. Forrester reported that the state had received funds for the use of convict labor to clear the lots in the subdivision. The report concluded that it was regrettable these "irregularities" took place.[39]

Forrester also alleged that the city of Baxley had not compensated the state for the use of convict labor in its paving projects and as a result billed the city $16,605. The Corrections Department also made news when a reporter for the *Atlanta Constitution* found one of the department's road scrapers that had been lost for eighteen months. A chagrined governor ordered the department to institute an inventory system in order to keep up with its equipment. Following revelations that state prisoners had illegally worked for several years on private construction projects in Gilmer County, state prison director Forrester established a daily reporting system informing him where convicts were working and for whom.[40]

On the last day of the 1958 legislative session, the state Senate created the Committee on Government Operations, charging it with the responsibility of conducting "any and all investigations" it deemed "proper and necessary." The lieutenant governor packed the committee with some of his staunchest supporters. Governor Griffin, claiming the interim committee had been created for political purposes, attacked the committee's existence as being unconstitutional because only one house of the legislature had created it. Since the regular appropriations for the legislature had been spent, the committee lacked funds to underwrite an investigation until the new fiscal year began on July 1 or unless the governor provided funding by transferring funds in the budget. The governor refused to do so, resulting in a Vandiver's claim that the governor was trying to undermine the committee out of fear of what it might undercover about his administration. When some committee members volunteered to serve without pay, the governor prohibited anyone in his administration from testifying before the committee. In April 1958 the chairman of the committee reluctantly conceded that the governor had stymied the committee—at least for the time being.[41]

Unfortunately for the governor, Fulton County solicitor general Paul Webb entered the fray by announcing in April 1958 that his office was planning to undertake an investigation of charges of improper conduct in state government. "The people of Georgia," he stated, "are familiar with the numerous charges of corruption and dishonesty in departments of our state government." The Fulton County Commission authorized the expenditure of fifty thousand dollars to finance the investigation, and Webb appointed Paul Cadenhead assistant solicitor in charge of the investigation. State attorney general Eugene "Gene" Cook expressed his approval of the investigation of state governmental activities by local authorities. According to Cook, state law gave him the responsibility of investigating criminal or civil wrongdoing in state government only if local solicitor generals failed to act. In response to Solicitor General Webb's investigation, Governor Griffin announced his own investigation to be headed by none other than former state highway board chairman Roger Lawson. In August 1958 newspapers reported that a Fulton County grand jury was even considering subpoenaing the governor to answer questions pertaining to alleged corrupt activity in state government. The governor stated that he would not appear, calling such action a "slur on the dignity of the office of governor." The same grand jury indicted revenue commissioner Williams on charges that he converted $46,902 in Revenue Department funds to his own personal use. Williams called the indictment part of a smear campaign against him by the Atlanta papers.[42]

By the beginning of May 1958, Ernest Vandiver enjoyed a commanding presence in the approaching gubernatorial election. In fact, he was the only candidate in the race with the withdrawal of Lawson, and some began to speculate whether he would even have an opponent. The rising tide of allegations of improper conduct and mismanagement against the Griffin administration provided Vandiver with an excellent opportunity to run on an honesty-and-integrity-in-state-government platform. His longtime goal of occupying the governor's office seemed easily within his grasp. Few contenders for the state's highest office had ever been in such an enviable position.

SIX

The 1958 Governor's Election

Ln the aftermath of the withdrawal of Roger H. Lawson Sr. from the governor's race in March 1958, the Griffin administration made a diligent effort to persuade former state representative Denmark Groover Jr. to become a candidate. Groover declined to do so, according to Vandiver, because of a friendship that went back to their days as fraternity brothers at the University of Georgia. Although publicly claiming that the demands of a busy law practice prevented his entering the race, he privately attributed his noncandidacy to Vandiver's commanding lead. Groover become the fifth potential candidate after Truman V. "Red" Williams Sr., Zachary D. Cravey, Ivan Allen Jr., and Lawson either to withdraw or to decline to enter the race. The *Atlanta Constitution* attributed the administration's failure to recruit a viable candidate to its sordid reputation and the realization "that to campaign as a Griffin man would be an invitation to humiliating defeat." In April 1958, former governor and anti-Talmadge faction leader Ellis G. Arnall denied reports of his possible candidacy and publicly endorsed Vandiver. Several months later, Arnall reiterated his decision not to enter the race, claiming that he lacked sufficient time to organize a statewide campaign. For the first time since its organization in the 1930s, the anti-Talmadge faction did not run a gubernatorial candidate.[1]

A candidate supportive of the Griffin administration, William T. "Bill" Bodenhamer Sr., finally entered the race in May 1958. Robert A. "Cheney" Griffin insisted that neither he nor his brother had encouraged Bodehamer's action, and neither publicly endorsed Bodenhamer or appeared at any of his campaign activities. However, in a letter to Governor Marvin Griffin written after the election, Mrs. Bodenhamer reminded him that her husband had become a candidate because of Griffin's "encouragement and promise of financial support." Vandiver attributed Bodenhamer's entry to the influence of revenue commissioner Williams, with whom he had never enjoyed a friendly relationship. Vandiver, who considered Williams to be dishonest and unethical, had earlier clashed over the existence of a special fund in the Revenue Department. Since the 1958 legislation session, Vandiver had repeatedly criticized the Revenue Department for alleged improper conduct. A strained relationship between the revenue commissioner and the lieutenant governor had seriously deteriorated.[2]

Peter Zach Geer Jr. cited Williams's personal animosity toward the lieutenant governor as the reason for his encouraging Bodenhamer to enter the race. Williams, according to Geer, may have considered Bodenhamer a viable candidate because of his contacts made throughout the state as a supervisor with the state Department of Education and his work as executive director of the States' Rights Council of Georgia. Bodenhamer pastored a Baptist church in Ty Ty in southwest Georgia at the time of his entering the governor's race, having previously held pastorates in several rural churches throughout south Georgia. A career in education included employment as a teacher, coach, county school superintendent, president of a Baptist college in south Georgia, and state school supervisor in the state Department of Education. Since 1953, he had represented Tift County in the state House of Representatives and had been appointed to the state board of education by Governor Griffin in 1955. From November 1955 until his resignation shortly before the primary, Bodenhamer served as executive director of the States' Rights Council of Georgia, an organization created to promote and preserve white supremacy in the state.[3]

Bodenhamer promised if elected to maintain segregation, preserve the county-unit system, establish the best rural roads program in the country, create the nation's best school system, increase old-age pensions, expand health department services, and reduce utility rates. Bodenhamer believed that the state collected sufficient revenue, which, combined with "business-like economics," could adequately fund his platform and even permit him to cut state taxes. In response to the numerous allegations of improper conduct against the Griffin administration, he assured voters that extravagance, graft, and corruption would not be tolerated if he was governor.[4]

To undermine Vandiver's commanding lead in the race, Bodenhamer attempted to portray the lieutenant governor as being weak on segregation, opposed to the county-unit system, and against building rural roads. He accused Vandiver of being the candidate of the Atlanta newspapers that were opposed to the county-unit system and segregation. He reminded rural voters that Vandiver and the Atlanta newspapers had fought Governor Griffin's rural roads program in the 1958 legislative session. He further charged that the Atlanta papers not only had endorsed Vandiver for lieutenant governor but had even endorsed black candidates for political office in Atlanta. Bodenhamer's campaign newspaper, the *Georgia Progress,* displayed a photograph of Vandiver inserted between photographs of two Atlanta black politicians. "These are the kind of candidates that the Atlanta newspaper monopoly would have the people of Georgia entrust with segregation, the County Unit system, Rural Roads, and Rural Progress," Bodenhamer charged. The *Georgia Progress* also reprinted the *Atlanta Journal* article entitled "Vandiver Takes Middle Road on Segregation," *Atlanta Journal-Constitution* editorials critical of the county-unit system, and a 1955 letter in which Vandiver had declined Bodenhamer's request to give speeches on behalf of the States' Right Council because of the lieutenant governor's "full schedule."[5]

Bodenhamer even accused Vandiver of allowing "race-mixing" at his campaign rallies by allowing blacks and whites to stand in the same line while waiting to be served barbecue at a political rally in Valdosta. The Baptist minister praised the Valdosta police chief for insisting on separate lines and thereby preventing Vandiver from "mixing the races on a social level." He accused Vandiver of permitting a similar transgression at another rally in Thomson—an allegation promptly denied by local officials. A Bodenhamer advertisement in the *Macon Telegraph and News* questioned whether Vandiver could maintain segregation in the state's public schools if he couldn't do so at his own political gatherings. Bodenhamer challenged Vandiver to a television debate to be broadcast statewide during which Bodenhamer promised to discuss Vandiver's weakness on segregation.[6]

In the opening speech of Bodenhamer's campaign in Moultrie, the candidate accused the "Vandiver camp" of bringing the Koinonia Farm, a racially integrated and controversial farming community located near Americus, to Georgia. He attempted to associate Vandiver with the farm through one of the lieutenant governor's former aides and close friends, Robert H. "Bob" Jordan, whose brother was director of the farm. Bodenhamer accused Jordan, while an aide to the lieutenant governor, of legally representing the farm and further charged that this "race-mixing group" had been "advised and directed from the lieutenant governor's office during 1955, 1956, and 1957." Bodenhamer promised as governor to close the controversial farm and take the same action against "any other such institution that the firm of Jordan, Vandiver, and Jordan [tried] to foster in any county in this great state." Vandiver considered Bodenhamer's Koinonia allegations demagoguery and the "meanest thing Bodenhamer did in the campaign" because of the hurt it caused the Jordan family.[7]

Bodenhamer also claimed that members of the Georgia branch of the NAACP had held a secret meeting in Macon and had endorsed Vandiver's candidacy.

When leaders in the Vandiver campaign organization accused revenue commissioner Williams of having "NAACP Endorsed" stickers attached to Vandiver campaign posters, Williams retorted that Vandiver was "entitled to the NAACP stickers on his posters because the leaders and members [of the NAACP were] supporting him." Bodenhamer also criticized Vandiver's "false plea for economy," claiming it had "the same hollow ring as his newfound attitude on segregation." The Baptist minister charged that the expense of operating the state's Defense Department and the office of lieutenant governor had "tremendously increased" under Vandiver's leadership. In fact, Bodenhamer claimed that his opponent's "experience in spending public money [had] been one of waste and extravagance" and warned of "a rising spiral of new taxes" if Vandiver was elected.[8]

While most of the high-ranking officials in the Griffin administration either remained neutral or supported the Vandiver candidacy, Williams played a highly visible and key role in the Bodenhamer campaign. In fact, Vandiver considered Williams to have been Bodenhamer's chief fund-raiser and credited him with raising "the necessary funds from liquor interests and other people under his control to [allow Bodenhamer to] run a pretty vigorous campaign." Critics of Williams accused him of forcing Revenue Department employees to contribute to Bodenhamer's campaign. Representative Edgar H. Wilson of Bibb County and Dr. Roy O. McClain, pastor of Atlanta's First Baptist Church, charged that Revenue Department employees had been told to contribute to the Bodenhammer campaign or run the risk of being fired. Another critic, Harold M. Dixon, who was the manager of the Atlanta regional sales tax office, accused his superiors of forcing him to obtain contributions from fellow employees. From whatever sources obtained, Bodenhamer had sufficient funding to finance a strong campaign against Vandiver. In fact, Sam Scheinman, whose firm had been retained by Vandiver to handle his media campaign, warned his client that Bodenhamer had already contracted by June for "more television network and radio network time than [he recalled] ever used in any gubernatorial campaign." During the primary, Bodenhamer gave several thirty-minute television addresses on Monday nights that were carried over eight stations and distributed 500,000 copies of the *Georgia Progress* throughout the state.[9]

Griffin administration officials, who joined Williams in support of Bodenhamer's candidacy, included Truman V. Williams Jr., executive secretary of the Georgia Commission on Education, and Roy F. Chalker Sr., chairman of the state highway board. So many employees and high-ranking officials in the Revenue Department attended Bodenhamer political events that the *Walton Tribune* complained of the "imported crowd of hooray-yelling state employees" present at his rallies. Williams M. Bates, political editor of the *Atlanta Constitu-*

tion, also commented on the large number of Revenue Department employees attending Bodenhamer's Saturday afternoons rallies. Despite such support, attendance at Bodenhamer's speeches was considerably lower than that present at Vandiver's rallies. Bodenhamer's opening speech drew only 2,500 supporters, whereas 15,000 were in attendance at Vandiver's kickoff address in Dublin. In the final weeks of the campaign, Bodenhamer cut back on the number of speeches he gave because of poor attendance. William Bates wrote in August 1958, "If crowds at political rallies are any measuring stick, William T. Bodenhamer is not making much of a stir in his quest of the governorship." Bodenhamer's Saturday rallies usually attracted around 500 supporters, and attendance during the week was considerably lower, with some speeches canceled because of poor attendance.[10]

A statewide poll among justices of the peace revealed in August 1958, according to the political editor of the *Atlanta Journal,* what most political observers had thought all along: "There is no governor's race." Although the poll indicated that Bodenhamer would carry only three counties, he predicted victory because only the "integrationists and a few deadhead, self-seeking, repudiated politicians" were supporting Vandiver. Williams even boasted of his candidate winning a landslide victory by carrying more than 135 counties. Despite such rhetoric, the Bodenhamer candidacy never posed a threat to Vandiver's march to the governor's mansion because his campaign started in a weakened condition and deteriorated rapidly thereafter.[11]

In contrast, a confident Vandiver opened his campaign on July 12 in Dublin to a large crowd of fifteen thousand supporters, who braved a drizzling rain to hear their candidate. His speech, carried live over a statewide radio broadcast, lasted forty-five minutes and was interrupted more than sixty times by the enthusiastic audience. Vandiver stressed the major planks in his platform of maintaining segregation, preserving the county-unit system, promoting economy and efficiency in the conduct of state business, and restoring honesty in state government. He promised a businesslike administration that would reorganize and streamline state government as well as end fraud, graft, and corruption in the conduct of the state's affairs. He assured Georgians that during his administration there would "be no need for investigators to investigate the investigators" and there would be no assistant governor—a promise that provoked cries of "No Cheneys!" Vandiver went on to assure rural Georgians of his commitment to build roads for them, but, unlike the Griffin administration, on a pay-as-you-go basis. The crowd loudly applauded his pledge to spend more for road maintenance, improve the quality of road construction, and pay highway contractors only for work actually completed. He assured voters that his administration would be one in which all Georgians would be proud and that they would not have to apologize for its conduct.[12]

Vandiver realized that his most important promise to the voters would be his commitment to preserving segregation in the state's public schools. However, the degree of that commitment resulted in intense discussion between Vandiver and his advisors prior to his opening speech in Dublin. Some of them, led by brother-in-law Robert L. "Bobby" Russell Jr. and Peter Zach Geer Jr., advocated Vandiver promising that schools would not be desegregated in his administration to counter Bodenhamer's charge of Vandiver's weakness on maintaining segregated schools. After all, Governor's Herman Talmadge and Marvin Griffin had made similar pledges. Other advisors, including Walter O. "Bee" Brooks Jr., Griffin B. Bell, and Henry G. Neal, favored a more moderate position of promising to use every legal means to maintain segregation in the state's schools. "Unfortunately," Vandiver conceded, "my advisors and I let Red Williams and Bodenhamer get under our skin, and we took his [sic] political goading too seriously." Vandiver went with the stronger position in his Dublin speech—"When I am your governor, my three children nor any of yours, will ever attend a racially mixed school in the state of Georgia." He used variations of the statement "As long as Ernest Vandiver is your governor, there will be no mixed schools or college classrooms in this State—no, not a single one!" in speeches given later in the campaign. In retrospect, the lieutenant governor explained that he went with the stronger position because of the "vitriolic campaign [he] was getting from Bodenhamer," but he conceded that such a promise was a mistake because of the inevitability of desegregation. He further conceded that his election would have occurred even if he had taken the moderate position.[13]

Vandiver did not confer with either of the state's U.S. senators about which position he should take prior to the Dublin speech. In fact, he never discussed this matter with Senator Richard B. Russell Jr., perhaps realizing the senator's adamant views on segregation and his opposition to yielding on the issue. Vandiver did discuss the matter with Senator Herman E. Talmadge after the Dublin speech. According to the senator, he told Vandiver that his position was a mistake: "Sooner or later probably the federal government would force a decision, and I knew we would have to decide whether we wanted to have schools or no schools, and I knew that we had to continue [public] schools in Georgia regardless." Glenn W. Ellard, a state representative at the time, agreed that the promise was a mistake but admitted that "it certainly didn't hurt him any in his campaign for governor." A colleague of Ellard's in the legislature, William D. Ballard, however, contended that Vandiver had to take such a position "if he wanted to be governor." Three other legislators who were Vandiver supporters, William L. "Bill" Lanier Jr., George D. Busbee, and Carl E. Sanders, considered Vandiver's position to have been a mistake.[14]

Bodenhamer's questioning Vandiver's commitment to segregation irritated the lieutenant governor because nothing in Vandiver's past indicated any wavering on his part in upholding segregation. He had spent his entire political career closely associated with Eugene and Herman Talmadge—two of the state's most ardent defenders of the "southern way of life." Vandiver was also associated by marriage and friendship with Senator Dick Russell, an unyielding defender of the old order. Another adamant segregationist, Roy V. Harris, played a major role in Vandiver's gubernatorial campaign and vigorously defended Vandiver against Bodenhamer's weak-on-segregation charge. Harris had earlier been instrumental in planning the state's anti-integration strategy and in creating the States' Rights Council of Georgia, an organization in which he currently served as president. He and Governor Griffin had even traveled to Little Rock in 1957 to shore up Arkansas governor Orval E. Faubus's resistance to school desegregation in that state. Both Griffin and Harris were frequent speakers at citizens councils meetings throughout the South. It seemed highly unlikely that Harris, one of the most adamant defenders of segregation in the South, could be supportive of a gubernatorial candidate "weak" on the issue.[15]

Public statements made by Vandiver throughout his career indicated his staunch commitment to segregation. During the 1948 gubernatorial election, Vandiver called for Herman Talmadge's election as a means of resisting the efforts "to destroy . . . Southern institutions and traditions." As a candidate for lieutenant governor in 1954, Vandiver stressed his commitment to public schools as long as they remained segregated and promised to never sign an appropriations bill for "mixed schools" if he ever became governor. Vandiver actively worked for the ratification of a constitutional amendment in 1954 sponsored by Governor Talmadge that permitted the dismantling of the state's public school system to avoid integration. While a candidate for lieutenant governor, he suggesting legislation to implement the proposed private school amendment that included the termination of public funds to integrated schools and tuition grants to students attending private schools in order to avoid integration. Vandiver later boasted in the gubernatorial campaign that the legislature had enacted his suggestions.[16]

Like most Georgia politicians in the 1950s, Vandiver vehemently opposed the *Brown v. Board of Education* decision, maintaining that it was not based on law or precedent, was contrary to the federal Constitution, and was based "in part on a Swedish textbook of sociology." On one occasion in 1957, the lieutenant governor called the Brown decision a "judicial monstrosity fabricated upon sociology and psychology rather than legal precedent." In the same year, he told an audience, "[There is] not enough money in the Federal treasury to force us to mix the races in the classrooms of our schools in Georgia." The lieutenant warned that if President Dwight D. Eisenhower sent federal troops to Little Rock, Arkansas, to carry out a federal court school desegregation order, "the sovereign states [would] be mere puppets of a central dictatorship." When the president did commit troops to Little Rock, Vandiver denounced him as a "modern-day Caesar" and lamented "the terrifying spectacle of Federal troops, in full battle regalia, invading a sovereign state seeking to enforce, with fixed bayonets, an illegal and preposterous decree of the United States Supreme Court." Vandiver even called for President Eisenhower's impeachment for his actions in Little Rock. The lieutenant governor also supported a resolution in the General Assembly calling for the impeachment of members of the U.S. Supreme Court for their antisegregation decisions and another calling for the repeal of the Fourteenth and Fifteenth Amendments. An opponent of the Civil Rights Act of 1957, Vandiver urged Senators Talmadge and Russell "to filibuster this monstrosity to a well-deserved death." [17]

Bodenhamer's accusations that Vandiver was a weak supporter of the county-unit system also irritated Vandiver, since he had consistently defended the county-unit system throughout his political career. He was politically associated with the Talmadges, who were ardent defenders of the system, and supported the two unsuccessful efforts by Governor Herman Talmadge to extend the county-unit system to general elections. Vandiver himself came from a two-unit county and had no reason to challenge an electoral system that gave the rural counties—the political base of the Talmadge political organization—their political clout in state politics. Vandiver had, in fact, won the state's second-highest political office in 1954 with 77 percent of the county-unit vote. [18]

Vandiver's strategy in dealing with Bodenhamer was to ignore him—a tactic Vandiver conceded "was hard." For the most part, Vandiver adhered to this strategy. He labeled Bodenhamer the "puppet candidate" of revenue commissioner Red Williams and accused his opponent of directing "an absurd campaign of vilification and utter falsehoods never before equaled in the whole history of this country." However, Vandiver decided that Bodenhammer's weak-on-segregation charge could not be ignored. He reminded voters of the Tift County representative's vote against the private school amendment that had been sponsored by Governor Herman Talmadge. The attack forced Bodenhamer to defend his vote by claiming that his plan of saving segregated schools was better than that of Governor Talmadge, one of the most vociferous defenders of the racial status quo in the state. The Vandiver campaign also widely distributed to rural voters—the most ardent supporters of the existing social system—a political newspaper stressing Vandiver's longtime support of segregation. In addition, the campaign assembled a panel of four prominent segregationists who presented a program televised statewide in which they extolled Vandiver as a strong political leader who would vigorously and successfully defend segregation. The panel consisted of the president of the States' Rights Council of Georgia, Roy Harris; former president of the States' Rights Council of Georgia, Carter Pittman; Governor Herman Talmadges' House floor leader, J. Robet Elliot; and the executive secretary to former governor Herman Talmadge, James L. "Jimmy" Bentley Jr.[19]

Bodenhamer's campaign also came under blistering attack from the media. The *Miller County Liberal* contended that Bodenhamer's "unfounded and irresponsible charges that Vandiver was weak on segregation and the county unit system" were ridiculous. In the editorial opinion of the *Camden County Tribune,* "Bodenhamer's smear, fear, scare and deceitful campaign tactics" had disqualified him as a candidate. The *Columbus Enquirer* editorialized, "Bodenhamer's tactics increased our desire for the nomination of Lieutenant Governor Vandiver." The *Macon Telegraph* condemned Bodenhamer's "low-level tactics," and the title of an editorial in the *Waycross Journal-Herald* read, "Campaign Tactics Insult Voters." The title of an *Augusta Herald* editorial simply stated, "A New Low in Dirty Campaigning." The Atlanta papers agreed that Bodenhamer's "unholy mud-slinging" had damaged his campaign, which the *Augusta Chronicle* characterized as "gutter type of politics at its worst." In a front-page editorial, James H. "Jimmy" Gray Sr., editor of the *Albany Herald* and a staunch segregationist, bitterly attacked the "nauseous deed" of the Bodenhamer campaign for affixing "NAACP Endorsed" stickers on Vandiver's campaign posters. In doing so, Gray claimed that Bodenhamer had hit a new low in dirty politics. The *Americus Times-Recorder* agreed and concluded that such activity was "even more deplorable when a man who calls himself a minister resorts to such tactics."[20]

Vandiver's campaign organization had a number of leaders with considerable political expertise, including James L. "Jim" Gillis Sr., Peter Zach Geer Jr., Bobby Russell, C. Dixon Oxford, and Roy Harris. Gillis, a prominent leader in the Talmadge organization, served as state campaign manager. Key advisors included Senator Talmadge, Bee Brooks, Griffin Bell, Henry Neal, Frank Twitty, George L. Smith II, and John S. Bell. Vandiver had the support of the powerful Talmadge organization, and Senator Talmadge, who, while publicly professing neutrality in the gubernatorial contest, supported his former campaign manager behind the scenes. Talmadge described his organization's support of Vandiver as "very active." Even though Talmadge declined to attend Vandiver's final campaign speech in Gainesville, the senator sent his mother, who sat on the platform, which sent an unmistakable message to voters. In addition, Bobby Russell persuaded his uncle, Senator Dick Russell, to attend the Gainesville speech, which likewise sent a message to the voters. Vandiver believed that Senator Russell's presence in Gainesville was probably "the only time he ever took part in somebody else's political campaign, and he didn't do anything except be there."

The presence of Senator Russell and Senator Talmadge's mother on the platform in Gainesville represented a symbolic unification of the two most powerful politicians in the state behind Vandiver's candidacy.[21]

In contrast to Bodenhamer's efforts, Vandiver's campaign enjoyed the overwhelming support of the press. The *Augusta Herald* expressed the sentiments of many of the editorials in support of the lieutenant governor in that he would maintain segregation while returning honesty and efficiency to state government. The *Atlanta Journal-Constitution* endorsed Vandiver as a reformer who would end "the free wheeling days and flagrant cronyism of the past." Even though the black-owned *Atlanta Daily World* expressed disagreement with Vandiver on the race issue, it praised his "constructive proposals" for reforming state government. The *Walton Tribune* endorsed Vandiver because he was "a good, clean, honest and sincere man," and the *Augusta Chronicle* endorsed him because he would provide a "clean, wholesome, and dynamic kind of leadership." Nevertheless, the *Savannah Morning News* expressed concern over his promise to preserve the county-unit system—a system detrimental to the growing urban areas of the state.[22]

In a time of weak campaign finance disclosure laws in Georgia, Vandiver estimated that his campaign raised about $500,000, "which was a lot of money in those days." Peter Zach Geer Jr. agreed that the campaign was "well financed" and never experienced money problems because contributors considered Vandiver to be the next governor. The campaign spent much of its money on television and radio; the 1958 campaign was the first in Georgia in which the candidates used television as a major means of reaching the voters. In a typical campaign week, Vandiver gave several speeches, visited with voters, met with local politicians, and attended campaign functions. The week's activities usually culminated in a major rally on Saturday at which he gave a speech that was broadcast over a radio station network of one hundred stations. Vandiver also gave several statewide television addresses on Monday nights from Atlanta. His presence in the capital city on Mondays also allowed friends and supporters to visit with him and to make financial contributions to the campaign.[23]

Even though most observers considered Bodenhamer's run for the governorship a failure even before it began, Vandiver nevertheless conducted a vigorous personal campaign by seeking votes in every county in the state. The Vandivers worked well together, as they had in the lieutenant governor's race, with Betty Vandiver accompanying her husband on his campaigning throughout the state. Although she disliked being away from her children, Betty Vandiver nevertheless spent most of the summer on the campaign trail with her husband. The Vandivers left the girls with either her mother or his sister, and Chip spent the summer at camp. Although enjoying talking with voters or passing out campaign literature, she refused to give campaign speeches, claiming an inadequacy in that type of political activity.[24]

Vandiver, who had heard political speeches since Gene Talmadge's day, could give a good stump speech. Although most observers did not think his oratorical skills were on the level of the Talmadges or that of Marvin Griffin, they nevertheless considered him more than adequate on the political stump. George T. Smith, a state representative at the time, saw Vandiver and Griffin as having two different styles of speaking. An entertaining and gregarious Griffin used levity and stories to illustrate his points in his speeches, whereas Vandiver rarely did. If Vandiver lacked the entertaining abilities of Marvin Griffin, he possessed other personal qualities to help him in the campaign. He was only forty years old—thirteen years younger than Bodenhamer—and had a handsome appearance with his black curly hair and penetrating blue eyes. In addition, Vandiver, in Geer's opinion, "had a sincerity about him that was not made up at all; it was genuine," a sentiment concurred in by those who knew him best—his wife and children.[25]

In comparison with previous gubernatorial campaigns, the 1958 election proved to be dull and lackluster, occasionally enlivened by a controversy. One such flare-up involved the Georgia Commission on Education. The agency's assistant executive secretary, Harvey H. Chandler, abruptly resigned in the midst of the primary, charging that the commission's executive secretary was utilizing commission personnel and facilities to prepare a political newspaper for the Bodenhamer campaign. Vandiver, who served as vice chairman of the commission, criticized Williams for allowing the commission to be involved in the publication of the newspaper in question, the *Georgia Progress*. Another member of the commission, state auditor Barton E. "B. E." Thrasher Jr., called for the agency's abolishment—a sentiment concurred in by the Atlanta newspapers and the *Macon Telegraph*. However, Governor Griffin, who served as chairman of the commission, opposed dismantling of the agency and even refused to convene the body to discuss the charges, perhaps because of his awareness that a majority of the commission supported Vandiver's candidacy. Instead, the governor directed his former chairman of the state highway board, Roger Lawson, to investigate the allegations.[26]

In the midst of the controversy, Executive Secretary Williams resigned, claiming his action was taken in an effort to prevent the Atlanta newspapers, Vandiver, and "other integrationists" from using the controversy to destroy the commission. Williams, while denying the allegations made by Chandler, charged that Vandiver's weakness on segregation was "so soundly documented" in the *Georgia Progress* to justify the commission's publishing the paper. Governor Griffin considered Williams's resignation as the end of the controversy, and the *Atlanta Journal* labeled the matter "another sordid chapter" of the Griffin administration. At first, Governor Griffin refused to release Lawson's report, but he finally agreed to do so late in August. Lawson's report concluded that Williams and his personal secretary at the commission had indeed prepared the *Georgia Progress* and that commission employees had even prepared a mailing list for the paper's distribution.[27]

The long campaign, whose first round had occurred in the 1958 legislative session, finally ended on September 10, 1958, when more than 620,000 Georgians nominated a gubernatorial candidate in the Democratic primary. As predicted, Vandiver won an overwhelming victory, carrying 156 counties, winning 400 county-unit votes, and obtaining 499,477 popular votes. Bodenhamer carried only three counties—his home county of Tift, an adjoining county to Tift, and Governor Griffin's home county—and received only 87,830 popular and 10 county-unit votes; another candidate, Lee Roy Abernathy, received 33,099 popular votes. A reporter for the *Atlanta Constitution* called Vandiver's victory—with almost 81 percent of the popular vote and 98 percent of the county-unit vote—"one of the greatest triumphs ever racked up in this state by a candidate for a contested political office." Governor Griffin, in trying to explain the outcome, told reporters, "Obviously you can't win a race if you wait until the year of the election to begin." While Senator Russell called Vandiver's victory "almost without parallel in Georgia politics," Vandiver called his win the greatest ever given to a politician by the voters. Revenue commissioner Williams expressed satisfaction that at least the Bodenhamer campaign had "succeeded in getting Mr. Vandiver to promise that there would not be a single mixed classroom for the next four years."[28]

Vandiver attributed his landslide victory to several factors: the electorate's desire to support a sure winner, the negative reaction to Bodenhamer's campaign, and the lack of bifactionalism that had characterized Georgia gubernatorial politics since the 1930s. In addition to conducting a vigorous personal campaign, Vandiver had the backing of the two most powerful politicians in the state—Herman Talmadge and Richard Russell—and he had assembled an outstanding campaign organization. He also had the backing of the state's political establishment, the overwhelming endorsement of the press, and a weak opponent who had neither the support of a statewide political organization nor the backing of a popular outgoing governor. Bodenhamer had never run in a statewide election, whereas Vandiver had served as Herman Talmadge's campaign manager in 1948 and had successfully run for the state's second-highest office in 1954. Vandiver had been in state office for almost ten years, which allowed him to make numerous contacts throughout the state as adjutant general and later as lieutenant governor. In contrast to Bodenhamer's last-minute entry into the race, Vandiver had been campaigning for governor for years. Vandiver's successful challenge of Governor Griffin on the rural roads issue in the 1958 legislative session plus the numerous allegations of misconduct against the Griffin administration had neutralized whatever influence the governor may have exerted against Vandiver in the primary. Perhaps most important, the voters rejected Bodenhamer's charges that Vandiver was weak on protecting the county-unit system and segregation.[29]

Vandiver officially became his party's gubernatorial nominee at the party's state convention in Macon in October 1958. In his acceptance speech, Vandiver warned of "the end of the public schools for both the white and the colored" if the federal courts ordered school desegregation in Georgia. He also warned that the state was on the verge of bankruptcy, with most of the state's surplus having been spent by the Griffin administration. He contended that the state's revenue for the present fiscal year had been $318 million while state expenditures had been $342 million, resulting in a deficit of $24 million. At the beginning of the last fiscal year, Vandiver noted that the state had a surplus of $35 million, which had been reduced to $5 million by the Griffin administration—the lowest surplus in ten years. Vandiver called depletion of the state's surplus by the Griffin administration "suicidal" and wondered "what other maneuvers [would] be made to financially embarrass the incoming administration."[30]

In December 1958, Vandiver, pledging to do "everything possible" to carry on state government without raising taxes, warned that his job had "been made far more difficult by spendthrift policies carried on in the past year." He attributed the prevailing lack of confidence Georgians had in their state government to the "graft, ineptitude, lost motion, waste, extravagance and irresponsible policies" of the outgoing "corrupt administration." As for whether the governor himself was corrupt, Vandiver concluded, "If you know the people around you are corrupt, and you don't do anything about it, you're corrupt." Many observers of politics in Georgia agreed with Vandiver that the Griffin administration left much to be desired in its running of the state government. Lester Velie, in an article in *Reader's Digest,* concluded that "never in Georgia's history had so many stolen so much." According to Velie, twenty-four state officials, employees, and conspiring businessmen were indicted on fraud, conspiracy, embezzlement, and other charges, fourteen of whom were convicted. Robert W. Dubay's study of the Griffin administration concluded that it was "fully deserving of its reputation as one of the most corrupt, amoral, mismanaged, and inefficient administrations in Georgia history." Historian Numan V. Bartley characterized the Griffin regime as one of "lax administration, alleged corruption, and an apparently rampant spoils system." Historian James F. Cook observed that although Griffin himself was "never convicted of any wrongdoing himself, his lax and careless administration allowed corruption to flourish all around him." One author, Robert Sherrill, estimated that state losses through corruption during the Griffin administration ranged from $10 million to $30 million.[31]

Clearly, Vandiver faced a challenge overcoming the mismanagement, inefficiency, and corruption associated with the Griffin administration. But even more important, the governor-elect faced the problem of living up to his promise of maintaining segregated schools in his administration. Neither of Vandiver's immediate predecessors, Herman Talmadge and Marvin Griffin, had to face a challenge to segregation in the state's public schools. Vandiver understandably hoped to "be that fortunate." However, events taking place outside the state threatened the racial status quo in Georgia's educational system. Arkansas's legislature, like the General Assembly of Georgia, had passed massive-resistance legislation. Vandiver later contended that Roy Harris had even carried copies of the Georgia massive-resistance statutes to Arkansas governor Faubus, who used them as the basis for his state's massive-resistance laws. Nineteen days after Vandiver's primary victory on September 10, 1958, the U.S. Supreme Court announced its decision in a case involving the state of Arkansas's resistance to the desegregation of Central High School. The Court unanimously held that *Brown v. Board of Education* could not "be nullified openly and directly by state legislators or state executives or judicial officers, nor nullified by them indirectly through evasive schemes." As a result of the *Copper v. Aaron* decision, Vandiver concluded, "I knew then that times would be tough."[32]

Unfortunately for the governor-elect, black parents had already filed suit in January 1958 challenging Atlanta's segregated public school system. A federal district court, after denying a motion to dismiss the suit, had promised a ruling prior to the opening of the city's schools in September 1959. As Governor Griffin warned of a desegregation crisis for the state "in the not-too-distant future," Atlanta mayor William B. "Bill" Hartsfield called for a referendum to allow Atlantians to determine the fate of their public schools. Fulton County representative Milton M. "Muggsy" Smith announced his intention to introduce local option legislation in the upcoming legislative season. Representative Smith, conceding that the segregation battle was lost, contended, "It's now simply a question of whether or not we want public schools." However, Senator Russell angrily attacked the "surrender group" and those who advocated "a little" integration, and Senator Talmadge likewise publicly expressed his opposition "to any surrender" in the state's efforts to maintain segregation. While Governor Griffin attacked Mayor Hartsfield for trying to "throw in the towel" on this issue, the governor-elect insisted that the Vandiver administration was not considering local option and reiterated his campaign pledge to continue segregation in the state's public schools.[33]

Despite the governor-elect's stance, many white Atlantans called for the preservation of the city's public schools even if they were desegregated. An unmoved Governor Griffin reiterated his opposition to desegregation and expressed his "utmost confidence" in the legislature and the governor-elect's commitment to upholding segregation in all the schools. On January 10, 1959, four days before Vandiver's inauguration, federal district judge William B. Sloan ruled against segregation at Georgia State College, a senior college in the state's university system located in Atlanta. It was becoming increasingly obvious that soon the political leadership of the state would have to make some crucial decisions concerning the future of public education in the state of Georgia.[34]

The governor-elect's hope of avoiding the desegregation issue appeared doomed, with the question no longer being whether the state would have to desegregate its schools but when. As Vandiver prepared to assume the reins of power in state government in January 1959, he realized that his administration would face some of the most difficult problems ever to confront an incoming governor—maintaining segregation in the state's public schools, overcoming a crisis in state finances, and cleaning up a state government racked by corruption and inefficiency. At least, the governor-elect could take satisfaction from his overwhelming victory in the gubernatorial election.

SEVEN

Vandiver's First Year

Samuel Ernest Vandiver Jr. took the oath of office as Georgia's seventy-third governor on January 13, 1959. More than eighty-five hundred chilly and windblown spectators, including outgoing governor Marvin Griffin, gathered at the capitol to witness the occasion. In his inaugural address, the new governor called the challenge to the state's segregated schools "the most overriding internal problem ever to confront the people of Georgia and the South" in the twentieth century. The governor told the assembled crowd that the guiding principles of his administration would be preserving "our way of life," conducting state government in the most economical manner possible, reforming and reorganizing state government, and restoring integrity in the conduct of state affairs. The *Macon Telegraph,* after noting the racial and financial problems facing the new administration, wondered "whether condolences might not be in order rather than congratulations." Lester G. Maddox, an unsuccessful mayoral candidate in Atlanta and a well-known segregationist, concluded that none of Vandiver's predecessors had had "to shoulder the load that [had] been placed upon this man."[1]

The new governor appointed Peter Zack Geer Jr. to be his executive secretary and Henry G. Neal to be the assistant attorney general assigned to the governor's office. Other key appointments included Atlanta attorney Griffin B. Bell to the position of chief of staff and Walter O. "Bee" Brooks Jr. as his press secretary. Governor Vandiver headed a state government in which most of the major department heads were either elected by the voters or appointed by boards or commissions. Elected officials included the attorney general, commissioner of agriculture, commissioner of labor, comptroller-general, secretary of state, public service commissioners, and state school superintendent. Nevertheless, a governor exercised influence over department heads, even those elected, since he had the constitutional responsibility of submitting their departments' budgets to the General Assembly for its consideration and adoption. Additionally, since the last appropriations bill adopted by the legislature was in 1956, the governor had discretionary power to spend money in the state budget that had not been appropriated. The governor also had other budgetary powers including item veto power over appropriations bills.[2]

Governor Griffin had demonstrated yet another means of influence that Georgia governors had over nonconstitutional boards and commissions: the threat of legislative reorganization. On assuming office in 1955, Governor Griffin decided to replace James L. "Jim" Gillis Sr. as the chairman of the state highway board. When Gillis refused to resign, the governor threatened to force him out by having the legislature reorganize the board. Even though Gillis had several years left in his term, he bowed to the inevitable and resigned, thereby allowing the governor to fill that position with a Griffin supporter.[3]

Governor Vandiver, even before he assumed office, let it be known that he wanted a state highway board acceptable to him. His choice for chairman of the board was his former campaign manager, Jim Gillis, who ironically was the same individual whom Governor Griffin had forced out of the position four years earlier. Even though state highway board chairman Roy F. Chalker Sr. still had two years left in his term, he decided to resign. The other two members of the board followed his example. The legislature unanimously approved Governor Vandiver's suggestions of Gillis, Robert H. "Bob" Jordan, and Willis N. Harden to fill the vacancies on the three-member board. Jordan, a close personal friend of the governor's, served as Senate president pro tempore in the 1959 legislative session. Hardin had earlier served on the Rural Roads Authority and the state highway board during the Griffin administration but had resigned as a result of his disagreement with Governor Griffin over the financing of rural roads.[4]

Executive positions filled by boards included the directors of the Department of Corrections, Department of Public Health, Department of Veteran Services, State Merit System, Forestry Commission, and the Game and Fish Commission. The governor did not made any effort to replace the holders of those positions. Governor Vandiver reappointed the state superintendent of banks and the directors of several state departments, including the Department of Public Welfare and the Department of State Parks, Historic Sites, and Monuments. Although the board of the Department of Public Safety had the authority to choose a director, Governor Vandiver's preference for state senator William P. "Bill" Trotter Sr., a close personal friend, to serve as director of the department received the support of the board of the Department of Public Safety.[5]

Governor Vandiver realized that his two most important appointments would be the state purchaser of supplies and the state revenue commissioner. Both of these officeholders had received intense criticism during the Griffin administration. The governor recruited William R. "Bill" Bowdoin, a young Atlanta banker known for his integrity, to head up the state Purchasing Department. At first Bowdoin resisted Vandiver's pleas, but finally he agreed to assume the position with the understanding that his tenure would be brief and that his successor would be Alvin C. Gillem, whom he intended to bring in as his deputy. Bowdoin had earlier served as chairman of the Georgia Ports Authority in the Griffin administration but had resigned over a disagreement with Governor Griffin. For the other key appointment, Vandiver turned to a former Talmadgite, state senator C. Dixon Oxford, to serve in the position of revenue commissioner. Oxford had served as chairman of the highway board in the Herman Talmadge administration.[6]

The new governor quickly moved to implement his promise of economy in the state government by ordering a 10 percent reduction in spending for most government departments. The governor warned of the state's having either to cut back on services or to increase taxes in order to maintain the existing level of services. He also issued an executive order prohibiting state officials and employees from doing business with the state. Such practices in the Griffin administration had been strongly criticized. In the spirit of reducing governmental expenditures, revenue commissioner Oxford fired more than 200 of his department's 1,100 employees, contending that his department was overstaffed. He also issued a directive prohibiting political fund-raisers in the Revenue Department as well as prohibiting the creation of any special fund accounts like that of Governor Griffin's revenue commissioner. In the spirit of reducing the cost of government, state highway board chairman Gillis announced the termination of almost 400 of his department's 5,500 employees.[7]

Even before Vandiver took office, opposition to the incoming administration surfaced in the state board of education. The ten-member board, eight of whom had been appointed by Governor Griffin, ignored Governor Vandiver's call for economy in government by approving a $23 million increase in its budget request for the upcoming fiscal year. The governor angrily criticized the increase as "utterly ridiculous." The board also voted to reelect George P. Whitman Jr., a strong Griffin supporter, as its chairman. The vice chairman of the board, James S. "Jim" Peters, criticized Whitman's election and the substantial increase in the board's budget as an effort to embarrass the new governor. Whitman had been criticized for his vast business dealings with the state in the Griffin administration. According to the state Purchasing Department, businesses owned by Whitman had sold more than three hundred thousand dollars' worth of merchandise to the state in 1958. Whitman's insurance company also provided the insurance coverage on the facilities of the Georgia Ports Authority. The *Macon Telegraph* urged Vandiver to remove Whitman from the board. Both the vice chairman of the House Education Committee, Representative William H. Mc-Whorter, and the Greene County Board of Education called for his resignation. Despite such demands, Whitman refused to resign.[8]

Chairman Whitman, although closely associated with Governor Griffin, had supported Vandiver in the 1958 election and had financially contributed to the Vandiver campaign. The governor, on learning of Whitman's plans for the board in his administration without Whitman's discussing it with him, had a tense meeting in the governor's office with Whitman. Vandiver told the chairman, "George, we both can't be governor, and I've got my plans for the State Board of Education, and you're not included in them." Whitman agreed to resign as chairman but insisted on continuing as a member of the board until his term expired. However, after Whitman refusal to appear before a Fulton County grand jury investigating state purchasing procedures in the Griffin administration, Governor Vandiver requested Whitman's resignation from the board—a request that was refused. An irritated governor ruled out calling a special legislative session to impeach Whitman but publicly hinted at legislative reorganization to remove him from the board. After all the board members except William T. "Bill" Bodenhammer Sr. urged their fellow member to resign, Whitman finally did so on March 8, 1959. The board then elected a Vandiver political supporter, Jim Peters, to the chairmanship.[9]

Governor Vandiver experienced far less difficulty from the leadership of the General Assembly. At the time of the Vandiver administration, legislative independence did not exist, and a governor exercised tremendous influence over the legislature, which included selecting its leadership. A governor's choice for Speaker of the House of Representatives historically had always been elected by the lower house. Vandiver designated George L. Smith II as his preference for Speaker, a choice unanimously agreed to by the House. Smith, a longtime Talmadge supporter, had represented Emanuel County in the lower house since 1945. He had long desired to be Speaker and had broken ranks with Governor Griffin because of his choice of Marvin E. Moate Sr. for the position. Vandiver asked Frank S. Twitty, a close personal friend and an effective legislator, to be his floor manager in the House. The governor considered Lieutenant Governor Garland T. Byrd, who presided over the Senate, a "good friend" and supporter. Another Vandiver supporter and friend, Robert H. "Bob" Jordan, served as president pro tempore of the Senate until his resignation in March 1959 to assume a position on the state highway board. A young senator from Augusta, Carl E. Sanders, with the backing of the governor, became president pro tempore in

Jordan's place. Robert Culpeper of Camilla served as Vandiver's floor leader in the Senate, and George T. Bagby, a key Vandiver supporter in the rural roads fight in 1958, became the Speaker pro tempore in the House.[10]

In his State of the State address on January 15, 1959, the governor discussed at length the two major problems confronting Georgia: the threat to segregated schools and the state's financial crisis. Vandiver meticulously listed the short-comings of the Griffin administration that he intended to correct, which included wasteful spending practices; the hiring of unqualified personnel by the state; the use of state material, equipment, and personnel for private purposes; abuses in state purchasing; the practice of state officials selling to the state; and scandals in highway construction. The governor assured lawmakers of his commitment to "a program of retrenchment" that would be carried out "with vigor and without relent" and requested the creation of an economy and reorganization commission to make recommendations concerning governmental reorganization and efficiency in state government. He proposed the abolishment of fifteen government agencies and the elimination of fourteen others by assigning their responsibilities to other governmental entities. The governor promised the introduction of a "honesty in government" bill, legislation reforming state purchasing procedures, and a bill abolishing the controversial Georgia Commission on Education.[11]

In order to shore up the state's defense of segregated schools, the governor asked the legislature to enact six segregation bills. One bill permitted the governor to close a public school ordered desegregated by the federal courts. Others prohibited cities with independent school systems from levying property taxes to support desegregated schools, permitted the state to pay legal counsel to defend segregated schools, permitted the closing of any unit in the university system to avoid desegregation, allowed state income tax credit for financial contributions to private schools, and established maximum age limits for admission to units of the university system. Five of the bills passed with only nine negative votes, but the age bill encountered stronger opposition.[12]

That bill established twenty-one as the maximum age for admission as an undergraduate and twenty-five for admission to a graduate program in any unit of the University System of Georgia. Representative J. Roy McCracken justified the proposed bill on the grounds that the NAACP had difficulty in finding young people to challenge segregated colleges and reminded his colleagues that the plaintiffs in the Georgia State desegregation case were in their forties. The president of the Georgia Institute of Technology, Dr. Edwin Harrison, however, expressed fears that such a law would devastate his school's graduate program, and Dr. O. Clyde "O. C." Aderhold, president of the University of Georgia, warned of the adverse impact it would have on his institution's enrollment. Representative Quimby Melton Jr., who also served on the state board of regents, contended the bill "would toll the death knell for every off-campus center in the state." Representative Melton M. "Muggsy" Smith asserted that the bill discriminated against students who pursued their education after they had married and entered the work force. Representative James A. "Jim" MacKay expressed opposition because the state should be encouraging rather than discouraging people to continue their education. Defenders of the legislation pointed out that the proposed law made exceptions for veterans, teachers pursuing additional education, and individuals who exceeded the age limits but who possessed "ability and fitness" to further their education. Speaker pro tempore Bagby, assuring members of the House that the bill would not discriminate against a single white student, bluntly told his fellow lawmakers that the bill was "designed to keep the nigger out!" He urged, "If that's what you want to do, then vote for it!" The bill passed the legislature with only twenty-eight negative votes.[13]

The legislature unanimously approved the governor's request to abolish the Georgia Commission on Education and to replace it with a new agency, the Governor's Commission on Constitutional Government. The new agency had the task of suggesting laws and recommendations to prevent the federal encroachment on the powers and rights of Georgia. The legislature also unanimously created the Governor's Commission on Economy and Reorganization, which had the responsibility of recommending to the legislature "efficient and economical methods and procedures" to improve state government and formulating reorganization plans to bring about a government structure that would "more efficiently and economically manage the affairs of the state." In response to the governor's request, the General Assembly abolished several state agencies, including the Georgia Recreation Commission, the Aeronautics Advisory Board, and the Civil Defense Advisory Council. Several state agencies, including the Oil and Gas Commission, the State Planning Commission, and the State War Ballot Commission, were abolished and their responsibilities transferred to other state agencies. The legislature also abolished the Rural Roads Authority, the pride and joy of the Griffin administration, and transferred its responsibilities to the state highway board.[14]

Vandiver considered the "honesty in government" bill his most important request of the 1959 legislative session. The proposed legislation, given the designation of HB 1, made twenty-five activities in dealing with state government illegal. State officials or employees could not receive compensation to help defeat or pass legislation or do business with the state or have any connection with firms doing business with the state. The bill made the making of false reports concerning quality of material or work by state officials or employees a felony offense. The proposed legislation also prohibited state legislators from holding

state jobs and made the bribery of judicial officials and witnesses felony of-
fenses. The legislature unanimously approved HB 1. The *Atlanta Constitution*
called the legislation "one of the most important reforms in state government in
this century," and Representative Charles L. Gowen called it the most progressive legislation in twenty years. Senator Sanders believed that the legislation
would "certainly go down as a landmark in Georgia legislative history." Governor Vandiver considered HB 1 "the most important bill passed by the legislature
in the last decade." [15]

Bruce Galphin, a reporter for the *Atlanta Constitution*, summed up the 1959
session succinctly: "Whatever Ernie wants, Ernie gets." The *Atlanta Constitution* praised the session for passing "a great deal of constructive legislation." The
Waycross Journal-Herald called it a "praiseworthy session" with governmental
reorganization, restoration of honesty in government, and an economical fiscal
policy as its major accomplishments. The *Dekalb New Era* praised Governor
Vandiver and the legislature's efforts "to rid the state of waste and graft and corruption." Jim Thomasson, a writer for the Associated Press, concluded that the
"legislature gave virtual rubber stamp approval to his [Vandiver's] legislative program, but did little else of note." Governor Vandiver called the session one of the
best in the state's history and hailed the passage of HB 1 and the segregation legislation as the session's outstanding accomplishments. [16]

Shortly after the legislature adjourned, reports circulated of the governor
calling a special session in order to raise taxes as his predecessor did in 1955.
Governor Griffin, in commenting on Governor Vandiver's rhetoric about the
deplorable financial conditions of the state government, observed that such talk
was "ordinarily salve for a tax session." However, Governor Vandiver told the annual convention of county commissioners in March 1959 of his commitment to
economizing rather than raising taxes as the best way to overcome the financial
difficulties inherited from the Griffin administration. The governor warned the
county commissioners that the state Highway Department's dire financial straits
left little money for county paving projects that were extremely important to the
political interests of the commissioners. Bruce Galphin, a reporter for the *Atlanta Constitution*, concluded that the consensus of the commissioners at the
convention was that additional state revenue had to be found to fund the activities of the Highway Department adequately. [17]

Shortly after the governor's address to the commissioners, the Senate Government Operations Committee released a report critical of the Griffin administration's failure to budget adequately for highway maintenance. The report
estimated that $32 million was needed to resurface 6,000 miles of state roads.
The chairman of the state highway board, Jim Gillis, called for a special session
to raise taxes, explaining, "The people want services and there isn't any way

to have them without taxes." Representative Charles Gowen, secretary of the Governor's Economy and Reorganization Commission, and Representative Robert C. "Bob" Mathews also favored a tax-raising special session. However, House Speaker Smith and Senate president pro tempore Sanders opposed such a session. Sanders contended that the legislature should not try to raise taxes "without making every effort to economize before unloading on John Q. Public again." He added, "I believe Governor Vandiver feels the same way." Lieutenant Governor Byrd likewise concluded that Georgians would oppose additional taxes, unless they were "thoroughly satisfied" that every effort had been made toward economy and efficiency in the state government.[18]

Governor Vandiver finally ended the speculation on June 1 by ruling out a special session and calling for department heads, county officials, and private citizens to assist his administration's economy drive in order to allow the state to live within its income. The state's newspapers, led by the Atlanta papers, supported the governor's opposition to a special session. The *Atlanta Constitution* concluded, "We do not believe the state of public opinion now would sustain a tax increase." The *Atlanta Journal* praised Vandiver's stand on a special session as "a bit of political heroism." The *Walker County Messenger* commended Governor Vandiver for refusing to raise taxes, and the *Carroll County Georgian* praised the governor for his "courage and determination" to operate state government without a tax increase. The Georgia Chamber of Commerce reported widespread opposition to increasing state taxes: over 77 percent of more than one thousand businesses surveyed throughout the state were against a special session.[19]

Late in June, a proud governor revealed that the state's budget for the fiscal year beginning on July 1, 1959, would be $348,102,000—an increase of $18 million over the present budget. The governor had cut spending in twenty-seven departments, bureaus, and commissions while increasing spending for the Department of Education by $8 million, for the Highway Department by $8 million, and for the university system by $2,275,000. In addition, the state surplus had been increased from $2.6 million at the end of the Griffin administration to more than $6 million. Vandiver attributed this financial turnaround to several factors, including his administration's stringent economic measures, the reorganization of various departments, and an increased revenue collection. He praised the Revenue Department for increased collections of 6.3 percent even though it sustained a budget reduction and a loss of one-fifth of its employees. He also praised the state Purchasing Department for instituting major savings as a result of open and competitive bidding in sales to the state. Examples of savings included two-ton trucks purchased for $2,322, compared with $3,378 in the Griffin administration; automobiles for State Highway Patrol use purchased for

$100 per car less than was paid in the Griffin administration; and tractors purchased for $1,242, compared with $2,245.[20]

In his State of the State address in January 1959, Governor Vandiver had requested the creation of a economy and efficiency committee to make recommendations on how to make state government more efficient and economical. The legislature responded by unanimously creating the Governor's Commission on Economy and Reorganization. The governor, Speaker of the House, and lieutenant governor served as ex officio members, with the governor designated as chairman of the commission. Membership included Senators Sanders and John W. Greer along with Representatives Twitty, Gowen, and Joe C. Underwood. Nonlegislative members included presidents of the Georgia Education Association, Georgia Farm Bureau, Association of County Commissioners, Georgia Municipal Association, and Georgia State AFL-CIO. Dr. Morris W. H. Collins Jr., director of the Institute of Law and Government at the University of Georgia, served as staff director. The commission, which held eight meetings from April through December, proposed thirty bills to be submitted to the 1960 session of the legislature to correct shortcomings in state government. In addition, the commission made numerous recommendations that could be implemented by governmental agencies without legislative action.[21]

One of the legislative recommendations called for a forty-four-hour workweek for state employees after the commission found that most state employees did not work a forty-hour week. The governor responded by issuing an executive order directing all state employees to work a minimum of forty hours per week and called for the legislature to mandate such a workweek for all state employees. However, two high-level officials, state treasurer George B. Hamilton and state auditor Barton E. "B. E." Thrasher Jr., expressed opposition to such a policy. Hamilton even accused the governor of being "ill-advised" on this matter and promised to continue to work the employees in his department on a thirty-five-hour week. Despite such opposition, the governor remained firmly committed to supporting such legislation "obstructionists to the contrary not withstanding." The *Savannah Morning News* believed that "a taxpayer who puts in 40 hours or more in his own work just doesn't look kindly upon paying the wages for a person who is getting by with fewer hours on the job."[22]

Within three months after the new administration assumed office, allegations surfaced concerning Milledgeville State Hospital, which housed almost twelve thousand Georgians suffering with mental illness. Dr. Thomas B. Phinizy, a senior physician at the hospital, publicly charged that several patients needing surgery had been neglected as a result of a backlog of surgery cases at Jones Hospital, the institution's medical hospital. Other allegations included a female nurse's performing major surgery at Jones Hospital with no doctors present, the administrating of unlicensed drugs to patients without their permission or the authorization of their families, and the employing of physicians who had a record of alcohol abuse or drug addiction.[23]

Governor Vandiver responded to the allegations by insisting that his administration was committed to "the proper care and treatment" of the mentally ill. Even though Luther Alverson, president of the National Association of Mental Health, urged the governor to appoint nonphysicians to an investigative committee, the governor believed that "doctors are best qualified to investigate doctors" and requested that the Medical Association of Georgia appoint a committee to investigate the allegations. The president of the Medical Association of Georgia appointed a five-member committee, all of whom were medical doctors, with Dr. W. Bruce Schaefer serving as chairman. In its report submitted to the governor on April 23, 1959, the committee concluded that Alan Kemper, who headed the Department of Public Welfare, the agency charged with the responsibility of overseeing the hospital, dominated the hospital's administration. The committee found that improvements had been made in the hospital's physical facilities under Kemper's direction but that there was no similar emphasis on psychiatric care and treatment of the patients. The committee urged that the superintendent of the mental hospital be a qualified psychiatrist and recommended that the mental hospital be transferred from the jurisdiction of the Department of Public Welfare to the State Department of Public Health. [24]

Other recommendations included decentralizing the hospital, creating an advisory committee on mental institutions, adding at least five qualified psychiatrists to the hospital staff, and instituting training programs for residents in psychiatry at the hospital. The committee called for the removal of Dr. Thomas G. Peacock, superintendent of the hospital, as soon as a qualified psychiatrist could be found to take his place. The committee concluded that Director Kemper and Superintendent Peacock had a policy of employing doctors who had alcohol and drug problems. It was recommended that such physicians not be employed at the hospital unless they were rehabilitated from alcohol or drug addictions. Finding that Jones Hospital had delayed some elective surgery to accommodate hospital employees who received medical and surgical services free of charge or at a nominal fee, the committee recommended that only mental patients should be treated at Jones Hospital. The committee concluded that Marion Garland, the supervisor of nurses in the operating room at Jones Hospital, had indeed performed operations on patients and that Dr. Wallace Gibson, the medical director at Jones Hospital, had not been truthful about Garland's conduct. It recommend Dr. Gibson's removal as medical director of Jones Hospital. The committee reasoned that the irregularities it found were only symptoms of the failure of the state to treat adequately Georgians coping with mental illness at

Milledgeville State Hospital. Governor Vandiver praised the Schaefer Report as "one of the finest, most authoritative and all-inclusive public documents" he had ever read and saw it as a chart for the state's future progress in the field of mental health.[25]

After receiving the report, the governor transferred administrative control of the mental hospital from the State Department of Welfare to the State Department of Public Health. He expressed general agreement with the report's recommendations and expressed his support for their implementation. The *Atlanta Constitution* hoped that the report would shock the state's residents out of 116 years of neglect of the mentally ill. The *Macon Telegraph* considered the report "a needed shock" necessary to improve Milledgeville State Hospital, and the *Thomaston Free Press* called the Schaefer Report "a great service" to the state. The House of Delegates of the Medical Association of Georgia unanimously expressed its approval of the Schaefer Report, and the association's journal praised the governor for calling for an investigation of the hospital.[26]

Several resignations from the hospital occurred in the aftermath of the report. They included Dr. Gibson, Marion Garland, and Dr. Peacock, who had served as hospital superintendent since 1949. State Health Department director Dr. Thomas F. Sellers appointed his assistant director, Dr. John Venable, superintendent until the position could be filled by a certified psychiatrist. Dr. Sellers expressed reservations about placing the hospital under the control of a separate department of mental health, but Dr. Rives Chambers, chairman of the Mental Health Committee of the Medical Association of Georgia, called for a separate department of mental health. Dr. Venable disagreed with Chambers, contending that he couldn't "conceive of a better organized group than the State Board of Health to administer the hospital." Governor Vandiver agreed and refused to create a new department of mental health, saying that the Health Department should continue to oversee the hospital as long as it continued to do the kind of job it was doing. The governor also gave another reason for his decision—his administration was attempting to eliminate and consolidate government agencies rather than create new ones.[27]

In July 1959, Governor Vandiver's advisory committee on mental institutions recommended the appointment of Dr. Irville H. MacKinnon, chairman of the Department of Psychiatry at Columbia University, as the new superintendent of the Milledgeville facility. The director of the Health Department concurred with the committee's recommendation. The appointment, which was praised by the governor, fulfilled the Schaefer committee recommendation that the superintendent be a pychiatrist.[28]

During the 1959 legislative session, both houses authorized their appropriate standing committees to inspect Milledgeville State Hospital. These two committees then created a joint committee entitled the Senate-House Mental Health Study Committee. Representative E. Culver Kidd Jr. of Milledgeville headed the joint committee, which toured the hospital in June. Jack Nelson, a reporter for the *Atlanta Constitution,* wrote that the tour "left many of the legislators shaking their heads at the state's inadequate facilities for treating the mentally ill." The *Atlanta Constitution* editorialized about the "State's Shame" at Milledgeville with its overcrowded facilities, inadequate treatment, lack of a chapel or a full-time chaplain, and only three psychiatrists on its staff.[29]

Governor Vandiver announced after the committee's tour that he and his wife also planned to tour the hospital. The governor stated that an objective of his administration was to "put Georgia among the top states in the union in treatment of mentally ill." After completing the tour, the governor remarked that the conditions at the hospital were worse than he thought they were, calling some of the facilities "shameful." In one ward, the governor found patients passing time by swatting flies that entered the building through unscreened windows. The Vandivers toured another ward—a fifty-eight-year-old building once used as a prison—and the governor commented that the building wasn't good enough for prisoners, much less mental patients. When asked about the food served the patients, Governor Vandiver declared, "I don't see how a dog could have eaten it." In another ward, he found 126 patients who shared three commodes and one shower in a bathroom lacking electric lights. The Vandivers walked through wards that smelled of urine and unwashed bodies and visited one building where one thousand male residents slept in beds so close that the mattresses touched. Attendants in one ward complained that wharf rats roamed the facility at night. The Vandivers saw patients sitting on benches starring vacantly at nothing, patients sprawled out on the floor as flies crawled over them, and old women rocking and singing to dolls. After visiting a ward housing children, Betty Vandiver, with eyes filled with tears, excused herself to go to an empty office to regain her composure. She later commented, "I can stand anything but to see the children![30]

After completing the two-day tour, the governor concluded that the state had to implement a long-range mental health program. However, he said some of the "terribly inadequate" facilities at the hospital had to be improved immediately. In order to do that, he transferred five hundred thousand dollars in building funds from the Welfare Department budget to the Health Department's budget. Betty Vandiver stated after the tour that she and her husband would never forget what they had seen that day and that they would "be haunted" by it until they had done all they could "to correct conditions here."[31]

In November 1959, a group of state legislators led by the lieutenant governor and the Speaker inspected the hospital. Speaker Smith expressed his belief that the upcoming legislative session would adequately fund the hospital. Another representative, William L. "Bill" Lanier Sr., even contended that Milledgeville State Hospital should be the first priority of the 1960 legislative session. Another lawmaker, Senator Carl R. Dykes, expressed the desire to improve the hospital even if the legislature had to "cut short some roads or whatever else [was] necessary." In commenting on the dismal housing quarters for patients, Senate president pro tempore Sanders stated, "Most Georgia farmers have better quarters for their livestock." Lieutenant Governor Byrd agreed, insisting that "they had better facilities in the Dacha prison camp in Germany." As a result of its tour, the Senate-House Mental Health Study Committee recommended increasing the mental health budget by $5 million each year for the next five years. Other committee recommendations included developing a long-range building program at the hospital, establishing scholarships for persons interested in psychiatry, establishing minimum wages for attendants, providing an educational program for patients, developing a full-time chaplaincy program, and hiring more attendants and social workers. Governor Vandiver had approved in June a million-dollar increase in the state's mental health budget for the next fiscal year. This increase provided for additional psychiatric personnel, increased salaries for hospital employees, and additional attendants and nurses.[32]

Jack Nelson, a reporter for the *Atlanta Constitution,* noted that six months after the Schaefer Report the "great majority" of its short-range and medium-range recommendations had been carried out. Lieutenant Governor Byrd and Speaker Smith pledged to work with the governor in promoting a mental health program "second to none in the nation." Speaker Smith endorsed the joint committee's recommendation of an increase in spending for the state's mental health program. However, the governor's Advisory Committee on Mental Institutions noted that even with the increased spending, the state would still fall short of the national average spent by states on mental patients. Proposed legislation endorsed by the Health Department, the Committee on Mental Institutions, and the Joint Senate-House Mental Health Committee included a constitutional amendment granting scholarships to physicians desiring to specialize in mental health, constitutional amendments allowing medical students to repay state scholarships by working at Milledgeville State Hospital, and the strengthening of the 1958 law pertaining to the procedures for admission to the hospital. Governor Vandiver committed his administration to making the state's mental health program "second to none in the nation."[33]

After it came to Betty Vandiver's attention that only half of the patients at Milledgeville State Hospital received Christmas presents, she suggested to the president of the Georgia Municipal Association that cities and towns collect Christmas presents for the patients. As a result, an organized effort directed by GMA executive director Elmer George involved more than sixty communities that sent thousands of gifts for distribution to the patients. Governor and Mrs. Vandiver, along with numerous mayors, celebrated Christmas in 1959 with the patients, at which time the governor pledged to transform the long-neglected and underfunded facility into "a great training institution, equipped to provide human care and the best modern psychiatric treatment." He assured the patients of his commitment to ask the legislature to provide more personnel and more buildings to improve the care and treatment of mentally ill Georgians.[34]

In another area of public policy, the Atlanta school desegregation case hung over the state awaiting resolution. Senator Talmadge had expressed the hope in March 1959 that the case would "not be brought to a head." The senator made it clear, however, that he preferred closing the public schools of the state rather than allowing their desegregation. However, a former Talmadge political opponent, former governor Ellis G. Arnall, threatened to run for governor in 1962 if the public schools were closed to avoid desegregation. Arnall suggested that Georgia's segregated schools could be maintained by a pupil placement law, local-option legislation, and grants-in-aids. He predicted political ruin for Georgia politicians who closed the state's public schools. Arnall's statements evoked a quick response from Governor Vandiver, who accused Arnall of inviting the NAACP to file a desegregation lawsuit in every county in Georgia. "For the past 20 years former Gov. Ellis Arnall has been giving aid and comfort to left wing organizations and the NAACP," Vandiver charged. The governor concluded that Arnall's recent statements indicated that he was "still following that line."[35]

The state experienced another threat to its segregated schools when ten Negroes obtained summer school registration information at Georgia State College and the Georgia Institute of Technology. The governor criticized their action as "another conspiracy on the part of the NAACP to destroy [the state's] schools." Even though three of the applicants returned their applications to Georgia State prior to the summer quarter's deadline, the school rejected their effort to enroll. Governor Vandiver stressed that his position remained unchanged—he would close a unit of the university system or public school rather than allow its integration. In the midst of the growing controversy, the governor testified before a subcommittee of the U.S. Senate's Judiciary Committee on behalf of Senator Talmadge's proposed constitutional amendment returning control of public school systems to the states. He praised Georgia's progress in the field of education since 1952, which included the construction of 481 new schools, 354 additions to existing schools, and 166 remodeling projects, accomplished at a cost of almost $163 million in state funds.[36]

Back home in Georgia, Vandiver denied speculation that his administration was considering abandoning the private school option of avoiding integration, and he insisted that the public schools would remain open—as long as they were segregated. "We don't plan," the governor stated, "to accept integration in Georgia." He disagreed with Virginia governor J. Lindsey Almond Jr.'s shift from a policy of massive resistance to one of accepting some desegregation in order to keep the schools open. The state of Virginia, like Georgia, had a policy of massive resistance that allowed the governor to close any public school ordered desegregated. Governor Almond had, in fact, closed the public schools in Norfolk in September 1958 in an effort to avoid desegregation there. However, a federal court of appeals had ruled in January 1959, six days after Vandiver had been sworn in as governor, that Virginia could not keep some of the public schools open and close others in an effort to maintain segregation. The beleaguered Virginia governor appointed a commission to hold public hearings on the future of public education in Virginia. The commission recommended to the legislature that the state shift from a policy of massive resistance to one allowing local option. Governor Almond supported the commission's report, which was enacted into law.[37]

About the same time that Virginia was abandoning massive resistance, district court judge Frank A. Hooper in June 1959 ordered the Atlanta Board of Education to cease operating a segregated system and prepare a plan to desegregate the city's school system. While the president of the board told reporters that such a plan would be developed, Governor Vandiver reminded Georgians of the state law requiring the closing of any desegregated school. The following month, Judge Hooper gave the city a deadline of December 1, 1959, for submission of its desegregation plan. In compliance with Judge Hooper's order, the Atlanta school board proposed a desegregation plan modeled after Alabama's pupil placement plan, which had been upheld by the federal courts. The proposed plan called for gradual desegregation beginning with the twelfth grade and the desegregation of one grade each year. While attorneys representing the Negro plaintiffs objected to the proposed plan, Governor Vandiver reiterated his position of maintaining segregated schools in the state.[38]

Atlanta's mayor, William B. "Bill" Hartsfield, argued that the closing of Atlanta's schools would be a "catastrophe of world-wide magnitude" detrimental to the city's future. Such an action, the mayor contended, would give Atlanta a black eye in the financial and business community that would be comparable to a bond forfeiture. He warned that thousands of home offices and national businesses that "had entrusted millions in investments [in the city] and sent thousands of employees would . . . immediately make arrangements to carry on their businesses elsewhere." The superintendent of the Atlanta public schools, Ira Jarrell, joined in Hartsfield's call for keeping Atlanta's public schools open. A meeting of the Atlanta Council of the Parent-Teacher Association, with four hundred representatives from the city's eighty-six PTAs, passed a unanimous resolution in support of open schools. Numerous organizations, including the League of Women Voters, American Association of University Women, Georgia Council of Churches, Council of Jewish Women, and the North Georgia Annual Conference of the Methodist Church, endorsed keeping public schools open. Citizens in Atlanta committed to the continuation of public schools also organized Help Our Public Education (HOPE) in December 1958.[39]

Judge Hooper emphasized in December 1959 that Georgians had the choice of either accepting gradual integration of their public schools or having them closed. If the 1960 legislature failed to adopt a school desegregation plan, the judge stressed that he would have no choice but to desegregate Atlanta's public schools. However, Representative Twitty maintained that the legislature would never pass legislation allowing integration in the public schools as long as Vandiver was governor. Representative Quimby Melton Jr., who was also a member of the board of regents, became the first legislator outside the Atlanta metropolitan area to favor local-option legislation to keep the schools open in order to "hold integration to a minimum." It seemed to many Georgians that the state was rapidly approaching, in the opinion of the *Walker County Messenger*, "That Fork in the Road" of either closing the public schools or allowing their desegregation in order to keep them open.[40]

As the first year of his administration drew to a close, Governor Vandiver could look back with considerable satisfaction and pride. His legislative agenda had easily passed the General Assembly, and the budgetary crisis inherited from his predecessor had been resolved. His Commission on Efficiency and Reorganization had undertaken an exhaustive examination of state government operations and had made numerous recommendations for the legislature's consideration in 1960. The Vandivers had taken a personal interest in improving the quality of life and the treatment of patients at the state's mental hospital. In his first year in office, at least, the governor had fulfilled his campaign promise of no integrated schools during his administration. However, despite the governor's firm commitment to that promise, the future of segregated schools in the state appeared dismal. A showdown on the issue between the federal judiciary and the state of Georgia appeared imminent in the near future. When that time arrived, Governor Vandiver would have to make a decision that none of his predecessors had ever had to contemplate seriously—should the state's public schools be closed to avoid desegregation, or should they be kept open even if desegregated?

EIGHT

A Year of Accomplishment and Stress

In January 1960, Governor Ernest Vandiver gave his second State of the State address, in which he pledged to use "EVERY LEGAL MEANS AND REMEDY" in the state's fight to maintain segregated schools. The reiteration of his commitment to cut off state funds to desegregated schools received the enthusiastic approval of the legislature. However, the governor didn't request additional legislation to protect segregation in the schools, perhaps realizing the futility of such laws, since the federal courts were invalidating them in other southern states. Instead, Vandiver devoted most of his address to urging the lawmakers to pass his legislative agenda. The governor praised the legislators for their cooperation in restoring "morality, economy and efficient operation to state government," which he claimed had resulted in a saving of more than $36 million. This unanticipated revenue helped the administration in its effort to balance the 1959 budget as well as to fund additional state services such as the building of new area vocational trade schools and providing additional funding for highway construction.[1]

The governor urged the legislators to correct a major defect in the appropriations process. A constitutional amendment, which had been adopted in 1952, required Highway Department allocations in the general appropriation act to equal the revenue collected from state motor fuel and vehicle license taxes in the preceding year. As a result, the last general appropriations act, which was enacted in 1956, allocated almost 25 percent of appropriated funds to the Highway Department. Any appropriations in excess of the 1956 act had to be approved by the legislature as an amendment to the act and were contingent on sufficient revenue being collected. Motor license taxes and fuel tax receipts had increased from $67 million in 1955 to more than $96 million by the last fiscal year of the Griffin administration. A new appropriations bill would automatically increase funding for the Highway Department, leaving fewer dollars for other state services. As a result, legislatures since 1956 either had to reduce funding for other state services or had to raise taxes to fund them. If a new appropriations act was passed in the 1960 legislative session, the Highway Department would gain an additional $29 million increase in appropriations. Governor Vandiver argued that the 1952 amendment had the practical effect of putting "the legislature out of the appropriations business." He recommended a constitutional amendment limiting allocations for the Highway Department to receipts from motor fuel taxes, which, he contended, would adequately fund the Highway Department without neglecting other essential state services. Such and amendment would allow, he told the lawmakers, the legislature to regain its rightful place in the appropriations process.[2]

The governor endorsed more than thirty recommendations of his Economy and Reorganization Commission, including requiring interest to be paid on idle state funds, reorganizing the State Merit System, and mandating employers to withhold state income taxes. Unlike the federal government, the state had not required employers to withhold state income taxes on employees on a monthly basis. The governor emphasized that withholding would not be a new tax but simply would be "an improved method of collecting an existing tax."[3]

In his first year in office, the governor had reduced state spending in order to force the state to live within its means. Contending that major capital needs of the state could no longer be ignored, he now proposed a new spending program of more than $134 million to be paid for without raising taxes. The governor asked the legislature to fund these capital projects by resorting to the authority method of financing. Governor Vandiver conceded that critics could attack his inconsistency on financing through authorities because he had fought Governor Griffin's efforts to use authority financing to fund rural roads construction. The governor endorsed authority financing for capital improvements of a "permanent nature" but opposed similar financing for "temporary improvements that would be worn out four times" before their cost was paid, a clear reference to rural roads built by the Griffin administration. He requested authority financing of about $100 million in capital projects, which included $60 million for new school construction, $8 million for the construction of new area trade schools, $12,370,000 for construction projects in the university system, and $6,460,00 for a building program at Milledgeville State Hospital, as well as funds for a new prison and additional money for a new state archives building. He also proposed more than $29 million for expansion of state services and $5 million for nonrecurring capital expenditures to be paid for out of revenue generated from the growing state economy and savings derived from his administration's frugality and efficiency. This expansion of state services included an additional $1,560,000 for maintenance and operation for the local school systems, $6.5 million for a pay raise for public school teachers, and $1.3 million for more personnel at Milledgeville State Hospital.[4]

Bruce Galphin of the *Atlanta Constitution* thought the request for increased state spending ironic, since it came from a politician who had built a reputation for saying "no" to spending in his first year in office. The *Atlanta Constitution* commended the governor for proposing "one of the most constructive programs for the future in recent Georgia history." The legislature, the *Macon Telegraph* observed, reacted positively to the governor's message of expanding state services without raising taxes. The *Atlanta Journal* praised the governor's plan and its method of financing. The *Cobb County Times* observed that even the governor's "severest critics credit[ed] his ingenuity in being able to chart such an ambitious program without an increase in taxes." Charles Pou, a political reporter for the *Atlanta Journal,* called the governor's request "a shrewdly conceived political package" in that it offered expanded services without raising taxes.[5]

The legislature responded favorably to Governor Vandiver's legislative requests. One reporter for the Atlanta papers, Gorden Roberts, wrote, "The governor got all of his bills through and had quite a say so in passing some others." Galphin concluded, "A baseball slugger would turn green with envy at the batting average Gov. Vandiver posted on his administration bills in the 1960 legislature." The legislature overwhelmingly approved the governor's requests for expansion of state services, authority financing of capital projects, and his economy and reorganization requests. Vandiver's request to modify the constitutional provision allocating revenue to the State Highway Department passed with only one negative vote.[6]

However, the governor's request for the withholding of state income taxes by employers ran into opposition. Charles Pou had even picked the withholding tax as the most controversial proposed legislation of the session. The governor noted that sixteen states had already enacted such legislation and had, as a result, benefited from an increase in income taxes collected. Senator William J. Crowe opposed the governor on this issue, he claimed, because Georgians were "fed up" with government red tape. Representative John T. Phillips agreed with the senator's sentiment, maintaining that it would place yet another requirement on overburdened small-business owners. Former governor Marvin Griffin argued that the bill would require "little business folks" to spend more than $2 million to hire bookkeepers to handle the additional burden. Despite such arguments, the bill easily passed the legislature, with only five "no" votes in the Senate and forty in the House.[7]

During the session, Governor Vandiver's proposed increase in teachers' salaries of $200 per year per teacher received criticism from a group of educators known as the United Teachers of Georgia. These teachers had organized as a result of their dissatisfaction with the Georgia Education Association's support of the governor's pay raise for teachers. The UTG, criticizing the governor's recommendations as insufficient, advocated a $1,000 per year increase and urged teachers to resign at the beginning of the next school year if they did not receive the increase supported by the UTG. The governor rejected the UTG's demand, claiming it would take a tax increase of more than $24 million to fund. Reminding teachers that his administration was diverting 53 percent of the state's income into education, the governor insisted the state was doing all it could for them.[8]

Some legislators also joined in the dispute over teacher raises. Representative Knox Bynum, expressing his sympathy for the underpaid teachers, introduced a resolution granting them a $300 pay raise above the governor's recommendation. Another legislator, Senator William Crowe, obtained the unanimous approval of a resolution in the Senate recommending a 15 percent raise for teachers as soon as revenue became available. As a result of a meeting between GEA and UTG leaders, the UTG dropped its advocacy of teacher resignations, and the GEA endorsed the Crowe resolution. The executive secretary of the GEA even suggested the raising of taxes to fund higher teachers' salaries, a suggestion that the governor immediately rejected. Relations between the governor and the GEA deteriorated to the point that delegates attending the organization's annual meeting shouted down a proposed resolution thanking the governor for the $200 pay raise.[9]

On March 18, 1960, the same day of the defeat of the proposed resolution, the governor suffered a heart attack while working at his office in the capitol. Other than experiencing "a little angina" previously, Vandiver had never experienced heart problems. The Atlanta Constitution editorialized that the very demanding job of governor had become even more stressful in recent months as a result of the school crisis. Betty Vandiver concurred and added that the GEA's rejection of the pay raise resolution "hurt him so badly." The governor recovered sufficiently to return to a daily work schedule in May. The issue of an additional raise for teachers faded from public attention as presidential politics and school desegregation increasingly dominated the news.[10]

The legislature and the governor had to decide how to respond to Judge Frank A. Hooper's ruling desegregating Atlanta's public school system. In compliance with Judge Hooper's order, the Atlanta school board had earlier presented a plan that called for desegregating the city's school system one grade per year beginning with the twelfth grade. The board's plan called for students' school assignments to be based on factors rather than race or color.[11]

In order for the board's plan to be implemented, the state's massive-resistance laws had to be repealed. Margaret Shannon, a reporter for the Atlanta papers, wrote that "no lawmaking body in Dixie has been put in quite the same boat as Georgia's General Assembly" because Judge Hooper had given the legislators an opportunity to save the state's schools. However, the mood of both the General Assembly and the governor was one of opposition to repealing the state's massive-resistance legislation. Twenty-four legislators who resided in the Second Congressional District signed a declaration expressing their "unilateral" opposition to desegregating the state's school system. Fifty lawmakers residing in the First and Third Congressional Districts signed similar declarations. The governor himself told an enthusiastic audience at a fund-raising dinner for the States' Rights Council of Georgia in Atlanta, "We must not let them run up the flag of surrender over our Capital City." Estimating that 95 percent of Georgians favored closing the public schools before allowing their desegregation, he assured Georgians of his intent to veto any bill permitting desegregation in the state's public schools. The governor insisted that he had a mandate from the voters to close the schools rather than to allow them to be integrated. Representative Frank S. Twitty, the governor's House floor leader, declared that any effort to repeal the state's massive-resistance laws would have "real rough sledding." Lieutenant Governor Garland T. Byrd expressed similar views, and Peter Zach Geer Jr., Governor Vandiver's executive secretary, boasted, "So long as Gov. Vandiver is governor of this great state, and so long as I am at his side, we will not capitulate, we will not surrender, we will not give up." [12]

Lobbying efforts by opponents of desegregated schools intensified. Cobb County representative Harold S. Willingham Jr. received a petition with more than two thousand signatures of his constituents in support of closing the schools rather than desegregating them. Governor Vandiver estimated that 99 percent of his mail on the issue favored the continuance of segregation in the schools. Lee Davidson, the Grand Dragon of the Georgia Ku Klux Klan, even urged the state to create a private school system for white students. More than a thousand Fayette County citizens petitioned the General Assembly to vote against integrating the state's schools. Legislators received numerous petitions calling on them to continue segregated schools. Robert Patterson, the executive secretary of the Citizens Council of Mississippi, speaking to an audience of more than a thousand in Atlanta, called for the closing of any white public school "the minute the first Negro child [put] his foot on the school house steps." Roy V. Harris, president of the States' Rights Council of Georgia, called the present desegregation crisis the "Second Battle of Atlanta" and encouraged the "decent white people" of Georgia to join together in a holy crusade to preserve segregation. [13]

Those who favored keeping the schools open also lobbied the policy makers in Atlanta. The organization Help Our Public Education, better known as HOPE, which led the fight to retain the public schools, had grown to approximately thirty thousand white citizens by 1960 with chapters in many of Georgia's larger cities. It contended that the state would suffer economically if the schools were closed, that the closing of the schools would deprive the children of the state of an education, and that private schools could not replace the state's public school system. Representatives from HOPE attended daily sessions of the 1960 legislative session to lobby on behalf of open schools. When Senators Talmadge and Russell spoke to the 1960 session, HOPE organized a lobbying effort in which almost a thousand women representing fifteen organizations packed the visitor's gallery of the state House of Representatives, displaying signs supporting their position. It also submitted to the legislature a petition with more than ten thousand signatures of Georgians supporting open schools.[14]

Other Georgians and organizations joined in the effort to save the public schools. More than 700 Hall County citizens and a similar number from Griffin submitted petitions in support of public schools. The governor received a telegram with 747 signatures from white voters in Athens appealing for "uninterrupted operation of public schools in Georgia." Similar petitions came from 2,000 citizens in DeKalb County, 230 citizens in Lumpkin County, and 600 students at Emory University. One mother wrote Governor Vandiver to encourage him to save the state's public schools and "go down in history as Georgia's savior in this crisis." She urged the governor to back down from his campaign promise to close the schools because it was a "bad promise." Another citizen pleaded with the governor to oppose closing the schools because closing them "would be a tragedy far outweighing all the good" he was accomplishing. A minister urged the governor to use his "wise and courageous leadership to maintain the public school system."[15]

Former Senate president pro tempore G. Everett Millican of Atlanta urged the legislature to keep the schools open. Mayor William B. "Bill" Hartsfield urged citizens of Atlanta to lobby members of the General Assembly on behalf of open schools. His city's board of aldermen passed a resolution calling on the legislature to pass local-option legislation. Grand juries in Fulton and DeKalb Counties made the same request. Prominent Atlanta bankers William R. "Bill" Bowdoin and Mills B. Lane Jr. warned of the detrimental impact that school closings would have on the state's economy. The Presbytery of Atlanta, representing ninety-five Presbyterian churches in the Atlanta area; the Atlanta Baptist Pastors Conference, composed of most of the Baptist ministers in the Atlanta area; and the Atlanta Jewish Community Council, representing thirty-seven affiliated organizations, expressed their support for public education. The Atlanta Council of PTAs, representing eighty white schools, unanimously passed a resolution urging the legislature to allow their schools to stay open. Delegates attending the Georgia Educators Association's annual meeting narrowly approved a resolution in favor of the continuation of the public school system and in favor of local option.[16]

Some lawmakers, even as they professed fidelity to segregation, endorsed the continuation of public schools. Representative Roscoe Denmark, although emphasizing in a speech in the House his opposition to integration, nevertheless told his colleagues that he opposed shutting down the schools: "That looks to me like that is where we are heading." Senator John H. Woodall Jr. favored local option as the best way to minimize the impact of integration, and Representative Ed Gobel told his colleagues that his commitment to segregation did not include closing the schools. Representative Herschel Lovett, who had been nominated to the state board of education by Governor Herman Talmadge, also joined the opposition to the closing of the schools. Even Marvin E. Moate Sr., the Speaker of the House of Representatives in the Griffin administration, spoke out against school closing, calling such a response one of the greatest mistakes the state could make.[17]

In the midst of this furor, James S. "Jim" Peters Sr., chairman of the state board of education, wrote another key Talmadgite, Roy Harris, to warn of the political consequences for the Talmadge political faction if the schools were closed. Peters, conceding that "some form of integration" was inevitable, warned that former governor Arnall and the proponents of integration were hoping that Governor Vandiver would close the schools once they were integrated by the federal courts. He warned that Arnall running for governor in 1962 on a platform of reopening the schools would be difficult to defeat and that Senator Talmadge, who was up for reelection in 1962, could very easily be defeated. Peters suggested to Harris that the leaders of the Talmadge faction come up with a solution to the crisis rather than closing the schools, which would deprive former governor Arnall of an issue with which to regain the governor's office. "Otherwise," he concluded, "we are headed toward defeat and the loss of our power and influence in the government of this state." Harris publicly disagreed bitterly with Peters's conclusion, but Governor Vandiver and Senator Talmadge remained silent on Peters's letter.[18]

As the fight intensified, some lawmakers proposed legislation to cope with the pending crisis. Baldwin County representative E. Culver Kidd Jr. introduced a resolution providing for a statewide referendum giving the voters several options on the school issue. Opposition to Kidd's resolution included House floor leader Frank Twitty and Senate president pro tempore Carl E. Sanders. Representative Twitty argued against the resolution, contending that 90 percent of the state's population supported the governor's uncompromising stand on segregation. The proposed referendum quietly died in committee, leading Representa-

tive Kidd to propose a repeal of the constitutional requirement mandating segregated schools. After the governor predicted that such a proposal would receive
no more than ten votes in the state, the proposed amendment died in subcommittee. Representative Milton M. "Muggsy" Smith of Fulton County introduced
two anti-school-closing bills that were never considered by the legislature. The
effort of the DeKalb County legislative delegation to pass legislation to give parents the right to vote on whether schools should remain open if the courts ordered them desegregated proved to be futile as well.[19]

Unfortunately for the governor, the Atlanta school desegregation case assured
his administration of confrontation with the federal judiciary. Ernest Vandiver
faced the most difficult problem of his young administration and his political
career in that, thanks to massive-resistance legislation, the state had only two
choices—segregated public schools or no public schools. A columnist in the *Atlanta Journal* asked, "Isn't there some way to extricate poor Gov. Vandiver and
the imperiled state of Georgia from this idiot dilemma?" The governor's campaign promise to close the schools rather than to allow their desegregation had
been well received among many whites, especially in the Black Belt section of
Georgia, home of the strongest defenders of the traditional racial order. However, among many whites in the areas of Georgia experiencing population and
economic growth, economic development overshadowed the effort to maintain
segregation. In particular, the political and business leaders of Atlanta had no
desire to have their city experience the negative publicity associated with other
southern cities, believing the turmoil associated with the turbulent desegregation in those cities detrimental to economic development. Historian Numan V.
Bartley concluded that most of the white businessmen and professionals in the
growing urban-surburban population areas of the state were "segregationists,
but their ideological commitment was to capitalist economic expansion."[20]

What many Georgians hoped would never take place—the clash between
state law and the federal judiciary on the issue of school segregation—appeared
to be imminent. In meeting with his advisers, Governor Vandiver struggled with
how to deal with the crisis. The governor agreed to the creation of a study committee to present the options available to resolve the crisis and to allow Georgians the opportunity to consider those options before abandoning public education. After taking the pulse of the state on this issue by holding hearings, the
committee would make recommendations to the legislature. The governor attributed the idea of a study committee to his chief of staff, Griffin B. Bell, who
saw the Sibley committee "as a way to let the people decide if they wanted to
have [public] schools."[21]

The governor believed that the key to the committee's success was to convince
a well-known and respected citizen to serve as its chairman. Governor Vandiver

had in mind John A. Sibley, who he contended "was probably the most respected man in Georgia at that time." The seventy-one-year-old Sibley, who had distinguished himself in the legal and banking professions in Atlanta, arrived in the capital city in 1918 to practice law with the King and Spalding firm, where he eventually became a senior partner. King and Spalding represented some of the largest commercial and industrial interests in the state, including the Coca-Cola Company and the Trust Company of Georgia. Sibley also served as general counsel for the Coca-Cola Company for a time and as president of the Trust Company of Georgia in Atlanta for thirteen years until his resignation in 1959. He had served as chairman of the bank's executive committee since 1959 and was preparing to retire to his fourteen-hundred-acre farm in north Georgia when Bell approached him about chairing the study committee.[22]

The banker-lawyer had supported Vandiver in the 1958 gubernatorial race, believing that Vandiver would "give the State an excellent administration." When the governor-elect expressed his appreciation to Sibley for his "effective work" in Vandiver's behalf, Sibley responded, "If there is any way at any time that I can help, please feel free to call me." During the first year of the Vandiver administration, Sibley had praised the governor for his "level-head approach and fidelity to duty in handling the State's affairs." Sibley, as chairman of the Trust Company's executive committee, had played a major role in the bank's releasing one of it officials, Bill Bowdoin, so he could serve as head of the state's Purchasing Department in the first year of the Vandiver administration. When first approached by Bell about the chairmanship, Sibley resisted, insisting that his age prevented him from getting involved in politics. Sibley also questioned whether the committee's creation was simply a delaying tactic to postpone the inevitable or a mechanism to allow the state to consider its options seriously. It took a personal visit and plea from the governor to persuade Sibley to agree to serve on the committee. Vandiver attributed the acceptance of the difficult responsibility to Sibley's love for his state. Sibley considered his service on the committee "the most important single thing that [he had] ever had any connection with."[23]

Behind the scenes, Bell wrote the resolution creating the committee, and the governor, realizing the committee's potential for sparking controversy, decided to get someone not associated with the administration to introduce it in the legislature. That task fell to George D. Busbee, a young state representative from Dougherty County, who saw himself as an "independent young Turk" and as one who was not identified in the public mind as an administration supporter. State party chairman James H. "Jimmy" Gray Sr., a constituent of Busbee's, had the responsibility of convincing his representative to introduce the resolution. The young lawmaker agreed to do so because he felt very strongly that the public schools should remain open. Bell later commended Busbee for having the courage to sponsor the resolution. However, Busbee didn't consider his sponsorship as demonstrating courage because at that particular time he did not envision "a political future."[24]

Behind the scenes the Vandiver administration played an instrumental role in the creation of the committee, but publicly the governor remained neutral, going so far as not even to suggest the creation of the committee in his State of the State address. After the fact that Representative Busbee was going to introduce the resolution became public knowledge, the governor publicly stated that he would remain neutral as the legislature considered creating the committee. Representative Busbee, denying being a front man for the administration, claimed that he had never discussed the committee's creation with the governor or the administration's legislative leadership. Chairman Gray also publicly denied any involvement in the committee's creation.[25]

Busbee's resolution proposed the creation of a committee to be called the General Assembly Committee on Schools. The legislature increased the size of the proposed thirteen-member committee by adding six positions to be filled with legislators. Even though the amended resolution easily passed with only two negative votes, the governor further separated himself from the committee by not signing the resolution The governor did not mention the committee in his comments at the close of the legislative session. Shortly after the resolution's passage, the Atlanta newspapers printed a story in which one of its reporters, Gordon Roberts, asserted that despite Vandiver administration denials "the school segregation study commission [was] its idea and [had] been since the very beginning." Roberts attributed the administration's position to the fact that it did not want to be associated with any committee recommendations that might threaten the racial status quo.[26]

The governor also distanced himself from the committee because the resolution did not authorize him to appoint members. The resolution instead spelled out membership, which, with the exception of the legislative members, was determined by leadership positions in several statewide organizations. However, the governor had influence in determining which leadership positions Bell listed in the resolution. When Bell found out that Sibley was serving as president of the Alumni Society of the University of Georgia, he included that position as one that would have membership on the committee. The other members consisted of the chairmen of the legislature's education committees, the chairman of the board of regents, the chancellor of the state's university system, the state school superintendent, and the presidents of the state chamber of commerce, the Association of County Commissioners, the Georgia Municipal Association, the Superior Court Judges' Association, and the Georgia Farm Bureau. In addition, the chairman of the Georgia Education Cabinet, representing several statewide educational organizations, served along with four House members appointed by the Speaker and two Senate members appointed by the lieutenant governor. The committee consisted of white males who were prominent in the state's business, political, and educational communities. The resolution required the committee to hold at least one public hearing in each congressional district to allow Georgians to express their opinion on whether they wanted to close their public schools. The resolution further mandated that the committee make its recommendations no later than May 1, 1960.[27]

In its first meeting, the committee elected Sibley as its chairman and John Duncan, the president of the Georgia Farm Bureau, as its vice chairman. Although viewing the *Brown* decision as being "devoid of legal reasoning and sociological validity," Sibley nevertheless stressed the decision's binding authority on lower federal courts and the state. He clearly spelled out the options Georgians had—abolish the public schools or change state law to allow desegregation in them. Sibley, leaving no doubt as to his position, warned of the state's losing control of the education of its young people if it closed its schools. He further observed that publicly owned school facilities could not legally be used by private schools and that the only financial assistance the state could provide to students attending private schools would be tuition grants. According to Sibley, each local community rather than the state retained the right to close individual schools under local-option plans used by other southern states.[28]

The committee held hearings during March and heard testimony from 1,800 witnesses purporting to represent more than 115,000 Georgians and received more than 600 letters and petitions. A three-to-two majority of the witnesses favored maintaining segregated schools even at the cost of doing away with public schools. The well-attended hearings, usually held at courthouses, began at nine in the morning and finished late in the afternoon. Committee staff members contacted local governments, civic organizations, and other groups to invite them to send representatives to the hearings and to share the views of their members with the committee. Individuals not affiliated with groups also had the opportunity to testify. Chairman Sibley opened each hearing with a statement explaining the purpose of the committee and the two options available to the state under existing law. Instead of allowing the witnesses to engage in speech making, the chairman asked each witness his opinion concerning the options and imposed a time limit of usually two minutes for a response. Sibley received praise for the fair and dignified but firm manner in which he conducted the hearings. Margaret Long, a reporter for the *Atlanta Journal,* praised Sibley's "suave, firm and humor-shot conduct of the hearings." One member of the committee who attended all of the hearings, Homer M. Rankin, couldn't recall any criticism of Sibley's conduct as chairman. Another member of the committee, Robert O.

Arnold, commended Sibley for presiding "in a masterful way." The League of Women Voters of Athens praised the chairman for his "spirit of fair play, of courtesy, and of infinite patience." The editor of the *Christian Index,* a publication of the Georgia Baptist Convention, commended Sibley "for the fine way" in which he discharged his responsibilities as chairman. State representative Quimby Melton Jr. commended Sibley for completing "an extremely difficult task with great credit to the state as well as to [himself]." West Georgia College president Irvine Ingram praised Sibley for his fair and able leadership on the commission.[29]

On April 28, 1960, the committee issued its report, which, despite Sibley's efforts, was not unanimous. Eleven members concurred in the majority report: Sibley, the state school superintendent, the chancellor of the University System of Georgia, the chairman of the board of regents, the president of the Georgia Press Association, the president of the state chamber of commerce, the chairman of the Georgia Education Cabinet, the president of the Georgia Municipal Association, the president of the Superior Court Judges' Association, and two of the eight members of the legislature on the committee.[30]

Even though the majority report condemned the *Brown* decision as "utterly unsound," it conceded that the federal judiciary would enforce the decision. The majority found a lack of unanimity in the hearings over what course of action the state should take. The majority report dismissed private schooling as an option because of problems concerning accreditation, funding, and the loss of state control over curriculum as well as the realization that private schools could not "provide adequately for the educational needs of the masses of the people of the state." The majority recommended a state constitutional amendment to prohibit children from involuntarily attending a public school with classmates of another race. The majority report recommended local option that allowed voters in each school district to decide whether their schools remained open "as the best and most democratic procedure" for coping with the desegregation issue. The majority further recommended that the legislature provide tuition grants to children withdrawn from desegregated schools and to children who had previously attended schools that had been closed to avoid desegregation. For the first time in the state's battle to maintain segregation, an official state governmental body had not only advocated abandoning massive resistance but had accepted the inevitably of desegregation in the state's public schools. "I believe," Sibley wrote to a state representative, "we turned loose a document that will be hard to get rid of, and in fact it should stand up against the most severe test." He went on to say, "[The groundwork has been laid] to get this difficult problem behind us without the necessity of closing our public schools; If this can be accomplished, Georgia will be on the road to progress again."[31]

The minority report, concurred in by eight members—the president of the Farm Bureau, the president of the Association of County Commissioners, and six members of the legislature—concluded that the hearings revealed "virtually unanimous sentiment" in support of segregated schools. The minority report called for the continuation of segregation in the public schools until the federal judiciary closed them, at which time the state would implement its program of providing tuition grants to students to attend private schools. Like the majority report, the minority report called for passage of a freedom-of-association constitutional amendment.[32]

Governor Vandiver reacted to the report by announcing his opposition to a special session to consider the recommendations of the committee, which meant that the legislature's first opportunity to take action on the committee's report would be in its next regular session in January 1961. Roy Harris bitterly attacked the majority report for allowing "race-mixing in the public schools." The *Augusta Herald* complained that the majority report did not reflect the "wishes of most Georgians, those in rural areas in particular." The *Albany Herald* agreed, calling the majority report "disappointing and contradictory in that it clearly cut across the expressed will of a majority of Georgians."[33]

However, the editor of the *Columbus Ledger* praised the majority report for recommending "a wise course" and one that would preserve public education. The *Macon Telegraph* commended the majority report for providing an "honest, helpful approach to Georgia's school crisis," and the *Valdosta Times* urged the legislature to make sure that Georgia children would not be denied the educational training to which they were entitled. The *Atlanta Constitution* endorsed the majority report as a way to preserve public education, and the *Griffin Daily News* expressed support for the majority report because it provided for local option. The majority report received the praise of Mayor Hartsfield and former governor Arnall, who reiterated his belief that politicians who closed schools would suffer at the polls. Commendation for the committee even came from Judge Hopper, who thought it had done "a great deal to educate the people of the State as to the dangers" that threatened the schools. One member of the committee, Robert Arnold, praised the majority report for arousing "people to thinking about a subject which they were willing to brush off or run from in the hope that it could never happen in Georgia."[34]

Ten days after the release of the committee's report, Judge Hooper held a hearing in which the plaintiffs in the Atlanta case pleaded for the immediate implementation of their plan. Judge Hooper delayed implementation until September 1961, stressing that the plan's implementation depended on the repeal of the state's massive-resistance laws. The judge, detecting "a great shift" in public opinion away from closing the public schools, speculated that the legislative candidates seeking election might reflect that attitude change. As a result, he intended to give the new legislature convening in January 1961 the opportunity to keep the schools open by repealing the massive-resistance legislation. The editor of the *Gainesville Daily Times* also detected a shift in public opinion on the issue, calling it "mind changing time all over Georgia."[35]

The delayed implementation of the plan gave supporters of the public schools additional time to lobby for their cause. The organization HOPE launched a new effort, dubbed Operation Last Chance, that created a statewide network of citizens to lobby legislators. It presented to the governor and legislators an open school statement signed by representatives of almost a thousand businesses located throughout the state. In conjunction with fifteen other organizations, HOPE sponsored legislative forums throughout the state to discuss the implications of closing the public schools. Several of the Sibley committee members, who supported the majority report, spoke to various gatherings in favor of their recommendations. Homer Rankin concluded that his audiences' attitudes changed after they realized that the committee recommendations were "not an effort to enforce integration, but rather a plan to maintain the maximum segregation under the law."[36]

Others calling for preservation of the public schools included Newell Edenfield, president of the Georgia Bar Association, who called for the repeal of the state's massive-resistance laws. Governor Vandiver dismissed Edenfield's suggestion, contending that the legislature would not "consider the repeal of segregation laws that [had] been on the lawbooks for many years." Delegates attending the Georgia School Boards Association's annual meeting in October 1960 passed a resolution urging the legislature "to alter the laws of the State of Georgia in accordance with the majority report of the Sibley Committee." State school superintendent Claude L. Purcell, who had signed the majority report, continued to speak out in strong support of public education. Ivan Allen Jr., president of the Atlanta Chamber of Commerce, called for the chamber to work actively for the passage of open school legislation. More than eighty-five organizations throughout the state endorsed maintaining the public school system. In the latter half of the year, Senate president pro tempore Sanders and House floor leader Twitty toured the state in a prelegislative forum sponsored by the state chamber of commerce. During the tour, Sanders and eventually Twitty expressed their support for keeping the schools open.[37]

In addition to the school crisis, another issue—the 1960 presidential election—competed for the attention of Georgians. Potential Democratic presidential nominees included Senators Hubert H. Humphrey, Lyndon B. Johnson, and John F. Kennedy. The Georgia delegation to the 1956 Democratic National Convention had supported Kennedy's unsuccessful effort to become the vice presidential nominee. In the aftermath of that defeat, Kennedy made a concerted effort to gain the support of the state's political leaders in his attempt to gain the party's presidential nomination in 1960. Robert B. "Bobby" Troutman Jr., who served as Kennedy's southern presidential campaign manager, had been actively working the Georgia political leadership on behalf of Kennedy for several years. After the 1956 convention, both Senator Kennedy and Robert F. "Bobby" Kennedy had visited the state on several occasions, and the senator had carried on an extensive correspondence with Georgia politicians including the governor. During Vandiver's gubernatorial campaign, Senator Kennedy expressed delight in the then lieutenant governor's "unhampered progress toward the Governor's chair" and later congratulated Vandiver on his "impressive victory" in the primary. Communications from the senator to the governor included Christmas cards, copies of speeches, a "get well" letter, and a copy of the statement announcing Kennedy's presidential candidacy.[38]

Despite Kennedy's active cultivation of the state's political leadership, Senator Johnson enjoyed a distinct advantage in Georgia in the quest for his party's presidential nomination—his friendship with Senators Russell and Talmadge. Both considered Johnson to be the best presidential nominee from the South's standpoint. Johnson, whose close friendship with Russell went back to the Texan's arrival in the Senate in 1949, assiduously cultivated his relationship with Russell, whom he considered his mentor in the Senate. Senator Russell played an instrumental role in Johnson's rise to the position of minority leader and later majority leader in the Senate. Johnson's friendship with Talmadge began with the Georgian's arrival in the Senate in 1957. Governor Vandiver concurred with the state's two senators that Johnson was the least objectionable of the prospective candidates seeking the Democratic presidential nomination.[39]

As head of the state Democratic Party, Governor Vandiver continued the traditional practice of handpicking the party's delegation to the national convention. The delegation supported Johnson's bid for the presidential nomination on the first ballot, according to Vandiver, "at the behest of Senator Russell and Senator Talmadge." The Georgia delegation, along with the other southern delegations, strenuously objected to the proposed civil rights plank, which called for elimination of literacy tests, creation of a fair employment practices commission, and "first-step" compliance with the *Brown* decision. Governor Vandiver attacked it as "the most vicious plank that [had] ever been proposed to any convention at any time" and directed state party chairman Jimmy Gray to draft a minority report in defense of the southern point of view. The report, which had the support of nine other southern states, was rejected on the convention floor. As a result, several southern delegations urged Governor Vandiver to seek the vice presidential nomination as a protest candidate against the civil rights plank.

In the meantime, Senator Kennedy asked several southern governors including Vandiver to discuss with him which vice presidential candidate would be most helpful in carrying the South in the presidential election. Vandiver warned Kennedy of the possibility of losing the South without Johnson on the ticket. To the governor's suprise, Kennedy offered and Johnson accepted the vice presidential nomination. As a result, Vandiver's potential vice presidential candidacy ended, since the southern choice for the position had been Johnson. Vandiver, still displeased with the treatment the South received at the convention, returned to Georgia without endorsing the national ticket.[40]

Some southerners, still grumbling over the civil rights plank, supported unpledged presidential electors as a way to force both parties to be more tolerant of the South's position on race. Georgia and four other southern states already had laws permitting unpledged presidential electors. Georgia's law, which had never been used since its enactment in the Herman Talmadge administration, allowed unpledged electors to cast electoral votes for their personal choice for president rather than for the presidential candidate of their party. In the event of a close presidential race, unpledged electors could deny either of the major presidential candidates a majority in the electoral college and throw the election into the House of Representatives. Governor Vandiver saw voters in Georgia as having three choices in the 1960 presidential race—the Democratic ticket, the Republican ticket, or unpledged electors. An angry former governor Arnall called the governor's failure to endorse the Democratic ticket "utterly disgraceful," and even former governor Griffin urged Governor Vandiver to support the ticket because it was "about as good as the Democrats could have selected." Undeterred by such criticism, the governor called a special session of the state Democratic Executive Committee for it to consider allowing a referendum on unpledged electors to be placed on the primary election ballot. After a Fulton County judge denied a petition to enjoin such a vote, the committee placed the referendum on the primary ballot.[41]

In August 1960, Governor Vandiver went to Washington seeking Senator Kennedy's promise never to use federal troops in Georgia if he was elected president. Kennedy agreed, and Vandiver returned to Georgia, where he announced his endorsement of the Democratic ticket and its slate of pledged electors. Senators Kennedy and Johnson called the governor to express their appreciation for his endorsement, and even former governor Arnall praised the governor, who had "at long last decided to support the national Democratic party." Roy Harris, who had led the fight for unpledged electors, denounced the governor's decision as a "surrender to the principle of integration and race-mixing." The governor's endorsement of pledged electors came too late to have the referendum removed from the September primary, in which 55 percent of the voters supported unpledged electors. The governor attributed the results to confusion among the voters over wording of the referendum as well as continued dissatisfaction with the party's platform. Even though it had no binding effect, the vote was a rejection of Governor Vandiver's position on pledged electors.[42]

Despite this temporary setback, the Kennedy presidential campaign made substantial progress in its efforts to carry the state. The governor selected two close friends and supporters, House Speaker George L. Smith II and his chief of staff, Griffin Bell, to serve as co-chairmen of the Kennedy-Johnson campaign organization in Georgia. The campaign organized in every county in the state and received an additional boost late in September when Senators Russell and Talmadge finally announced their support for the Democratic ticket. Senator Kennedy's candidacy had the backing of most of the state's Democratic political leadership, with Governor Vandiver playing a major role in behalf of the senator's campaign in Georgia. Griffin Bell claimed that such support by the state's political leadership was rare because the state's Democratic politicians had not actively backed national tickets in the past.[43]

In response to a request by the governor, Senator Kennedy brought his campaign to Georgia in October and spoke to a crowd of more than ten thousand at the Little White House in Warm Springs. Governor Vandiver introduced Kennedy as a man of outstanding qualities who would provide the same type of leadership that Franklin D. Roosevelt had. The governor also campaigned for the ticket by boarding the "LBJ Special" campaign train in South Carolina as it whistle-stopped its way to Atlanta. There he gave an enthusiastic introduction of the vice presidential candidate to a large crowd of partisan Democrats. Senator Johnson later wrote Vandiver, "With folks like you on our side, we'll make it." Other political activities by the governor on behalf of the Kennedy-Johnson ticket included speeches at a Jefferson-Jackson Solid South Dinner in Atlanta and at the Henrico County, Virginia, Democratic Executive Committee's annual banquet. Not since the efforts of Ellis Arnall on behalf of President Franklin D. Roosevelt in 1944 had a governor of Georgia worked so diligently on behalf of a Democratic presidential candidate. The governor boasted of Georgia continuing its tradition of voting Democratic in presidential elections "unless something catastrophic" occurred.[44]

Then, in late October 1960, an incident occurred that had the potential of being catastrophic for Kennedy's support among white voters in the South. It began when Atlanta police arrested Dr. Martin Luther King Jr. for participating in a sit-in demonstration. Dr. King chose to remain in jail rather than pay bail. Mayor Hartsfield obtained the dismissal of charges against Dr. King and in the process incorrectly claimed that someone in the Kennedy campaign had intervened on behalf of Dr. King. Hartsfield believed that his statement, made without authorization by the candidate or his campaign, would "throw the Negro vote" to Senator Kennedy. The mayor downplayed fears that the senator's association with King could be politically detrimental to Kennedy's support among the state's Democratic politicians and white voters. Hartsfield dismissed such concerns by claiming that Georgia would continue its tradition of always voting Democratic even if the party's nominee were "a one-legged Chinaman who couldn't speak English." Bobby Troutman expressed concern when he confronted the mayor over his statement about the Kennedy campaign's involvement in Dr. King's release. According to Morris B. Abrams, who witnessed the exchange, Troutman accused the mayor of having "just blown" the election. "We had it sewed up, but now you're going to lose the South." [45]

As soon as Dr. King was released from jail in Atlanta, DeKalb County authorities took him into custody, charging him with probation violation. The civil rights leader had been charged in 1959 with driving without a valid Georgia license and had been given twelve months of probation by DeKalb County judge James O. Mitchell. The same judge deemed Dr. King's sit-in arrest as a violation of his probation and sentenced him to several months of hard labor at the state's maximum security prison. Wofford Harris, Senator Kennedy's civil rights adviser, urged him to issue a public statement in support of the civil rights leader "to increase the pressure for King's release and improve Kennedy's standing among Negro voters." However, Governor Vandiver and Bell warned that such a statement would result in Kennedy's losing Georgia and other southern states. [46]

Senator Kennedy finally decided against making a statement, opting instead to solicit Governor Vandiver's assistance in securing Dr. King's release. At first glance, it seemed highly unlikely that the segregationist governor would lend assistance to the state's most vocal opponent of segregation. Historian Taylor Branch had even characterized the governor as "King's most aggressive political enemy of the moment," noting that "Vandiver's antipathy for King was a manner of public record." When the media reported Dr. King's decision to move back to Atlanta to head the Southern Christian Leadership Conference, Governor Vandiver stated that Dr. King was not welcome in Georgia. He stated further, "Until now, we have had good relations between the races." Vandiver, whose future political ambitions included another gubernatorial term and a possible U.S. Senate race, responded to the request by stressing that his personal intervention on behalf of Dr. King would be "political suicide" for him. Nevertheless, he assured the nominee of his willingness to do what he could "under cover" to secure the release of the famous prisoner. After conferring with Bobby Russell, the governor asked one of Judge Mitchell's closest friends, George D. Stewart, to intervene with the judge on behalf of the president. Stewart discussed the matter with Judge Mitchell, who agreed to release King if Senator Kennedy or Bobby Kennedy personally made such a request. [47]

After Governor Vandiver informed Bobby Kennedy of the Mitchell-Stewart conversation, Bobby Kennedy called Judge Mitchell, who then released Dr. King. Senator Kennedy had called Mrs. King prior to the release to express his concerns about her husband's well-being. Governor Vandiver called it a sad commentary "when the Democratic nominee for the presidency makes a phone call to the home of the foremost racial agitator in the county." Although believing that the calls to Mrs. King and Judge Mitchell damaged the senator's campaign in Georgia, the governor still stood by his prediction of Kennedy's carrying the state in November. His prediction proved to be correct when the Democratic ticket received 62.5 percent of the vote—a higher percentage of the total vote cast in any state except Rhode Island. Several factors contributed to the Democratic landslide in addition to the state's tradition of voting Democratic in presidential elections since before the Civil War. The ticket benefited from the endorsement of three of the most powerful politicians in Georgia—Senator Russell, Senator Talmadge, and Governor Vandiver—in addition to a well-organized campaign in the state. John Sibley, in a letter to Bobby Kennedy, contended that Griffin Bell and Ernest Vandiver "contributed more than any two men" to Senator Kennedy's victory in Georgia. Although the King incident proved to be beneficial to Kennedy among black voters in the North, it failed to shake white Democrats loose from their traditional loyalty to the Democratic Party. The presence of Lyndon Johnson on the ticket—a fellow southerner who had the endorsement of the three most powerful segregationist politicians in the state—reassured white Georgians that the national ticket was safe on the race issue. Vandiver later told President Kennedy that he had "laid his future political career on the line" in support of Kennedy's candidacy.[48]

The majority of white Georgians may have remained loyal to the national Democratic Party in the 1960 presidential election, but many of their younger black counterparts were growing increasingly impatient with the slow rate of desegregation in the state. Even though the U.S. Supreme Court had ruled against segregation in Atlanta's public parks, playgrounds, and golf courses in 1955 and federal judges had ended segregation in the city's public library and transportation systems in 1959, segregation still remained firmly entrenched in Georgia. Younger blacks, criticizing the NAACP's legalistic approach, increasingly looked to direct action to speed up the dismantling of Jim Crowism. A new phase of the civil rights movement began on February 1, 1960, when black college students sat in at a white-only lunch counter in Greensboro, North Carolina. Activism by black students challenging Jim Crow laws quickly spread throughout the South. Governor Vandiver attributed sit-ins to "subversive influences" and praised the "good judgment" of Georgians for not engaging in them. Even as he spoke, however, college students who attended the six black private colleges in Atlanta were organizing a direct-action campaign challenging Jim

Crowism in the state's largest city. They published a statement in the Atlanta newspapers on March 9, 1960, entitled "An Appeal for Human Rights," which expressed their dissatisfaction with "the discriminatory conditions under which the Negro" was living in Atlanta at the time and "with the snail-like speed at which they [were] being ameliorated." The students pledged to use every legal and non-violent means at their disposal to secure their citizenship rights.[49]

Atlanta mayor Bill Hartsfield praised the "Appeal" as an expression of "the legitimate aspirations of young people throughout the nation and the entire world." He commended the students for their commitment to achieving their goals by nonviolent and peaceable means. In contrast, Governor Vandiver contended that the only purpose of this "left wing statement" was "to breed dissatisfaction, discontent, discord and evil." He asserted that "all Georgians were working diligently to increase and expand job opportunities for all of [the state's] people" and reminded the students that salaries for public school teachers had been equalized and that in many cases school facilities had been built for Negro students that were "better and more modern than provided for white children." Contending that Georgians rejected the false charges that Atlanta and the state of Georgia were "a land of 'inequality and injustice,'" the governor maintained that human rights could be gained "only through individual initiative and individual achievement, not by discord and strife." He denounced sit-ins as unorthodox tactics that were unacceptable to the majority of the state's citizens and urged students not to engage in such activism.[50]

The students ignored the governor's plea and held a sit-in on March 15, 1960, six days after the "Appeal" had been published. Approximately two hundred black college students sought service at white eating facilities in Atlanta, and seventy-seven of them were arrested for refusing to leave after being requested to do so. The governor denounced the protests as "subversive in character," which could lead to violence and anarchy. Despite the governor's objections, the sit-ins continued, and one of the city's most famous residents, Dr. King, was arrested in October 1960 for challenging segregation at a Rich's Department Store restaurant. Under increasing pressure from sit-ins, boycotts, and adverse national publicity, representatives of the Atlanta business community eventually negotiated a plan with black leaders in which desegregation of eating facilities in the major businesses in downtown Atlanta would occur in September 1961.[51]

Eventually the passage of the Civil Rights Act of 1964, a law that Vandiver and the state's political establishment opposed, ended racial discrimination in public accommodations in the state. Vandiver opposed the law and, in particular, the public accommodations portion of the legislation. He strongly expressed his views in a two-page letter to President Kennedy in 1963 for including such a provision in proposed legislation that eventually became the Civil Rights Act of

1964. Vandiver believed that the solution to racial problems would come about when people voluntarily tried to work out their own problems, but, he said, "They damn well resent being forced to work them out under the proposed new federal statutes." He reminded President Kennedy that prejudice couldn't "be whisked away by a federal statute. The only way that you can make progress in the field of racial relations is in the minds and hearts of men of good will." As long as public funds were not involved in operating a private business, Vandiver deemed it fundamental that the owner had the right to determine whom his business served.[52]

Some years earlier in testimony before a congressional subcommittee, Vandiver, then governor, had expressed a view held by many of his fellow white southerners that the South was making racial progress without interference by the federal government or "professional agitators." He criticized civil rights legislation being considered by Congress in 1959 as "dangerous" because it destroyed more rights than it created and because it concentrated power in the federal government at the expense of the reserved powers of the states. He warned that racial progress could not be achieved by enactment of punitive and unconstitutional federal legislation reminiscent of Reconstruction statutes that were "so base that no American can read them now without a sense of shame." Vandiver told the subcommittee members, "For over a decade now, it has been the policy of the State government to equalize and to improve education, welfare, health, employment, economic, and other opportunities for all of our people." In fact, Vandiver insisted that Georgia, without federal interference, had made "steady advancement in job opportunities, personal incomes, housing and other meaningful benefits accruing in everyday living. That [was] the Georgia civil rights program." Such progress had occurred, Vandiver insisted, because members of both races in the state had mutual respect for each other and shared "a common determination" to work out their problems "within the framework of Georgia authority."[53]

However, blacks disagreed with the governor's claim that the state was making "steadfast advancement" in ensuring equal treatment and opportunities for all its citizens. They complained of the "snail-like pace" in obtaining equal treatment and pointed to inequities such as the employment of only 35 black officers in the 830-member Atlanta police force in 1960. Despite the fact that blacks made up almost 39 percent of that city's population, blacks were restricted to the use of 680 hospital beds out of 4,000. The General Assembly had enacted numerous laws detrimental to equal treatment for black Georgians such as a law in 1956 reinforcing segregation on state property and in public accommodations. In the follow year, the legislature had even urged Congress to repeal the Fourteenth Amendment. Since the early 1950s, the state had improved black public schools to undermine allegations that they were not equal to white schools. The gap between state educational expenditures for black and white students had narrowed as a result of this effort to shore up the separate-but-equal doctrine as it underwent increasing scrutiny by the federal courts. Still the state in 1958 spent $226.35 per white student, compared with an expenditure of $187.78 per black student. Contrary to the governor's optimistic assessment of race relations in the state, historian Numan V. Bartley concluded that the relationship between blacks and whites had actually worsened by 1959.[54]

The year 1960 proved to be an eventful year for Governor Ernest Vandiver. He obtained the legislature's approval of a major capital projects program and the expansion of state services without raising taxes. He played a major role in Senator Kennedy's victory in Georgia in the 1960 presidential election and in opposing the unpledged elector movement, which could have been detrimental to the senator's presidential campaign in the state and in the South. More important from the state's standpoint, he orchestrated the creation of a study committee that prepared the state to accept the inevitability of the desegregation of its public school system. However, the stress and strain of being governor in such turbulent times took its toll on him, and he suffered a heart attack at the age of forty-two. The year 1961 looked to be even more eventful and just as stressful for the young governor from Lavonia, for the state had to decide whether it would continue its system of public education.

Ernest Vandiver as a young boy. Courtesy of Governor Vandiver.

Governor Vandiver's parents, Samuel Ernest and Vanna Bowers Vandiver. Courtesy of Governor Vandiver.

Sybil Elizabeth "Betty" Vandiver at the age of sixteen. Courtesy of Betty Vandiver.

Betty Vandiver's parents and grandmother, Judge Robert L. "Bob" and Sybil Nannette Millsaps Russell with Blandina "Ina" Dillard Russell. Courtesy of Betty Vandiver.

Ernest and Betty Vandiver at their wedding reception in 1947. Courtesy of Governor Vandiver.

The Vandiver's wedding party. Best Man, James C. "Jim" Owen Jr. is on Vandiver's immediate left, groomsman Robert L. "Bobby" Russell Jr. is two positions to the right of his sister, and groomsman Herman E. Talmadge is on the far right. Courtesy of Governor Vandiver.

Sybil Elizabeth "Betty" and Lieutenant Governor S. Ernest Vandiver with Mary Elizabeth "Lib" and Governor S. Marvin Griffin at the Governor's inaugural ball. Courtesy of the *Atlanta Journal* and the *Atlanta Constitution*.

Lieutenant Governor S. Ernest Vandiver, Governor S. Marvin Griffin, and House Speaker Marvin E. Moate. Courtesy of the *Atlanta Journal* and the *Atlanta Constitution*.

Lieutenant Governor S. Ernest Vandiver presiding over the Georgia Senate. Courtesy of Edwin H. Friend Sr. and the Georgia Department of Archives and History.

Governor S. Marvin Griffin, Lieutenant Governor S. Ernest Vandiver, and Senator Herman E. Talmadge. Courtesy of Edwin H. Friend Sr. and the Richard B. Russell Library for Political Research and Studies.

Part of the crowd at Vandiver's campaign kickoff rally in Dublin in July 1958. Courtesy of Richard B. Russell Library for Political Research and Studies.

Gubernatorial candidate Vandiver at a Saturday afternoon political rally in his 1958 campaign.
Courtesy of Richard B. Russell Library for Political Research and Studies.

Gubernatorial candidate Vandiver at a political rally in Albany in 1958. Courtesy of Richard B. Russell Library for Political Research and Studies.

Gubernatorial candidate Vandiver speaking at a Gainesville rally in 1958 with Senator Richard B. Russell Jr. and S. Ernest "Chip" Vandiver III looking on. Courtesy of Edwin H. Friend Sr. and the Richard B. Russell Library for Political Research and Studies.

Senator Richard B. Russell Jr. mingling with Vandiver supporters at a political rally in Gainesville in 1958 campaign. Courtesy of Richard B. Russell Library for Political Research and Studies.

The Vandivers with Roy V. Harris and Robert L. "Bobby" Russell Jr. checking vote totals at the Vandiver gubernatorial campaign headquarters in 1958. Courtesy of the *Atlanta Journal* and the *Atlanta Constitution*.

S. Ernest Vandiver being sworn in as governor while outgoing Governor S. Marvin Griffin listens. Courtesy of Edwin H. Friend Sr. and the Georgia Department of Archives and History.

Governor and Mrs. Vandiver as he waits to address the General Assembly. Courtesy of Richard B. Russell Library for Political Research and Studies.

The State's First Family: Vanna Elizabeth "Beth," Jane Brevard, the governor, Sybil Elizabeth "Betty," and Samuel Ernest "Chip" Vandiver III. Courtesy of Edwin H. Friend Sr. and the Georgia Department of Archives and History.

Governor Vandiver swearing in William R. Bowdoin as Supervisor of Purchases. Courtesy of Edwin H. Friend Sr. and the Georgia Department of Archives and History.

Lieutenant Governor Garland T. Byrd and his wife, Gloria Elizabeth, and Governor Vandiver and his wife, Betty. Courtesy of the *Atlanta Journal* and the *Atlanta Constitution.*

Governor Vandiver conferring with Assistant Attorney General Henry G. Neal and Executive Secretary Peter Zack Geer. Courtesy of the *Atlanta Journal* and the *Atlanta Constitution.*

Governor Vandiver addressing the General Assembly as Lieutenant Governor Garland T. Byrd looks on. Courtesy of the *Atlanta Journal* and the *Atlanta Constitution*.

Governor and Mrs. Vandiver, accompanied by Atlanta *Constitution* reporter Celestine Sibley, touring Milledgeville State Hospital. Courtesy of the *Atlanta Journal* and the *Atlanta Constitution*.

Governor and Mrs. Vandiver with Christmas presents gathered by the Georgia Municipal Association for patients at Milledgeville State Hospital, a program suggested by the First Lady. Courtesy of the *Atlanta Journal* and the *Atlanta Constitution*.

Governor and Mrs. Vandiver at the groundbreaking ceremony for chapels at Milledgeville State Hospital. Courtesy of the *Atlanta Journal* and the *Atlanta Constitution*.

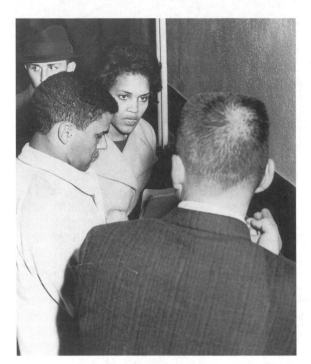

Hamilton E. Holmes and Charlayne A. Hunter attempting to register at the University of Georgia in January 1961. Courtesy of the *Atlanta Journal* and the *Atlanta Constitution*.

The General Assembly Committee on Schools with chairman Judge John A. Sibley in the center seat on the first row. Courtesy of Governor Vandiver.

Governor Vandiver addressing the General Assembly with (*left to right*) House Speaker George L. Smith II, Senator Herman E. Talmadge, Lieutenant Governor Garland T. Byrd, and Senator Richard B. Russell Jr. Courtesy of Edwin H. Friend Sr. and the Richard B. Russell Library for Political Research and Studies.

Governor and Mrs. Vandiver and Governor-elect Carl E. Sanders and his wife, Betty Foy. Courtesy of the *Atlanta Journal* and the *Atlanta Constitution*.

Vice President Lyndon B. Johnson, Governor S. Ernest Vandiver, and Senator
Herman E. Talmadge campaigning for the Kennedy-Johnson ticket in Atlanta in
1960. Courtesy of the *Atlanta Journal* and the *Atlanta Constitution*.

Senatorial campaign photograph, 1972.
Courtesy of Richard B. Russell Library
for Political Research and Studies.

The Ernest Vandiver family in 1998 in front of the Vandiver home: (*left to right, front row*) Vanna Elizabeth "Beth" Vandiver, Samuel Ernest Russell (son of Samuel Ernest "Chip" Vandiver III), Samuel Ernest Vandiver Jr., Sybil Elizabeth "Betty" Vandiver, Jane Brevard Kidd, and David Alexander Kidd Sr.; (*left to right, back row*) "Chip" Vandiver, Michelle Flemming Vandiver, Regina Leigh (daughter of Chip Vandiver), Elizabeth (daughter of Jane Kidd), and David Alexander "Alex" Kidd Jr. (son of Jane Kidd). Courtesy of Governor Vandiver.

Samuel Ernest Vandiver Jr., in 1985. Courtesy of Herb Pilcher, Tifton.

NINE

School Desegregation

After years of delay and postponement, it seemed certain that the public schools in Atlanta would finally be desegregated. Federal district judge Frank A. Hooper had delayed the inevitable until the fall of 1961 to give the legislature one last opportunity to allow the public schools to remain open by repealing the state's massive-resistance laws. The 1961 legislative session had to decide whether to permit desegregation or to end public education in the state. Governor Ernest Vandiver faced the most difficult decision of his political career—what course of action would he recommend to the legislature? Understandably, Georgians, both white and black, anxiously awaited the governor's decision.

On the eve of that momentous legislative session, another issue—the possibility of the governor's being appointed to a high position in Washington—temporarily gained public attention. According to newspaper reports in the latter part of December 1960, President-elect John F. Kennedy intended to nominate a southern governor to the position of secretary of the army. Governors Vandiver and E. Buford Ellington of Tennessee, both of whom had supported Kennedy in the presidential election, headed the list of possible appointees. According to Vandiver, Robert B. "Bobby" Troutman Jr., on his own initiative, had been actively lobbying for the appointment of Vandiver to the position of secretary of the army in the incoming administration. Troutman, a prominent Georgian and an influential political supporter and friend of the Kennedys, had two major arguments in support of a Vandiver appointment—the governor's critical support of Kennedy's campaign in Georgia and his key role in the release of Dr. Martin Luther King Jr. from the DeKalb County Jail. Roy V. Harris had another reason for a Vandiver appointment, claiming that the president-elect owed his election to the governor's opposition to the independent elector movement in the South. According to Harris, Vandiver's opposition killed the movement in the South, allowing Kennedy to carry the South and win the election. Certainly the governor saw himself as being "in a good position" for an appointment in the new administration. Although the governor was noncommittal when Troutman discussed the possibility of his appointment as army secretary, Vandiver later admitted, "I considered it very strongly." He conceded that the position held "some attractions" for him because of his military background and service as adjutant general.[1]

On the first day of 1961, one of the state's most influential members of Congress, Representative Carl Vinson, publicly stated that the president-elect and the governor had agreed on the appointment. According to the congressman, who held the position of chairman of the House Armed Services Committee, Governor Vandiver had sought his advice on whether he should take the appointment. "I told him," Vinson stated, "that I would be delighted to see him accept the appointment." The congressman even publicly expressed his pleasure that President-elect Kennedy had "seen fit to give it [the appointment] to him."[2]

The *Atlanta Journal* editorialized, "Georgia is proud and happy over Mr. Kennedy's choice." While Roy Harris conceded that Vandiver was "entitled to a political pay-off from the Kennedys, the editor of the *Atlanta Constitution,* Eugene Patterson, saw the appointment as a way out for Governor Vandiver from his "no, not one" promise made as a gubernatorial candidate. "He has come to the place as governor," Patterson wrote, "when he must break his word on school segregation or stultify his intelligence, and to him this is a tearing experience. The only alternative to making this choice is to give the governorship to a man less bound than he." That man, Lieutenant Governor Garland T. Byrd, remained silent on the possible appointment except to praise the governor for his outstanding record of public service. According to the publisher of the *Atlanta Constitution,* Ralph E. McGill Sr., the politicians who wanted to prevent Griffin's election as governor in 1962 wanted Byrd in the governor's office to give him time "to use the patronage and the power of incumbency to establish himself against Governor Griffin." Again, according to McGill, Troutman told him that he had urged members of the president-elect's staff to name Vandiver secretary of the army in order to get Byrd in the governorship and "and that he had cleared this with Senators Russell and Talmadge but not with Congressman Vinson." McGill also believed that "neither Senators Russell nor Talmadge wanted their man in office" when the Atlanta public schools were desegregated and that the Russell family did not want "one of their kinsman to preside over the desegregation" of the state's public schools.[3]

The governor finally ended his public silence on the appointment on January 3, 1961. He stated that Kennedy had not offered the position to him and that neither he nor any one representing him had even discussed the nomination with the president-elect or anyone on his staff. Nevertheless, he deemed it a "distinct honor" to have himself mentioned as a possible nominee. Later that day, the president-elect telephoned the governor to discuss a *New York Times* story claiming that Senator Russell and Congressman Vinson had used "congressional pressure" on behalf of Vandiver's appointment. According to the governor, the president-elect denied the allegation and claimed that he had never discussed the possible nomination with either Senator Russell or Congressman Vinson. During that conservation, the president-elect did ask Vandiver whether he would be interested in the nomination. "I emphasized to him," the governor explained, "that I had not sought the post, was not now seeking it, and would not seek it."[4]

By this time, Vandiver's possible appointment had drawn opposition from two prominent black Georgians, Dr. Benjamin E. Mays, president of Morehouse College, and Dr. Samuel Williams, president of the Atlanta chapter of the NAACP. Both pointed to the governor's well-known segregationist views as disqualifying him from serving as head of an army that was racially integrated. Roy Wilkins, executive secretary of the NAACP, sent President-elect Kennedy a letter expressing his organization's opposition to the appointment because of Vandiver's segregationist views. According to press reports, liberals in the Democratic Party also opposed the nomination for the same reason. Eugene Patterson even called it courageous "for a Southerner with Vandiver's vulnerable racial record to choose an inquisition by Senate liberals at confirmation." Ralph McGill noted that Vandiver's record included opposition to integrating the army and the National Guard as well as making "the typical Southern defiance statements about the Supreme Court." More recently, the governor had returned from a good-will tour of South America and told reporters that 80 percent of the people in Brazil had Negro blood, which was "an example of what could happen in the event of integration in this country."[5]

Governor Vandiver ended the speculation on January 5, 1961, by withdrawing his name from consideration. In doing so, he criticized the "irresponsible journalism" of the *New York Times* for falsely accusing Senator Russell and Congressman Vinson of lobbying for his nomination. He called such allegations "embarrassing to two of Georgia's greatest statesmen and to me." Vandiver attributed his decision to remain as governor to his obligation to the people of Georgia to serve a four-year term. In addition, he recalled, "The situation at that time was almost explosive because of the integration issue, and to have left my office under those conditions would have been an act of cowardice." The *Atlanta Jour-*

nal called the governor's withdrawal "the right thing to do," and the *Americus Times-Recorder* praised the governor for choosing "not to run out on the job to which the voters of Georgia elected him two years ago." Nevertheless, the *Waycross Journal-Herald* expressed regret that the appointment was not made because the governor "would have made an excellent Secretary of the Army." National columnist Drew Pearson attributed the nonappointment to the governor's remarks about the Brazilian people. Ralph McGill contended that Vandiver's remarks about Brazil and his segregationist views "would have made his confirmation hearings a very unfortunate spectacle" and thanked God that the appointment was not made. He even suggested in a letter to Robert F. "Bobby" Kennedy that the governor had been "steadily losing popularity" and should resign. Even though dismissing the whole affair as a "comedy of errors," the *Macon News* speculated that the governor would receive an offer for a position in the Kennedy administration in the future. In fact, in his conversation with the governor on January 3, the president-elect offered Vandiver "a position of responsibility" in Washington when his "work" in Georgia was done.[6]

The day after the governor withdrew his name from consideration, federal district judge William A. Bootle ordered the University of Georgia to admit two black plaintiffs, Hamilton E. Holmes and Charlayne A. Hunter. Blacks had tried unsuccessfully to integrate the university previously, and as recently as February 1959, a federal judge had turned down Horace T. Ward's request to desegregate the university, an effort that had begun nine years earlier. In the summer of 1959, Holmes and Hunter, both recent high school graduates from Atlanta, applied for admission to the university in the fall. The university's registrar denied their request, contending that university rules required freshmen students to live on campus and that the dormitories were already full for the fall quarter. As a result, the two applicants enrolled at other colleges, but both sought admission to the university for the winter quarter. Again the university claimed that lack of dorm space prevented their enrollment—a rationale repeated in the denial of their request for admission for the spring quarter. After being turned down for the 1960 fall quarter, the plaintiffs went into federal court, claiming racial discrimination as the basis for their rejections. Judge Bootle held a trial on their complaint and issued a decision on January 6, 1961, that upheld the plaintiffs' discrimination claim and ordered the university to enroll them for the 1961 winter quarter.[7]

However, a major obstacle—the General Appropriations Act of 1956—stood in the path of the judge's order. Instead of adopting a new appropriations bill every year, legislatures simply extended the 1956 act, in which Section 8 (a) specified that only racially segregated units in the university system could receive funding from the state. Section 8 (d) of the law further provided for the termination of state appropriations to any desegregated state college or university. The Budget Bureau, which consisted of the governor and the state auditor, distributed appropriated funds and had the responsibility of enforcing the termination provision of the 1956 law.[8]

In reaction to Judge Bootle's decision, Governor Vandiver refused to say whether he planned to cut off state funds to the university if the two black plaintiffs were enrolled. House floor leader Frank S. Twitty predicted the governor would not cut off state funds because "the great majority of the people" did not want the university closed. One of the plaintiffs, Charlayne Hunter, later succinctly stated the reason why she believed the university would not be closed: "If there was one symbol of pride that personified the aspirations of white Georgians of every class and stripe, it was the 176-year-old state university." Senate president pro tempore Carl E. Sanders believed that the legislature would do "everything possible to keep the university open." House Speaker George L. Smith II concurred. *Atlanta Constitution* reporter Celestine Sibley suggested a major reason for keeping the university open: many of the legislators were either alumni or had children attending or planning to attend the university. Prominent alumni included the governor, Betty Vandiver, both of the state's U.S. senators, House Speaker Smith, and Senate president pro tempore Sanders. Governor Vandiver later wrote: "Almost every family in Georgia has some connection with the University of Georgia. A father, mother, brother, sister, uncle, or aunt, somebody in the family group had attended."[9]

Support for keeping the university open came from editorials in numerous newspapers in the state including the Atlanta papers, the *Macon Telegraph and News,* the *Waycross Journal-Herald,* the *Marietta Daily Journal,* the *Brunswick News,* the *Savannah Morning News* and the *Columbus Enquirer.* The *Atlanta Constitution* noted that universities in seven other southern states had already desegregated. The *Macon Telegraph and News* concluded that Georgians were "more concerned with the possible closing of the university than the mixing of two Negro students with some seven thousand white students." A young state senator from Young Harris, Zell B. Miller, agreed and called for the university to remain open even if it meant "two Negroes going to the university." A petition signed by more than one-third of the student population at the university urged the legislature not to close their school. Dr. O. Clyde Aderhold, president of the University of Georgia, urged the state's political leaders to keep his institution open.[10]

On January 7, 1961, the governor directed Attorney General Eugene Cook to request that Judge Bootle grant a stay of his order admitting Holmes and Hunter to the university. The motion, contending that the university could not operate without state funds, urged Judge Bootle to give the legislature the opportunity to delete Section 8(d) of the Appropriations Act of 1956 so that state funds to the school would not be cut off. Two days later, on January 9, Holmes and Hunter arrived at the university to register, a process that ended when Judge Bootle issued a stay of his order admitting them to the university. A disappointed Holmes and Hunter, prevented from registering again, left campus, and their attorneys immediately sought to overturn the stay in the Fifth Circuit Court of Appeals.[11]

As these events were taking place in Athens, the legislature convened in Atlanta at noon on January 9, 1961, to hear the governor give his third State of the State address. He devoted most of his speech to the accomplishments of the first two years of his administration, which included a building program that already had exceeded the Griffin administration's expenditures for construction by $100 million. The governor also boasted of his administration's $55 million increase in support of state services. At the end of his speech, he briefly addressed the situation at the university, criticizing Judge Bootle's "sweeping edict" of January 6, which he claimed "threatened to destroy or disrupt the University of Georgia." Then shifting his attention to the state's public school system, he told the lawmakers, "We cannot abandon public education." He reminded the legislators that the federal judiciary had invalidated every law requiring segregation in the public schools that had been challenged. He went on to criticize federal judges for moving against the southern way of life "with a viciousness peculiar only to tyranny and dictatorship." The governor observed that legal defenses devised by the state to maintain segregated schools were "not presently enough in light of developments to afford all possible protection to the people." In light of that reality, he called on the legislature to "provide a new plate of armor" for protection "against the sweeping and insidious onslaught of forced integration in Georgia schools." His new "plate of armor" consisted of a child protection amendment, which was one of the recommendations of the Sibley committee. The proposed amendment assured children in the public schools of the right to freedom of association to prevent them from being forced "to attend a school where intolerable conditions" existed.[12]

Representative Pierre Howard Sr. complained that the governor's solution for keeping the schools open was "a little old constitutional amendment" saying that a child didn't have to go to school with a child of another race. "This legislature is going to have to do more than that!" The *Macon Telegraph* likewise criticized the governor for failing to offer solutions to save the public school system. Even lawmakers praising the governor for endorsing open schools complained of his failure to provided details on how to accomplish such a goal. One lawmaker, Representative William Killian, expressed the views of many of his colleagues by stating, "On the school situation he leaves a lot of questions unanswered." Nevertheless, a freshman representative, Thomas B. "Tom" Murphy, commended the governor for at least giving the "first signs" that he was giving some thought to the theory that the state could not afford to close its public schools. Within hours of the governor's address, federal circuit judge Elbert P. Tuttle set aside the stay of Judge Bootle's order directing the admission of the plaintiffs, and they returned to the university to complete registration and to begin classes on the following day, January 10.[13]

In response to Judge Tuttle's decision, Vandiver called a meeting at the governor's mansion of more than fifty individuals including department heads, some close personal friends, and legislative leaders. The governor asked each of them whether they would recommend "integrated schools or closed schools." With the exception of House floor leader Twitty and Senate president pro tempore Sanders, those in attendance recommended closing the schools. Following the meeting, the governor directed Attorney General Eugene Cook to seek a stay of Judge Tuttle's decision from the U.S. Supreme Court.[14]

The governor released a statement at midnight on January 9 in which he contended that Section 8 of the Appropriations Act of 1956 left him with no alternative except to cut off state funds to the university. "[It is] the saddest duty of my life to sign an order recognizing that such a condition as contemplated by the statute does in fact now exist in that state fund support must be withheld from the university." He called Section 8 "an albatross" whose effect would be to close the university and deprive students of an education. Proclaiming that he would "not be a party to defiance of law, as a few would wish, or do anything which might foment strife and violence," he urged the legislature to repeal Section 8 of the law. Eugene Patterson wrote in the *Atlanta Constitution* that Vandiver could have responded like some other southern governors: "He could have defied the law, appealed to the public passions, and crippled the university as well as the state's good name—for no possible gain other than his own vanity and political fear." Commending Vandiver for realizing that integration of the university could not be prevented, Patterson contended that in asking the legislature to repeal Section 8 the governor had risen to the "heights of political courage."[15]

Even though his statement indicated that a cutoff order had been signed, the governor stated on the morning of January 10 that he was waiting for the plaintiffs actually to enroll before signing such an order. Attorneys for the plaintiffs in the meantime had sought a temporary restraining order to prevent the cutting off of state funds to the university. Judge Bootle granted the request and called a hearing to determine whether the temporary order should be made permanent. He justified the restraining order on the basis that the governor had cut off state funds to the university. An angry governor responded to the order by sending Judge Bootle a telegram protesting his "interference in the administration of state law and what amounted to usurpation of the legislative prerogatives of the General Assembly of Georgia." Calling the allegation that state funds had been cut off false, the governor criticized the judge for issuing judicial orders based on newspaper accounts and affidavits from plaintiffs' lawyers. Despite his strong protest, the governor announced his intention to abide by the court order out of his "respect for lawful process and [his] oath as governor."[16]

The state's effort to maintain a segregated university suffered a devastating blow on that same day, January 10, when the U.S. Supreme Court denied the state's request to overturn Judge Bootle's decision ordering the admission of Holmes and Hunter. The two plaintiffs finally completed registration on January 11, becoming the first black students to attend classes at the University of Georgia. The following day Judge Bootle permanently enjoined the governor from complying with Section 8 (d) of the 1956 appropriations act.[17]

University officials assigned Hunter a room in Myers Hall, and Holmes took the option of residing off campus. Other than taunts and jeers, no serious incidents occurred on the students' first day of class. However, on the preceding two nights protests had occurred. On the night of January 9, 1961, a small group of students had peaceably gathered at the University Arch to protest the pending desegregation of their university. The following night, a larger crowd of protesters, estimated by a special House committee investigating the university's desegregation at between 500 and 1,000 individuals, became "boisterous," with fireworks set off and two students taken into custody. Following a basketball game in which the university lost to arch rival Georgia Tech on the night of January 11, a crowd, according to the special House committee report, consisting of between 1,000 and 1,500 students and nonstudents gathered at about ten o'clock at Myers Hall to protest the black students' desegregation of the university. Some of the protesters shouted obscenities, set off fireworks, started a fire in the wooded area near Myers Hall, and broke windows in the dorm. University officials requested and received assistance from the Athens Police Department. In their efforts to break up the crowd, five law enforcement agents suffered injuries, the most serious of which was the fracturing of a kneecap. City and university personnel endured various objects being thrown at them. As the situation deteriorated, the police department finally resorted to tear gas, and firemen doused the protesters with water to encourage them to disperse. Calm finally returned to the campus by midnight as a result of the combined efforts of city and university personnel, in particular dean of men William Tate. According to one observer, Dean Tate "waded in and started grabbing identification cards" of protesting students. The police arrested twenty protesters, of which twelve were university students and eight nonuniversity students who were also Klan members. Shortly after the protest ended, the university's dean of students, Dr. Joseph A. Williams, suspended Holmes and Hunter for their safety as well as for the welfare of the student population. Governor Vandiver concurred with the suspensions and directed the State Patrol to transport the students to their homes in Atlanta.[18]

In the aftermath of the disturbance, questions arose concerning the absence of the State Patrol during the turmoil. Colonel William P. "Bill" Trotter Sr., director of the Georgia Department of Public Safety, had ordered additional state patrolmen to the Athens post to be available if needed during the desegregation crisis. He insisted that local officials had been "thoroughly briefed that the use of the State Patrol would be with the orders of the Governor" through Trotter's office. However, he "perceived from the events that both the University officials and the Athens Police Department intended to handle this matter without [state] intervention." According to Colonel Trotter, the Athens Police Department made a request for tear gas around ten o'clock that night to the commander of the Athens post. Trotter, who was on duty at the State Patrol headquarters in Atlanta, approved the request, although he was "surprised" that troopers had not been asked for "because events were getting out of hand around Myers Hall." According to the colonel's recollection several years later, a request for troopers was finally made, but he could not recall the "exact time" of the request. "At no time," he insisted, "was there the least hesitation on the part of the Governor to use the troops we had assembled." In a memo to the governor sent the day following the disturbance, the director estimated the time of the request from Mayor Snow "at about 10:50 P.M. or 11:05 P.M." Colonel Trotter, according to his memo, immediately contacted the governor, who called him back within ten minutes to authorize the patrol's assistance. He then issued the orders to carry out the governor's instructions to the commander of the Athens post at 11:15.[19]

However, Athens mayor Ralph M. Snow and Dean Williams had a different recollection of what transpired. They claimed that they had requested assistance from the Athens Patrol Post around ten o'clock the night of the disturbance. Mayor Snow contended he went to the Athens post seeking troopers and even called Colonel Trotter to ask for assistance. Mayor Snow conceded that troopers arrived on campus twenty minutes after the crowd had been disbursed. For his part in this episode, Governor Vandiver denied any hesitancy in ordering the State Patrol to the Athens campus. According to the governor, Mayor Snow at 11:05 P.M. called Colonel Trotter, who immediately relayed the request to him. Ten minutes later, according to the governor, he ordered the State Patrol on campus. Governor Vandiver blamed Mayor Snow for failing "in his legal duty to notify the governor of conditions which existed," citing the Public Defense Act of 1955, which required local officials to seek state assistance from the governor in the breakdown of law and order in their communities. The governor stressed that it was "imperative that local officials perform their legal duty of notifying the governor" if they were unable to maintain order.[20]

Despite his explanation, Governor Vandiver received criticism concerning the response of the State Patrol in dealing with the disturbance. In a front page editorial, the *Athens Banner-Herald* asked, "Why was the State Patrol not immediately available to assist local officers in preventing trouble?" The *Macon News* editorialized that Georgians were not proud of a governor who could not "offer an adequate explanation of why state troopers were not on the scene to break up the mob before the demonstration was over." The *Atlanta Constitution* criticized state officials who "failed unforgivably to provide state police when only they could keep the law from being broken. Gov. Vandiver should have foreseen and prepared." One irate Georgian telegraphed the governor asking why it took more than two hours to get the State Patrol on campus when a patrol station was only five minutes away. "A military commander," another critical Georgian wrote in a letter to the governor, "who would let such things as this slip up on him would be court-martialed." Joseph Parham, editor of the *Macon News,* even contended that the governor was "dead politically" for not sending the patrol to the university sooner. Eugene Patterson, editor of the *Atlanta Constitution,* expressed remorse over the "heart-sickening breakdown of law enforcement on the part of the state." The faculty of Morehouse College, a black institution in Atlanta, complained that the riot was "aided and abetted by what appears to [have been] the planned negligence" by those in authority. More than three hundred faculty members at the University of Georgia signed a resolution expressing regret that state officials "were unable or unwilling to protect the rights and property of the University and its students."[21]

On January 13, 1961, Judge Bootle ruled that the university had to readmit Hunter and Holmes. In response to the judge's mandate, Governor Vandiver pledged to use such forces as were "needed and available to protect lives and property and to quell any disorder." However, the governor insisted that state intervention would occur only when the mayor of Athens informed him that local law enforcement officials could not maintain the peace. The Clarke County grand jury adopted a resolution calling on the governor to allow the State Patrol to work with local police to prevent a recurrence of the "shameful riot" of January 11. The governor responded that he had placed one hundred state patrolmen on standby duty in Athens and that they would be ordered on campus if law enforcement in Athens broke down. He stressed his desire not to set a precedent by sending state law enforcement officers into local communities unless local authorities requested them. On January 16, the two suspended students returned to class without any major incidents.[22]

Although the issue of desegregating the university had been settled by the federal courts, the fate of the state's public schools still remained to be resolved. The time for delay had passed. Now the governor and legislature had to determine whether to allow the schools to be desegregated or to close them. During the 1958 campaign, Vandiver had promised that no white child would ever attend an integrated school in his administration. If he backed down from that pledge, would the politician who had aspirations of serving in the U.S. Senate be committing political suicide? Betty Vandiver considered this decision to be the "biggest" of her husband's political career. Senator Talmadge called it "the most difficult decision probably any governor . . . had to make since the War Between the States." The governor solicited advice from legislative leaders, government officials, friends, and politicians. He also turned to his wife, who he admitted had a great influence on him as he struggled with his decision. Finally, after much soul-searching and prayer, the staunch segregationist, who had promised to maintain segregated schools in his administration, came to the conclusion that he could not recommend the closing of the schools, which would put "a million children out on the streets, not going to school." In making that decision, Vandiver accepted the fact that he "never would be able to be elected to anything again." Betty Vandiver agreed that from a political standpoint, the decision "hurt him; it was political suicide some people say, but he was willing to do it for Georgia and for the children of Georgia." Having made the most momentous decision of his political career, he now had to convince the legislature to go along with him.[23]

Governor Vandiver returned to the capitol on January 18 to address a rare night meeting of the legislature. He had requested the session in order to present his plan of action for the schools to the lawmakers and to the much larger audience of concerned Georgians watching or listening over a statewide television and radio hookup. The last night session had occurred fourteen years earlier when the legislature, embroiled in the state's infamous three-governors controversy, elected Herman Talmadge governor. At that time, Vandiver, as a young aide to Herman Talmadge, actively lobbied lawmakers to elect Talmadge governor. Now, under different circumstances, Governor Vandiver asked the legislature to convene so he could address the lawmakers and the citizens of the state on the future of their schools. Lieutenant Governor Byrd recalled that there was a "lot of tension" in the House chambers that night; the visitors' gallery was so crowded that many of the spectators had to stand. Betty Vandiver remembered the mood in the House chambers as being one of "dreaded gloom," and Speaker Smith described the mood in the capitol that night as a mixture of uncertainty and unrest.[24]

A somber governor spoke not only as the state's chief executive but also as a father who had three children in public schools. He told his audience that the state's fight to maintain segregation in the schools had finally come down to a simple choice of deciding whether the state would have "public education or no education." He commended the past efforts of legislators for passing laws to maintain segregation in the schools but pointed out that such laws in other southern states had been transformed by recent federal court "decisions and events, from possible instruments of defense, to instruments of doom at the onset." If the massive-resistance laws remained in place, the governor warned that they could be used to justify federal intervention in local affairs. Rejecting defiance of the law or violence as an appropriate means to fight the federal judiciary, he called for new legislation to prevent the state's schools from being "taken over and run by federal injunctions." The chief executive proposed preserving public education while at the same time maintaining segregation in schools on a voluntary basis. To accomplish this goal, the governor urged the legislature to pass his freedom-of-association constitutional amendment so the voters could vote on it in the next general election. Unlike in his State of the State address, in which he had proposed only the freedom-of-association amendment, the governor now suggested several bills to cope with the crisis. One would allow for local referenda though which voters could determine the fate of their schools, which was a recommendation made earlier in the majority report of the Sibley committee. Other bills repealed the state's massive-resistance laws, provided tuition grants for students who wished to attend private schools to avoid desegregation, and added procedures pertaining to the appeals of local boards of education to the state board of education.[25]

Lieutenant Governor Byrd endorsed the governor's plan as the "best known solution" to the state's school crisis, and House Speaker Smith praised the governor for charting "the best possible course for Georgia." One senator, H. Erwin Mitchell, commended the governor "for his courageous, farsighted and aggressive leadership" in the school crisis. The *Macon Telegraph* urged the legislators to pass the governor's plan because it offered "a bright hope of keeping most, if not all, of the public schools open." The *Columbus Enquirer* opined, "Georgians generally are happy over the fact that the state's chief executive has taken a positive approach to providing a solution of the school problem." The *Atlanta Journal* called the governor's proposal a "reconciliation of the fact of life with what [had] become an impossible legal situation." Pat Watters, city editor of the *Atlanta Journal,* emphasized the importance of the governor's historic turn from massive resistance to allowing local option to deal with the desegregation crisis, calling the governor's plan "the first voluntary retreat from massive resistance in the South." Robert D. Fowler, a columnist in the *Marietta Daily Journal,* described Vandiver's speech as "his finest hour. For he provided outstanding leadership when it was needed most." The *DeKalb New Era* editorialized, "No one can help but admire Governor Vandiver's effort to keep the schools of Georgia open." The *Carroll County Georgian* commended the governor for choosing the nonviolent method of coping with the integration of its schools and concluded that "in making that choice Gov. Vandiver quickly became a statesman."[26]

The governor's plan gained the endorsement of one of the state's most ardent defenders of segregation—Attorney General Eugene Cook. If the state opted to continue massive resistance, the attorney general warned of massive integration with the federal courts taking over the public schools. Even if the legislature refused to appropriate money to operate them, the attorney general pointed out, Atlanta could still continue to operate its schools with local funds, but a majority of the school systems could not. Cook called the governor's plan one that would minimize the problem of integration in the state's school. State school superintendent Claude L. Purcell likewise endorsed the governor's plan, and Ivan Allen Jr., president of the Atlanta Chamber of Commerce, telegraphed the governor expressing the chamber's support. The chairman of the state board of education, James S. "Jim" Peters Sr., backed the governor's plan because, he noted, it allowed each community to decide the issue of closing or desegregating its schools. Dr. Clyde Aderhold, president of the University of Georgia, wrote the governor in support of his school proposals and praised him for his "courageous stand" and the fact that he met the issues "squarely and forthrightly."[27]

Not unexpectedly, the governor's plan drew criticism from one of the state's most vocal segregationists, Roy Harris, who alleged that the "surrender to the NAACP" began with the creation of the Sibley committee, whose purpose was, according to Harris, "to lay the foundation to surrender Georgia to the race mixers in 1961." Harris regretted that the governor had "swallowed the Sibley Report hook, line and sinker and openly advocated that the State of Georgia legalize the mixing of the races in the public schools." Former governor Marvin Griffin also criticized the governor's plan, which, he claimed, provided for "mass integration without firing a shot." He reminded Georgians of statements made by Vandiver as a gubernatorial candidate and later as a governor pledging "no mixing of the races in Georgia schools." State Democratic Party chairman James H. "Jimmy" Gray Sr., a staunch segregationist who had been made party chairman by the governor, also criticized Vandiver for capitulating on the issue of school integration. Unfortunately, Jimmy Gray complained, the governor had altered his strong stand on segregation by responding "to the bleeding-heart appeal to 'save our schools' by proposing to keep them open whatever the cost to principle and to Southern tradition." The governor later conceded that he had "caught hell" from those who attacked him for not living up to his campaign promise.[28]

In defending his decision, the governor contended that he would not be so irresponsible as to urge "defiance of lawful processes and subject the teachers and children of Georgia to bodily harm." Instead, he intended to offer the state responsible leadership on the issue and urged the legislature to pass his plan with a unanimous vote to demonstrate to the nation that Georgia was "acting positively to protect her children and protect her good name." The governor later conceded that his decision was a reversal of his campaign pledge but confessed, "I have not regretted it. I have had no sleepless nights nor pangs of conscience. I knew that what I had to do was committing political suicide, but I also knew that what I was doing was right, and I didn't look back. Perhaps I could have gotten some temporary political gain had I stood in the schoolhouse door or something similar, but I would have had trouble living with myself." [29]

The legislature passed the local-option legislation with only twenty-two negative votes, and the freedom-of-association amendment received only twenty-four no votes. The bill repealing massive-resistance legislation and authorizing tuition grants easily passed with only two negative votes. The *Atlanta Constitution* praised the governor and the legislature for taking "this farsighted step," which saved public education in the state. One *Atlanta Journal* reporter, Margaret Shannon, called the passage a "historic step" in that the state was abandoning school segregation by law for what it hoped would be segregation by choice. A pleased governor called the bills and the proposed constitutional amendment the "most important measures signed this century." [30]

Although the university and school issues overshadowed the 1961 session, the legislators grappled with other important issues as well. Early in the session, the governor proposed a $100 million bond program to finance the widening and resurfacing of the state's primary and secondary roads. Whereas Governor Griffin's bond request in 1958 proposed the building of rural roads, Governor Vandiver called for a road maintenance and repair program that he justified by contending that the state had built roads in the past three decades "with scant thought given to repairs." Even with the increase in his administration's maintenance budget by almost 40 percent, the governor conceded that the additional money "came too late to catch up with the years of neglect." Lieutenant Governor Byrd endorsed the bond request, contending that the state's lack of emphasis on maintenance had left highways in "conditions of near catastrophe." The *Gainesville Daily Times* agreed: "Every Georgia motorist who has ever crossed a state line knows that Georgia 'really oughtta do something about our roads.'" [31]

Not surprisingly, former governor Griffin dismissed the governor's plan as nothing more than "pork barrel" legislation and claimed that the governor's change of mind on bonds was understandable, since he had "already been on both sides of every public issue at least twice." The bond proposal also received criticism from the *Macon Telegraph,* which reminded its readers of Lieutenant Governor Vandiver's strong opposition to Governor Griffin's rural roads bond proposal because of its long-term financing. Representative James H. "Sloppy" Floyd Sr. reminded his colleagues in the House of Vandiver's opposition to Griffin's roads bond proposal because it was not "on a pay-as-you-go basis." Undeterred by such criticism, administration leaders in the legislature introduced legislation to implement the bond program. HB 1, creating an authority to issue the bonds, easily passed with only seven negative votes, and SB 1, providing procedures to retire the bond certificates, passed with only one no vote.[32]

In his 1961 State of the State address, the governor boasted of the success of his administration's efficiency and economy program, which had allowed the state to accumulate a surplus and to balance the budget without raising taxes. Governor Vandiver proudly pointed to the fact that Georgia was one of only nine states that had not raised taxes in the past two years. He recommended a budget of $406 million—an increase in the regular state budget of $8.5 million—and predicted that the proposed budget could be financed by regular growth in state revenue. The governor proposed $18 million in contingency spending for services, including a $200 pay raise for teachers if revenues exceeded that needed to fund the regular budget. The *Atlanta Journal* urged the General Assembly to adopt the proposed budget even though conceding that "essentially it [was] one of austerity."[33]

Although the governor easily gained legislative approval for his bond proposal and plan to save the schools, he received strong opposition in the House to his budget, which was highly unusual because governors had dominated the budgetary process in the state in recent years. Vandiver described the existing process as one in which "the state auditor, working with the governor during that era, prepared an executive budget, who presented it to the legislature for adoption, and usually within a thirty to forty-five minute period it was passed just as the governor had presented it." William D. Ballard, a member of the House during the Vandiver administration, described the process as one in which the chief executive dominated and the legislature simply rubber-stamped his budget without even hearing from department heads. Peter Zach Geer Jr., who served as the governor's executive secretary, agreed that "the General Assembly was pretty much a rubber stamp for the governor." Augustus B. Turnbull III concluded in his study of the state's budgetary process that "the years from 1931 to 1961 showed a rather steady decline in the degree of legislative control over the budget." Former House Speaker Roy Harris claimed that the governor was "the absolute boss" of state surplus funds. Another member of the House during Vandiver's administration, George T. Smith, referred to the power of a governor having what was called "hip-pocket financing of government": "The appropriations laws at that time were written in such a way that unless you enacted a new appropriations bill every two years, you continued to travel on the old appropriations bill, and you did not have to account for how the money was spend except for the amount that was included in the last appropriations bill. Well, the income of the state was increasing. So all that money over and above that set out in the last appropriations bill, the Governor could spend it as he pleased, as long as it was legal. We called it a 'hip pocket government'—the hip pocket financing the government because he could spend it on roads, wherever he wanted to, any thing like that. And the legislature was trying to stop that."[34]

Ironically, candidate Vandiver had promised during the 1958 election to work for the restoration of the budgetary powers of the legislature. Carrying out that pledge, the governor succeeded in getting the General Assembly in 1960 to propose a constitutional amendment that would, in the governor's words, restore the legislature to its "rightful responsibility of appropriating money." The voters approved the amendment in the general election in 1960, and, as a result, the governor submitted a new appropriations bill to the 1961 legislative session—the first since 1956. The governor told the lawmakers in his 1961 State of the State address that passage of the amendment restored the legislature's prerogatives in the appropriation of public tax funds. Early in the session, Speaker Smith praised the governor as a chief executive who did not attempt "to stifle legislative independence."[35]

Hints of trouble for the governor's budget appeared early in the session. Teachers, and in particular members of the Georgia Education Association, criticized the governor's inclusion of teachers' pay raises in the contingency budget rather than the regular budget. The contingency budget provided for expenditures to be funded provided the state had sufficient revenue to do so. The GEA's legislative committee urged the lawmakers to disregard the governor's pay recommendation and include a five-hundred-dollar raise for teachers in the regular budget. Teachers flooded the capitol with ten thousand telegrams in support of the GEA's position. Although the *Atlanta Constitution* called the GEA-suggested pay raise "an unrealistic request that could not be financed without a tax increase," Representative Jack B. Ray, chairman of the House Appropriations Committee, announced that his committee would do "everything possible" to give teachers more money. Chairman Ray's comment provoked a warning from the governor against "unwise moves" to increase teachers' salaries beyond the recommendations in his appropriations bill. The governor expressed confidence that the House Appropriations Committee would not be part of any "slick, dishonest purely political maneuver" of adopting an appropriations act without providing revenue to fund it. Despite the governor's concerns, several legislators introduced legislation providing a pay raise for teachers in the regular budget. Such demands provoked a stern warning from the governor to the legislature to be prepared to raise taxes in order to finance raises in excess of his recommendation.[36]

The House and Senate appropriations committees held a joint meeting on January 26, 1961, to begin consideration of the governor's budget. At the request of the committees, the legislature voted on February 2 to recess until February 20 in order to allow the appropriations committees more time to examine the governor's budget. Over the objections of the governor, the joint committee held its meetings and hearings in executive session with department heads appearing to explain and defend their agencies' budgetary requests. "For the first time," one student of the state's budgetary process wrote, "the General Assembly was taking the departments to task, and members began to enjoy their work." Agriculture commissioner J. Philander "Phil" Campbell Jr. claimed that for the first time in his service as commissioner the legislature asked him how he spent his money and for what it was needed. In fact, the commissioner stated, "I don't recall that the legislature has ever done anything like this before." Chairman Ray revealed, "Most department heads stated to the committee that the Budget Bureau [the governor and state auditor] had never contacted them, nor had they appeared before the Budget Committee." [37]

Over the governor's objections, the joint committee continued to hold hearings behind closed doors. Even more ominous for the governor, it issued a statement asserting that the legislature intended to regain its control of the state's financial affairs. The statement contended that since 1941 the governor and the state auditor had had "complete control over the financial affairs" of the state and had exercised the authority "to transfer funds from department to department and spend surplus funds at their discretion." State auditor Barton E. "B. E." Thrasher Jr. denied having authority to spend surplus funds, insisting that only the governor had that power. [38]

On the same day the committees issued a statement declaring their intention of regaining control over state finances, the governor endorsed a teacher pay raise of $100 to be included in his proposed regular budget. According to the governor, his appropriations bill had contained a clerical error that had erroneously listed a $4.5 million expenditure in the regular budget when it should have been included in the contingency budget. The correction of this error, the governor insisted, provided sufficient revenue to finance a $100 pay raise for teachers in the regular budget. The *Atlanta Journal* criticized the clerical error as indicative that something was "dreadfully wrong" with the state's method of budgeting. The *Atlanta Constitution* agreed and called for the "overhauling" of the state's inadequate budgetary process. [39]

On February 20, the joint committee released its substitute appropriations bill. It totaled over $600,000 more than that of the governor's and included a $250 pay raise for teachers. Unlike the governor's appropriations bill, the substitute bill did not have a contingency budget. It increased the budgets of thirteen agencies and cut the budgets of three agencies. The Welfare Department took the largest reduction, while the Agriculture Department gained an additional $945,000. The bill also limited the governor's expenditure of surplus funds to $10 million; previously there had been no such restriction in appropriations bills. Although the pay raise for teachers and bus drivers totaled $9 million, the substitute bill allocated only $5.5 million additional money to the Department of Education to pay for the increases. The committee proposed to raise the remaining money needed to pay for raises from a state Department of Education fund designated "School Building Hardship Cases" and from surpluses it believed existed in the department's budget.[40]

The governor countered by asking Attorney General Eugene Cook for an official opinion on whether the state could divert money in the "Hardship Cases" school building fund to teachers' pay raises. The attorney general ruled against such a diversion, contending that those funds had been earmarked for capital expenditures by the Department of Education. The governor then charged that the substitute bill actually provided for a smaller pay raise than $250, since a substantial portion of the raise was to come from Department of Education funds that could not be spent for teachers' salaries. Governor Vandiver also criticized the substitute appropriations bill cuts in the Welfare Department's budget and stated that Georgians were "shocked and dismayed" at the lack of concern for the state's less fortunate and needy. He urged citizens to contact their legislators to protest the proposed reduction in essential state services and criticized the attempt to "trick [the] teachers into believing that they [had] a $250 pay raise when sufficient money [had] not been provided for it."[41]

The governor's comment provoked criticism from Frank Hughes, the executive secretary of the GEA. Hughes accused the governor of ignoring the needs of teachers and contended that the only friends teachers had in the capitol were in the legislature. Hughes attributed the governor's opposition to higher pay raises for teachers to his continuing resentment over the vote at the association's annual convention in 1960 against a resolution thanking him for a pay raise. House Appropriations Committee chairman Ray expressed shock and dismay that the governor would accuse his committee of being "guilty of trickery" in the funding of its appropriations bill. The chairman defended the committee's recommendations on pay raises as well as its proposal for funding the raise. Chairman Ray also argued that the committee's use of the school building fund for raises had been approved by none other than state school superintendent Purcell and state auditor Thrasher. He dismissed Attorney General Cook's opinion as a deliberate act "to deny the teachers and bus drivers a salary raise and to embarrass the General Assembly." House floor leader Twitty denied that the committee's substitute bill cut essential services and dismissed the attorney general's opinion by observing that he "had a habit of ruling like somebody wanted him to."[42]

In the midst of the growing controversy, the governor requested that the House action on the substitute bill be delayed for two days. The House, ignoring the request, adopted the committee's substitute bill with only eight negative votes—a bold act of defiance against the governor on the part of the lower house. Speaker Smith considered the vote "historic" and indicative of the lawmakers' commitment to legislative independence. Reg Murphy, political editor of the *Atlanta Constitution,* called the vote Governor Vandiver's "worst defeat" in the legislature. A reporter for the *Macon Telegraph,* Gene Britton, went even further by calling the vote "the first crushing defeat" in the governor's political career. Even more significant than the outcome of the vote was the leadership in the House challenging the governor's budgetary power. It consisted of Vandiver's own legislative leaders, including Speaker Smith, Appropriations Committee chairman Ray, Speaker pro tempore Robert L. "Bob" Scoggins, and floor leader Twitty. It in the opinion of Charles Pou, political editor of the *Atlanta Journal,* the vote was "a rare and raw power struggle between a governor and his lieutenants." The *Atlanta Journal* called the vote "a rebellion against the governor's authority and his power over the legislature by his control of state funds."[43]

Governor Vandiver believed that the rebellion against his budget was aimed at his possible successor, Lieutenant Governor Byrd, rather than at him personally. Even though Vandiver had withdrawn himself from consideration for the position of secretary of the army, the leaders of the revolt in the House, according to the governor, still thought that he was going to resign his office as governor and go to Washington. "And they were afraid that my successor . . . would be in charge and . . . they were not willing to work with him on the budget. They wanted the legislature to take control of the budget rather than having to deal with him."[44]

Although Lieutenant Governor Byrd professed ignorance as to why the House leadership challenged the governor on the budget, Henry G. Neal, who served as an assistant attorney general assigned to the governor's office in the Vandiver administration, considered the revolt "a genuine effort on the part of some legislators to have more 'say-so' in the budget process." Former House Speaker Harris attributed the challenge to legislators' being "tired of having to be rubber-stamps and vote as they [were] told by the governor's office." Interestingly, former governor Griffin surmised that the legislators were tired of being threatened by the governor with loss of roads, patronage, and state support for their local institutions unless they voted with him. In short, the former governor saw the legislature trying to regain control over "the purse strings of the public pocketbook." Speaker Smith believed that governors had too much power over the spending of surplus funds. Contending that such discretion was not "good government," the Speaker declared that although he had "the utmost confidence in Vandiver," he did not know who the next governor would be. Perhaps David C. Jones, then a member of the House, gave the best explanation as to why so many representatives opposed the governor's budget: "It didn't fit my nature to serve on the appropriations committee and get a 200-page bill and hold up my hand and vote yes when I didn't even know what was in it and not have any input whatsoever, you know. I knew that process was not conducive to good spending habits, and that people elected members of the General Assembly to go up there and direct how the money was spent and we weren't doing it."[45]

In an effort to salvage the governor's budget, the governor, his floor leader in the Senate, and the lieutenant governor proposed an appropriations bill in the Senate. It restored cuts in the governor's appropriations bill and removed the $10 million limit on surplus spending by the governor in the House substitute. The new administration bill, which gave teachers a pay raise of $300, totaled more than $412 million—an increase of $6 million over the governor's proposal. Governor Vandiver claimed the state could finance the increased expenditures without a tax increase by funding it out of the state's surplus. The governor strongly objected to two provisions in the House appropriations bill: the limiting of the chief executive to $10 million in spending of surplus funds and the prohibiting of the governor transferring surplus funds to state agencies. While still supporting the principle of legislative independence, he opposed making the office of governor nothing more than a "figure head" in the budgetary process.[46]

Vandiver and Byrd, who had a vested interest in protecting the budgetary powers of the governor because he was considered a likely gubernatorial candidate in 1962, decided to fight the House bill on the Senate floor rather than in the Senate Appropriations Committee, which eventually recommended adoption of the House substitute bill. Governor Vandiver engaged in intensive lobbying on behalf of his bill prior to its consideration on the Senate floor. Charles Pou wrote that the governor "probably spent his busiest weekend since the governor's race" lobbying senators to adopt the administration's bill, which was scheduled for a vote on Tuesday, February 28. "It is a fine display of power politics," the *Atlanta Journal* editorialized, "with each side applying all the pressure it can." Vandiver recalled that he fought "day and night for several weeks" in an effort to turn back the challenge to his budgetary powers. After more than six hours of debate on February 28, 1961, the Senate passed the bill by a vote of forty-one to twelve—a welcome victory for the governor after the devastating defeat in the House several days earlier.[47]

The struggle then shifted back to the House, where the governor asked Representative Charles A. Pannell to lead the effort to pass the administration's bill. In an effort to gain support, during debate on the House floor Representative Pannell read a letter from the governor that called for the creation of a joint legislative committee to make recommendations on improving the state's budgetary system. The letter also recommended the creation of a staff to assist the governor and legislature on budgetary matters. Debate on adopting the substitute bill lasted more than four hours. The Speaker himself took the well of the House to speak against the bill, an act called by Celestine Sibley "the most dramatic repudiation of a governor by a House Speaker since the days of the Roy Harris–Ellis Arnall split in the early 1940s." In his remarks, Speaker Smith sarcastically thanked the State Patrol "for bringing in so many of our friends" from throughout the state to lobby for the administration's bill. According to the Speaker, House members had told him that state jobs of relatives or paving projects in their counties could be in jeopardy if they voted against it. The Speaker, tracing his political association with the governor back to Herman Talmadge's administration, reminded the members of the House of his diligent efforts in support of Vandiver's campaigns for public office. On the issue of the legislature's budgetary role, however, he stated, he differed with his longtime political associate. Representative Ray also took the well of the House to plead with his fellow House members to stand by the appropriations committee's bill. Another opponent of the Senate bill, Representative "Sloppy" Floyd, dismissing the governor's claim for support of the General Assembly's reassuming its proper role in the budgetary process, declared that the governor wanted "legislative independence like Herman Talmadge wanted Martin Luther King, Jr., to serve as his executive director." Another representative, Robert Andrews, complaining of intense lobbying by the governor and his supporters, urged the members of the House not to sell their votes for promises of roads or jobs.[48]

Following the spirited debate, the House passed the substitute bill by a vote of 137 to 56—a significant victory for the governor. A bitter Roy Harris attributed the outcome to the governor's political clout, charging, "No king and No dictator has greater power." Like Speaker Smith, Harris accused the governor of threatening lawmakers with loss of future roads in their counties and loss of patronage unless they voted for the administration-backed appropriations bill. The *Atlanta Journal* called the effort of the House leaders in challenging the governor's budget "a power play that failed. The governor won and his ex-best friends and former most trusted lieutenants were the losers." The *Journal* also considered the taxpayers winners as a result of the fight because the governor had promised reform of the "sloppy budgetary procedure." Following the governor's suggestion, the legislature created a joint committee to study the budgetary systems of other states in order to make recommendations for changes in the state's budgetary system. The resolution mandated a report to the legislature by December 1, 1961.[49]

Following the adjournment of the General Assembly in March 1961, the state's attention began to shift to the pending desegregation of the Atlanta public schools in the fall of the year. The city's leadership hoped to avoid the turmoil that had accompanied desegregation of schools in other southern cities. Organizations Assisting Schools in September (OASIS), consisting of fifty-three civic, religious, and professional organizations, was formed to work for a peaceful transition to desegregated schools. Atlanta mayor Bill Hartsfield considered the peaceful desegregation of the city's schools critical to maintaining the city's progressive image. Atlanta police chief Herbert Jenkins capably directed his department's preparation to ensure a peaceful school opening. Chief Jenkins had earlier sent officers from his department to observe desegregation in other southern cities, and his department had prepared an extensive school desegregation action plan.[50]

In June 1961, Atlanta school superintendent John Letson announced that ten black students had been selected for transfer to four formerly white high schools in Atlanta. Shortly after that announcement, Governor Vandiver stated in a news conference his intentions of acting quickly to quell any violence that might occur during the desegregation of the Atlanta public schools. "Anytime the life or property of any citizen is endangered," Vandiver stated, "whatever forces that are necessary to preserve the peace will be used." While criticizing the *Brown v. Board of Education* decision as wrong when handed down in 1954 and still wrong today, he stated his intentions of complying with Judge Hooper's desegregation court order, explaining, "No matter how much I might disagree with it, that court order in fact exists. I think my feelings are well known on this." He reiterated his objections to integration but told reporters, "Unless the State of Georgia wants to secede from the United States and fire on Fort McPherson . . . , we'll have to obey that court order."[51]

Governor Vandiver insisted that although state forces would be used to protect schoolchildren and teachers from lawlessness or violence, neither the State Patrol nor the National Guard would be used to assist in the desegregation of the Atlanta schools. Noting that other southern governors had refused to maintain law and order in desegregation confrontations, the *Atlanta Journal* editorialized, "Gov. Vandiver is to be respected and commended for facing up to a situation not to his making or liking, and for declaring that Georgia will not tolerate lawlessness and rioting." In a statewide television address early in August 1961, the governor called for "restraint and caution on the part of every citizen" in the school desegregation crisis in Atlanta. He again assured Georgians that demonstrations would not be tolerated and that lives and property would be protected in the state's capital city. The governor pleaded for a peaceful school opening in Atlanta, pointing out that the state had been relatively free of racial violence and insisting that it be kept that way: "Outbreaks of violence could set us back a hundred years."[52]

As a result of the city's preparation combined with Mayor Hartsfield's and Governor Vandiver's commitment to maintaining law and order, the four Atlanta high schools were peaceably desegregated on August 30, 1961. Governor Vandiver expressed gratification that violence had not occurred, and Mayor Hartsfield praised his city for peaceably complying with Judge Hooper's desegregation order. President Kennedy commended Governor Vandiver and Atlanta's public officials for the "responsible, law-biding manner" in which desegregation occurred in Atlanta. Attorney General Robert F. Kennedy called the governor to praise the peaceable desegregation in the city. Governor Vandiver, in commenting on the call, stated that he told the attorney general that he and most Georgians were still "strenuously opposed to any integration" but would fight their battles "in the courts and not on the school grounds." Despite his opposition to integration, the state's public school system had been desegregated. To the governor's credit, he insisted that disorder would not be tolerated in the desegregation of Atlanta's schools. He later wrote President Kennedy, "We have handled our difficulties here in Georgia with reference to school integration with dignity and honor. We do not agree with the Court order, but we are law-biding people and we complied with the decree with a minimum of publicity and no violence. I felt that the best interest of my State and Nation would be served by handling our dilemma in that manner. In addition to this, the people of my State have gone about handling other racial difficulties on a voluntary basis—setting down with the interested parties and attempting to work out solutions to problems that have been with us for more than a hundred years."[53]

Governor Vandiver had achieved some notable accomplishments in the 1961 legislative session. The governor easily obtained legislative approval for a highway bond program that was twice as large as that of his predecessor, whose defeat he had engineered in the 1958 session. The governor also overcame a serious challenge to his budgetary powers in the House of Representatives. Although opposing desegregation in the public schools and at the University of Georgia, he refused to resort to defiance of the federal courts to maintain segregation. Most important, Ernest Vandiver provided the necessary leadership to ensure the continuation of pubic education in the state even though he fully expected his stand to end his political career. E. Freeman Leveritt, an attorney who advised the governor on desegregation of the schools, credited him with guiding the state through desegregation of its schools without the disorder and turmoil accompanying desegregation in other southern states. Even with these successes, the governor, understandably, welcomed the adjournment of the 1961 legislative session. It had been a difficult and trying year for both the state and its governor.[54]

TEN

The Final Year

On the eve of the 1962 legislative session, the political editor of the *Atlanta Journal* predicted few requests from the governor, since he had already "completed the bulk of his legislative program." The governor agreed with that assessment, cautioning that the state's budget was a "delicately balanced" one that could not fund additional expenditures. In his State of the State address on January 10, 1962, Governor Ernest Vandiver stressed the accomplishments of his administration and boasted that Georgia was one of only five states that had not had a tax increase in the past three years. The governor, assuring legislators that he would not ask for a tax increase in his last year in office, expressed his appreciation to the lawmakers for joining him in opposing "oppressive tax increases." The governor reminded the lawmakers of his administration's $89 million increase in spending for services without raising taxes—an accomplishment attributable, he claimed, to efficient operation of government, reforms in purchasing, and improvements in the enforcement of revenue laws. Governor Vandiver took pleasure in reminding the lawmakers that his predecessor had expanded state services by only $76 million while raising taxes $60 million.[1]

The governor saw the main task of the 1962 session as putting "the General Assembly back into the appropriating business." He pointed out that a "workable, overall plan" to restore the legislature's appropriations powers had never been presented to the General Assembly until the Pannell committee had submitted its report in November 1961. That committee, officially known as the Budget Study Committee, had been created by the 1961 session and had been chaired by Representative Charles A. Pannell. The governor, drawing on that report, made several recommendations concerning the budgetary process in his State of the State address. The governor pointed out that the legislature had passed only six appropriations bills in the past twenty-five years, resulting in nearly one-fourth of the state expenditures during those years being spent at the discretion of governors. Such a process, he stressed, limited the legislature in its rightful fiscal responsibility. To correct this problem, he recommended a constitutional amendment requiring biennial appropriations bills, limiting appropriations to no more than state revenue and surplus, capping debt obligations of state authorities to no more that 15 percent of the total budget, and creating a system of legislative budgetary controls. He called for the establishment of a "modern-day and universally-acceptable, functioning Budget Bureau," an office that he deemed essential in any effort to restore responsibility and accountability to the budgetary process.[2]

The *Atlanta Journal* responded favorably to the governor's address and praised him for his opposition to raising taxes and for his administration's honest, efficient, and economical handling of state funds. Nevertheless, the *Journal* saw the administration as still having one major unfinished job—the establishment of a "strong budgetary system." The *Macon Telegraph* also praised the governor's speech, contending that it "itemized a record of which he [could] be proud." The *Atlanta Constitution* editorialized that the reforming of the governor's request to reform the budgetary process would be "a magnificent monument topping all other achievements."[3]

Both Lieutenant Governor Garland T. Byrd and House Speaker George L. Smith II quickly endorsed the governor's request for budgetary reform. One frequent critic of the governor, Representative James A. MacKay, praised Vandiver for giving the legislature the most "golden opportunity in 30 years to restore its appropriating function." Other lawmakers praised the governor's speech as well. However, the announced Republican candidate for governor in the upcoming elections, A. Edward "Ed" Smith, thought the governor's speech emphasized complacency in state government at a time when Georgia had the worst highway system, the highest illiteracy rate, and the lowest per capita income of any state in the nation. Nevertheless, Smith conceded, "Vandiver has had a good administration. It has been far superior to what preceded."[4]

The governor's budgetary reform legislation, which House Speaker Smith called "one of the most important bills ever to reach the floor of the House," unanimously passed the legislature. Differences between the two versions of the bill resulted in a conference committee report that both houses unanimously adopted. The new law created a budget bureau with the governor designated ex officio director of the budget. The law also created an administrative head of the agency, the state budget officer, a position that was to be filled by the governor.

The agency had the responsibility of assisting the governor in preparing the state's budget for submission to the legislature. The law specifically limited general appropriations acts to two fiscal years.[5]

In addition, the legislature proposed two constitutional amendments necessary to implement the governor's budgetary reform request. The first provided for split legislative sessions in odd-numbered years to allow the legislature more time to consider a governor's budget. According to the proposed amendment, legislative sessions would last for twelve days, followed by a recess until the second week in February to give the legislature's fiscal committees adequate time to analyze the budgetary request of the state's chief executive. Following the recess, the legislature would reconvene for no more than thirty-three additional days, during which time action would be taken on the budget. The second proposed amendment required governors to submit general appropriations bills to the legislature every odd-numbered year. The legislature unanimously proposed both amendments, which were approved by the voters in the 1962 general election. The *Atlanta Journal-Constitution* claimed that the General Assembly "made history in enacting budget reform." Governor Vandiver hailed the restoration of the legislature's budgetary powers as the most significant event to have taken place in the state in the past fifty years.[6]

Whereas budgetary reform proved to be noncontroversial, a state industry tax proved to be one of the most contentious issues in the 1962 session. New or expanding industries had to pay a 3 percent tax on new equipment and machinery. The Georgia State Chamber of Commerce, viewing the tax as a deterrent to attracting new industries to the state, urged its repeal. On this issue the two highest elected officials in state government disagreed, with the lieutenant governor favoring repeal and the governor supporting retention of the tax. The governor claimed repeal would make it impossible to finance the state's budget without raising taxes. The *Atlanta Journal* endorsed repeal even if it resulted in "a brief dip in revenue," a loss that the paper argued would be offset by increased tax revenue from the economic development generated by the repeal of the tax. Governor Vandiver, in defending his position on the tax, reiterated his commitment to industrial development, noting that more than 300 new industries had moved to the state and 271 expansions of existing industries had occurred in his administration. The governor feared that repeal of the tax could lead to increased demands for exemptions to state tax laws and thus undermine the state's ability to raise revenue. He considered the tax fair and argued that it was not a high-priority item industries considered when contemplating relocating to another state.[7]

State revenue commissioner C. Dixon Oxford predicted that the repeal of the tax would result in an annual loss of $6 million to $10 million in revenue. However, Jack J. Minter, director of another state agency, the Commerce Department, claimed the reduction would cost less than $3 million—a loss that he insisted would be made up by tax revenue generated from increased industrial development and expanded payrolls. Harry C. Jackson, chairman of the Senate's Industry and Labor Committee, claimed that a study made by his committee concurred with Director Minter's assessment. The *Atlanta Constitution*, commenting that the governor was "a conservative who recoil[ed] from fiscal gambles," urged the governor to reverse his position on the tax and reminded him that the repeal or partial exemption of new industries from similar taxes by neighboring states had proved to be beneficial in their industrial recruitment.[8]

Early in the session, the governor met with members of the Senate Industry and Labor Committee, which was considering a compromise proposal supported by Lieutenant Governor Byrd to reduce the tax to 1 percent. After the meeting, Chairman Jackson told reporters that the governor was still "unalterably opposed" to modifying the tax. Despite the governor's opposition, the committee nevertheless voted to reduce the tax to 1 percent. Senator Jackson contended that the reduction would put the state in a more competitive position in its efforts to attract new industries. Senator Spencer M. Grayson went even further by offering a substitute bill to repeal the tax, which the Senate passed with only four negative votes. That action provoked a strong response from House Speaker Smith, who agreed with the governor on the tax issue. He threatened to rule the Senate bill out of order when it reached the House, arguing that the state constitution required all revenue bills to be introduced in the House first. Seeking to overcome the impasse, Representative George D. Busbee proposed a compromise bill allowing new and expanding industries to deduct taxes on new machinery from state corporate income taxes over a six-year period. Representative Busbee claimed the governor was "in sympathy" with his bill, which had also gained the endorsement of the Georgia State Chamber of Commerce. The House Ways and Means Committee recommended approval of the Busbee Bill, and Governor Vandiver said that he would sign it—providing no additional tax exemptions were added to the bill. None were, and the legislature unanimously adopted the Busbee bill, which the governor signed. The governor commended the lawmakers for a productive session, which, he claimed, stood in "sharp contrast to the political division" that hampered their progress in past years.[9]

The governor did not have long to enjoy the tranquillity of the recent session. Within weeks of the session's adjournment, the U.S. Supreme Court handed down a decision with significant implications for the state's political status quo. The Court, in the *Baker v. Carr* case from Tennessee, held in March 1962 that malapportionment in state legislative districts was a federal constitutional issue. The Court had earlier ruled in the *Colegrove v. Green* case in 1946 that federal courts lacked jurisdiction in malapportionment disputes. Georgia, like other states, had malapportioned state legislative and congressional districts that now stood in jeopardy as a result of the *Baker* decision. The state's political establishment had another problem. Georgia had a unique system of nominating state officials—the county-unit system—in which unit votes in counties determined Democratic Party nominations for state offices. Since representation in the malapportioned House governed the allocation of unit votes to counties, it seemed reasonable to assume that the unit system of nomination also stood in jeopardy of invalidation by the federal judiciary. The *Atlanta Journal* hailed the *Baker* decision as one that "could topple Georgia's longtime standing political structure." Former Atlanta mayor Bill Hartsfield, a longtime foe of the county-unit system, proclaimed that the *Baker* decision "opened the way for the unit system to be thrown out."[10]

V. O. Key Jr., a prominent scholar of the political systems of the southern states, had once described the county-unit system as "the most important institution affecting Georgia politics." In the era of one-party domination in state politics, the system of nominating state officials in the Democratic Party maximized the influence of rural and small-town residents, who were the most conservative voters in the state. The unit system, enacted into law with the passage of the Neill Primary Act in 1917, governed the nomination of federal and state officials. Representation in the malapportioned House determined voting strength in the county-unit system, with each county having two unit votes for each representative in the House. Since 1920 the 8 most populous counties had received three representatives and six unit votes each. The next 30 most populous counties had received two representatives and four unit votes each, while the remaining 121 counties had one representative and two county unit votes each. The total unit vote for the state consisted of 410 votes. All nominations required a plurality of unit votes, with the exception of senatorial and gubernatorial elections, which required a majority of the unit votes. By 1960 the 8 most populous counties in the state had 41 percent of the state's population but only 12 percent of the county-unit vote. In contrast, the 121 least-populated counties possessed only 32 percent of the state's population but cast 59 percent of the state's unit votes. In 1960, the six unit votes of Echols, Quitman, and Glascock Counties, with a combined population of 6,980, equaled the unit votes of Fulton County, the largest-populated county in the state, with 556,326 residents.[11]

Opponents assailed the unit system as undemocratic and detrimental to citizens living in urban counties because it assured rural voters of political dominance in a state that now had more urban than rural residents. The unit system rewarded those candidates running for state office who appealed to the rural voters, and, as Key observed, it became "possible to use the cities as whipping boys, to inflate rural pride and prejudice, including that against the Negroes who vote[d] most frequently in the cities." Eugene Talmadge, elected governor four times, epitomized the politician who benefited from the unit system. He couched his appeal for votes in the rural idiom, championed the small farmers, and preached the values of rural life—rugged individualism, hard work, frugality, individual initiative, governmental economy, segregation, laissez-faire government, low taxes, and balanced budgets.[12]

Following his father's death in 1946, Herman Eugene Talmadge had inherited the leadership of the Talmadge faction. Like his father, the young Talmadge had defended segregation and opposed civil rights for black Georgians. However, unlike his father, the young Talmadge had viewed government as an instrument to bring about improvements in the quality of life for Georgians. During his administration, state government had played a major role in modernizing the state's economy and improving the well-being of Georgians. By the time Herman Talmadge had left the governorship in 1955, expenditures for state services had increased dramatically—spending for public education had soared 310 percent, and spending for public health had risen by 436 percent. The Talmadge administration's support of economic development had resulted in the creation of more than fifteen thousand new jobs in the private sector and the expenditure of more than $50 million in new plant construction. Although Tamadge had broadened his appeal to include urban voters, his greatest political support had come from rural and small-town residents. Like his father, he had championed the county-unit system and had even supported a constitutional amendment on two separate occasions extending the unit system to general elections. Unfortunately for Talmadge, constitutional amendments had to be approved by a majority of popular votes rather than by unit votes in general elections, and his efforts to obtain passage of these amendments had failed.[13]

Not surprisingly, the unit system had been challenged in both federal and state courts on numerous occasions. The first legal challenges had occurred in 1946. Helen D. Mankin, congresswoman from the state's Fifth Congressional District, had received a majority of the popular votes, but challenger James C. Davis had won the nomination with a majority of the unit votes. A federal district court, citing *Colegrove v. Green* as precedent, had refused to overturn Davis's victory, claiming it lacked jurisdiction. In the same year, plaintiffs also had challenged the use of the unit system in the hotly contested gubernatorial primary. Even though James V. "Jimmy" Carmichael had won a plurality of the popular vote in the 1946 primary, former governor Eugene Talmadge had gained the nomination by winning a majority of the unit votes. A federal district court had ruled against the plaintiffs, claiming that the suit was moot because it had been filed after the election. The U.S. Supreme Court had refused to overturn the lower federal courts in both cases.[14]

In 1950, plaintiffs had challenged the unit system, and again a federal district court had refused to intervene, citing lack of jurisdiction. The following year, 1951, the Georgia Supreme Court had unanimously affirmed the dismissal of two suits that had been filed in state superior courts challenging the unit system. The U.S. Supreme Court refused to hear appeals in these cases "for want of a substantial federal question." Eight years later, in 1958, Atlanta mayor Bill Hartsfield had brought suit challenging the unit system and had requested the appointment of a three-judge panel to hear the petition. Federal district judge William B. Sloan had refused to request the panel's appointment, which led Hartsfield's attorney, Morris B. Abram, to seek a writ of mandamus to force Judge Sloan to do so. The U.S. Supreme Court had refused his request, however, in a five-to-four vote.[15]

Thus far, defenders of the unit system had been successful in turning back numerous legal challenges to their unique nominating system, but the *Baker* decision gave them grounds for increased concern, which intensified even further with the filing of the county-unit suit. On April 2, 1962, Governor Vandiver expressed his opinion that the *Baker* decision did not pose a "clear and imminent danger" to state legislative districts because a suit had not been filed challenging their apportionment. He believed the federal courts would allow the state the opportunity to pass a constitutional amendment to correct any deficiencies if the present apportionment was challenged in court. However, since a suit had been brought against the unit system, the governor directed attorneys Burket D. "Buck" Murphy and E. Freeman Leverett to assist Attorney General Cook in the defense of the unit system in federal court. Although seeing no need to convene the legislature to take immediate action to protect the unit system in response to the *Baker* decision, the governor did not rule out doing so in the future.[16]

Ivan Allen Jr., who had succeeded Bill Hartsfield as mayor of Atlanta, disagreed with the governor on this issue and urged the members of his county's legislative delegation to request a special session for the purpose of abolishing the county-unit system. Former governor Griffin also favored a special session and urged the "state leadership to quit taking tranquilizing pills, pulling up the covers and hoping after the 'big sleep,' the problem [would] have resolved itself." Lieutenant Governor Byrd, an announced gubernatorial candidate, agreed with the governor and opposed a special session at that time. The politically powerful Association of County Commissioners at its annual convention adopted a resolution reaffirming its longtime support of the county-unit system. However, the resolution stated that the association's support of the unit system did not preclude change in the system and even suggested that some reapportionment might be needed "to meet changing conditions." The adoption of that resolution came after Senator Herman E. Talmadge had addressed a closed meeting of the association's leadership. According to press reports, the senator told the leaders that the Supreme Court would invalidate the unit system as it presently existed. Talmadge had first suggested revision of the unit system in April 1959 in order to give populous counties more unit votes, a suggestion endorsed by Senator Richard B. Russell.[17]

In response to the filing of the unit suit, Elbert Tuttle, chief judge of the Fifth Circuit Court of Appeals, appointed a three-judge panel to hear the case; the panel consisted of Judge Tuttle, federal district judge Frank A. Hooper, and Fifth Circuit Court judge Griffin B. Bell. Ironically, Judge Bell had been Governor Vandiver's chief of staff until his resignation in October 1961 to assume a seat on the federal appellate court in Atlanta—an appointment strongly endorsed by the governor. Judge Tuttle scheduled hearings for April 27 on whether to grant an injunction against the use of unit votes in the September 12, 1962, Democratic primary. Shortly after Judge Tuttle's announcement, attorneys representing residents of Fulton and Dekalb Counties filed suit challenging the apportionment of seats in the General Assembly. The plaintiffs requested an injunction preventing legislative elections until the General Assembly was "validly reapportioned." The suit also challenged the constitutionality of the 3-2-1 ratio of representation in the House, the basis for the allocation of unit votes. It appeared now that both the unit system and the existing apportionment of seats in the legislature were in jeopardy.[18]

On the same day that Judge Tuttle scheduled hearings in the county-unit suit, Governor Vandiver issued a proclamation convening a special session of the legislature to begin April 16. The proclamation listed consideration of revising the unit system and the reapportionment of the legislature as the two reasons for the special session. However, in remarks to reporters, the governor stated, "This session is being called for one purpose only—to preserve and protect the county unit system." The proclamation condemned the U.S. Supreme Court's departure from the *Colgrove* precedent in order to engage in "judicial experimentation" concerning the "distribution of power" within a state. The *Atlanta Journal* editorialized that although apportionment of the legislature was important, the issue of "greatest importance" in the special session was to make sure "that whoever [was] elected to constitutional office [would] be responsible to all the people and not just to one group," as under the county-unit system. The *Atlanta Constitution* called for "fair apportionment" in the special session and predicted the invalidation of the unit system by the federal courts if the legislature did not abolish it.[19]

According to the press, the governor had a tentative plan to modify the unit system. It called for increasing the size of the 205-member House by 12 seats, thereby increasing the number of unit votes by 24. The eight most populous counties would gain the additional House seats and unit votes, while each of the thirty existing 4-unit counties lost a seat in the House and 2 unit votes. Prior to the session, the governor held several days of briefings with legislators and representatives of organizations including the Georgia State Chamber of Commerce, Association of County Commissioners, Georgia Municipal Association, and Georgia Farm Bureau. Governor Vandiver told the lawmakers that "our house is on fire" and the legislature had to revise the county-unit system in order to save it. By now, the proposed plan to revise the unit system as reported in the press had itself been revised as the governor struggled to advance a plan that could be passed by the legislature. Vandiver still supported shifting House seats and unit votes from middle-sized to large urban counties. According to the revised plan, the House would remain at 205 seats and the number of county unit votes at 410. Each county would receive 1 representative and 2 unit votes, with the remaining 46 House seats and 92 unit votes distributed among the eight most populous counties. The new plan proposed using a formula that the national House of Representatives employed in its allocation of seats following each census. Under this plan, only four of the thirty counties that currently had 4 unit votes and 2 representatives would retain that status.[20]

Understandably, the governor's plan ran into strong opposition from the 4-unit counties. Senator Earl Staples, representing one of those counties, clearly stated his position: "I'll fight anything that takes a representative away from any county in my district." Representative Quimby Melton Jr., also representing a 4-unit county, claimed that the inequity of the proposed plan "would be on the shoulders of [his] county and on the shoulders of other middle-sized counties." Representative George W. Potts, who likewise represented a middle-sized county, complained, "The fat's in the fire and we don't like it." Representative Edgar Blalock stated his opposition to the governor's plan, which, he claimed, would make the county-unit system "more unfair and more unjust in order to appease some other counties." The *Atlanta Journal* editorialized that penalizing the large cities of the state was "such an old thing" that it was generally accepted. "But reducing Clarke County and Athens, for instance, to the two-unit, one-representative level of Echols County and Statenville to save our politicians' way of life, puts a new perspective on the matter."[21]

The governor also came under criticism for not including consideration of reapportioning the Senate in his proclamation convening a special session. He attributed the omission of Senate reapportionment in his call for the special session to his preference for keeping senatorial districts based on a geographical basis. Legislators from the Fourth and Fifth Congressional Districts urged him to amend his call for the special session to include reapportioning the Senate. The governor, after receiving requests from sixty legislators, modified his call for a special session to include consideration of reapportioning the upper house.[22]

Attorney General Gene Cook urged the legislators to amend the unit system before the court hearing on April 27 or face the possibility of the federal courts invalidating it. The governor concurred, warning that the legislature had the opportunity to save the county-unit system. "If you don't," he told the lawmakers, "then I have done everything in my power to preserve the county unit system." On April 12, Governor Vandiver, yielding to the pressure of the 4-unit counties, presented yet another plan to save the county-unit system. The new plan increased House membership to 225 and modified earlier suggestions for giving the eight most populous counties more representation in the House and more unit votes. The new plan called for each county to retain its present number of seats in the House, with twenty new House seats to be apportioned among the seven most populous counties using the "equal proportions" formula used to allocate seats in the national House of Representatives. Under this plan, 26.7 percent of the population would elect a majority of the House and cast the majority of the unit votes in a statewide primary. The headline for an *Atlanta Constitution* article about the proposal stated that the small county was still "King in Vandiver's New Plan," and the editor of the paper, Eugene Patterson, criticized the new Vandiver plan as a "transparent evasion designed to make it look as if [Vandiver was] making changes without making any." The *Atlanta Journal* also disapproved of the governor's plan because it left things "basically the same."[23]

As the lawmakers contemplated what should be done to protect the unit system, the special session—the first in Vandiver's administration—convened on April 16, 1962. Former governor Griffin, who at first had concurred with the governor's decision to call a special session, now dismissed the special session as "premature." That criticism provoked an angry retort from the governor, who accused his old nemesis of preferring federal judges to modify the unit system to members of the General Assembly. Representative John E. Sheffield Jr., a longtime supporter of former governor Griffin, denounced the special session on the House floor as "a manufactured crisis" created by the Atlanta political machine to do away with the county-unit system in order to take over the state Democratic Party. In addition to the Vandiver proposal, there were at least ten bills to revise or to abolish the unit system. Lieutenant Governor Byrd, instead of unveiling his own save-the-county-unit-system proposal, announced his support of the governor's plan, at least for the time being. As the special session convened, the district court heard arguments by the state requesting the postponement of the hearing on the county-unit system until after the special session. The judges refused the request and left the hearing date scheduled for April 27.[24]

Governor Vandiver addressed the General Assembly in another night session, this time on April 16, 1962, with a speech televised throughout the state. A sober General Assembly listened intently to the governor's remarks, which lasted about thirty minutes. He defended the unit system by insisting that it did not dilute "a voter's vote" because popular votes in general elections determined the actual election of public officials and because the people voted on Democratic Party nominations in statewide primaries. In light of these facts, he asked, "In the name of common sense, how could anyone claim that a candidate can or cannot win an election at the hands of the people?" He conceded that recent population gains in "a very few of the State's most populous counties" had brought about imbalances in the population of some legislative districts. The governor asked the legislature to correct this problem by increasing the size of the House by twenty seats, which would be distributed using the "equal proportions" method employed by Congress to apportion seats in its lower house. He also requested the legislature to propose a constitutional amendment to increase the size of the lower house and to pass a law "to give immediate effect" to increasing the unit votes of those counties receiving additional representation. Passage of such a law, he claimed, would allow the Democratic Party's primary scheduled for September to be held under a revised unit system. Governor Vandiver argued that his plan was the fairest of those under consideration by the legislature and warned that "drastic judicial decrees" harmful to the unit system would be forthcoming if the legislature refused to take action.[25]

According to a headline in the *Atlanta Constitution*, "cheers and jeers" greeted the governor's speech. Senator Harry Jackson of Columbus called the Vandiver plan a "reasonable approach," and Senator Zell B. Miller praised it as being "the most feasible plan of all" the various plans presented. Floor leader Frank S. Twitty predicted, "If adopted, [the governor's] plan will save the county unit system." However, Republican gubernatorial candidate Ed Smith dismissed the Vandiver plan as "mere token reform" that would not satisfy the federal courts. Mrs. Fleming Law, president of the Georgia League of Women Voters, criticized the governor's plan because even if it passed "[the state] would still have government by the minority." Senator H. Erwin Mitchell urged the legislature to adjourn because he had witnessed no effort "to work for something fair and just for all the people." Fulton County representative Milton M. "Muggsy" Smith concluded that the governor's plan would not receive the approval of the federal courts, and an *Atlanta Journal* editorial headline simply stated, "Not Enough, Governor."[26]

Speaker Smith introduced HB 1, the governor's plan to modify the unit system, and the proposed constitutional amendment increasing the size of the House. Other bills were also introduced pertaining to the unit system, including several to abolish it. The State of the Republic Committee scheduled a hearing on April 18 on the various plans. On that occasion, William Gunter, an attorney and former legislator, criticized the governor's plan. "The proposition of giving 40 unit votes to a few more counties," he stated, "is not going to make the county unit system any more valid." Atlanta mayor Allen pleaded with the lawmakers to "bury the tired, out-worn, out-moded county unit system." However, Walter Dyal, immediate past president of the Association of County Commissioners, defended the system before the committee as "the only means of giving the voters of your county . . . a continual and effective voice in state affairs." He urged the passage of the Vandiver plan as the fairest and most workable proposal before the legislature.[27]

The next day, April 19, 1961, Speaker Smith proposed a substitute to the governor's plan. Former House Speaker Roy Harris, one of the authors of the plan, and Speaker Smith insisted that the substitute had the governor's support. The Speaker attributed the need to revise the governor's plan to remarks made by Judge Griffin Bell at the hearing at which the state had asked for a delay in the unit case. J. Roy MacCracken, chairman of the House State of the Republic Committee, described the Smith plan as being "along the lines that Judge Bell intimated might be acceptable to him." Speaker Smith insisted that his substitute had nothing to do with reapportionment and expressed the view that the administration would not support any efforts to reapportion legislative districts during the special session. The Smith substitute added 135 unit votes to be distributed among the thirty-five counties, with the eight most populous counties receiving 96. This plan gave the eight most populous counties, which contained 41 percent of the state's population, 26 percent of the unit votes—an increase of almost 15 percent. The 121 two-unit counties, which had 32 percent of the population and 59 percent of the unit votes, would see their share of the unit votes reduced to less than 45 percent.[28]

Lieutenant Governor Byrd expressed opposition to the Smith substitute, contending that rural counties would be better off with a popular vote than the plan proposed in the Smith bill. Byrd then unveiled his suggested reform of the unit system, which increased the number of unit votes to 930 and allocated them to candidates based on county popular votes received. If the legislature refused to support his plan, the lieutenant governor supported a nomination system based on popular votes. Byrd believed his plan to be an improvement over that presented by the Speaker and an alternative that would be acceptable to the plaintiff in the case. According to the lieutenant governor, he had discussed his plan with Morris Abram, attorney for the plaintiff, who told him that the Byrd plan "was one he could sell to his people and that he could influence the courts to accept."[29]

The House State of the Republic Committee substituted its version of a plan for the Smith bill, which the House approved by a vote of 163 to 30. The bill gave two unit votes to each county for the first fifteen thousand residents and allocated additional unit votes to counties according to twenty-six population brackets. However, the Senate Rules Committee substituted the Byrd plan for the House proposal, and the Senate adopted it on April 26 with only seven negative votes. Two conference committees failed to reach consensus during the afternoon and night of April 26. The following day, Governor Vandiver went to the legislature to make a dramatic plea for the lawmakers to revise the unit system, addressing the legislature thirty minutes prior to the convening of the federal district court's holding hearings on the unit system. The governor told the assembled lawmakers that unless the two houses resolved their differences, attorneys would have to defend the unit system in federal court "without armor, naked and alone." He proposed a compromise that used the allocation of votes proposed in the House bill while requiring nominees for state House positions to have a majority of both the popular and the county-unit votes. House members, believing that the governor's proposal reflected the House's position more than the Senate's bill, quickly passed the Vandiver compromise by a vote of 147 to 37. Lieutenant Governor Byrd endorsed the compromise bill, and the Senate passed it with twelve negative votes. Although having reservations whether the new law could save the unit system, the governor remarked, "At least, it gives us a weapon, and I hope it will be an effective weapon." The *Atlanta Journal* dismissed the new law as nothing more than a "laboriously constructed curiosity" designed to perpetuate political dominance of rural voters in state politics.[30]

Unfortunately for the governor and the legislators, their efforts proved futile. One day after the adjournment of the special session, the federal district court rendered its decision on the unit system. The unanimous opinion, ironically written by Judge Bell, concluded that the unit system as it existed prior to the recently passed Vandiver compromise clearly denied the plaintiff equal protection of the law. While conceding that the legislative action recently taken was an "improvement," Judge Bell nevertheless held that the revision still discriminated against urban counties by denying them a reasonable proportion of county-unit votes. The district court held that the state could still use the county-unit system "if the disparity against any county [was] not in excess of the disparity that exist[ed] against any state in the most recent electoral college allocation or under the equal proportions formula for representation of the several states in the Congress." Judge Bell concluded, "We do not strike down the county unit system as such. We do strike it down in its present form." The opinion, according to the judge years later, "was written in a way, if they wanted to have a county unit system, they could have one, but it had to be based on population, and it [would have] ended up like the electoral college." Margaret Shannon, a reporter for the *Atlanta Constitution*, called the decision "one of the most historic developments in the history of Georgia politics." Senator Talmadge described it as "appalling," and Lieutenant Governor Byrd lamented that the state did not have a county unit system because his suggestions had not been followed. Whereas Marvin Griffin reacted to the decision by calling it "sorry mess," an *Atlanta Constitution* editorial headline proudly proclaimed, "This Is a Day for Celebration." Former state senator, governor, and president of the United States James E. "Jimmy" Carter Jr. later described the ruling as "one of the most momentous political decision of the century in Georgia."[31]

The governor responded to the decision by saying that he intended to wait for the U.S. Supreme Court's decision on the state's appeal before making a recommendation to the party's executive committee on how to conduct the September 12 primary. He refused to reconvene the legislature for another effort to save the unit system, contending that the U.S. Supreme Court would probably invalidate elections held under modifications of the unit system as suggested by the district court. Former governor Griffin requested that the party's executive committee hold the upcoming primary on a popular vote basis with a plurality vote sufficient for nomination. The governor, mindful of Griffin's winning the gubernatorial nomination in 1954 with only 37 percent of the popular vote, responded that the election, whether by popular or unit vote, would be decided by a majority and not a plurality of the votes.[32]

While the state and its politicians were still contemplating the county-unit decision, a federal court handed down a decision on May 25, 1962, that further jolted the state's political status quo. The decision, concurred in by circuit judge Tuttle, circuit judge Bell, and district court judge Lewis R. Morgan, concluded that one house of the state's legislature had to be reapportioned on a population basis prior to the 1963 legislative session. The court held that the existing system discriminated against urban citizens in that senators from the twenty-eight least populated districts had less than 22 percent of the state's population but elected a majority of the senators. The decision further noted that representatives from the 103 least populous counties with less than 23 percent of the state's population elected a majority of the membership of the lower house. Nevertheless, the court refused to issue an injunction to force the legislature to reapportion one of the houses prior to the September 12 primary. In response to the decision, Governor Vandiver declined to call a special session to deal with reapportionment prior to the September 12 primary. "Nothing could be done," the governor explained to reporters, "with a politically charged legislature in the middle of a political campaign." The *Atlanta Constitution*, concurring with the governor's rationale, claimed that calling a special session in the midst of an election would be nothing more than "a costly political forum."[33]

On June 18, 1962, the U.S. Supreme Court announced its decision to hear the state's appeal in the unit case in its next term, ending the possibility of a district court decision invalidating the county-unit system being overridden prior to the September 1962 primary. As a result, the governor announced his intention to ask the State Democratic Committee to adopt a rule allowing the September primary to be conducted on a popular vote basis. Former governor Griffin urged Vandiver to seek a stay on the federal court's prohibition on the use of county-unit votes in the September primary. He accused the governor of not wanting a stay because he thought Griffin could not "win the race under a federally controlled primary." The governor declined to do so, contending that the only revision of the unit system acceptable to the federal courts would be "so close to a popular vote that there would be little practical difference." He also claimed that an effort by the state to seek a stay "would cast a cloud on all primary nominations." On June 27, the executive committee unanimously concurred with the governor's session to conduct the September primary on a popular vote basis— the first primary to be held on such a basis since 1908.[34]

On September 14, 1962, the governor called another special session, this one for the purpose of dealing with apportionment. The governor, considering reapportionment a legislative responsibility, did not address the legislature or recommend a reapportionment plan to it. The legislature finally chose to reapportion the Senate and divided the senatorial districts on a population basis. In signing the bill, Governor Vandiver praised the legislature for its work in coping with "more vital and crucial issues than any other General Assembly in history."[35]

The state's last effort to save the unit system took place in Washington at the U.S. Supreme Court. Oral arguments occurred on January 17, 1963, with attorneys Murphy and Leverett arguing for the state. Even before going through the motions of defending the system before the high court, Leverett conceded that both he and Murphy realized the unit system "could not be saved." Morris Abram, who had represented Bill Hartsfield in the 1958 suit, represented the appellee in the case, assisted by Attorney General Robert F. Kennedy, who argued the case for the federal government as a friend of the court. In addition to former Atlanta mayor Hartsfield being present for the historic occasion, a large number of the Kennedy family attended to watch the attorney general in his first appearance in any court, as well as to witness Edward M. Kennedy's admittance to the bar of the U.S. Supreme Court. The Court, with only one justice dissenting, agreed with the district court's enjoining the use of the unit system in the September 1962 primary, ruling that the county-unit system was not compatible with the equal protection clause of the Fourteenth Amendment under any circumstances.[36]

As his administration began to wind down, Ernest Vandiver faced the reality

of becoming a private citizen once again. He had held appointive or elected public office in state government since becoming an aide to Governor-elect Eugene
Talmadge in 1946. Vandiver later held the positions of aide to Governor Herman
Talmadge, adjutant general, lieutenant governor, and finally governor. Under
the provisions of the state constitution, however, governors could not succeed
themselves, and Vandiver would have to wait four years before seeking the office
again. While the still young Vandiver contemplated his course of action in both
public and private life, Marvin Griffin, seeking to return to the governor's mansion, made the Vandiver administration an issue in the 1962 Democratic gubernatorial primary.

ELEVEN

Well Done

As the Vandiver administration began to wind down in 1962, the forty-four-year-old governor contemplated his political future. He could not seek reelection because the state constitution prohibited governors from succeeding themselves. Samuel Ernest Vandiver Jr. had aspirations to serve in the U.S. Senate, but, unfortunately for him, both Senate seats were held by individuals whom he would never oppose—Richard B. Russell Jr. and Herman E. Talmadge. He could have sought a seat in the U.S. House of Representatives but apparently never had any interest in doing so.[1]

When his longtime political adversary S. Marvin Griffin Sr. finally qualified as a gubernatorial candidate in the 1962 Democratic primary, Vandiver had something else to consider as well. He believed that Griffin's return to the governorship would be a "disaster" for the state. He had made misconduct in the Griffin administration a major issue in his gubernatorial campaign in 1958 and, as governor, had led a concerted effort to correct abusive practices that had occurred in his predecessor's term in office. Vandiver had no intention of sitting idly by while Griffin campaigned to replace him in the governor's office. He told one of his closest political supporters and advisers chairman of the state highway board James L. "'Jim" Gillis Sr. that they had to do everything in their power to defeat Griffin, who, though tarnished by allegations of misconduct that occurred in his administration, remained a formidable candidate. Griffin, well known as a result of his service as adjutant general, lieutenant governor, and governor, was one of the best political campaigners in Georgia. His flamboyant personality, folksy style, excellent communication skills, and campaign experience gave him distinct advantages in a governor's race—even one conducted on a popular vote basis.[2]

Vandiver could take some comfort knowing that a political ally, Lieutenant Governor Garland T. Byrd, planned to run against Griffin. Byrd had begun a career in state politics with his election in 1946 to the Georgia House of Representatives, where he had aligned himself with the Talmadge faction. Although suffering defeat in a race for commissioner of agriculture in 1954, he had bounced back by carrying all but six counties in his campaign for the lieutenant gubernatorial nomination in 1958. Byrd, generally considered a staunch supporter of the Vandiver administration, appeared to be the candidate to continue Vandiver's style of honest and fiscally responsible government. However, he lacked the charisma of Griffin and, as one historian observed, "generated little enthusiasm among the voters." Nevertheless, Vandiver felt some obligation to Byrd, whom he considered "a good friend" and one who "had done everything" Vandiver asked him to do in his administration. Senate president pro tempore Carl E. Sanders believed Vandiver had another reason for supporting Byrd—a fear that Griffin, if elected, would undertake a strenuous effort to "besmirch and destroy" Vandiver in retaliation for his administration's investigation of alleged wrongdoing in Griffin's governorship.[3]

At first, it seemed that the major candidates in the 1962 governor's race would be Griffin and Byrd. At the last minute, however, a third major candidate qualified. Carl Sanders, then only thirty-six years of age, had originally planned to run for lieutenant governor against Peter Zach Geer Jr., the governor's former executive secretary. However, some of Geer's supporters had enticed a relatively unknown Atlanta resident named Carl F. Sanders to enter the lieutenant governor's race. His entry created a problem for Carl E. Sanders, since two candidates with similar names would cause confusion among the voters and make the senator's efforts to gain the nomination difficult, if not impossible. As a result, Sanders decided to switch to the governor's race. His decision presented a dilemma for Governor Vandiver—should he support Byrd, or should he back Sanders? Vandiver considered both candidates capable politicians and strong supporters of his administration.[4]

Though aware of the governor's leanings toward Byrd's candidacy, Sanders nevertheless met with Vandiver to explain his entry into the governor's race and to solicit his support. Sanders left the meeting with the impression that the governor would support Byrd. However, Vandiver's dilemma ended when Byrd suffered a heart attack in May 1962 and subsequently withdrew from the race. "I was not glad," Vandiver recalled, "that Garland had sickness, but it sure made my path easier." Sanders then met again with the governor to solicit his backing in the race. Vandiver told the senator of his intentions to vote for him and then offered to do his best to throw his "complete administration behind him as a candidate," provided that he would promise never to run against Senator Russell. Vandiver believed that the state's aging senior senator, who was experiencing health problems and who had provided outstanding service to the state, should be spared the rigors of campaigning. According to the governor, Sanders agreed in that meeting never to run against Senator Russell, but Sanders recalled the meeting differently, denying ever making any such promise to Vandiver or to Russell.[5]

Assistant state attorney general Henry G. Neal, who attended that meeting at the request of Vandiver, later recalled that a meeting between Vandiver and Sanders took place during which senatorial politics were discussed: "But insofar as what was said with respect to who would or would not do what, I simply cannot recall." Vandiver, pointing out that Neal later served as assistant state attorney general in the Sanders administration, attributed Neal's lapse of memory to "his friendship with Sanders and [him], he did not wish to offend either one of [them]." Russell's biographer, Gilbert C. Fite, does not mention such a promise in his discussion of the 1966 senatorial race. Sanders's biographer, James F. Cook, concluded that "the available evidence strongly suggests that Sanders made no promise regarding Russell in 1962" and contended, "Vandiver had no choice but to support Sanders enthusiastically; if Sanders lost, Vandiver's enemy would succeed him as governor." Vandiver strongly disagreed with that argument. Although conceding his intentions of voting for Sanders in the governor's race, Vandiver insisted that his strong support of Sanders had been motivated by his promise of never running against Russell. Both Vandiver and Sanders still adhere to their versions of the meeting that occurred in 1962.[6]

What is certain is that Vandiver used the power of the governorship to promote Sanders's candidacy. In fact, the governor claimed that he "went all out" to help Sanders, including raising money and encouraging appointees in his administration to support him. However, the governor began to have doubts about Sanders's electability when Senator Talmadge told him that his sources throughout the state were predicting a Griffin win. Vandiver attributed much of the problem to Sanders's state campaign headquarters, which, in his opinion, "was in pretty bad shape." He blamed the faltering Sanders campaign on Wyck Knox Sr., Sanders's campaign manager, who lacked experience in running a statewide campaign. The governor asked state highway board chairman Jim Gillis, whom he considered one of the state's best politicians, to assist Knox. Gillis agreed to step in, and, according to the governor, "from that time on, things just smoothed out."[7]

Vandiver also boosted the Sanders's campaign by raising teachers' salaries. Dipping into the state's surplus, Vandiver gave the thirty-six thousand public school teachers a two-hundred-dollar raise to take effect eleven days before the Democratic primary. The governor believed the pay raise "helped Carl tremendously" because of the senator's well-known association with the Vandiver administration in the public mind. The governor also revealed his intentions to use surplus state funds to raise the salaries of the faculty members in the University System of Georgia. In another exercise of gubernatorial power, Governor Vandiver announced the distribution of a million dollars in state funds to municipalities. Voters had approved a constitutional amendment in the 1960 general election authorizing the state government to make grants directly to cities and towns, but the governor had not previously released any state funds to municipalities. Former governor Griffin denounced Vandiver's release of these state funds on the eve of the primary election as a political gesture to help Sanders in the urban areas. Mayor Roswell Hair, president of the Georgia Municipal Association, conceded that the release of funds to the municipalities "had considerable influence" in the outcome of the governor's race.[8]

Griffin, believing that the governor was unpopular because segregated public education and the county-unit system had ended in his administration, made Vandiver an issue in the 1962 governor's race. He associated Sanders with the Vandiver administration in his campaign rhetoric, calling his opponent "a puppet" of Vandiver and criticizing the "Vandiver-Sanders administration." Griffin charged that Sanders had no record of accomplishment "except as the toadying mouthpiece" of the Vandiver administration. Apparently unknown to Griffin, a confidential Louis Harris survey of the state's political climate taken in July 1962 indicated that Vandiver was not as unpopular as Griffin thought. In fact, the survey gave Vandiver a 57 percent favorable rating, which the report concluded was "quite good compared to other Governors nearing the end of a four year term of office." The report concluded that Georgians liked the way Vandiver had "conducted himself in the Capitol" and recommended that "Sanders should not run away from Vandiver, but rather pledge to build on Vandiver's record in office." Sanders did not "run away" from the governor in the race and welcomed Griffin's effort to associate him with Vandiver.[9]

Even though Vandiver and Griffin were in the Talmadge faction in state politics, a hostile relationship between the two had existed for a long time. Vandiver had not voted for Griffin for governor in 1954, and they had sparred frequently while Vandiver served as lieutenant governor during Griffin's governorship. Griffin supported William T. "Bill" Bodenhamer Sr. against Vandiver in the 1958 governor's race. The sharp-tongued Griffin even nicknamed the governor "Buster," claiming it was an appropriate designation as a result of Vandiver's "inability to make a decision and his immaturity in the Governor's office." Griffin had never forgiven Vandiver for his role in engineering the defeat of the rural roads bond issue in 1958, and Vandiver's 1958 campaign promises to clean up the misconduct in the Griffin administration further irritated the former governor. Griffin accused the governor and the Atlanta newspapers of conspiring to uncover improper conduct in his administration to keep him from being elected governor again. "Never in the history of Georgia," Griffin claimed, "has one Governor spent all his waking hours attempting to persecute and prosecute his predecessor in office." [10]

Early in his administration, Governor Vandiver had directed Attorney General Eugene Cook to establish a criminal division in the state Law Department to investigate alleged illegal activities in the Griffin administration. The governor picked Robert H. Hall to serve as assistant state attorney general to direct the division's activities. According to press reports, twenty-eight state officials, state employees, and businessmen had been indicted by August 1962 as a result of the various investigations into wrongdoing during the Griffin governorship. Although a Fulton County grand jury had indicted the governor's brother, Robert A. "Cheney" Griffin, at the urging of the criminal division, a trial jury in May 1961 had acquitted him. The criminal division had also tried to convince another Fulton County grand jury to indict the former governor on charges of conspiracy to defraud the state. However, under existing state law at that time, public officials facing possible indictment by grand juries had the right to appear personally before the grand jurors to defend themselves. Griffin, who had a reputation as one of the state's best stump speakers and storytellers, went before the grand jurors and convinced them not to indict him. [11]

During the campaign, Griffin called Vandiver a "miserable failure" as governor, claiming that he had spent most of his time investigating the Griffin administration. Griffin charged that Vandiver had wasted $250,000 of the taxpayers' money in a futile effort to get him indicted on some "trumped-up" charges. "If I had been guilty of anything," the former governor told a crowd of campaign supporters, "they would have found it." Griffin pledged to make the Vandiver administration's record an issue in the governor's race, even though he claimed that the record wouldn't be "big enough to furnish landing space for a tomtit to light on." [12]

Griffin attacked Vandiver for his "indecision, inaction and idleness" as governor and claimed that he headed a "do-nothing administration" that had done little to improve the state or the well-being of its citizens. He told a crowd of supporters that the "do-nothing governor" wanted "to hand-pick his crown prince" in the 1962 governor's race so his successor would "do nothing for another four years." Claiming that the Vandiver administration had spent millions more than his administration, Griffin asked, "Where did it go?" He alleged, "About the only thing I can find is that they went over the state widening roads two feet and spreading a little black dirt." Griffin further charged the governor with padding the state payroll with five thousand "useless employees" who were "sapping the public treasury like hoards of locusts eating a crop." If elected, he promised to exterminate these "political parasites," which were costing the taxpayers millions of dollars. Griffin also accused Vandiver of doing an inadequate job in industrial recruitment and promised in his second term to "take the Governor's office off the nail keg of inactivity and go industry seeking again." [13]

Nor did Griffin let the voters forget the "no, not one" promise, which he claimed was just one more of Vandiver's long list of broken promises to the voters of Georgia. In the opening speech of his campaign in Americus, Griffin accused Vandiver of inaugurating a plan of token integration that was the "first step toward massive race-mixing in Georgia." Mississippi, South Carolina, and Alabama, Griffin argued, did not have integrated schools because they had "had Governors who had courage and were resolute" in defense of segregation and did not throw "in the towel of surrender." While promising to preserve and protect the Georgia way of life, the former governor accused Vandiver and Sanders of being the puppets of the advocates of racial integration in the state—the Atlanta newspapers, the NAACP, and Dr. Martin Luther King Jr. In another campaign speech, he accused Sanders of being supported by "the most injurious political elements in Georgia"—Atlanta banker Mills B. Lane Sr., Dr. King, Atlanta mayor Ivan Allen Jr., *Atlanta Constitution* publisher Ralph E. McGill Sr., "and their stooge, 'Buster' Vandiver." He even accused Vandiver of being "friends of Martin Luther King and his agitators." Griffin, speaking to a large crowd in Marietta, took delight in playing a recording of what was purported to be the voice of Martin Luther King Sr. praising Vandiver for having "one of the best records of any Governor that's been in that chair." Griffin agreed that Vandiver had been "great for the integrationists and the left-wingers." The former governor reminded a crowd of cheering supporters in south Georgia that the Griffin administration had kept the public schools open and segregated.[14]

Vandiver, who had promised to defend his administration if Griffin made it a campaign issue, did so, publicly calling on Griffin to explain how fraud and corruption in his administration had cost the taxpayers $30 million. The governor denied Griffin's allegation of padding the state payroll, attributing the increase in state jobs to the need for more employees as his administration provided additional services. In contrast to the operation of state government under Griffin's watch, Vandiver called his administration the most efficient and honest in the state's history and reminded voters that Griffin left office in 1959 with the "state teetering on the brink of bankruptcy." Vandiver attributed part of Griffin's fiscal problems as governor to his "abysmal ignorance of budgetary matters which made it impossible for him to run the government without raising taxes."

The voters, according to Vandiver, had to decide in 1962 whether to continue his policies of honesty and efficiency in the conduct of state business or to revert to the cronyism, graft, and corruption that had flourished in the Griffin years.[15]

Griffin's campaign claim of having done more for education than Vandiver provoked an angry governor to issue a seven-page statement "to set the record straight." The statement contended that expenditures for education in Vandiver's administration were higher than those during the Griffin administration and were at the highest level in Georgia's history. In fact, the statement pointed out that the Vandiver administration's expenditures for education in fiscal year 1962 would be $71 million more than those in the last year of the Griffin administration. Vandiver's statement also questioned Griffin's claim of raising teachers' salaries by $700. Although conceding that teachers did receive a pay raise under Griffin, Vandiver contended that only $530 in state funds had been allocated for each teacher's raise and that the Griffin administration had forced local school districts and local taxpayers to contribute $170 per teacher to ensure each teacher a $700 raise. In contrast, Vandiver pointed out that his administration had allocated $700 per teacher in state funds to fund his administration's pay raise. In addition, the governor's statement reminded teachers that Griffin had "conveniently forgot that he left a $750,000 bill for teachers retirement when he left office," an obligation that the Vandiver administration had assumed. Griffin dismissed Vandiver's seven-page response as "a childish statement" and labeled Vandiver and Sanders the "two biggest foes of education in Georgia."[16]

The long and bitter governor's race finally ended on September 12, 1962, when the voters gave Sanders an overwhelming victory with 58 percent of the popular vote. Even if the county-unit system had still been in place, Sanders would have won the nomination. He ran best in the state's urban areas, receiving more than half of his popular votes from the eleven city counties. A pleased governor called Sanders's win "a victory for honesty and morality" and "a complete vindication of what the Vandiver administration [had] done to serve the people of Georgia." Governor Vandiver praised Sanders for his "unstinted and unreserved affiliation with the principles and policies of the Vandiver administration." He also viewed the outcome of the election as a rejection of Griffin's negative campaign against him. Clearly, Griffin had made a tactical misstep in attacking the popular governor and associating Sanders with him. Sanders's biographer concluded that instead of hurting the senator's candidacy, "Griffin merely enhanced Sanders' standing among the people by his criticism of the Vandiver administration." With the defeat of Griffin, Vandiver could look forward to a political ally in the governor's office who would continue his style and philosophy of government. He could also be assured that his successor would not be investigating and trying to discredit the Vandiver administration. Perhaps most satisfying for Vandiver was his knowledge that he had played a major role in denying his old political adversary a second term in the governor's chair.[17]

To Vandiver it seemed that his administration had become the defender of lost causes—segregation in public education, malapportionment, and the county-unit system. He even called his governorship, with some justification, the "most crisis ridden administration in state history." Reg Murphy, political editor of the *Atlanta Constitution*, even thought it understandable if Vandiver developed an "intense hatred for his predecessors" because they had avoided the "whirlwind of so many political crises." The governor wanted his administration to be re-membered as one that had been "able to accomplish something lasting." In his last news conference as governor, Vandiver discussed the legacy of his admin-istration: expanding state services by more than $100 million without raising taxes, implementing a building program of more than $850 million, preserving the public schools, saving the state from disgrace and violence, restoring the confidence of the people in their state government, implementing a sound state budgeting system, and leaving a surplus in the state treasury for his successor. Asked shortly before leaving office what had been his most beneficial act as gov-ernor, Vandiver replied that it had been "protecting the good name of Georgia" during the integration crisis.[18]

During Vandiver's gubernatorial term, the state's budget had increased from $324,718,000 in fiscal year 1958 to $419,988,000 in fiscal year 1962—a 29.3 per-cent, or $95,270,000, increase. Vandiver attributed the increase in revenue, which permitted the expansion in state services without a tax increase, to his ad-ministration's improved enforcement of revenue laws, more efficient operation of the government, and reforms in purchasing. The governor claimed that in-creased state expenditures in the areas of public school and university system operations, support for the Milledgeville State Hospital, and the state's contri-bution to the Teachers' Retirement System were "the greatest increases ever made in a comparable period" in Georgia's history. State support of education received the largest share of dollars in the state budget, with appropriations for education increasing from 52.4 percent of the state budget in fiscal year 1958 to 53.9 percent in fiscal year 1962. Comparison of expenditures in the state's five largest spending units in the last year of the Griffin administration and the last year of the Vandiver administration indicated a steady increase in spending in those areas. The Highway Department had the greatest growth (35.3 percent), followed by the Department of Public Health (33.6 percent), the University System of Georgia (29 percent), the state Department of Education (24.8 per-cent) and the Department of Public Health (14.8 percent).[19]

The governor took pride in the fact that his administration had undertaken a building program of $854 million without a tax increase, compared with the

Griffin administration's $550 million building program, which had required a tax increase to fund fully. The Vandiver administration had spent $105 million dollars for capital expenditures for public schools, including building more than forty-five hundred classrooms. It had spent more than $29 million in new construction for the university system, including dormitory facilities for four thousand students, a $4 million coliseum at the University of Georgia, a $900,000 visual arts building, and a $1,680,000 pharmacy building at his alma mater. When Vandiver had come into office, state funds had been allocated to build five area vocational-technical schools. His administration, having a goal of building vocational-technical schools within fifty miles of prospective students, had obtained $20 million in state funding to build twenty-one additional vocational-technical schools. Vandiver believed the state had an obligation and responsibility to provide the facilities to train skilled workers for existing industries and to attract new industries. In appreciation of his commitment to vocational and technical education, the Georgia Vocational Association honored Governor Vandiver with an award of merit. His administration had also funded the Department of Education's first educational television station and had appropriated $600,000 to build a system of five educational television stations throughout the state. In appreciation of his support of educational television, the state board of education gave one of its educational television stations the call letters WVAN.[20]

The governor, believing that good highways contributed to the economic development of the state and to the enhancement of the growing tourist industry, had obtained the passage of a $100 million bond program to finance the widening and resurfacing of the state's primary and secondary highways. In addition, the progress of construction of the state's share of the federal interstate highway system had increased significantly in the Vandiver administration. The Griffin administration had awarded only $78 million in interstate highway construction contracts, compared with the Vandiver administration's awarding of $165 million in construction contracts by July 1961. Under the Vandiver administration, Georgia had gained the rank of seventh in the nation in interstate highway construction. Overall, the Vandiver administration had spent more than $600 million on highways.[21]

The governor had taken a strong interest in the state's port system, which he saw as a vital component in his effort to promote economic growth in the state. His administration had spent more than $21 million in expanding and improving Georgia Ports Authority facilities, a larger state investment in ports than the total of all previous administrations combined. Expansions and improvements had included building a new port at Columbus and upgrading the facilities at the ports at Savannah, Brunswick, and Augusta. The state also had provided $41 million to assist in the construction of seventy-six hospitals and related health facilities. In order to make the state park system more enticing to Georgians and to out-of-state visitors, state parks had received needed rehabilitation and improvements at a cost of more than $3 million. In addition, the Vandiver administration had spent $6 million for the development of the Stone Mountain Memorial Park, a facility that had been authorized by the Griffin administration.[22]

Another $4 million had gone to the construction of a state archives building to replace an inadequate facility, and the state had spent $18 million in a much needed program to renovate existing buildings and to construct additional buildings at the state's mental health facilities. New construction at Milledgeville State Hospital had included a 500-bed rehabilitation facility, an 627-bed addition to a housing facility for patients, and a new central kitchen, as well as extensive repairs and renovations of existing buildings. Other improvements had included the addition of two 50-bed dormitories and an infirmary at the Gracewood State School and Hospital for children and the establishment of the Georgia Mental Health Center in Atlanta for the treatment of emotionally disturbed children. The Vandiver administration had also built a $4 million state prison and had added 500 maximum security cells at the overcrowded state prison at Reidsville. In addition, the administration funded the construction of a school at the Georgia Industrial Institute to allow juvenile offenders to participate in an accredited educational program. Nor had the former state adjutant general ignored the state's National Guard—his administration had contributed $3 million in its share of building twenty armories.[23]

Like his predecessors, Governor Vandiver had played an active role in promoting economic development of the state. Historian Numan V. Bartley called Vandiver "one of the region's most enthusiastic industrial promoters" following his shift from massive resistance in 1961. In fact, Bartley contended that the governor "spent much of his remaining tenure recruiting northern investment." Vandiver had gone on numerous industry-seeking trips and on one occasion had traveled to New York City to meet with and encourage presidents and board chairmen of some of the nation's largest industries to consider Georgia as a site for their companies' expansion or relocation. Vandiver believed that a governor had a distinct advantage in industrial recruitment: "If you send an industrial representative to these places, he talks to his counterpart in the business, but a governor—any governor—gets to the president and chairman of the board where the final decisions are made." The governor also had headed the state's first trade mission to Europe. As part of the administration's plan to promote Georgia products in the international market, the Georgia Ports Authority had established offices in West Germany and Japan. The Georgian State Chamber of Commerce, with the support and participation of the governor, began its annual Red Carpet Tours of the state for out-of-state business executives whose companies were contemplating moving to Georgia. At Vandiver's suggestion, the tours concluded at the Masters Tournament in Augusta, and, as a result, Vandiver observed that the tours never "had a shortage of executives."[24]

Governor Vandiver attributed the state's successful efforts in industrial expansion to the existence of "a good business climate" in which industry could prosper and its employees could live "profitably in peace and contentment." He claimed that his administration had "insisted upon the maintenance of public education and obedience to law and the courts rather than futile defiance of federal force and authority." Vandiver believed that another major factor that accounted for the state's industrial growth was the confidence the business community had in the administration's "conservative system of government and its adherence to established principles of honesty, economy and frugality." Specifically, he stressed to industrialists considering plant relocations or expansion of existing facility expansions his opposition to rasing taxes. He told a group of industrial executives on a Red Carpet Tour that his administration was avoiding " the 'spend-to-bankruptcy' and the 'exodus-of-industry-from-high-taxation' policies" made by irresponsible politicians. He believed that his administration had struck "a delicate balance of fostering growth . . . but not jeopardizing business and expanding job opportunities . . . through oppressive taxation." Vandiver claimed that almost one thousand industries had been created or expanded in his administration, and more than thirty-five thousand additional jobs had been established in the state through capital investments totaling nearly $600 million.[25]

The governor believed that the state government should play a major role in economic development and looked upon state government as "the catalyst— the activating agent . . . with the *resources* and *authority* necessary for bringing together the ingredients of economic development." In an effort to help local communities recruit new industry, the Vandiver administration had successfully supported adoption of a constitutional amendment permitting local governments to issue revenue bonds for the construction of facilities that then could be turned over to private companies through lease-purchase agreements. The administration also held the state's first Governor's Conference on Trade and Commerce, with attendees from numerous states and foreign countries. The governor insisted, however, that in recruiting industries the state wanted the kind that were "willing to pay all the required taxes," rather than those that came to the state "only at the price of tax inducements."[26]

Nor had the Vandiver administration ignored another potential economic growth area—tourism. The governor had pledged that his administration would "leave no stone unturned" in promoting tourism in a state that he claimed had more tourist attractions "than almost any other state." For too long, he complained, Georgia had "sat idly back" as tourists passed through on the way to Florida—an attitude he intended to change. Under the Vandiver administration, the state had initiated a comprehensive program to attract "these 'passers-through' to become 'stay-awhilers'" and to ensure that the state received its rightful share of tourist dollars. As a result, his administration had conducted the state's first large-scale survey of tourists to determine the strengths as well as the shortcomings of the state in this area and had created a tourist division in the state Department of Commerce to promote tourism. The newly created division undertook the state's first-ever comprehensive tourism promotional campaign, placing advertisements in national magazines as well as state and regional publications. The Tourist Division also sent representatives to national trade fairs to promote Georgia as a travel destination—another first for the state. The Department of Commerce began the state's first outdoor advertising program by putting up almost a thousand billboards in Georgia and surrounding states publicizing the state's tourist attractions. The Tourist Division sent representatives to several states and Canada to promote Georgia and also established bureaus in Washington, D.C., and New York City. Again, such efforts were firsts for the state.[27]

The administration had built Georgia's first welcome stations for tourists and, in order to encourage increased visitation of tourists to the state-owned Jekyll Island, had paid off the debt of the Jekyll Island toll bridge connecting the island to the mainland. He took the same action for the Sidney Lanier Bridge, a toll bridge at Brunswick, in an effort to encourage tourist visitation to Jekyll Island and travel on U.S. 17, which at the time was the state's major coastal highway. The governor believed that his administration's efforts to improve the state's highways would enhance the state's growing tourism business. The Vandiver administration had held the state's first Conference on Tourism in 1961, an event that attracted more than 175 individuals representing organizations interested in promoting tourism in the state. Clearly, no previous governor had shown the level of commitment to tourism that Vandiver had.[28]

Governor Vandiver took pride in the fact that his administration had undertaken a significant expansion of state services without raising taxes. During his tenure as governor, the state had added almost three thousand public school teachers and had begun an educational loan program to encourage top students to enter the teaching profession. The administration had implemented a school bus safety program that met or exceeded national guidelines. In an effort to improve the treatment of patients suffering from mental problems, the governor had transferred the state's mental health program from the Department of Welfare to the Department of Public Health. Improvements at Milledgeville State Hospital had included adding personnel, raising personnel pay, ensuring adequate medical care for patients, upgrading admissions standards, and implementing a chaplaincy training program. The Vandiver administration had so significantly upgraded the treatment given to these patients and improved its mental health facilities that Georgia had moved from near the bottom to being one of the top-ranked states in mental health treatment. Concern over the lack of places of worship at Milledgeville State Hospital had led to the governor and the first lady's initiating an effort to raise private funds to build chapels at the facility. When initial fund-raising among churches proved insufficient, First Lady Betty Vandiver had successfully headed up a statewide campaign to raise additional private funds to build six chapels at the Milledgeville facility. At the suggestion of Betty Vandiver, the Georgia Municipal Association began an annual "Mayors Motorcade," which brought Christmas gifts from residents in cities and towns throughout the state for patients at the state's mental health facilities.[29]

An increase in state employment had accompanied the expansion of services in the Vandiver administration. Excluding employees of the public schools and public corporations, state employment increased from 22,514 in fiscal year 1958 to 26,943 in fiscal year 1962 — an increase of 19.7 percent. Public school teachers had received increases of $200 in 1960, $300 in 1961, and $200 in 1962 — a $700 increase in pay. As a result, the average teacher's salary had risen from $3,767 in the 1958–59 school year to $4,595 in the 1962–63 school year. The average salary of faculty members in the university system increased from $5,794 in the 1958–59 academic year to $7,372 in the 1962–63 school year. School bus drivers had received a $200 pay raise, and State Merit System employees had obtained a 3.9 percent hike in pay. In an effort to retain good employees and to enhance the recruitment of higher-quality employees in the state's correctional system, the administration had placed state Board of Corrections personnel in the Social Security system, enrolled them in the state's retirement system and health insurance program, and increased their salaries.[30]

Some significant changes occurred in state governmental operations in the Vandiver years. Vandiver had campaigned for governor promising to reorganize state government and to eliminate useless governmental agencies. Once he reached the governorship, he had created an economy and reorganization commission, which made numerous recommendations for reorganizing and streamlining state government, many of which he implemented. Vandiver claimed that as a result of this reorganization the state abolished more than 120 governmental boards, commissions, and bureaus. Other reforms included the placement of idle state funds into interest-bearing accounts, the implementation of a self-insurance program for state property, and the withholding of employees' state income taxes by employers on a monthly basis. Vandiver claimed that under the leadership of his commissioner of revenue, C. Dixon Oxford, the state installed computers to allow the Revenue Department to compare state income tax returns with federal tax returns to ensure compliance with state income tax laws. Ivan Allen Jr., in a letter to Governor Vandiver, commended Commissioner Oxford for his "excellent job in collecting taxes for the State," adding that his fiscal policies (and their administration) had "added a new high to the fiscal integrity of the State." Although the constitution prohibited the state from incurring debt, previous administrations had created state authorities that could. The governor successfully supported changing the state constitution to allow the state to incur debt as long as it did not exceed 15 percent of the state's revenue. At the recommendation of the governor, changes took place in the state's budgetary process, including recessing the legislature during its regular session to allow it more time to study the governor's budget requests, creating a bureau in the executive department, and requiring a biennial state budget.[31]

Prior to the Vandiver administration, few laws had existed to assure honesty in the conduct of state business. The governor had obtained passage of legislation clearly defining crimes against the state by state employees as well as individuals or businesses conducting business with the state. As a result of abuses in the state Purchasing Department in the Griffin administration, the governor had reformed the agency to make it efficient, honest, and businesslike. The governor had also led efforts to reform the state's budgetary process and restore the legislature's appropriations powers. Another major change occurred in state government with the adoption of a constitutional amendment permitting state grants to municipalities. Vandiver became the first governor to allocate state aid to municipalities, where, according to the 1960 census, 53 percent of Georgians resided. Other changes in state policies benefiting urban Georgia included municipalities' receiving a portion of the state-collected user fees and the state assumption of maintenance expenses of its highways that traversed municipalities. W. Elmer George, executive director of the Georgia Municipal Association, praised the Vandiver administration for its accomplishments: "More progress was made toward helping our towns and cities than during any other [administration] we can recall."[32]

In assessing the Vandiver administration, Cheney Griffin concluded that Vandiver had the "poorest record" of any governor the state had ever had. "In two short years we lost our segregation, we've lost our county unit system and our entire legislature as far as rural counties of Georgia are concerned." Most Georgians, however, had a more positive opinion of the seventy-third governor of the state. In fact, one historian, James F. Cook, concluded that "both his political colleagues and the press agreed that Vandiver had given Georgia four years of honest, competent leadership." The *Columbus Ledger* lavished praise on Vandiver for having restored honesty and efficiency in the operation of state government as well as expanding state services and undertaking a major building program without a tax increase. But most important, the *Ledger* commended the governor for restoring the "the confidence of the people of Georgia in their state government." The *Atlanta Journal-Constitution* praised the governor "for helping bring [the state] through a series of social and emotional crises with honor and dignity intact" and called the Vandiver administration "one of the most progressive of the century" because of its "great many reforms" in state government. Author and newspaper reporter Bruce Galphin praised Vandiver for coping with the state's crises in a manner "that won him much respect in Georgia, even among those resisting the changes." [33]

One newspaper, the *Athens Banner-Herald*, called Vandiver's governorship one of the most progressive in the state's history. The *Macon Telegraph*, likewise praising the governor for having achieved an outstanding record, concluded, "History's verdict must be well done, Gov. Vandiver, well done." Eugene Patterson, editor of the *Atlanta Constitution*, commended the governor for having cleaned up a corrupt state government, having kept the public schools open, having upgraded the state's treatment of its citizens with mental disabilities, and having improved the state's highways. Patterson also praised the governor for having implemented "a revolutionary fiscal system for the state which resulted in an almost magic ability to raise revenue without raising taxes." [34]

Even Sid Williams, publisher of the *Austell Enterprise* and a supporter of Griffin in the 1962 governor's race, praised Vandiver for having established "a pattern for progress and advancement in the Empire State of the South." The *Savannah Morning News*, while conceding that it had differed with the governor on some issues, nevertheless concluded that his administration had been "one of the most successful in modern history." The journal of the Georgia Municipal Association praised the Vandiver administration and the legislature for their "many accomplishments." W. H. Montague Jr., editor of the *Georgia State AFL-CIO News*, expressed the opinion that Vandiver was leaving office "with the overwhelming respect and admiration of the majority of Georgia people." Charles Pou, political editor of the *Atlanta Journal*, agreed that the governor left office "right popular with the people, and respected, if not liked, by most politicians." [35]

Citizens throughout the state likewise praised the governor for his service to the state. An Augusta resident, Odell Dyer, wrote Vandiver to express appreciation for a chief executive whom he did not "need to feel sorry for having." A juvenile court judge in Albany, Hudson Malone, expressed pleasure in being "in a position of hating to see the Governor leave office instead of rejoicing at his going." The chairman of the board of the Moultrie Banking Company boasted, "We can hold our heads up and be proud we are Georgians." In the opinion of one citizen, Mrs. H. M. Dixon, Vandiver had restored Georgia "to its proper place as the Empire State of the South," and another citizen commented the governor for doing "a superb job during the most difficult times in Georgia since Reconstruction days." A Methodist minister in Colquitt County predicted, "History will accord you the Number One place in the long list of Chief Executives of this state." Buckner F. Melton, a Macon attorney, wrote the governor, "The great majority of Georgians are proud of your administration and the splendid progress which has been made during these 4 years." The director of public affairs at WRBL-TV in Columbus hailed the Vandiver governorship as "one of Georgia's finest and most constructive administrations."[36]

Public officials joined in praising Vandiver as well. According to University of Georgia president O. Clyde Aderhold, "Few men have gone into public office with such overwhelming support—and few have gone out of office with such respect." State representative P. Theodore McCutchen commended the governor for his achievements, which had been "far above all other administrations." The clerk of the state House of Representatives, Glenn W. Ellard, claimed that "no Governor since the Civil War faced and solved so many problems." Vandiver even received praise from federal district judge William A. Bootle, who wrote the governor that the state was in his debt for the leadership in a time of crisis. The chief justice of the Georgia Supreme Court, William H. Duckworth, commended Vandiver's governing with "a superlative degree of success, honesty, and decency." State representative W. Frank Branch of Tift County called him "one of the greatest Governors in the history of this state." Fielding L. Dilliard, the director of the Income Tax Unit of the state Department of Revenue, praised the governor for restoring public confidence in the administration of the state's government.[37]

Despite the praise and acclaim bestowed on Vandiver and his desire to serve another term, the state constitution prohibited a governor from serving two consecutive terms. The last effort by a governor to repeal that constitutional provision had occurred when Ellis G. Arnall had led two bitter and unsuccessful efforts so that he could seek reelection in 1946. Since Vandiver had no desire to fight that battle, he had to wait at least four years before seeking the office again. While waiting, Vandiver had no intention of living in Atlanta because he wanted to raise his three children in Lavonia "with the same hometown virtues and values" with which he had grown up. Likewise, Betty Vandiver had grown weary of the "rat race" life in Atlanta and wanted to go back to the small-town tranquillity of Lavonia. Vandiver, although moving his family back to Lavonia, decided to practice law in Atlanta and joined the legal firm of Wilson, Branch, and Barwick, commuting between the capital city and his hometown. Professionally, Atlanta provided the former governor with more opportunities to practice law than

Lavonia; in addition, it was where he could best promote efforts to return to the state's highest political office in four years.[38]

Vandiver, shortly after leaving the governor's office, became involved in one of the major issues in the Atlanta metropolitan area—the increasing need for a rapid transit system. Even before leaving the governorship, Vandiver had spoken out in favor of such a system to alleviate the area's growing traffic congestion. A report issued by the Metropolitan Atlanta Transit Study Commission in 1962 had called for the development of a rapid transit system for the Atlanta metro area. However a proposed statewide constitutional amendment allowing counties to tax to operate such a system had been defeated in the 1962 general election.[39]

In response to the amendment's defeat, the five metro counties and the city of Atlanta created the Metropolitan Transit Committee of 100 in 1963 to lead another effort to change the state constitution to permit the creation of a metro rapid transit system. Atlanta mayor Allen asked Vandiver in March 1963 to serve as chairman of the executive committee of the Committee of 100. Although Vandiver had reservations about assuming such a responsibility because of his "fairly active law practice," he nevertheless accepted the position. At the executive committee's first meeting, he raised the question of whether his residency in Franklin County precluded him from serving as chairman. Dr. Howard Menhinick, who had served as chairman of the Metropolitan Atlanta Transit Study Commission, responded, "I think it is the feeling of this gathering that the matter of your prestige and competence outweighs any minor matter of residence." The chairman of the DeKalb County Commission, C. O. Emmerich, agreed, contending that Vandiver's serving as the committee's chairman would assure its success.[40]

Vandiver and his committee focused their attention first on gaining passage of federal mass transit legislation that would provide needed federal financial assistance in order to build a rapid transit system in Atlanta. The Kennedy administration had first proposed the Urban Mass Transportation Act, which now had the backing of President Lyndon B. Johnson. As chairman of the Metropolitan Transit Committee of 100, Vandiver actively lobbied members of the Georgia congressional delegation on behalf of the bill, contending that the creation of an Atlanta metro rapid transit system would be "extremely difficult" without federal financial assistance. The bill passed, with the entire Georgia congressional delegation voting for it. "Our 'win' and the Georgia delegation's vote," Atlanta's congressman Charles L. Weltner wrote Vandiver, "are certainly the results of your leadership of the Committee of 100 and your personal concern."[41]

In the 1964 session, the General Assembly proposed a constitutional amendment permitting the creation of a rapid transit authority, an agency that was necessary in order for the Atlanta metro area to obtain federal mass transit funding. Unlike the statewide amendment that had been defeated two years earlier, only voters in the five Atlanta metropolitan counties would determine the fate of this amendment, which was designated Amendment 16 in the 1964 general election. However, the legislature required approval by the voters in all five affected counties in order for the amendment to go into effect. Vandiver assured those who had reservations about rapid transit that passage of the amendment only established a rapid transit authority that could seek federal funds. Stressing that passage of Amendment 16 did not mean automatic membership for counties in the authority, Vandiver endorsed referenda to allow voters in each of the affected counties to decide that issue. Dick Herbert, a reporter for the *Atlanta Constitution,* wrote, "Vandiver put the weight of his position as former governor and head of the Rapid Transit Committee of 100 behind any such referendum clause in rapid transit legislation." The strongest opposition to the amendment emerged in Cobb County, leading Vandiver and other key supporters of Amendment 16 to meet with politicians and civic leaders in that county to alleviate their concerns.[42]

Mayor Allen had charged Vandiver's committee with the responsibility of conducting "an extensive informational and promotional program" to ensure the passage of an amendment permitting the establishment of a metro rapid transit system. The committee launched, in Vandiver's words, "an intensive educational effort" in October 1964 to accomplish its assigned goal. It retained a public relations firm to plan and direct the publicity campaign. Chairman Vandiver solicited money from the business community to help the metro governments fund the committee's publicity campaign. He even asked business executives to contribute space on their companies' billboards for committee advertisements. The chairman warned that defeat of Amendment 16 would mean federal grant money that was "rightfully" Georgia's would go to other states "to pay for major improvements to their cities and counties."[43]

The amendment passed in all five metro counties, although it did so in Cobb County by only 403 votes. Vandiver boasted that its approval placed the Atlanta area "in a better position" than any other southern metropolitan area to obtain federal rapid transit funding. Mayor Allen thanked Vandiver "for the very fine job" he had done in obtaining the adoption of Amendment 16. The Atlanta Board of Aldermen passed a resolution expressing appreciation to Vandiver and the members of the Committee of 100 for their role in obtaining the amendment's adoption. Richard H. Rich, chairman of the board of Rich's, a chain of department stores headquartered in Atlanta, wrote Vandiver, "[It was evident that] Cobb County was going to be our problem, and had you not stepped into the breach and made the outstanding contribution that you did, I am certain that it would have been defeated." Another prominent Atlanta businessman, Rawson Haverty, president of Haverty Furniture Company, commended Vandiver and the Committee of 100 for their effort, "which apparently did the job," in passing Amendment 16. Fulton County representative Wilson Brooks also praised Vandiver for his "good work" and that of his committee on behalf of Amendment 16. Shortly after the general election, the executive committee met and, since it had accomplished its objectives, voted to disband the Committee of 100. Chairman Vandiver wrote each member of the committee, congratulating them for their contribution to "a most important and worthwhile project." [44]

State senator Benjamin F. Johnson Jr., the author of Amendment 16, correctly predicted that "the real hard work" would be in passing legislation in the 1965 session to create a transit authority. Differences over details in the legislation proved to be quite contentious, and the needed legislation appeared to be stalemated. Late in January 1965, Vandiver publicly urged the legislators to iron out their differences and pass the implementing legislation. "Economic prosperity cannot be sustained in any state or in any city," Vandiver declared, "in which free movement is strangled by traffic jams." He also lobbied members of the legislature to pass implementing legislation, which it eventually did. The legislature required a referendum to be held in the five metro counties on June 16, 1965, to determine which county would participate in a rapid rail transit system. Local governmental and civic leaders asked Vandiver to reactivate the Committee of 100 to ensure a favorable vote in the referendum. This time, however, the former governor declined, contending that he would be out of the state during much of the time prior to the referendum. With the exception of Cobb County, the voters in the other four metro counties and in the city of Atlanta approved their governments' participation in the rapid transit authority. [45]

In addition to playing a major role in the adoption of Amendment 16, the former governor engaged in a wide range of civic responsibilities in the years from 1963 to 1965. He, along with twenty-one mostly local and state government officials, participated in a People-to-People tour of seven European countries in June 1963 as part of a program that had been started in the Eisenhower administration. In the same year, the former governor agreed to serve as vice chairman of the legislative committee of the National Guard Association and gave the principal address in February 1964 at the dedication ceremony for the Chapels of All Faiths at Milledgeville State Hospital. Vandiver also served as chairman of the state March of Dimes Foundation and the Metropolitan Atlanta Mental Health Association in 1964 but reluctantly declined an appointment in the same year to be a University of Georgia Foundation trustee, claiming that a "crowded" schedule would prevent his attendance at foundation meetings. Although not an alumnus, the former governor accepted an appointment in 1964 to serve on the steering committee to oversee the expansion of the Walter F. George School of Law at Mercer University. The former governor also delivered the commencement address at the June 1964 University of Georgia graduation ceremonies and dedicated the university's new coliseum, which his administration had built. The former chief executive chaired the 1964 annual Georgia Exposition of Commerce and Industry, which was sponsored by the Georgia State Chamber of Commerce, and continued to participate in the chamber's Red Carpet Tours. The former governor also accepted an appointment to a statewide committee in 1965 to raise funds to build a Baptist church on Jekyll Island as part of a missionary project of the Georgia Baptist State Convention. He served as fundraising chairman of the Georgia Society for the Prevention of Blindness campaign in 1964 and chaired a committee in 1965 soliciting contributions to the O. C. Aderhold Library Endowment Fund at the University of Georgia. However, Vandiver's participation in civic matters began to taper off in 1965 as his campaign for governor took more of his time and energy.[46]

Vandiver had assumed office following an administration whose reputation had been tarnished by charges of misconduct. In contrast, his administration had conducted state government in an honest and efficient manner and had achieved a solid record of accomplishments, including keeping the public schools open when some had advocated their closing to avoid integration. Leaving the governorship in 1963 well thought of by the majority of his constituents, Vandiver had no intentions of ending his political career with a single term in the governor's office.

Family Life

Ernest Vandiver considers politics to be a worthy calling, and he takes pride in his more than fifteen years of public service to the state. Nevertheless, for him there is an even higher calling—his family. He prays every night that the Lord will allow him to be a good husband, father, and grandfather. Vandiver insists that he could not have found a better wife if he had searched a hundred years: "I couldn't have found anybody that could have been sweeter and more understanding than she has been." He appreciates Betty Vandiver's 100 percent support of whatever he undertakes, as well as her talent for being a good mother and grandmother. Betty likewise is most complimentary of her husband, whom she considers "so sincere and so sweet and basically good." In reminiscing about her mother's love for her father, she seems to be describing her own relationship with her husband: "Mother worshipped Daddy. It's amazing really how Daddy was her guiding star. Everything centered around Daddy. And we all knew it. We knew she loved us, but she centered around Daddy, and it was a wonderful thing to watch." [1]

The Vandivers' youngest daughter, Jane Brevard Kidd, describes her parents' marriage as one in which her mother has been "totally devoted" and in love with her husband "every moment." She cannot remember "a time when they weren't adoring and gracious and kind and sweet and loving toward each other." According to Jane, her mother quickly accepted the role as "Daddy's helper, and she would do anything to help him in any way as a budding politician." Jane maintains that her mother had stayed in the background and played a supporting role during her father's holding of public office. However, she detects a change in that relationship as they grow older, with them becoming "more equal and more side-by-side companions." Jane describes her father as serious and reserved, while her mother is more emotional and outgoing and has a lively and "jubilant" personality.[2]

Jane thinks the label "Steel Magnolia" appropriately describes her mother. "She's as gracious as anyone could ever be and loving and giving," Jane maintains, "and would never hurt anyone, but there is an underpinning strength there that she would give her life to save any of us." As indicative of that determination, she recalls her mother's successful battle with cancer, during which Betty Vandiver decided that the illness was not going to take her life. Jane attributes her mother's victory over cancer primarily to her determined drive to survive and her positive attitude toward life: "She wasn't going to leave Ernie, and she wasn't going to miss out on grandchildren."[3]

Jane considers her father a strong but loving parent, who has always stressed the values of integrity and perseverance to his children. She remembers his encouraging them to do the best in whatever they attempted and to be helpful to others less fortunate than them. Her father, Jane recalls, was always "very concerned" about the children and "interested in what was going on and supportive of the good things that [they'd] done, and corrective of the things he thought were mistakes." Jane claims that she had "a real happy childhood" because of her loving and caring parents.[4]

Vanna Elizabeth "Beth" Vandiver views her parents' marriage as a traditional one and believes her mother happily accepted her stay-at-home-with-the-children role. Beth always thinks of her parents as being happy in their marriage, and she can't envision "either one of them without the other one." She considers her mother a person who "always knows how to have lots of fun" and who, at the same time, emphasizes being kind and considerate of others and their feelings. Beth recalls that in her childhood the family was "pretty happy all of the time." Like Jane, Beth remembers her father stressing the values of integrity and honesty, and she thinks that he is "probably the most honest person" she has ever known. She considers her father more serious and reserved than her mother and describes him as more "cautious in his dealings with people." However, she insists that her father can be "a lot of fun once you get to know him," conceding, however, that her mother has a more outgoing personality than her father. Beth praises her mother and father for being loving and supportive parents.[5]

Samuel Ernest "Chip" Vandiver III looks upon his father as being "a loving and sensitive person" who was very demanding of his children when they were growing up and who always urged them to be the best in whatever they undertook. Chip recalls his father's telling him "'at least a hundred times'" to be "'the best damn garbage man there is'" if that's what he wanted to be. He considers his father as being a supportive parent who has always helped his children find solutions for their problems. Chip recalls his father's stressing to his children the values of honesty and integrity. He agrees that individuals who don't know his father well may consider him reserved and serious. However, Chip insists that his father's family and close personal friends know him as he really is—"a very happy fun-loving" individual who can be "a good friend" and "a fun person to be with." Chip happily remembers the many occasions that his father, while governor, had taken him along on hunting trips or golf outings.[6]

Chip considers his mother a unique person who has "an infinite capacity for patience and sweetness and understanding and sensitivity." He credits her with cultivating in her children a sensitivity of other people and a sense of humor. Chip sees his mother as having been a definite asset to his father's political career, calling her the "consummate politician" who had the ability to remember everybody's name and who enjoyed campaigning. He describes his parents' marriage as one in which his father was the traditional "women-in-the-kitchen kind of guy" and his mother was one of those "smart women [who] really run the show and just make the man think that he's running the show." Chip believes that his parent's relationship has matured from one in which the husband dominates the family decision-making process to "the point where they have pretty much of an equal decision-making capacity." He even views his mother as becoming more independent in recent years and becoming more insistent on her point of view. Chip insists that his mother, although supportive of equal rights and equal pay for women, would reject the label of feminist. In Chip's opinion, his parents have a strong marriage because they "complement each other well."[7]

The children agree that their father took care of the major disciplinary problems while their mother handled day-to-day minor disciplinary matters. Both parents believed in corporal punishment and resorted to it when the offense merited it. "I'm sort of an old-time believer in warming the seats of their pants occasionally," Vandiver admits. Betty concurs in that philosophy and disagrees with the let-them-do-as-they-please attitude of child rearing. However, Chip found his mother a "more gentle, forgiving person" than his dad when it came to punishment when he and his siblings were growing up. His parents supported each other in handing out punishment; Chip recalls that he and his sisters were not successful in trying to play one parent against the other when it came to discipline.[8]

Both Betty and Ernest Vandiver had grown up in small towns, and neither wanted to live in Atlanta on a permanent basis. However, with his appointment as Talmadge's adjutant general, Vandiver had to comply with a state law that required adjutant generals to reside in Atlanta. They found a two-bedroom apartment for $125 a month. The position of adjutant general had a fringe benefit that Betty greatly appreciated—an official car. Prior to this time in their marriage, the young couple had been a one-car family, but now Betty could keep the family car. Never again would the Vandivers be a one-car family.[9]

Nor would they continue to be a one-child family. Chip was born in 1948, and two years later Betty was pregnant with Beth. The Vandivers decided that they needed more room to accommodate their growing family and purchased a house in Atlanta in 1950 for thirteen thousand dollars. Two years later, after the death of Dr. S. B. Yow, they had the opportunity to purchase his house in Lavonia. It was a large white wooden Colonial-style two-story house, and, as a young boy, Vandiver had boasted of living there some day. Betty liked the house because of its spaciousness and because of its similarity to her childhood home. Vandiver, intending on remaining adjutant general until Herman E. Talmadge left the governorship in 1955, decided to commute to Atlanta on a weekly basis to allow his family to stay in Lavonia. The Vandivers sold their home in Atlanta and used that money to purchase the Yow house. Their new home consisted of twelve rooms, including four bedrooms, a living room, a dinning room, a large kitchen, a family room, and several bathrooms. It was located on sixteen acres of well-landscaped grounds. The following year, 1953, the Vandivers' last child, Jane Brevard, was born.[10]

With Vandiver's election to the lieutenant governorship, he and his wife decided that Betty and the children would continue to live in Lavonia while he commuted to Atlanta. He spent the week in Atlanta during the legislative sessions and returned to Lavonia on the weekends unless official responsibility required his presence in Atlanta. When the legislature was not in session, he usually spent one or two days in Atlanta attending to state business and the rest of the week in Lavonia taking care of personal business matters. Vandiver had already assumed the responsibility of looking after his father's business and farming operations even before the death of his father in 1951.[11]

Following Vandiver's election as governor, the family moved into the Governor's Mansion at 205 The Prado, which was located in the Ansley Park section of Atlanta. The eighteen-room, three-story granite-stone mansion had been built more than fifty years earlier and unfortunately had not been properly maintained by the state. "It had some places in the roof where it was very difficult to repair," Governor Vandiver recalled, and pans and pots had to be placed at various locations when it rained. After several years of residing there, Vandiver concluded that the state either had to build a new mansion or buy another house for the first family's residence. At his suggestion, the legislature appointed a study committee in the 1961 session to make recommendations pertaining to the mansion. The legislative committee reported the following year that the mansion was no longer suitable for use by the first family and recommended the building of a new mansion. The General Assembly agreed with the report.[12]

However, the Vandivers never lived in the new mansion, residing instead in the mansion where Betty Vandiver's uncle, Richard B. "Dick" Russell Jr., had resided almost three decades earlier as governor. After Dick Russell's election as governor in 1930, the bachelor chief executive asked his mother, Blandina D. "Ina" Russell, to move to the mansion and serve as his hostess. "She hated leaving Winder," Betty recalls, so her grandmother Russell invited each of her grandchildren to spend a week with her during the summers. Because of the large number of grandchildren, she staggered the invitation list and had double-decked beds installed in the guest bedrooms to accommodate her overnight visitors. As a young girl, Betty recalls spending several summers at the mansion under the watchful eye of her grandmother. She compares those visits to a summer house party and fondly remembers the good times she enjoyed there with her cousins.[13]

Like their parents, the Vandiver children had thoroughly enjoyed living in small-town Lavonia and had reservations about leaving, even to live in the Governor's Mansion. An article in the January 1959 issue of the *Atlanta Journal-Constitution Magazine* quotes Betty as saying: "The children love Lavonia—a friendly little town. Chip played on a midget football team, and he's afraid he won't be able to play in Atlanta. All three hate to leave their playmates and their two big dogs, Currahee and King." The parents decided not to bring the family's big dogs because the mansion's grounds were not fenced, but they allowed the children to take their two house pets—a black cat named Sootie and a Chihuahua named Wamo for the legislator who had given it to the Vandivers. Unfortunately, Sootie got into some insect spray and died—a death that Betty considered the worst thing that happened to the family while they resided at the mansion.[14]

Ernest Vandiver enjoyed living in the mansion despite its age and need of repair because "it was a comfortable place and [they] felt at home there." The family never was awed by living in the mansion, nor did the parents view it as a museum where they had to worry about their children damaging the furniture because, according to Betty, "there was nothing there that fine to hurt." Betty succeeded in her efforts to allow her family to live as normal a life as possible while living in the mansion. Jane certainly did not consider the mansion a museum: "It was our home, and the den was our den, and the living room was our living room." She remembers the mansion as "really a home": "We had friends spend the night, and we had parties, and we had a normal childhood."[15]

During the family's residence in the mansion, the children attended a public school that was nearby. The Vandivers enrolled Chip in the fifth grade, Beth in the third grade, and Jane in kindergarten at the Spring Street Elementary School. Betty took her children to school, and the Vandivers participated in the school's Parent-Teacher Association activities and attended school functions with their children just like other parents. Betty continued to buy the family groceries even though she was now the state's first lady; nor did she ever use state patrolmen to take the children to school or to pick them up at after school activities. Chip credits his mother primarily for ensuring a sense of normalcy in her children's' lives: "I think Mama made it as normal as possible. I think Daddy tried too, but Daddy was busy trying to do his job." Nor did she think of herself as making a great sacrifice to stay at home with the children because she enjoyed staying at home and doing, in Chip's opinion, exactly what she wanted to do, which was "running the house and being Mama." Jane remembers her parents' striving to make sure that she and her siblings had a normal childhood while they were living in the mansion. They were told by their parents, Jane recalls, that they were not any better than anyone else.[16]

At first, the two girls shared a bedroom, but their constant bickering led to the conversion of an upstairs den into a bedroom for Jane. Chip had his own bedroom, and there were two guest bedrooms in addition to the master bedroom. One of the guest bedrooms had a king-sized bed and a queen-sized bed that, pulled together, made, in Jane's opinion, "the biggest bed you've ever seen." It also had served as a makeshift trampoline for the children and their visitors. When the children had overnight company, they would all sleep in that room, which also served as a "sick room" for the children because it was conveniently located next to the parents' bedroom.[17]

The Vandiver children enjoyed living in the mansion. Jane distinctly remembers the first day that she and Beth and Chip walked into the mansion and started running "around like crazy children" because they were so excited about their new home. Beth recalls a long hall on the second floor and remembers that the children would run the length of the hall while jumping over suitcases. In particular, they enjoyed playing on the two large stairwells and pulling each other down the stairs on quilts. Upon reflecting on the experience of living in the governor's mansion, Beth concludes that the Vandiver children "were pretty happy all of the time." Chip likewise enjoyed life at the mansion, which he characterized as "a great old house." In particular, Chip enjoyed visiting with the state patrolmen assigned to guard the mansion, whom he called his "buds." He had a go-cart, and the patrolmen helped him keep it running. Jane enjoyed putting on shows for the attentive patrolmen, and on report-card days she insisted that they give her a quarter for every A she made. On several occasions, the enterprising Jane even offered, to the consternation of her mother, to give visitors tours of the mansion for a quarter.[18]

Betty also has fond memories of the family's living in the mansion: "We en-joyed it, and the children loved it." Betty enjoyed playing the role of traditional housewife and mother, and that role did not change when she became first lady of the state of Georgia. She was an excellent cook and enjoyed preparing the governor's favorite dishes, one of which she called "Southern Chicken"—a com-bination of chicken, mushrooms, and sherry, cooked slowly in the oven. The gov-ernor had a problem maintaining his weight, Betty confesses, because "he likes to eat!" Meal times were always important at the Vandiver household because they gave the family members opportunities to be together and share their daily experiences. Vandiver made every effort while governor to be home for the eve-ning meals. The Vandivers had a ritual of holding hands at the dinner table while one of the children prayed a blessing. "They love saying it," Betty recalls. "If we had [had] another child, we would have had to start having tea so that there would be four times for the blessing."[19]

Betty had a staff of two to help her run the mansion. A black woman, Fanny Smith, helped with the cooking, cleaned the house, and did the laundry. Fanny, however, was more than just a paid employee. She had started working with the Vandivers when Vandiver had been adjutant general. Jane describes her as "an-other mother" who loved and cared for the Vandiver children and who had the authority to discipline them if they needed it. Betty also had the assistance of David Walker, a black state prisoner, who had been assigned duty at the man-sion. Walker enjoyed working for the Vandivers, and, after completing his prison term, he moved to Lavonia to help cook and take care of the grounds at the Van-divers' home there. He became involved in the civic affairs of Lavonia, includ-ing once serving as president of the elementary school's Parent-Teacher Associ-ation even though he had no children. Betty had only one regret about living in the mansion—she wished that she had had someone to help her with the mail.[20]

In an interview granted shortly before the Vandivers moved into the mansion, the first lady stated that the members of her family were "pretty much stay-at-homes at heart"; she continued, "I hope that we can continue our normal, in-formal way of living for the next four years in the Governor's Mansion." For the most part, the first family managed to do both because of their preference and because the mansion itself was not designed to accommodate large groups for formal entertaining. The Vandivers' entertaining activities included dinner par-ties at the mansion for members of the legislature during legislative sessions and buffets for friends before home football games. Occasionally they invited friends to the mansion for dinner. However, Betty recalls, "We never did any big, ex-tensive entertaining, and we didn't do a lot of socializing." Big events at the man-sion were family birthday parties and holiday parties, and out-of-town relatives descended upon the mansion to help the first family celebrate them.[21]

A State Patrol station had been located at the mansion for security purposes long before Vandiver had been elected governor. The Vandivers' youngest daughter, Jane, never considered security a major concern for the children: "We walked home from school. We stopped in at the drugstore on the way home. We rode our bikes everywhere 'cause in Ansley Park there are all of those little parks in between neighborhoods, and we knew each one." On one occasion, the Ku Klux Klan had a protest in front of the mansion. Prior to the event, Jane had ridden her tricycle to a friend's house, and the Klan members in the meantime had gathered on the sidewalk in front of the mansion to protest. When Jane returned home, she found the sidewalks taken over by the protesting Klan members. Undeterred, she pedaled through them, clearing a path, recalling proudly that they got out of her way and "all ran off into the street." On another occasion, she had accompanied her mother to the mansion's front door, where they found a man who wanted to talk with "General Motors." Her mother discreetly locked the screen door while talking to the stranger and kept him occupied until state troopers could be summoned.[22]

Although the mansion lacked such amenities as a swimming pool and an indoor gymnasium, it did have tennis courts and a large yard where the children could play and a long, steep, curvy driveway on which they could ride their bicycles or Chip could drive his go-cart. On the weekends, weather permitting, the family usually went to Lake Lanier, where the Vandivers had a houseboat, and did some fishing, skiing, swimming, and boating. The entire family enjoyed bowling as a family activity and, being avid Georgia Bulldog fans, faithfully attended University of Georgia football games. Vandiver received numerous invitations to go on hunting and fishing trips while serving as governor, which he frequently accepted because he was an avid fisherman and hunter. Both Ernest and Betty enjoyed playing bridge, and he occasionally golfed. He also enjoyed watching sports programs on television and kept up with current events by reading newspapers and newsmagazines.[23]

Although the governor tried to leave his work at his office at the capitol, the demands of being the state's chief executive sometimes forced him to bring work home, especially when the legislature was in session. Assistant State Attorney General Henry G. Neal recalls that the governor often had to take work home because interruptions by visitors and by telephone calls prevented him from completing his official responsibilities during the day. He sometimes brought aides and advisers to the mansion for dinner, followed by a night work session. If the governor brought his advisers home, Betty usually prepared food that ranged from a full-course meal to eggs and sausage for them. Assistant Attorney General Neal, whose assignment was to provide legal advice to the governor, frequently went to the mansion in the evenings. Neal's responsibilities included reading every bill passed by the legislature and, according to Betty Vandiver, making "sure that what Ernie was signing was what Ernie wanted to sign." As a result, the assistant attorney general spent many hours at the mansion at night going over the bills with the governor. Betty even told Neal on one occasion that "he might as well move in the other bedroom," since he stayed at the mansion so much.[24]

Betty had been involved in several community activities in Lavonia, including membership in the Women's Club, president of the community's elementary school, head of the nursery department at the Lavonia Baptist Church, parent volunteer with the Cub Scouts, and even a Civil Defense plane spotter. Although Betty attended Lavonia Baptist Church with her family, she never joined the congregation, retaining her membership in the church she joined as a child, the First Presbyterian Church in Winder. As first lady, she continued to be active in civic affairs, serving as honorary chairman of numerous fund-raising drives sponsored by organizations such as the Heart Association or the Muscular Dystrophy Association. She received the Atlanta Woman of the Year Award in 1963 for her civic service. Many of the conventions in Atlanta invited the first lady to luncheons, and she usually attended. However, she tried to limit her civic responsibilities as first lady to daytime activities in order for her to be at the mansion when her husband and children came home. She enjoyed accompanying her husband to numerous governors' conferences. However, she spent the greatest effort as first lady on improving the conditions at Milledgeville State Hospital and leading the drive to raise private funds to built chapels at the hospital.[25]

The Vandivers raised three children who have been successful in life. Chip, like his father, graduated from Darlington School in Rome and from the University of Georgia with a liberal arts degree and a law degree. He worked for two years as chief clerk for one of the members of the Georgia Court of Appeals, Robert Henry "Bob" Jordan, a longtime friend of the governor. Chip and his first cousin, Robert Lee Russell III, decided to move to Alaska, in the governor's opinion, "to see if they could make it on their own, without the Russell and Vandiver name." They both had passed the bar exam and opened a law office in Anchorage, where they practiced for ten years. While in Alaska, Chip met a native of California, Michelle Fleming South, whom he eventually married. They have two children, Regina Leigh and Samuel Ernest Russell. Chip and his family now live in Lavonia, where he practices law in the firm Vandiver & Vandiver. His father practiced with his son for several years but then stepped down from being an active partner in the firm. The Vandivers' middle child, Beth, who has not married, continued the Vandiver tradition of graduating from the University of Georgia. She worked for the Department of Family and Children Services in

Athens for a number of years before deciding to return to the University of Georgia to earn an additional degree. She now works as a media specialist at a middle school in Franklin County and lives in her home outside Lavonia. The Vandivers' youngest daughter, Jane, attended Queens College and later graduated from the University of Georgia. She married David Alexander Kidd Sr., who had grown up in Lavonia. The Kidds, who started going together in grammar school, have two children—Elizabeth and David Alexander Jr.—and reside in Athens. Of the Vandiver children, Jane is the only one who has demonstrated any interest in politics. She served on the city council of Lavonia, managed Congressman Don Johnson's campaign in 1992, and worked as director of the congressman's district office until his defeat in 1994.[26]

The Vandivers, who celebrated their fiftieth wedding anniversary in 1997, take great pride in their children and grandchildren. Certainly, Both Ernest and Betty Vandiver were good parents in a close-knit family who enjoyed life and sharing life together. Although the members of Vandiver's family appreciate his sincere commitment to public service, they appreciate him even more for being a good husband, father, and grandfather. Perhaps Beth best expressed the Vandiver children's affection for their father in her response to a third-grade classmate who had asked if she was proud of the fact that her father was governor. Beth hesitated for a moment and then replied, "I don't know, but I am glad he's my daddy."[27]

THIRTEEN

Vandiver's Last Hurrahs

The election of 1964, in which President Lyndon B. Johnson had sought a full presidential term, temporarily diverted the attention of Georgians from state to national politics. Shortly after the tragedy that occurred in November 1963, which resulted in Johnson's elevation to the presidency, Ernest Vandiver had written the president to express his shock "at the tragic turn of events" and his relief Johnson was "in the position to assume the leadership of the Nation." He recalled his pride as chairman of the state's delegation at the 1960 Democratic National Convention in casting Georgia's votes for Johnson to be the party's presidential nominee.[1]

Democratic presidential candidates had fared well in elections in the state. In fact, Georgia had never cast its electoral votes for a Republican presidential candidate. In the aftermath of the Civil War, the Democratic Party had become the dominant political party in Georgia and the South in an effort to maintain a united front against threats to white supremacy. During the New Deal, the national Democratic Party had shifted to the political Left, resulting in the irony of the most conservative region of the nation—the South—providing the greatest electoral support for the presidential candidates who were more liberal than their Republican challengers. Franklin D. Roosevelt had overwhelmingly carried the state in his four presidential elections, and Harry S. Truman had managed to win 61 percent of the state's popular vote in 1948 despite the presence of a third-party ticket headed by a southerner. Adlai E. Stevenson had easily carried the state in the 1952 and 1956 elections, and the Democratic Party's presidential nominee in 1960, Senator John F. Kennedy, had won 63 percent of the state's popular vote. However, Vandiver warned President Kennedy in June

1963 that support of a public accommodations section in civil rights legislation being considered by Congress would seriously jeopardize his carrying the South in 1964. The former governor insisted that the president could not have been elected in 1960 without the support of the South and warned that inclusion of a public accommodations section in civil rights legislation "would make it impossible for any "respectable leader in this part of the country to give [him] any support in the campaign next year." Until now, Vandiver told the president of his "great admiration" for Kennedy's presidential decisions, including sending federal troops to carry out federal court desegregation orders at the universities of Mississippi and Alabama. Such action, he conceded, was necessary because it was "the responsibility of the Chief Executive Officer of the Nation to enforce the orders of the courts." However, Vandiver confessed that the president's decision on public accommodations left him "at a complete loss to understand." [2]

In the 1964 presidential election, Senator Barry M. Goldwater became the first Republican presidential candidate in the twentieth century to make the South a major factor in his strategy to gain the presidency. Senator Goldwater believed that his economic and social conservatism, his states' rights stance, and his vote against the Civil Rights Act of 1964 assured him of becoming the first Republican presidential candidate to carry the South. The senator from Arizona calculated that the electoral votes of the southern and western states would give him the electoral majority needed to win the presidency. Senator Goldwater enjoyed an additional advantage in his efforts to carry Dixie in that President Johnson's popularity among southern whites had declined precipitously as a result of his liberal domestic agenda and his vigorous support of the Civil Rights Act of 1964. Among Georgia's Democratic officeholders on the state level, only Governor Carl E. Sanders actively campaigned for President Johnson. Former Speaker of the state House of Representatives Roy V. Harris, who supported the Goldwater candidacy, claimed that Sanders and Vandiver were the only prominent state politicians backing the president in Georgia. According to Harris, they "did everything in their power to swing the state to Johnson" and made the presidential election "a real race in Georgia." Vandiver, disputing Harris's assessment of his role on behalf of Johnson, denied being active in President Johnson's campaign. [3]

Vandiver, while conceding that Senator Goldwater would run stronger in the state than past Republican presidential candidates, nevertheless believed that the senator's "reckless statements" about abolishing the Rural Electric Authority and the Tennessee Valley Authority as well as his criticism of Social Security would "overshadow his momentary popularity in the South." Vandiver attributed that popularity to the senator's vote against the Civil Rights Act of 1964, which, in his opinion, was "a direct attempt" by the senator to gain white southern support. Vandiver reminded white voters of the senator's past support of civil rights legislation and his boast of being "an integration leader in Arizona." Claiming to be "very much a Democrat" who had "always stood by the party," Vandiver contended that the South had "gotten along just fine all these years under the guidance of the Democratic party." He praised Johnson as "a great president" even though he disagreed with him over the Civil Rights Act of 1964, which Vandiver considered to be unconstitutional. Vandiver predicted that this legislative effort was doomed to failure because the solution of the nation's civil rights problems lay "in the minds and hearts of people of both races" rather than in legislation. Despite this disagreement with the president, Vandiver voted for him in 1964 and remained a Democrat while some conservatives in the party abandoned it. Senator Richard B. Russell Jr. even told President Johnson that Vandiver and Robert L. "Bobby" Russell Jr. were "two of the most loyal friends [he had] on earth."[4]

Senator Goldwater ended the state's Democratic tradition in presidential elections by winning 54 percent of the popular vote in 1964. The president, despite losing the state and the lack of support for him in the election by the state's Democratic politicians, invited several of them to go deer hunting with him at the LBJ Ranch in Texas. Those attending included Senator Russell, Senator Herman E. Talmadge, Governor Sanders, Vandiver, and his brother-in-law state court of appeals judge Bobby Russell, whom Vandiver had appointed to fill an unexpired term on that court in 1962. Vandiver, who previously had hunted at the LBJ Ranch, described such excursions as being "about the plushest hunting" he had ever done. The president had the participants flown by helicopter from the LBJ Ranch to a location that had been amply stocked with deer. The hunters then were transported in Lincoln Continentals to areas where deer stood around "just like cattle, so you got out of the car and rest[ed] your gun on the white Lincoln Continental" and shot. "Your hospitality was wonderful," Vandiver wrote the president, "and I don't know when I have had so delightful an experience except two years ago when we did the same thing." As a token of their appreciation, Vandiver and Judge Russell sent the president a painting of the old Governor's Mansion in Milledgeville, which was hung at the LBJ Ranch.[5]

The following year, Bobby Russell, only forty years old and father of five children, tragically died of cancer. Vandiver lost not only a brother-in-law but also one of his closest political advisers and someone whom he loved as a brother. President Johnson attended the funeral service in Winder, and Vandiver, on behalf of Judge Russell's family, wrote the president to express appreciation for his taking time to devote "an entire day paying tribute to an old friend." He assured the president that he would "always hold a warm, affectionate spot in the hearts of the Russells and the Vandivers."[6]

Something else held an "affectionate spot" in Vandiver's heart—his desire for another term as governor. Speculation about the possibility of Vandiver's entering the 1966 governor's race had surfaced years prior to the election. Reg Murphy, political editor of the *Atlanta Constitution,* wrote in September 1963 that Vandiver "was in the early stages of asking for the job again." At an appreciation dinner for Vandiver early in 1963, state game and dish commissioner Fulton Lovell had referred to the guest of honor as "Georgia's next governor," and Senator Russell had told President Johnson in November 1963 that Vandiver was "running for Governor next time" and that he would be elected. Beryl Sellers, assistant city editor of the *Savannah Evening Press,* concluded that the consensus of the political talk during the 1964 legislative session was of Vandiver's winning "an easy victory" in 1966. State senator Zell B. Miller wrote Vandiver in mid-1964 to tell him, "During the past year, I have said hundreds of times that S. Ernest Vandiver should be, and is going to be, our next Governor in Georgia." Roy V. Harris wrote in his newspaper in November 1964 that Vandiver had been running for governor "for many months now." The chairman of the board of commissioners of the Georgia Department of Industry and Trade, Peter S. Knox Jr., referred to Vandiver as the state's next chief executive in remarks at a Georgia Chamber of Commerce Red Carpet Tour banquet in April 1965. Tom Sellers, a reporter for the *Columbus Enquier* covering the banquet at Callaway Gardens, thought it had the "trappings that resembled a political rally" for Vandiver, who "mingled happily with the guests, shaking hands and chatting with all the appearances of an aspiring candidate." Ralph E. McGill Sr., the publisher of the *Atlanta Constitution,* predicted in February 1965 that Vandiver would not have any serious opposition in the governor's race.[7]

Well before the 1966 election, Vandiver began a vigorous personal campaign to ensure his victory. He believed that personal contact with elected officials as well as with private citizens was essential in winning elections for a statewide office. The former governor sent congratulatory letters to legislators elected in 1964 and invited members of the 1964 legislative session to breakfast meetings in order to solicit their support. The federal courts had mandated special elections in 1965 to allow voters to elect members of a newly reapportioned state House of Representatives. Taking advantage of this opportunity, Vandiver sent congratulatory letters to the winners of those elections, urging them to visit him at his law office when they were in Atlanta. He also wrote citizens who had received honors and appointments or who had suffered deaths or illnesses in their families. The former governor engaged in an extensive letter-writing campaign to local officials, expressing appreciation for their "continuing friendship and support" and urging them to visit him when they were in Atlanta or Lavonia. The Vandivers sent hundreds of cards in the 1964 and 1965 Christmas seasons.

Vandiver also undertook a hectic speech-making schedule, making more than one hundred talks to civic groups throughout the state from May 1965 through April 1966.[8]

Vandiver's early campaigning gave him a distinct advantage in the upcoming race. *Atlanta Constitution* editor Eugene Patterson concluded in May 1965 that Vandiver was "considered to have the inside track in his unannounced race for governor." Most of the attendees at the 1965 Georgia Press Association Convention considered him the leading candidate in the upcoming gubernatorial race. A 1965 poll of the membership of the boards of directors of Citizens and Southern banks throughout the state also overwhelmingly showed Vandiver to be the leading gubernatorial candidate. A poll commissioned by Vandiver in early May 1966 indicated that more than 70 percent of the electorate favored his return to the governor's office.[9]

Vandiver anticipated criticism for his failure to carry out the "no, not one" promise made in the 1958 campaign. In an interview with Reg Murphy in 1965, he discussed his strategy for dealing with that promise. He intended to remind Georgians of the U.S. Supreme Court's invalidation of the state's massive-resistance laws by the time of his inauguration. Without the federal courts' action, Vandiver insisted, "I would have been able to keep that promise. But we had a fundamental decision to obey the law or to recommend secession from the country and be a demagogue." Vandiver did not believe that standing in the schoolhouse door or going to jail in defiance of the federal courts would have been beneficial to the state. "The fact remains," Vandiver told Murphy, "that the people of Alabama and Mississippi—with all of their statements and actions—are in the same position with regards to desegregation. And Georgia has kept its reputation."[10]

Unlike the 1958 campaign, Vandiver anticipated major opposition in 1966. Possible candidates mentioned in the press included Atlanta banker William R. Bowdoin, House Speaker George T. Smith, former governor Ellis G. Arnall, former lieutenant governor Garland T. Byrd, and Congressman Howard H. "Bo" Callaway Sr. In addition, Senator Talmadge, according to newspaper reports, had asked Vandiver in 1965 not to enter the governor's race because of his plans to run for the office. Denying making such a request, Senator Talmadge publicly stated in July 1965 that he would not enter the governor's race. Vandiver told reporters that Senator Talmadge had not approached him on this issue but that some of the senator's supporters had. According to Vandiver, these supporters had told him of the senator's inclination to enter the race because "he was sick and tired of Washington" and "would look forward to running for governor again." Despite these pleadings, Vandiver had informed the Talmadge supporters of his intentions of remaining in the race.[11]

While the state's junior senator declined to become a gubernatorial candidate, former governor Arnall announced his candidacy for the gubernatorial nomination in July 1965. Arnall, a leader in the anti-Talmadge faction of the state Democratic Party in the 1930s and 1940s, had served as governor from 1943 to 1947. He enjoyed the distinction of being the only candidate ever to have defeated Gene Talmadge in a governor's race. The Arnall administration had achieved a remarkable record, which included repealing the state's poll tax, lowering the voting age, reforming the state's infamous penal system, paying off the state's debt, revising the state's constitution, establishing a teachers' retirement system, and creating the Georgia Ports Authority. The young governor had also been successful in gaining the reaccreditation of several units of the state's university system. Governor Gene Talmadge's political interference with the board of regents in 1941 had resulted in the loss of accreditation, providing Arnall with an issue that he skillfully used to defeat Talmadge in the 1942 governor's race. Although fifty-eight years of age, the former governor possessed the drive and energy of a much younger man and had many advantages as a politician. In addition to enjoying politics, Arnall was intelligent, articulate, personable, outgoing, and wealthy. Certainly he presented a greater obstacle to Vandiver's election as governor in 1966 than William T. "Bill" Bodenhamer Sr. had in 1958.[12]

However, Arnall brought with him some major political liabilities and baggage as well. Carl Sanders saw his greatest drawback as being "labeled as a rich Atlanta lawyer" who had some very liberal ideas. "I don't think that the political climate in the state of Georgia at that time favored that type of candidacy." As governor, Arnall had been a strong supporter of President Franklin D. Roosevelt and had befriended one of the most liberal and controversial members of the Roosevelt administration, Vice President Henry A. Wallace. Arnall had even led the unsuccessful fight for Wallace's renomination at the 1944 Democratic National Convention despite the vice president's lack of popularity in Georgia. The former governor eventually had disassociated himself from Wallace because of his controversial foreign policy views and his hostility toward segregation.[13]

Nor had the Talmadgites ever forgiven Arnall for defeating Eugene Talmadge in the 1942 governor's race and for opposing Herman Talmadge in the infamous three-governor controversy in 1947. Arnall's numerous out-of-state speaking engagements, his two successful books, and his numerous articles in national publications in which he addressed some of the problems of the state and the South further alienated many Georgians. He outraged many whites by complying with a federal court mandate in 1946 allowing blacks to vote in the state's primaries at a time when other liberal or progressive politicians in the South were distancing themselves from that issue. During the state's desegregation crisis in

1961, Arnall had supported keeping the public schools open while many were advocating closing them to avoid desegregation. He had even publicly expressed his opposition in the early 1960s to the county-unit system, which further alienated him from rural and small-town white voters in the state, who benefited the most politically from that malapportioned nominating process.[14]

Another candidate, Lester G. Maddox, entered the race in September 1965, conceding that most political observers at that time did not think much of his candidacy. At that time, Vandiver considered him "an absolute radical" who was not taken seriously by anyone. Unlike the upper-class background of both Arnall and Vandiver, Maddox had been born into a low-income family in Atlanta and had dropped out of high school to help support his family. A hard worker, Maddox had opened a restaurant in Atlanta in 1947 that eventually became well known for its home-cooked meals and its owner's segregationist views. As his interest in politics increased, the outspoken segregationist ran unsuccessful races against Atlanta mayors in 1957 and 1961. Undeterred by these losses, Maddox ran for the Democratic lieutenant gubernatorial nomination in 1962 against Peter Zack Geer Jr. Geer, labeling Maddox a "radical extremist," gained the endorsement of Carl Sanders and Marvin Griffin, the two major gubernatorial candidates in the 1962 Democratic primary. Geer won the nomination and handed Maddox his third political electoral defeat.[15]

Undeterred by his string of electoral defeats, Maddox continued to play an activist role in politics. Although denying membership in the Ku Klux Klan, Maddox had the endorsement of one of the largest Klan organizations in the state in his race for lieutenant governor. He had publicly endorsed the John Birch Society, had joined a chapter of the Citizens Council, and had picketed the White House to protest President Johnson's support of civil rights for blacks. He strenuously opposed the Civil Rights Act of 1964 and denounced the "white renegades in public office" who refused to oppose "the sell-out to the communist inspired race-mixers." Maddox denounced those individuals, which included "a governor," for boasting of their role in integrating the University of Georgia. He thought that they "should hang their heads in shame and ask the people to forgive them." Maddox adamantly opposed the election of President Johnson in 1964 and formed, along with former state Democratic Party chairman James H. "Jimmy" Gray Sr. and former governor S. Marvin Griffin Sr., an organization of disgruntled conservative Democrats who were not yet ready to leave their party but supported the election of Goldwater. Maddox's vociferous opposition to racial integration, along with his well-publicized denial of serving blacks at his restaurant by threatening them with ax handles and a pistol, made him one of the best-known segregationists in the state. A feisty and confident Maddox predicted his election as governor in 1966 against "cowardly political leaders who ask you to follow their programs of cowardice into the pits of hell and destruction—integration and amalgamation."[16]

Thus by the end of 1965, two candidates—Lester Maddox and Ellis Arnall—had announced their candidacies to challenge Vandiver for the Democratic gubernatorial nomination. Of the two, former governor Arnall posed the greatest threat to Vandiver's return to the governor's mansion. He undertook a vigorous campaign to cut into the commanding lead held by Vandiver, promising "to run him ragged": "Wherever he speaks today, I'll speak tomorrow." Vandiver saw Arnall's bitter campaign against him as an effort to destroy his reputation of being an honest politician. "I think he thought that in order to run a credible race or to have a chance in beating me he had to destroy that image," Vandiver concluded. "So he took things that were absolutely nothing . . . and twisted them around and ran a very bitter campaign against me in an effort to destroy the image that I had." In addition, Arnall, as Vandiver had anticipated, reminded voters of Vandiver's "no, not one" promise. "Governor Vandiver knew when he promised that," Arnall charged, "he could not defy the law of land. He knew when he made those pledges he was not telling the truth." Arnall announced his intentions of playing a recording of Vandiver's statement throughout the state to remind the voters how Vandiver had gotten "elected governor by lying to the people" and called him "a fool" for making such a promise.[17]

Arnall also attacked Vandiver for compiling "one of the most disgraceful records a governor ever had." He called Vandiver's claim of not raising taxes in his administration "an unadulterated and unmitigated lie," charging that Vandiver had lowered the sales tax bracket, which forced consumers to pay additional taxes. Arnall also questioned the propriety of the Louisville and Nashville Railroad Company's hiring Vandiver as its legal counsel upon his leaving the governorship. According to Arnall, the state had been attempting to force the railroad to pay taxes on profits made from its lease of the state-owned Western and Atlantic Railroad until Vandiver became governor, when the tax claim was dropped. He accused the railroad of retaining the former governor as counsel for thirty thousand dollars a year to keep it "from paying its just due and past due income taxes on the profit from the Western and Atlantic Railroad." Arnall further alleged that the railroad wanted its "political agent" Vandiver back in the governor's office because its lease of the state-owned Western and Atlantic Railroad would be up for renewal in the next governor's term. Vandiver strongly denied Arnall's allegations of any impropriety concerning his relationship with the L&N Railroad. He admitted to having represented it upon leaving the governorship "just like Ellis Arnall represented the big interests up east and Walt Disney in Hollywood" after his departure from the governorship. As for the tax claim allegation, Vandiver insisted that it was he who had signed an executive order that "kept the suit alive" and insisted that collection could be made by the state if the courts ruled in favor of the state's tax claim. Vandiver contended, "There was nothing done during my administration that was beneficial to the railroads at all." [18]

Arnall also charged that Vandiver, while governor, had engaged in unethical conduct concerning the routing of Interstate 85. He alleged that Vandiver had received advanced information on the routing of the interstate that allowed him to purchase land through which it would traverse. Arnall further accused the governor of having the route changed so it would go through some of his land in Franklin County. Vandiver strongly denied the allegations, while conceding that a member of the state highway board had tried to change the route to one closer to Gainesville. However, Vandiver claimed that he had responded to this effort by directing the "Highway Board to run it [I-85] as straight as they could from Atlanta to Greenville [South Carolina] because that was the most economical and most direct route" and that he further directed the highway board to make sure that the interstate did not go through any of his property. Despite his directive, he admitted, the routing of the interstate had taken "a little piece" of his property for which he received three hundred dollars, which was donated to the chapels at Milledgeville State Hospital. Arnall also attacked state highway board chairman Jim Gillis, accusing him of using his position to award highway construction projects to further Vandiver's candidacy. Denouncing Gillis as the "czar" of the Highway Department, Arnall promised to fire him if elected. Vandiver defended the chairman, who had managed his 1958 gubernatorial campaign, by calling Arnall's criticisms of Gillis a "dastardly and cowardly brand of politicking" against a public servant "whose long and honorable life had been notable for honest, efficient and loyal service to the people of the state." [19]

Vandiver sought a second term as governor by running as a conservative, noting that the people of Georgia were "still basically conservative, politically speaking." Vandiver called his candidacy to regain the governorship a "crusade for responsible government" based on the principles of "responsibility, honesty, compassion, progress, integrity, efficiency and economy." He released a platform entitled "Platform for Progress for Georgia," which spelled out the goals of his second administration. The platform listed education as his "top priority" and promised to implement a comprehensive educational program to provide students with an education second to none in the nation. The platform further promised that the state's public school system would have the best-qualified teachers, who would be paid "not less than the national average." He also promised "to work for dramatic advancement in higher education," including raising professors' salaries to national standards. His platform also pledged a continuation of the "compassionate mental health program" begun in his first administration, a "maximum effort" to complete the interstate system in Georgia, the four-laning of major state highways, and a state industrial development of at least $200 million a year. Unlike his 1958 promise of no tax increases, Vandiver this time only pledged to "exert every effort—practice every economy—install every efficiency—to avoid seeking increased taxes." His platform also called for creating an equitable state revenue system, reforming the state's correctional and probation systems, increasing the promotion of tourism, revising the constitution of 1945, and reorganizing state government.[20]

Normally, the struggle over the governorship in one-party Georgia would have been settled in the Democratic primary. However, the Republican Party in 1966 presented a threat to Democratic control of that office when Republican congressman Bo Callaway became a gubernatorial candidate. Callaway, who had been born into a well-to-do family of textile mill owners, had assisted his father in the development of Callaway Gardens, a popular resort near Columbus. He had supported the Talmadges in state politics and had backed the gubernatorial bids of both Vandiver and Griffin. Governor Herman Talmadge had placed him on the Board of Regents of the University System of Georgia. Despite his past association with the Democratic Party, Callaway switched to the Republican Party in 1964 and, in the same year, became the state's first Republican congressman since Reconstruction.[21]

At first, it seemed that only Democrats would fight over who would be the next governor. Congressman-elect Callaway even told reporters shortly after the 1964 presidential election that the Republicans would not run anyone against Vandiver in 1966, an indication of Vandiver's overwhelming lead in the governor's race. The congressman shortly thereafter announced his intentions to seek reelection in 1966. However, in February 1965, the chairman of the Georgia Republican Party announced the possibility of Bill Bowdoin's seeking the Republican gubernatorial nomination. After Bowdoin declined to enter the race, Callaway qualified as a Republican gubernatorial candidate.[22]

Health problems posed a greater obstacle to Vandiver's returning to the governor's mansion than his political opposition did. The former governor, since experiencing his heart attack in 1960, had been taking medication that had allowed him to lead an active life. Nevertheless, he suffered from occasional attacks of angina pectoris, and the frequency and severity of the angina attacks increased as the tempo of the campaign increased. To ease the pain, Vandiver began "eating nitroglycerine like it was going out of style." He realized that the stress and demands of a statewide campaign for governor were taking a toll on his health: "I would try to go from one end of the state to the other, and I wasn't eating right. I was eating barbecue and civic club food . . . and losing sleep." Betty Vandiver remembered that it was "always just panic when he would have his heart troubles." On May 16, 1966, the former governor, after experiencing a severe angina attack, had an examination by Dr. Carter Smith, who had been treating him since his heart attack. He warned Vandiver that "the stress and strain of a vigorous political campaign and then the stress of another possible four years as governor" could cause "serious injury" to his health. Vandiver, mindful of Bobby Russell's death, which left his wife with five young children to rear, reluctantly concluded that he had no choice but to withdraw from the race.[23]

Prior to making his decision public, Vandiver flew to Washington to discuss his withdrawal with Senator Talmadge. He urged the senator to enter the governor's race to keep "Ellis Arnall or Lester Maddox or somebody like that" from being governor. "Their philosophy is entirely different from my own." Vandiver, returning to Atlanta without a definite commitment from Talmadge to enter the race, held a news conference on May 18, 1966, to announce his withdrawal from the governor's race. He expressed appreciation to the people for allowing him to serve in the state's two highest political offices and told reporters that his health would dictate his future political plans. For the time being, however, Vandiver said, he planned to practice law, oversee his farming operations in Franklin County, and catch up on his hunting and fishing.[24]

On the same day of Vandiver's withdrawal, Senator Talmadge held a news conference in Washington to tell reporters that he tentatively had decided to run for governor. However, he insisted that a final decision had not been made, and he urged the people of Georgia to let him know their views on what he should do. Congressman Callaway reacted to the senator's news conference by accusing President Johnson of persuading Talmadge to enter the race to save the governorship from the Republicans, an allegation that Vandiver dismissed as "completely and utterly untrue." Some of Talmadge's closest political advisers, including his wife and mother, urged him to remain in the Senate. His mother candidly stated that "the big business people wanted him to stay up there because he was for their interests." Carl Sanders likewise concluded that Talmadge's strongest financial backers and supporters wanted him in Washington because "his position in the United States Senate was far more valuable to the state and to them." These prominent supporters, according to Vandiver, included Atlanta banker John A. Sibley and Coca-Cola executive Robert W. Woodruff. Talmadge finally decided not to run for governor and so informed Vandiver. On May 23, 1966, Senator Talmadge publicly announced his intention to stay in the Senate, where, he claimed, the "overwhelming majority" of Georgians who had expressed their views wanted him.[25]

Shortly after Talmadge's announcement, Jimmy Gray, conservative editor of the *Albany Herald* and state Democratic Party chairman in the Vandiver administration, entered the governor's race, hoping to replace Vandiver as the Talmadge-backed candidate. Former lieutenant governor Byrd and state senator James E. "Jimmy" Carter Sr. also qualified. Thus five major candidates— Ellis Arnall, Garland Byrd, Jimmy Carter, Jimmy Gray, and Lester Maddox— sought the 1966 Democratic gubernatorial nomination. Vandiver felt obligated to vote for Gray out of gratitude for the Albanian's service as party chairman during his administration and because of Gray's friendship and past political support. However, Vandiver, as a result of his health problem, declined to play an active role in the Gray campaign. Interestingly, Vandiver agreed to provide some political guidance for Carter, one of Gray's opponents in the primary. William B. Gunter, a close friend and active supporter of Carter's, had asked Vandiver to give the senator some advice on running a statewide campaign. Vandiver agreed to the request of his friend and former university classmate, and Carter spent several hours in Lavonia discussing campaign strategy with the former governor.[26]

As a result of the crowded field of contenders in the race, neither of the candidates won a majority of the votes in the primary election. State law prior to 1966 had required gubernatorial candidates to receive only a plurality of the votes for nomination. However, the legislature during the 1966 session had changed the requirement for nomination to a majority vote. If a candidate failed to receive a majority of the votes in the primary election, the reform mandated a runoff election between the two candidates with the greatest number of votes. Arnall received a plurality of 29.4 percent of the votes, and Maddox came in second with 23.5 percent of the vote; Carter came in third with almost 21 percent of the votes. To the shock and dismay of many Georgians, Maddox won 54.3 of the runoff vote, prompting him to call his win one of the greatest political victories in the history of humankind. Certainly, the victory of a three-time political loser over former governor Ellis Arnall qualified as one of the major political upsets in the state's political history. [27]

Vandiver voted for Maddox in the runoff, calculating "that 'Bo' would have had an easier time beating a political clown than he would have beating Ellis Arnall." He concluded that "Georgians couldn't vote for Arnall so they voted for Maddox figuring that Bo Callaway would defeat him" in the general election. "We would suffer four years under the Republicans and then get it [the governorship] back." Arnall attributed his defeat to Republicans voting in the Democratic primary for Maddox, who they believed would be the weaker candidate against Callaway in the general election. Vandiver, Carter, and Sanders agreed with Arnall that Republican votes had influenced the outcome of the Democratic runoff. Vandiver voted for Callaway in the general election, believing the congressman to be more qualified than Maddox to lead the state.[28]

Although Callaway received a plurality of more than three thousand votes in the general election, a write-in effort on behalf of Arnall, which the former governor never repudiated, denied the Republican candidate a majority of the popular vote as required by the state constitution. In such a situation, the legislature had the constitutional responsibility of electing the next governor. Disgruntled Georgians quickly filed suits in federal and state courts challenging the General Assembly's authority to elect the state's next chief executive. However, both the United States Supreme Court and the Georgia Supreme Court upheld the legislature's authority to elect the governor, and the General Assembly, with only twenty-nine Republican members, overwhelmingly elected Maddox governor.[29]

Four years later, Carl Sanders and Jimmy Carter emerged as the leading candidates seeking the Democratic Party's gubernatorial nomination in 1970. Two Republicans, Comptroller General James L. "Jimmy" Bentley Jr. and Atlanta television news commentator Hal Suit, fought for the right to take on the Democratic nominee. The candidates realized that the next governor would probably have to appoint someone to complete the term of Richard Russell, the state's senior United States senator, who was suffering from acute pulmonary emphysema. Although Senator Russell had publicly stated his intentions to seek reelection in 1972, some wondered whether his health problems would prevent him from completing his term of office. The seventy-three-year-old senator, experiencing increasing difficulties in performing his senatorial duties as a result of his declining health, told Senator Talmadge that he wasn't "going to be around much longer."[30]

Both Carter and Sanders sought Vandiver's support in the 1970 Democratic primary. Sanders had unsuccessfully solicited Vandiver's backing through a mutual friend, James A. "Jim" Dunlap, who, according to Vandiver, relayed a message from Sanders—"that if I supported him that he would appoint me to the Senate." However, Vandiver refused to back his former Senate floor leader: "Sanders, after telling me that he would never run against Senator Russell, became a candidate [in 1966] to the extent that Senator Russell had to get out and start raising campaign funds. So, I still had that in my craw." Sanders denied promising to appoint Vandiver to the Senate but alleged that Carter had made such a promise in an effort to obtain Vandiver's support in the 1970 race.[31]

Vandiver considered Carter "a likable sort of fellow, very friendly," and requested a meeting with him before making a decision on whether to back him in the race. Two of Carter's major supporters in Lavonia, Robert Meredith and Andrew Hill, flew Carter to Lavonia to meet with the former governor. According to Vandiver, "[Hill and Meredith told] me before I talked with Carter that he said that he was going to appoint me. I didn't ask him to appoint me. That wouldn't have been the right thing to do. . . . I never did politics that way in my life. But certain things are understood." Vandiver believed that he had an "understanding" with Carter that the governor would appoint him to the Senate in the event of Senator Russell's death. Griffin B. Bell also believed that a "commitment" had been made for Vandiver's support of Carter in return for Vandiver being appointed to the Senate by Carter in the event of Senator Russell's death. According to Bell, the commitment had been made in a meeting to Robert H. "Bob" Jordan, who was representing Vandiver, and Charles Kirbo, who was representing Carter.[32]

Vandiver also claimed that Carter visited Russell during the primary to seek his support. During that meeting, Carter, according to Vandiver, "indicated" but "didn't say outright he was going to appoint [Vandiver] to Senator Russell's [seat], but that was the basis of Senator Russell's coming out and supporting him." Vandiver also recalled having a conversation with Senator Russell in which the senator told him that he would like for Vandiver to succeed him. "So I thought Carter understood that." However, Carter emphatically denied making any commitment to Vandiver concerning an appointment to the Senate. "If there had been a commitment to Vandiver," Carter stated in an interview several years later, "he would have been senator." Carter insisted that he had "entered the governor's office, and had made public statements to the effect that [he] did not have a single outstanding commitment." Carter emphatically stated, "I didn't promise anyone anything."[33]

Nevertheless, Vandiver, believing that he had an understanding with Carter, endorsed his gubernatorial candidacy by praising him as a candidate of "splendid qualifications" and "a man of great character and integrity." Vandiver also helped Carter raise about three hundred thousand dollars, contending that Carter "had absolutely no idea how to raise campaign funds." He actively urged his supporters to vote for Carter and gave him campaign advice. Vandiver concluded that Carter could not have defeated Sanders "if [Vandiver] hadn't worked with him and for him." Almost winning the nomination without a runoff, Carter easily defeated Sanders in the Democratic runoff and Republican Hal Suit in the general election. Shortly thereafter, the governor-elect, Vandiver, and his law partner Cook Barwick went on a fishing trip to the Everglades during which Carter asked Vandiver to serve in his administration as adjutant general. Reasoning that serving in this position would be a good way to get back into politics, Vandiver accepted the offer. The *Atlanta Journal* praised the appointment, noting that Vandiver had been "a good governor" and that it would be "fine to have him back in public life."[34]

Less than two weeks after Carter had been sworn in as governor, Senator Russell died of pulmonary emphysema. His death increased speculation over whom the governor would appoint to complete his unexpired term. Bill Shipp, political editor of the *Atlanta Constitution*, considered Vandiver the leading candidate, followed by state Democratic Party chairman David H. Gambrell. Harry Murphy, a writer for the *Atlanta Journal*, reported that most political observers believed that either Vandiver or Gambrell would get the appointment. Hal Gulliver, a columnist for the *Atlanta Constitution*, looked upon Vandiver as the leading candidate despite questions about his health. Although a *Constitution* editorial praised Vandiver as "a competent man who made the state a solid governor," the paper reminded its readers of Vandiver's past heart problems while endorsing Vandiver for the vacancy if he felt "up to taking it." At least twenty-five individuals—including Vandiver; Gambrell; the governor's chief of staff, Charles H. Kirbo; his campaign adviser, Philip H. Alston, and his second cousin Hugh A. Carter Sr.—had, according to Carter, been proposed for the appointment. Although the governor never asked Senator Talmadge whom he should appoint, the senator thought Vandiver would have been a good choice because he "could have easily been re-elected if he had been appointed."[35]

Vandiver, assuming the senatorial appointment was his, anxiously awaited the call from the governor to offer him the position. The Vandiver household, already in a state of stress precipitated by the death of Senator Russell, had something else to cope with as well. The Vandivers' youngest daughter, Jane, was competing in the Georgia Junior Miss contest in Atlanta, and the family was staying in a hotel in the capital city during the competition. "It was the most horrendous week," Betty Vandiver recalled anxiously, "waiting any minute to get the call from Jimmy Carter and never getting it and seeing Ernie waiting." She thought the governor might have even tried to telephone her husband in Lavonia, not knowing that they were in Atlanta. After several days of anxious waiting, Vandiver finally went to the governor's mansion to talk with Carter about the appointment. Even though he indicated his "renewed interest in the appointment," Vandiver left the mansion without a commitment from the governor.[36]

Governor Carter finally ended eleven days of speculation on February 1, 1971, by appointing David Gambrell to the Senate. A devastated Betty Vandiver called the appointment "quite a let-down": "I hated seeing Ernie being hurt like that." The forty-one-year-old Gambrell, whom Carter had earlier appointed chairman of the state Democratic Party, had never sought nor held an elected public office. Gambrell's father, E. Smythe Gambrell, was a prominent Atlanta attorney and former president of the American Bar Association, who had given Emory University $1 million toward the construction of a new building for the university's law school. David Gambrell had graduated from Davidson College and Harvard University's law school. He had practiced in his father's law firm and later worked in one of Atlanta's largest legal firms, King and Spalding. Gambrell had assisted Charles Kirbo, a senior attorney in King and Spalding, in representing state senatorial candidate Jimmy Carter in his successful legal effort to throw out the tainted results of a voting precinct. Carter had become acquainted with Gambrell as a result of his work with Kirbo in this case. Gambrell, who later established his own law firm in Atlanta, had a record of assisting political campaigns, including participation in the gubernatorial campaigns of Herman Talmadge, Vandiver, Sanders, and Carter. Gambrell had even held the position of campaign treasurer in Carter's 1970 gubernatorial campaign. Shelby McCash, a reporter for the *Macon Telegraph,* credited Gambrell with being "among several insiders" who plotted Carter's successful election strategy against Sanders. Gambrell had also served as president of the Atlanta and Georgia bar associations, a director of the National Legal Aid and Defenders Association, a trustee of the Atlanta Commission on Crime and Juvenile Delinquency, a trustee of the Westminister Schools of Atlanta, and vice president of the state Young Men's Christian Association.[37]

Governor Carter knew Gambrell's family and considered his appointee an "up and coming young leader who was not deeply involved in Georgia politics." Carter believed that Gambrell would be a "good choice" to fill the senatorial vacancy, contending that he had the potential of becoming "a dynamic senator." However, former state representative William L. "Bill" Lanier Sr. speculated that the governor picked the unknown Gambrell as "a seat-warmer" because he intended to run for the office himself. The governor's leading critic, Lieutenant Governor Lester Maddox, criticized the appointment of "one of the aristocrats," contending that Gambrell could not even be elected to a full senatorial term. Maddox even hinted of his interest in running for the seat in 1972. Another frequent critic of the governor, the *Atlanta Constitution,* expressed regret that Carter had appointed a "seat warmer" to the vacant Senate position. However, the *Atlanta Journal* endorsed the nomination of the successful attorney, who was a "good friend" of the governor. However, the "good friend" was not well known in the state, as indicated in a survey commissioned by Senator Gambrell in July 1971. The survey of the state's political opinion found that Senator Gambrell had a favorable rating of only 29 percent, whereas Governor Jimmy Carter's favorable rating of 71 percent surpassed the favorable ratings of Lieutenant Governor Lester Maddox's 66 percent, former governor Carl Sanders's 62 percent, and former governor Ernest Vandiver's 48 percent. Although Senator Gambrell had only a 7 percent unfavorable rating, 64 percent of those surveyed either had no opinion of him or did not recognize his name. Former governor Vandiver had a 17 percent unfavorable rating, and 35 percent of those surveyed had no opinion of him or did not recognize his name. The survey concluded that Gambrell had not yet made "a major impact" on Georgia voters, which was understandable because he had been in the Senate for only four months and had never been a candidate in a statewide race. "At the same time, it allows the Senator," the survey concluded, "the flexibility of molding his image over the next year."[38]

Shortly after Gambrell's appointment, a disappointed Vandiver issued a statement stressing that he had not asked the governor for the appointment and that the governor had not "made any commitment to [him] personally either before, during or after his campaign for governor." The statement promised an announcement on his future political plans at "the appropriate time." Governor Carter refused to tell reporters why Vandiver, who he conceded had been among the "top three or four contenders" for the appointment, had not been appointed. Carter later revealed that he had "never really seriously considered Ernie Vandiver" for the appointment even though he looked upon him as "one of the finest governors [the state] had in the past despite the fact he was in the no, not one category when racism was prevalent." Vandiver attributed his failure to get the appointment to Carter's presidential ambitions, contending, "If he had appointed someone who had been associated with segregation, that would have hurt his chance to be president." He also viewed the appointment as a payback to Gambrell's father for his financial support given to Carter's 1970 campaign.[39]

Vandiver continued to serve as adjutant general in the Carter administration until his resignation in November 1971. Four months later, on February 16, 1972, he announced his senatorial candidacy to a large crowd of friends and supporters in the state Senate chambers. Stressing that no one could take Senator Russell's place, Vandiver claimed to possess the ability, experience, and maturity needed to represent the state effectively in the Senate. He later explained why he had entered the race: "mainly because I was still upset because with Carter for not appointing me." Early in the campaign, Vandiver addressed the concerns among voters that his past heart problems would prevent him from serving in the Senate. "My doctor tells me," Vandiver told members of the Atlanta Press Club, "that I am in far better physical condition today than when President Johnson and President Eisenhower [both of whom had previously suffered heart attacks] ran very strenuous campaigns for the presidency." Certainly, he contended, a "one-time physical disability" should not be a disqualification for someone who had "many good years left" and who wanted to serve his state and nation in the Senate.[40]

Voters in the Democratic primary election on August 8, 1972, had a choice of fifteen senatorial candidates. Although both former governors Maddox and Sanders considered entering the race, they eventually declined to do so. Vandiver viewed Maddox's decision not to enter the race as being beneficial to his candidacy in that they both would have appealed to the same conservative vot-

ers. The former governor believed that Gambrell would get the most votes because of his incumbency status but would fall short of the majority needed for
nomination. Vandiver thought that his experience and record in public service
plus a vigorous personal campaign on his part would get him in the runoff, in
which he could defeat Gambrell. Other major Democratic contenders included
state treasurer William H. Burson, former congressman W. M. "Don" Wheeler,
and state representative Samuel A. "Sam" Nunn. Congressman S. Fletcher
Thompson ran as the front-runner of the four senatorial candidates in the
Republican primary.[41]

Vandiver sought to portray Gambrell as someone who was not representative
of the political views of the majority of the Georgia electorate. He accused him
in his tenure as state party chairman in the Carter administration of "father-
ing the selection system" used by the party in choosing its delegates to the 1972
Democratic National Convention. "Not since the black days of reconstruction
and the carpetbaggers," Vandiver charged, "have the ultra-liberals taken over so
much of the state's delegation." Vandiver also accused Gambrell of being a "political bedfellow" of the 1972 Democratic presidential nominee, George S. Mc-
Govern, whom he considered "dangerous" to the country because of his calls for
drastic cuts in defense spending. He accused McGovern and his liberal supporters of not just wanting to change America : "They want and mean to destroy
it." He insisted that Senator McGovern's positions on most issues were "totally
repugnant to the rank-and-file people" of the state. Vandiver accused Gambrell
of embracing "some of McGovern's pet causes in Washington," compiling an
"ultra-liberal voting record in the Senate," and voting on the side opposite Senator Talmadge at least thirty-eight times. Denouncing Gambrell as a politician
who talked "like a conservative in Georgia" and voted "with the flaming liberals
in Washington," he urged voters to reject the "wild-eyed, irresponsible liberalism" of both McGovern and Gambrell.[42]

In particular, Vandiver lambasted Gambrell's vote to limit a filibuster by Senator Talmadge and other southern senators against legislation expanding the
power of the Equal Employment Opportunities Commission. Vandiver contended that Gambrell became the first senator in the state's history to end a filibuster in the U.S. Senate and "then he voted for the bill, the only member of the
Georgia delegation to do so." That vote, according to Vandiver, "was a vote to
send hundreds of federal agents swarming over Georgia threatening private
citizens and businessmen, unions and management with persecution if they
[didn't] hire the people the bureaucrats want them to." Vandiver, criticizing
Senator Gambrell's vote against the continuation of the supersonic transport
program, contended that the vote not only endangered America's leading position in the aerospace industry but also threatened the jobs of thousands of em-

ployees of Lockheed-Georgia. If he had been in the Senate, Vandiver assured voters that he would have voted for the continuation of the program.[43]

In addition to attacking Gambrell's Senate record, Vandiver took a conservative position on court-ordered busing, law and order, foreign aid, national defense, the welfare system, and big government. He also opposed the nomination of Senator McGovern as his party's presidential nominee, telling voters that he "just might not vote in the presidential election" if McGovern received the nomination. Vandiver considered former Alabama governor George C. Wallace his pick of the Democratic candidates seeking the presidential nomination in 1972: "His thinking is more like mine than any of the other candidates." Reg Murphy, political editor of the *Atlanta Constitution,* concluded that the major candidates in the Democratic primary were taking similar conservative positions on the issues, which made it "difficult to tell one's platform from another's." Another reporter, Sam Hopkins of the *Atlanta Constitution,* noted that the major candidates in the race stood "should-to-shoulder on most matters."[44]

Vandiver denounced busing mandated by federal judges as the domestic issue that was "doing the most" to tear the country apart. He condemned the "legal whiz-kids" in the Justice Department, bureaucrats in the Department of Health, Education, and Welfare, and federal judges for busing children "all over the landscape." The former governor supported a constitutional amendment to allow the voters to decide whether they wanted "their children bused from here to Timbuktu to satisfy some social theory." He reminded Georgians of his administration's freedom-of-choice plan for students in the state's schools and promised, if elected, to work for a similar plan on the national level.[45]

The former governor called the breakdown in law and order a major societal problem that had to be addressed. "To survive, we must reestablish our society as one of law and order," Vandiver stated in a newsletter, "[and] begin to seriously *enforce* our laws." In particular, he called for the rigorous enforcement of laws regulating illegal drugs. The former governor endorsed capital punishment as a deterrent to crime and supported legislation making the killing of law enforcement agents a federal crime. Vandiver, although still professing to be a believer in states' rights, nevertheless endorsed federal aid to train state and local law enforcement agents and to supplement their salaries.[46]

In the area of foreign policy, Vandiver criticized the government for underwriting massive foreign aid programs while running up a staggering deficit. He called for cutting foreign aid "to the bone" and limiting it to efforts either to strengthen the nation's defense posture or to meet humanitarian purposes. Most of the $200 billion in foreign aid spent by the federal government since the end of World War II, the former adjutant general insisted, had "been poured down the rat holes of the world." He suggested that foreign aid money be spent at home to rebuild the economy and "rural and main street America." Vandiver called for a strong military as the best means of preserving peace and preventing aggression against the United States. He urged the nation's political leaders to reverse the trend to make America a second-rate power. Vandiver questioned American involvement in Vietnam but supported the war effort because President Johnson had put the U.S. flag there. However, he called for the United States to get out of the conflict as soon as possible. Vandiver favored legislation in Congress that would limit presidential authority to commit troops in overseas conflicts without congressional approval.[47]

Vandiver also criticized the nation's welfare system and urged Congress to reform it. If elected, he promised to support legislation to force able-bodied welfare recipients off the welfare rolls and to put them on payrolls. Although conceding that most welfare assistance was being "spent wisely" on those who truly needed help, he favored ending it for recipients who didn't work, and he endorsed legislation making welfare fraud a federal crime. He feared that the welfare system was indicative of the nation's drifting away from its puritanical work ethic.[48]

Vandiver embraced the conservative view that the federal government was getting too large, warning that everyone would be "working for some level of government by the year 2049" if the present trend continued. Accusing politicians of using "government as the catch-all for all problems" facing society, Vandiver promised to downsize the federal government by holding down taxes and finding solutions to societal problems in the private sector. Vandiver expressed concern at the federal government's intervention in the lives of citizens and, in particular, objected to the Voting Rights Act of 1965, which required state and local governments in the South to have the approval of the Justice Department prior to making changes in electoral districts and laws. If elected, he promised to introduce legislation to change that section of the law.[49]

Vandiver stressed his record of experience as mayor, adjutant general, lieutenant governor, and governor. Although calling Senator Gambrell a "fine fella and a good lawyer," the former governor attacked him for a lack of experience "except as a bond lawyer in Atlanta." He reminded the voters that, unlike himself, the "appointed senator" had never held elective office and observed that this inexperience had been costly to the state. "No other candidate," the *Rome News-Tribune* editorialized, "offers the combination of experience in government at the administrative and legislative levels." Shelby McCash, a reporter for the *Macon Telegraph-News,* concurred, "No one else matches Vandiver's political experience and success in the race."[50]

Vandiver ran his senatorial campaign as he had his previous races for statewide offices by personally campaigning in every county in the state. He added one new wrinkle to his people-to-people style by touring the state with his wife in a mobile home dubbed the Vanwagon. After three months of crisscrossing the state, Vandiver had put more than fifteen thousand miles on the Vanwagon and talked with more than three hundred thousand Georgians in visits in cities and towns in every county in the state. He described his campaigning style: "I just drove from town to town, walking the streets and shaking hands. It's the way I campaigned when I first ran for office." As he campaigned throughout the state, Vandiver carried with him a thick black notebook that contained the names of citizens and local public officials to be contacted. He wrote public officials seeking their support, a practice that resulted in one state representative telling him that he had been the only senatorial candidate "thus far" who had thought enough to send out a letter. "As far as I am concerned that goes a long way, and I shall remember it." Vandiver believed his personal campaign would enable him to get in the runoff. Bill Montgomery, a reporter with the *Atlanta Journal*, described Vandiver's campaign strategy as one based "largely upon old law school classmates, former legislators, local office holders and sheriffs" who remembered him, as well as one appealing to the newer voters by stressing his decisions to keep the schools open and not raising taxes.[51]

As most expected, Senator Gambrell led in the Democratic senatorial primary held on August 8, 1972, receiving 31.5 percent of the votes cast for a six-year senatorial term. To the surprise of many, Representative Nunn came in second with 23.2 percent of the votes, and former governor Vandiver came in third with 20.5 percent of the votes, an outcome he described as "depressing." The *Atlanta Constitution* called the results "a sad day for former Gov. Ernest Vandiver," a man who had served the state "honorably and well." Nunn lead Vandiver by 2,832 votes in rural precincts and 4,973 votes among town voters while surpassing him by 10,976 votes in the state's metropolitan areas. Even though Vandiver led Nunn in the mountain and Piedmont regions of the state, the young representative outdistanced the longtime supporter of the Talmadges in the Black Belt and south Georgia, areas that had been the backbone of the Talmadge faction in the bifactional period of recent Georgia politics. Nunn led Vandiver in the Black Belt by 26,647 votes and by 19,709 votes in south Georgia. How had a young state representative, who had never been in a statewide race, defeated a politician who had been Herman Talmadge's gubernatorial campaign manager, had won two statewide campaigns, and had been the front-runner in the 1966 governor's race until his health problem forced him to withdraw?[52]

Although many Georgians remembered Vandiver for having had a successful administration, he had entered the race with several major liabilities. He had to overcome the opposition of four former governors—Marvin Griffin, Ellis Arnall, Carl Sanders, and Lester Maddox—and that of an incumbent governor, all of whom opposed Vandiver in the primary. Certainly, Griffin had justification for opposing Vandiver's efforts to return to the governor's mansion. As lieutenant governor, Vandiver had led the opposition to the Griffin administration's rural roads bond proposal in 1958 and, while governor, had actively supported an investigation of alleged improprieties in the Griffin administration. Nor had Griffin forgiven Vandiver for supporting Sanders against him in the 1962 governor's race. Ill will also existed between Arnall and Vandiver, who had been in opposing political factions since the 1940s and who had bitterly fought each other for their party's gubernatorial nomination in 1966. After health problems forced Vandiver to withdraw from the race, he threw his support behind an anti-Arnall candidate. Vandiver believed that Sanders "was still mad" at him because of his support of Carter in the 1970 governor's race. Vandiver also contended that former governor Maddox, who had assured him of his neutrality in the primary, had been persuaded to support Nunn by Griffin. Although Carter publicly remained neutral in the Senate race, Vandiver believed that Carter was supporting Gambrell. Maddox even told Vandiver that "Carter was doing everything to get Gambrell elected." Vandiver concluded that he had every former governor in Georgia against him except Talmadge, who had promised to support him in the general election.[53]

Other problems hampered Vandiver's candidacy. He later admitted that his decision not to name a campaign manager in the 1972 race had been a mistake. He had tried to convince his 1958 campaign manager, James S. "Jim" Gilllis Sr., to manage his campaign, but the eighty-year-old former state highway board chairman declined, claiming his health and age prevented his taking on such a responsibility. Vandiver insisted that he would have been in the runoff if Gillis had managed his campaign. Instead of designating a single campaign manager, he had asked several supporters, including his former assistant adjutant general, Homer T. Flynn, and his former executive secretary, Wallace L. Jernigan, to head his campaign efforts. Others helping with the campaign included Robert L. Russell III, Keith Allen, George Woelper, Doug Kidd, and S. Ernest "Chip" Vandiver III. Former lieutenant governor Geer detected a difference in the organization of Vandiver's senatorial campaign compared with his earlier political efforts. Geer recalled receiving a call from Vandiver prior to a campaign visit to Albany: "He just called me and I met him and what little we did . . . it wasn't much. I told him . . . 'Governor, this ain't the kind of campaign we used to run.'" Another problem, according to Vandiver, was that many of his political friends who had campaigned so actively for him in the past has gotten old and preferred to stay home and watch television. Betty Vandiver concurred that the core group of supporters who had helped in previous campaigns "had gotten too old" to play an active role in her husband's senatorial campaign.[54]

Vandiver conceded to having made a "wrong decision" by promising to campaign in every county rather than concentrating on the heavily populated metropolitan counties. In retrospect, Vandiver believed that he could have made the runoff by spending more time in the metropolitan areas. Instead he concentrated on the small rural counties, believing such a strategy would give him "enough votes to get in the runoff." Vandiver's son, Chip, observed that his father "treated Columbus like Ty Ty" in his campaigning. The younger Vandiver thought his father should have been conducting "more of a media-based campaign" concentrated on the "population centers because that was where the people were that were going to vote." In the last weeks of the primary, Chip Vandiver observed that while Gambrell and Nunn were flying around the state visiting the urban counties, his father was campaigning in the rural counties of the state, practicing "the old type of politicking. It was county unit politics in a time when the county unit system wasn't there." The younger Vandiver concluded that his father "lost that Senate race in '72 because of that philosophy of campaigning."[55]

Vandiver's frugal nature stood in the way of his spending more on media publicity in his campaign. He later expressed regret that he had not borrowed one hundred thousand dollars to underwrite a media campaign to get his message out, conceding that television rather than the personal contact had become the "all important thing in politics today." James C. "Jim" Owen Jr., a close personal friend of the governor's, likewise thought Vandiver had made a mistake by not spending more money on television "to get his message out to the people better." Other supporters such as Griffin Bell and Chip Vandiver observed that many new voters had moved into the state since Vandiver had left the governorship in 1963 and they were not aware of his accomplishments. Even longtime residents had needed reminding of the accomplishments of Vandiver's administration, which had ended almost a decade earlier.[56]

Other difficulties hampered Vandiver's efforts to get in the runoff. According to the former governor, Reg Murphy, the editor of the *Atlanta Constitution,* had assured him of the paper's endorsement in the primary. However, the *Constitution* had endorsed Nunn instead, resulting in an irritated former governor calling Murphy to ask: "What the hell's going on? You said you were going to support me." Murphy, according to Vandiver, told him that he would be in the runoff without the paper's endorsement and therefore decided to endorse Nunn because "he was an up and coming politician and might be a good candidate for governor next time." Vandiver believed that the endorsement had knocked him out of the runoff because the newcomers to the state "didn't know what kind of governor" he was and the *Constitution's* endorsement had influenced them to vote for Nunn.[57]

Several additional factors hindered Vandiver in his senatorial bid. He accused Gambrell of putting former congressman Don Wheeler, who had represented the Eighth Congressional District in south Georgia, into the race to pick up support from voters in that area who would have voted for him. Betty Vandiver agreed with her husband that many people voted against him because of his decision to keep the public schools open. One of Vandiver's longtime supporters, James A. "Jim" Dunlap, who had played an active role on Vandiver's behalf in 1958, attributed Vandiver's failure to get in the runoff to voters' concerns over a candidate who had withdrawn from the governor's race in 1966 because of health reasons. Betty Vandiver concurred in the belief that "a lot of people worried about his health." Even Vandiver conceded that many voters thought his heath was not good enough to serve in the Senate. Vandiver gave another reason for his defeat. "Maybe I've been away too long," he told reporters on election night. "My last statewide race was 14 years ago." Others including Jim Dunlap, Griffin Bell, Peter Zach Geer Jr., and Henry Neal agreed with that assessment. Former state representative David C. Jones contributed another reason for Vandiver's defeat in the primary: Vandiver's political "base that had carried him to the lieutenant governorship and the governorship really no longer existed." A survey of public opinion taken in June 1972 for Senator Gambrell concluded that Vandiver was "generally popular" but that there appeared to be "little depth to his image." Senator Talmadge observed that most former governors had difficulty returning to the governor's office and that Nunn had a slogan about getting tough in Washington that "probably had more to do with it [Nunn's being in the runoff] than anything else. Everybody was mad with Washington." Former governor Sanders concluded simply that the voters "wanted a new fresh type of political leadership."[58]

Prior to the election on August 8, Vandiver and Nunn met and concluded that Gambrell would be in a runoff. They agreed that whichever one of them managed to get in the runoff would have the support of the losing candidate. Vandiver carried out his commitment by sending out twenty thousand letters to his supporters as well as telephoning many of his supporters to encourage them to vote for Nunn. In the runoff election, Nunn defeated Gambrell with more than 54 percent of the vote and then went on to defeat the Republican senatorial candidate easily. Vandiver has never regretted supporting Nunn in the runoff and in the general election in 1972 and believes that Nunn had "made a fine senator."[59]

With his defeat in the 1972 senatorial election, Vandiver realized that he would never hold elective office in Georgia again, but his avid interest in politics continued. In both the 1974 and 1978 gubernatorial elections, he actively supported George D. Busbee, who, as a young representative, had introduced the bill in the legislature creating the Sibley committee. Vandiver also actively supported Senator Talmadge's effort to turn back Zell B. Miller's challenge in the 1980 Democratic primary. Although Talmadge eventually won renomination, Vandiver contents that the senator was "so damaged by the race that Zell Miller ran against him that . . . an unknown Republican" defeated him in the general election. Vandiver voted but did not actively campaign for state representative Joe Frank Harris in the 1982 and 1986 gubernatorial races.[60]

In the 1990 election, Lieutenant Governor Zell Miller won the Democratic gubernatorial nomination and went on to defeat the Republican candidate, Guy Millner, in the general election. Miller had been a senator in the Vandiver administration and had been very supportive of the governor. However, Miller did not have Vandiver's backing in 1990 because of something that had happened years earlier when Miller had campaigned for the lieutenant governorship. At the time, Vandiver was president of the Georgia Independent Bankers Association, and Miller had contacted him seeking the support of the independent bankers in his race for lieutenant governor. The independent bankers had long considered the Senate's banking committee opposed to their interests. Miller told Vandiver that independent bankers would get "a fair shake" in his appointments to the banking committee if they supported and contributed to his campaign. As a result, Vandiver and the independent bankers actively supported Miller. Following Miller's election, Vandiver presented the lieutenant governor–elect with a list of senators friendly to independent bankers for his consideration in appointing members to the banking committee. To Vandiver's dismay, Miller, according to the former governor, appointed "the bitterest enemy of the independent bankers" chairman of the banking committee. An irritated Vandiver conceded that he "had a long memory and a tendency to hold a grudge," which accounted for his opposing Miller in 1990. Miller's campaign against Talmadge in the 1980 senatorial race probably contributed to Vandiver's opposition as well.[61]

Vandiver opposed Governor Miller's unsuccessful effort to change the state flag and his successful effort to establish a state lottery. He strongly disputes the governor's contention that the state flag was changed in 1956 to protest the *Brown v. Board of Education* decision and the federal government's support of desegregation. Vandiver, who served as lieutenant governor at the time of the flag change, contends that the change occurred "to honor Civil War veterans" and that there were "no racial overtones" motivating the change. Vandiver has always opposed a state lottery and still opposes it. However, he has commended the governor for making sure lottery funds went specifically for education. In recent years, Vandiver contends that he and Miller have put their differences aside and have become friends again.[62]

The early 1970s were not good years in Ernest Vandiver's political career. In fact, he experienced his biggest political disappointments since he had gotten involved in state politics in the days of Gene Talmadge. Vandiver had believed that Governor Carter would appoint him to the Senate in 1971 to complete Senator Russell's unexpired term. Such an appointment would certainly have made him the front-runner in the 1972 election to elect someone for a full senatorial term. Unfortunately for Vandiver, the governor had appointed Gambrell. Vandiver then entered the race to unseat the appointed senator but failed for a number of reasons: doubts among voters over his health, lingering resentment by some over his decision to keep the public schools open, opposition by former governors, his county-unit campaign strategy, his failure to spend more on media publicity, a strong campaign by Nunn, and the *Atlanta Constitution*'s failure to endorse him. In retrospect, Vandiver believed that his defeat in 1972 was "probably the best thing that happened" to him because it spared him from having to deal with the growing Watergate crisis. He also concluded, "My health is better and I have lived longer because I didn't go to Washington." However, Chip Vandiver gave a different perspective, noting that his father loved politics and practicing the art of governing: "It was the only thing he [Governor Vandiver] cared a whit about doing. He didn't care about being a lawyer. . . . That was boring." The younger Vandiver believed that his father never considered his successful business and banking career as satisfying as politics. He compared his father's involuntary removal from the political arena to "putting away a thoroughbred racing horse . . . when he's got another season left in him. It's just a lot of wasted potential."[63]

FOURTEEN

A Solid Sort of Fellow

Samuel Ernest Vandiver Jr. rose to political power in Georgia closely associated with the Talmadge faction. Vandiver's father had been a strong supporter of Eugene "Gene" Talmadge in his numerous campaigns for state office and had been appointed by Talmadge to the powerful state highway board. Vandiver joined his father in actively supporting Gene in his two unsuccessful senatorial races in the 1930s and his successful gubernatorial campaign in 1946. Not surprisingly, the younger Vandiver and Gene's son, Herman E. Talmadge, became close personal friends and political allies, a relationship that continued after both had left public office.

Governor-elect Gene Talmadge, impressed with Vandiver's efforts on his behalf, asked him to work in the governor's office as his chief aide. Talmadge's untimely death in December 1946 not only deprived Vandiver of that opportunity but also threw the state into a constitutional uproar as to who the next governor would be. Vandiver pitched in to help his friend Herman Talmadge obtain the governorship by being elected to that position by the legislature. When their efforts succeeded in January 1947, the new governor asked Vandiver to serve him as his chief aide, a position Vandiver readily accepted. Less than three months later, however, the Georgia Supreme Court invalidated Talmadge's legislative election. It held that Lieutenant Governor Melvin E. "M. E." Thompson should hold the office of governor until the general election of 1948, at which time the voters would elect someone to complete Gene Talmadge's unexpired term. Vandiver, then only thirty years of age, managed Talmadge's gubernatorial campaign in 1948, and the voters chose Talmadge to complete the remaining two years in his father's term. In appreciation for Vandiver's services as chief aide and campaign manager, Governor Talmadge appointed Vandiver to the position of state adjutant general, an appointment that made him the youngest adjutant general in the nation. He held that position for almost six years in the Talmadge administration.

However, Vandiver had higher political ambitions than adjutant general—he wanted to be governor and eventually a U.S. senator. As adjutant general Vandiver traveled extensively throughout the state and made numerous personal contacts with local politicians, a networking that proved to be of immense benefit when he sought higher office. He entered the race for his party's nomination for lieutenant governor in 1954, winning the primary with 77 percent of the county-unit vote. Four years later, he sought the Democratic Party's gubernatorial nomination and had only token opposition. The outcome of that race had already been decided in the 1958 legislative session in a power struggle between Lieutenant Governor Vandiver and Governor S. Marvin Griffin Sr. over the latter's proposed rural roads program. Vandiver easily became the party's gubernatorial nominee in 1958 by carrying all but 3 of the state's 159 counties. As governor, Vandiver succeeded in providing four years of competent and honest government but failed in his efforts to maintain segregation in the state's educational system and to save the county-unit system.

The state constitution prohibited gubernatorial succession, and Vandiver left the governorship in 1963. Unwilling to run for the U.S. Senate against two individuals he respected and admired, Vandiver turned his energies toward returning to the governor's office. Unfortunately, a heart condition forced him to withdraw from the 1966 election, a race in which he had clearly been the frontrunner. Vandiver returned to public service in 1971, when the incoming governor, James E. "Jimmy" Carter Jr., appointed him state adjutant general, a position he had held more than two decades earlier.

At first, it appeared that Senator Richard B. "Dick" Russell Jr.'s death in 1971 would provide the opportunity for Vandiver to achieve his goal of serving in the Senate. However, Vandiver again suffered a major setback in reaching a political objective—this time as a result of a governor's appointment rather than a physical ailment. Vandiver had hoped that Governor Jimmy Carter would appoint him to fill Senator Russell's unexpired term; instead, the governor turned to David H. Gambrell. Disappointed at this turn of events, the fifty-four-year-old Vandiver conducted a vigorous but unsuccessful campaign to win a full six-year senatorial term in 1972. A disappointed Vanidiver realized that his political career was over.

Vandiver ran for governor in 1958 pledging to restore the state's reputation, which had been damaged by the scandals associated with the Griffin administration. As governor, he successfully led efforts to clean up the abuses, mismanagement, and corruption that had plagued state government in the Griffin years. He pushed a tough Honesty in Government Act through the legislature, and his administration implemented competitive biding in state purchasing. The governor also created for the first time in the state's history a criminal division in the state Law Department specifically for the purpose of prosecuting corruption in state government. In addition, he obtained the creation of an economy and reorganization commission and obtained the implementation of many of its recommendations. At the urging of the governor, the state government provided financial assistance to municipalities—again, another first in Georgia's history. While protective of the powers and prerogatives of the office of the governor, Vandiver led the effort to restore the legislature's appropriation powers, which had gradually been taken over by his predecessors in the governor's office.

Governor Vandiver, a careful and prudent money manager, insisted on efficient operation of state government and governmental services. Owing in large part to his administration's success in this effort, the governor increased state spending by almost 30 percent in four years without raising taxes. His administration also undertook a significant building program and a major expansion of state services, again without a tax increase. To its credit, the Vandiver administration focused attention on an area of state government that had been too long ignored and neglected: its treatment of its citizens with mental problems. The state began the process of upgrading its mental health treatment program and made it one of the best in the nation.

At the direction of the governor, the state also stepped up its efforts to recruit industry and to expand foreign trade. Vandiver, realizing the importance of providing vocational education as an integral part of economic development, committed the state government to expanding significantly the number of vocational educational schools. In order to expand trade with foreign countries, the Vandiver administration also substantially improved and enlarged the state's port facilities. The governor, realizing the economic benefits of the tourist industry, substantially increased the state's efforts to attract tourists to the state and, for the first time, made tourism a major focus of state government. Vandiver took pride in the fact that, although the state had been on the verge of bankruptcy when he took office, his administration managed to get the state financial house in order and left his successor with a substantial surplus in the state treasury.

Many of Vandiver's contemporaries in public service praised him for his decisions to keep the state's public schools and university system open rather than resorting to the tactic that some southern governors had unsuccessfully tried of closing them to avoid desegregation. Former governor George D. Busbee called the decision to keep the schools open the major accomplishment of the Vandiver administration. Former lieutenant governor George T. Smith agreed, calling Vandiver's decision to keep the schools open "courageous" in light of his campaign promise to close them rather than allow their desegregation. Zell B. Miller, who served in the state Senate during the Vandiver administration, concurred, contending that Vandiver "had the courage to change his mind on integrating the University of Georgia. If he had 'stood in the door' Georgia would be more like Alabama today." [1]

Others, such as William R. "Bill" Bowdoin, former head of the state's Purchasing Department in the Vandiver administration; former governor Carl E. Sanders; former assistant state attorney general Henry G. Neal; former governor Herman Talmadge; and former state attorney general Robert H. "Bob" Hall acclaimed Vandiver's restoring integrity in state government as his administration's most significant accomplishment. Homer M. Rankin, former president of the Georgia Press Association, considered Vandiver's greatest accomplishment to have been putting "the government of the state back on a totally respectable basis." Former assistant state attorney general E. Freeman Leverett believed that the Vandiver administration had begun "an enlightened period in state government that did put a high degree of credence . . . in honesty in government." Bill Bowdoin, who later served as chairman of the Governor's Commission on Efficiency and Improvement in Government during Carl Sanders's tenure as chief executive, called Vandiver an "able and conscientious" governor whose "administration laid the cornerstone for a more efficient and modern government." [2]

Herman Talmadge called Vandiver a strong governor who was "far better than the average governor and better than most people thought." Another former chief executive of the state, Carl Sanders, also considered Vandiver a strong governor who provided the state with honest and able leadership. Former lieutenant governor Garland T. Byrd, former chairman of the Georgia Ports Authority Robert C. "Bob" Norman, former board of regents member James C. "Jim" Owen Jr., and former Governor George Busbee likewise characterized Vandiver as a strong governor. Busbee considered Vandiver "strong willed," a trait that made it "kind of hard to make him change his mind." Former lieutenant governor George Smith described Vandiver as one who could be considered "stubborn," hastily adding however, "If a governor's not stubborn he ain't a governor." [3]

Vandiver never considered himself "a very good politician" because of his being "a little bit too outspoken" and his not finding campaigning "pleasurable." Former senator Herman Talmadge characterized Vandiver as a politician who "was not a flashy type" or "a dynamic political leader, but he was a solid sort of fellow like the man you wanted to be executor of your estate." Sanders agreed that Vandiver was not a charismatic leader, but Vandiver's former executive secretary, Peter Zach Geer Jr., disagreed, contending that his former boss had "charisma. He was a very handsome man. He had coal black curly hair, and he had very penetrating blue eyes, and he was clean cut and well spoken. He had a sincerity about him that was not made up at all; it was genuine." Ralph E. McGill Sr., publisher of the *Atlanta Constitution*, considered Vandiver "a nice fellow with gentlemanly manners" who had a quiet personality but lacked political appeal and "has not exhibited much ability."[4]

Charles Pou, political reporter for the *Atlanta Constitution*, conceded that Vandiver was "not the baby-tickling, rollicking, I-knew-your-Aunt Fanny type politician; he was, nevertheless, easy to talk to, a good listener, ruggedly handsome, and, above all, patently sincere in what he said and promised." Longtime friend Bob Norman admitted that, while Vandiver was not a typical backslapping politician, he was friendly and cheerful and had "a warm, inviting way about him." Former state senator DeNean Stafford Jr. concurred that Vandiver was not as extroverted as most politicians, and Busbee described him as someone who was reserved but was, nevertheless, "very enjoyable to be around" because he liked people. Longtime friend Jim Owen contended that Vandiver had a good personality even though he would never qualify as the "jester of the court." A former state representative in the Vandiver years, William D. Ballard, considered Vandiver "a good politician" who was "one of the most likable people" he had ever met.[5]

Former lieutenant governor George Smith commended Vandiver for his political skills, contending, "Any man that can get elected governor is a good politician." He agreed that Vandiver tended to be reserved and serious and lacked the "happy-go-lucky" personality of former governor Griffin. Federal district judge Bob Hall, who had headed the criminal division in the state Law Department in Vandiver's administration, concurred that Vandiver did not have the "hail-fellow-well-met" personality of Marvin Griffin. Betty Vandiver agreed that her husband tended to be on the serious side: "He says what needs to be said, and he's not much of just idle talk." Vandiver's former chief of staff Griffin B. Bell contended that Vandiver had a "very warm personality" but one that was not as colorful as Marvin Griffin's because he was "a serious-minded person" who never developed "a colorful approach to life." Former state representative David C. Jones, who served in the legislature while Vandiver was governor, concluded that Vandiver's more reserved nature gave some people "the idea that he was sort of pompous." Former state assistant attorney general Freeman Leverett conceded that Vandiver lacked the humor or contagious personality of an outgoing politician like former governor Griffin.[6]

Certainly Vandiver qualified as a fiscal conservative. Former senator Herman Talmadge attributed Vandiver's frugality to the influence of his father. According to Talmadge, Vandiver spent "the state's money just like he would've his own, which was frugal." Geer agreed, calling Vandiver "a thrifty man. You might call him tight." Others, including longtime friend James A. Dunlap, former state representative Glenn W. Ellard, former lieutenant governor Garland Byrd, and former chief of staff Griffin Bell, attested to Vandiver's fiscal conservatism. Chip Vandiver concurred that his father was "tight, tight, tight from a financial standpoint, and he carried that frugality into office." Former state representative William L. "Bill" Lanier Sr. described Vandiver as being "as tight on money as bark is on oak. Some politicians have trouble saying no, and Ernie had trouble saying yes."[7]

During the period of the 1930s through the 1950s, some of Georgia's most flamboyant politicians—Eurith Dickinson "Ed" Rivers Sr., Eugene Talmadge, Ellis Gibbs Arnall, Herman Eugene Talmadge, and Samuel Marvin Griffin Sr.—pranced across the state's political stage. Vandiver, who had heard the rhetoric of these politicians, insisted that his speaking style was his own and not an imitation of anyone else's. Freeman Leverett considered Vandiver a good speaker even though he was not a spellbinder or eloquent. Former senator Talmadge deemed him a good speaker but not "a great flaming orator." Bill Lanier noted that Vandiver never put much emotionalism in his speeches, unlike most of his political contemporaries. Garland Byrd classified him as a "good speaker" even though he had a tendency to rely on prepared speeches. Bell considered Vandiver "a very good speaker" who was capable of giving "a good solid speech." Henry Neal described Vandiver as "a strong speaker with a deep resonant voice that you could hear without the use of microphones" and one who spoke "clearly and distinctly, and commanded the attention of the audience."[8]

George T. Smith, while classifying Vandiver a "good speaker," did not consider him "an orator in Herman Talmadge's field" or a speaker as entertaining as Marvin Griffin. He contended that Vandiver, unlike Griffin, "never did put much foolishness in his talks. His talk was all meat, and he went straight to the point and covered it that way." William Ballard succinctly contrasted Vandiver's speaking style with that of Marvin Griffin's: "Ernie talked business. Marvin, he'd talk to you about the catfish pond." Betty Vandiver agreed that her husband's speeches tended to be serious, explaining that it was not his nature "to bring in a whole lot of levity in his speaking." Chip Vandiver compared the tone of his father's speeches to the tone that his father used with him when he had done something wrong. Bill Bowdoin called Vandiver a "mediocre, not a bombastic, hell-raising speaker." He contended that while Griffin's performance on the political stump resembled "an old-time medicine show," Vandiver was "not a particular showman." Former congressman Robert G. Stephens described Vandiver as not being "an orator in the sense of a spellbinder. He got his points across, and he wasn't stumbling or mumbling, but he was not known as a real orator."[9]

Throughout his public career, Vandiver took great pride in his reputation for honesty and for being a man of integrity. Although Vandiver's father has always been interested in politics, his mother considered politics corrupting and discouraged her son from a political career. Vandiver promised his mother that if he ever was elected to office he intended to be an honest politician and that he was not going to do anything that she would be ashamed of. Vandiver believes that he has lived up to his promise to his mother. One of his daughters, Jane B. Kidd, agreed, contending that her father had more integrity than anybody she had ever known. His other daughter, Vanna E. "Beth" Vandiver, called him probably the most honest person she had ever known. Chip Vandiver called his father "very honest, direct, very little guile about him." Henry Neal called him "scrupulously honest," and Geer credited Vandiver with setting a high standard of ethics and honesty in state government that has endured. One longtime friend, Jim Owen, described Vandiver as one who "doesn't have anything to sweep under the rug or to go lock up. His life is an open record." George T. Smith contended that Vandiver reestablished the people's confidence in state government in the aftermath of the Griffin scandals. Smith further contended that Vandiver was able to do so "because he was an honest, upright man." Bill Lanier described Vandiver as a "clean and honest and honorable man." One of Lanier's colleagues in the House, David C. Jones, agreed that Vandiver "had a reputation for integrity." Ralph McGill agreed that Vandiver was "personally honest." One of the state's leading authorities on Georgia governors, James F. Cook, concluded, "No hint of scandal was ever associated with the Vandiver administration."[10]

Vandiver always insisted on ethical conduct by those in state government during his administration. Ivan Allen Jr., who later served as mayor of Atlanta, had supported Vandiver in the 1958 governor's race. Early in the new administration, Allen expressed his desire to the governor for an appointment to the state board of regents. However, Vandiver had just recently obtained legislative approval of his Honesty in Government Act, which prohibited businessmen who sold to the state from serving on state boards or commissions. Vandiver offered to appoint Allen, head of one of the state's largest office supplies companies, if the Ivan Allen Company ceased doing business with the state. Allen declined to do so, and Vandiver never appointed him to the board of regents.[11]

There were numerous examples of Vandiver taking action on what he considered improper conduct. On one occasion, Governor Vandiver forced Guyton Deloach, director of the Georgia Forestry Commission, to resign because of alleged improper conduct on his part. The governor had suspected Deloach, who had been director of the Forestry Commission since 1949, of receiving kick-backs on machinery purchased by the Forestry Department. After gathering sufficient evidence against DeLoach, Vandiver called him to the governor's office, presented him with the evidence, and obtained his resignation. George P. Whitman Sr., an appointee of Marvin Griffin, also was called on the carpet by Vandiver. Whitman, who was chairman of the state board of education, had contributed twelve thousand dollars to Vandiver's 1958 gubernatorial campaign. After the election, Whitman met with members of the state board of education and without discussing the matter with Governor Vandiver told them what the board would do in the new administration. Upon learning of this discussion, the governor summonsed Whitman to his office and demanded his resignation, telling him that only one of them could be governor. After receiving the requested resignation, Vandiver returned Whitman's financial contribution to his 1958 campaign. Mills B. Lane Jr., the president of the largest bank in the state at that time, offered to back Vandiver in the 1958 gubernatorial race provided he could name the state banking superintendent, who was an appointee of the governor. Vandiver refused the offer, telling Lane that he would not be much of a governor if he gave up the right to make appointments to fill positions in his administration. Betty Vandiver recalled that on several occasions her husband returned campaign contributions to supporters after they made demands on the governor. Vandiver returned more than fifteen thousand dollars in campaign contributions in his 1958 campaign: "I was fearful that these contributions were made in an effort to tie my hands and prevent me from acting in the public interest." [12]

Certainly no one ever accused Vandiver of making rash or quick decisions. Betty Vandiver describes her husband's decision-making process as "slow and deliberate." She observes that if her husband "says something, you know he's thought about it, and he wouldn't say it if he didn't mean it." After he considers an issue from every angle and makes up his mind, Betty Vandiver insists, "it's over, and then we don't have to worry about that anymore." The youngest of the Vandiver children, Jane Kidd, considered her father as a person who was very thorough "and detail oriented and fact oriented" rather than "emotional and feelings oriented" in making decisions. George T. Smith described Vandiver as a leader who "really listened to his advisors, and that's one of the hardest things in the world to do in a place of leadership." Vandiver agreed: "[I] always sought as much advice as I can [obtain] when I had decisions to make. Didn't always follow it. But I did . . . what I thought was best." [13]

Like the state's other chief executives since the 1930s, Vandiver believed that the state government should promote economic development and support programs for the betterment of the lives and well-being of its citizenry. Governor

Eugene Talmadge, however, had rejected such positive governmental roles. He had believed that the most important functions of state government were protecting the state's racial status quo, safeguarding the county-unit system, keeping taxes low, and minimizing state economic regulation. Whereas Gene Talmadge had favored a minimalist government, his successor in the governor's office, Ed Rivers, had a more liberal philosophy and had enthusiastically embraced New Deal programs as the means of improving the lives of citizens in one of the poorest states in the Union. However, the legislature had refused to raise taxes to fund his "Little New Deal" adequately, and Rivers had left office with the state heavily in debt and his administration damaged by allegations of corruption. In contrast, Ellis Arnall, who served as governor during World War II, had paid off the state debt, expanded state services without raising taxes, led the state's efforts to promote economic progress, and left office with his administration untainted by corruption charges.[14]

Herman Talmadge, although a staunch defender of the racial status quo, had not held his father's negative role of state government and had supported policies and programs that had contributed to the economic modernization of the state. In fact, expenditures for services and infrastructure had increased dramatically in his tenure as chief executive. His successor in the governor's chair, Marvin Griffin, had further expanded state services but had left office, like Rivers, amid allegations of misconduct in his administration and with the state burdened with debt. While neither Gene Talmadge nor Ellis Arnall had sought tax increases, Ed Rivers had—but without success. Tax increases had taken place in the administrations of Herman Talmadge and Marvin Griffin. The fiscally conservative Vandiver had expanded state services and promoted economic development without raising taxes. Unlike Griffin and Rivers, Vandiver had departed from the governor's office without allegations of misconduct and with a surplus in the state treasury.[15]

Carl Sanders had been elected governor in 1962 promising to continue the Vandiver style of honest, progressive, and responsible government. He had likewise fostered economic and industrial progress in the state. Unlike the more conservative Vandiver, however, Governor Sanders successfully obtained a tax increase to pay for his expansion of services. By the end of the Sanders's administration, the chief function of Georgia's state government had clearly shifted from protecting white supremacy to promoting economic progress. As a result of Vandiver's leadership in keeping the state's schools open, Sanders and future governors and legislators had the opportunity to devote their time and energy to issues rather than defending segregation.[16]

Vandiver, like his political contemporaries in Georgia and other southern states, had entered public life in the 1940s as a segregationist. He had become an active member of the Talmadge faction, the most conservative faction in the state's bifactional politics. This group—whose leadership included Herman Talmadge, Roy V. Harris, and Marvin Griffin—included some of the staunchest defenders of segregation, who willing to close the state's schools rather than to see them desegregated. Unlike the Talmadges, Marvin Griffin, and Ernest Vandiver, Ed Rivers, one of the principal organizers of the anti-Talmadge faction in the 1930s, never used the race issue in his political campaigns. Another leader in the anti-Talmadge faction, Ellis Arnall, promised in his 1942 gubernatorial campaign to protect segregation in Georgia. However, Governor Arnall had earned the condemnation of the Talmadgites for complying with the federal judiciary's mandate to allow black participation in the state's primaries. Nor did Arnall's friendship with Vice President Henry A. Wallace, a liberal and outspoken critic of segregation, endear Talmadgites to him. Arnall's national speaking tour after leaving the governorship and his many publications, including two books in which he discussed the problems of the state and the South, further alienated many whites. Vandiver considered Arnall a politician who was "extremely liberal" and who was too liberal for Georgia. To the consternation of Talmadgites, Arnall had threatened to run for governor in 1962 on a platform of keeping the state's schools open and had even publicly attacked the county-unit system before the federal judiciary's invalidation of it.[17]

When the Supreme Court handed down its decision in *Brown v. Board of Education,* most southern liberals had urged gradual compliance and acceptance of desegregation. Ralph McGill, editor of the *Atlanta Constitution* and one of the best-known liberals in the state and the South, had defended the separate-but-equal doctrine as having been best for the South, but he had urged his fellow southern whites to accept the Court's decision. Vandiver had joined the racial conservatives in the state—which included Senator Russell, Senator Talmadge, former state House Speaker Roy V. Harris, state House Speaker pro tempore George L. Smith II, Garland T. Byrd, and Governor Griffin—in opposition to complying with the decision. Conservatives in the state and in the South had attempted to nullify the *Brown* ruling by enacting massive-resistance legislation, which included closing the public schools to avoid their desegregation. Vandiver had supported, as did most southern politicians during this time, massive resistance and had verbally assailed those calling for the end of segregation.[18]

Nevertheless, Vandiver had on occasion criticized defenders of segregation. While lieutenant governor, he had criticized Arkansas governor Orval E. Faubus for using the Arkansas National Guard in a hopeless effort to prevent the implementation of a federal court order desegregating an all-white high school

in Little Rock. To counter this challenge to federal authority, President Eisenhower had ordered federal troops to Little Rock to bring about compliance with
the federal court order. Lieutenant Governor Vandiver had complained to a reporter that Governor Faubus's actions were "going to speed up integration here
and elsewhere" five to ten years. "They are cheering him, when actually he's cutting our throats." On the other hand, Vandiver, while governor, had criticized
Virginia governor J. Lindsey Almond Jr., a staunch massive-resistance advocate,
for reversing his position on school desegregation in 1959 and successfully urging his state's legislature to keep the state's schools open and to enact a local-
option policy. Interestingly, Vandiver had duplicated Almond's course of action
two years later.[19]

By the end of 1959 massive-resistance efforts in the South had collapsed, and
only the states of Alabama, Georgia, Louisiana, Mississippi, and South Carolina
had not experienced school desegregation. Those states had almost exhausted
their delaying tactics, and it was only a matter of time before school desegregation would occur even in those states. Louisiana governor Jimmie H. Davis, a
militant segregationist, had taken over control of the New Orleans public schools
in 1960 in a last-ditch effort to prevent desegregation. The governor's efforts
failed, and desegregation finally occurred in Louisiana following the state legislature's refusal to appropriate money to finance tuition grants and the U.S. Supreme Court's ruling against the state's last attempts to maintain segregation.[20]

Desegregation occurred in Mississippi in 1962 despite the strong opposition
of Governor Ross R. Barrnet, who invoked the doctrine of interposition in an
effort to nullify a federal court order admitting a black applicant to the University of Mississippi. He, like numerous other southern diehards, had promised
never to yield to federal judiciary tyranny. Governor Barnett's failure to exercise
responsible leadership came at a high cost: 160 federal marshals were injured,
2 individuals were killed, hundreds had been arrested, and more than 6,000 federal troops had been sent to the University of Mississippi by President John F.
Kennedy to restore law and order and to carry out the federal court order. The
"Battle of Oxford" ended the most serious confrontation between a state government and the national government since the Civil War.[21]

In Alabama, George C. Wallace had been elected governor in 1962, promising to maintain segregated schools in the state by refusing to abide by federal
court desegregation orders "even to the point of standing at the school house
door." The governor had pledged segregation forever in his inaugural address
and had preached defiance of the federal judiciary efforts to enroll two black
students at the University of Alabama in 1963. As promised in his campaign, the
governor literally stood in a doorway at the university in a symbolic effort to pre-

vent the black student from enrolling at the university. Wallace's defiance collapsed after President Kennedy federalized the Alabama National Guard, and shortly thereafter desegregation occurred at the University of Alabama.[22]

Desegregation occurred in South Carolina with the peaceable desegregation of Clemson College in 1963. Outgoing governor Ernest F. Hollings, who like Vandiver had been elected to the state's highest public office as a militant segregationist, told the legislature in 1963 that the state was running out of legal remedies to maintain segregation. Hollings urged the legislature to accept the pending desegregation with dignity and with law and order for the good of the state and nation. Shortly after his remarks, Harvey Gantt quietly enrolled at Clemson College and became the first black to attend a previously all-white educational facility in South Carolina.[23]

Vandiver, like governors Almond and Hollings, reversed his position on school desegregation and accepted with dignity the inevitable ending of segregated schools. Like Almond and Hollings, Vandiver feared the detrimental effect the closing of schools would have on the state's children and the negative impact that it would have on the state's economic development. Vanidiver declined to adopt the option used by governors Faubus, Wallace, and Barnett of defying the federal courts in a desperate effort to save segregated schools. To his and the state's credit, Vandiver provided the necessary leadership to allow the desegregation of schools to take place in Georgia without the intervention of federal troops, without the federalizing of the state's National Guard, without bloodshed, and with the state's reputation intact.

A significant transition in the state began in the Vandiver administration. The old order based on racial segregation and rural political domination endured fatal blows from the federal judiciary in the early 1960s. The state, bowing to the pressure of the federal judges, began the difficult process of dismantling a dual school system with the support of Governor Vandiver. Another change occurred when the federal courts held that the county-unit system of nominating state officials was unconstitutional. Vandiver led an effort to make the malapportioned nominating system more equitable in order to save it, but that attempt was unacceptable to lower federal judges. After the U.S. Supreme Court announced its intention of reviewing the invalidation of the county-unit system but only after the 1962 primary elections, Governor Vandiver accepted the inevitable and concluded that the state had done all it could do to save the county-unit system. The executive committee of the state's Democratic Party, adopting his recommendation that the 1962 Democratic primary be based on popular rather than county-unit votes, held the first primary based on a popular vote basis in the state since 1908. As Vandiver had anticipated, the nation's High Court invalidated the unit system in 1963.

When Vandiver had entered the governor's office in 1959, the old order had been solidly entrenched. When he departed four years later, it had been demolished, and a new order was in the process of coming into existence. Black Georgians had voted in increased numbers, the legal structure of segregation in the state's schools had been dismantled, and urban citizens had replaced their rural counterparts as the dominant influence in state politics. The governor who held office during this turbulent period in the state's history considered himself an "average person" who had "the qualities of a good person." Vandiver was a member of the First Baptist Church of Lavonia since he was twelve years of age. Vandiver tried his "best to live a good life," admitting that he was not perfect, readily conceding his tendency to hold grudges. After leaving the governorship, Vandiver had practiced law first in Atlanta and later with his son in Lavonia but eventually gave up being an active partner in the firm. He served several terms on the board of trustees of the Southern Baptist Theological Seminary in Louisville, Kentucky, and continues to serve as president of Georgia Seed Company, Inc., a company his father started. Other business activities include serving as chairman of the board of directors of the Northeast Georgia Bank of Lavonia, president of the Georgia Association of Independent Bankers, president of the board of directors of the Lavonia Development Corporation, and member of the executive council of the National Independent Bankers. He has also served as president of Roadside Sales, Inc., president of Bar Q Ranch Inc. and president of Stuckey's Franchise Advisory Board. A proud alumnus of the University of Georgia, Vandiver has been very supportive of the university, including being a member of the President's Club.[24]

Ernest Vandiver gave the state fifteen years of dedicated, responsible, and competent public service. Although he could point with pride to a long list of major accomplishments, the defining moment of his political career occurred with his decision to keep the state's public schools and institutions of higher education open. He made that decision despite a campaign promise to the contrary, anticipating that it would end his political career. Nevertheless, Vandiver believed that his political interests were secondary to the state's well-being and future. He concluded that further resistance to the federal judiciary on the school desegregation issue would damage the state's reputation and be injurious to its economic growth and development. Despite his strong opposition to school desegregation, he believed that the state had reached the point where it could no longer resist and had to comply with the federal judiciary's mandate to desegregate. Refusing to following the examples of some southern governors, who bitterly resisted the federal courts' school desegregation efforts, Vandiver accepted the inevitable with dignity and grace and made a conscious effort to abide by something he found totally objectionable. He took pride in the fact that desegregation of the state's educational systems took place without loss of life and without the intervention of federal troops. His efforts to return to the governor's office and to serve in the U.S. Senate proved to be unsuccessful, and he would never hold public office again. Such a loss was unfortunate, for it deprived the Empire State of the South of his vast experience, his political courage, and his willingness to accommodate change for the good of the state.

NOTES

ONE. Franklin County Roots

1. *Lavonia Times,* February 23, 1934; Franklin County Historical Society, *History of Franklin County,* 40, 49.

2. Samuel Ernest Vandiver Jr., interview by author, September 15, 1993, Samuel Ernest Vandiver Jr. Oral History Collection 4G, pp. 16–21, S. Ernest Vandiver Papers, Richard B. Russell Library for Political Research and Studies, University of Georgia Libraries, Athens (interviews in the Samuel Ernest Vandiver Jr. Oral History Collection hereafter cited as OH Vandiver; all interviews in the Vandiver Oral History Collection were done by the author); Wellington Vandiver to ————, January 25, 1922, copy of letter in possession of Vandiver; Franklin County Historical Society, *History of Franklin County,* 535–36.

3. Franklin County Historical Society, *History of Franklin County,* 536; Vandiver, OH Vandiver 4G, p. 26; Samuel Ernest Vandiver Jr., September 14, 1993, OH Vandiver 4A, pp. 6–7.

4. Vandiver, OH Vandiver 4A, pp. 6, 10, 12; "Facts about the NEW Heavy Fruiter 5 Cotton," Georgia Seed Company brochure in possession of Vandiver.

5. *Lavonia Times,* October 30, 1931; Ernest Vandiver Sr.'s cotton acreage stated in an advertisement in *Lavonia Times,* August 29, 1930; advertisements in *Lavonia Times,* September 15, 8, 1933, September 25, June 8, 1931, February 12, 1932, and May 22, 1936.

6. Vandiver, OH Vandiver 4G, pp. 29–30; ibid. 4A, p. 3.

7. Ibid. 4A, pp. 2–3; ibid. 4G, pp. 22–24; Franklin County Historical Society, *History of Franklin County,* 403–4; *Lavonia Times,* September 15, 1911.

8. Vandiver, OH Vandiver 4G, pp. 26–28.

9. Ibid., p. 30; Louise Dixon Akin, September 14, 1993, OH Vandiver 32, p. 2; William Herbert Bonner, March 19, 1994, OH Vandiver 20, p. 3; Sybil Elizabeth "Betty" Vandiver, January 22, 1994, OH Vandiver 13A, pp. 49–50; Vandiver, OH Vandiver 4A, p. 17; *Lavonia Times,* May 11, 1951; Franklin County Historical Society, *History of Franklin County,* 194, 275–76, 371.

10. Bonner, OH Vandiver 20, p. 2; *Lavonia Times,* January 10, 1941; Vandiver, OH Vandiver 4A, pp. 4–5; *Lavonia Times,* January 10, 1941.

11. Vandiver, OH Vandiver 4A, p. 12; Marie H. Williams, *Lavonia, Gem of the Piedmont,* 10–11; U.S. Bureau of the Census, *Tenth Census of the United States, 1880: Statistics of the Population of the United States,* 55, 123; U.S. Bureau of the Census, *Fifteenth Census of the United States, 1930, Population, 3, Part 1, Alabama-Missouri,* 534, 548, 514.

12. Vandiver, OH Vandiver 4A, pp. 14–21; *Lavonia Times,* September 22, 1933, and May 17, 1935; Bonner, OH Vandiver 20, p. 6; Akin, OH Vandiver 32, p. 2.

13. Interview of Samuel Ernest Vandiver Jr. by Melvin T. Steeley and Theodore B. Fitzsimons, June 25, 1986, Georgia Political Heritage Series, Special Collections, Irvin S. Ingrams Library, State University of West Georgia, Carrollton. This interview has been transcribed by the Richard B. Russell Library for Political Research and Studies, University of Georgia Libraries, Athens (hereafter cited as Russell Library) and is henceforth cited as OH Vandiver 1; Vandiver, June 25, 1986, OH Vandiver 1A, pp. 4–5; Vandiver, OH Vandiver, 4A, pp. 7, 14; Samuel Ernest Vandiver Jr., interview by Charles B. Pyles, April (n.d.) 1990, pp. 6–7, Georgia Government Documentation Project, Special Collections, Pullen Library, Georgia State University, Atlanta (hereafter cited as Pullen Library); Bonner, OH Vandiver 20, p. 4.

14. Vandiver, OH Vandiver 4G, pp. 33–35.

15. Ibid., 4A, pp. 15–16.

16. Ibid., 4G, pp. 31–33.

17. Ernest Vandiver Jr. to Ernest Vandiver Sr., August 15, 1933, and October 18, 1935, letters in possession of Vandiver; Vandiver, OH Vandiver 4G, pp. 31–32; Samuel Ernest Vandiver Jr., interview, name of interviewer not given, June 23, 1987, pp. 5–6, Vandiver interview transcript folder, "Dawn's Early Light: Ralph McGill and the Segregated South," 1988 documentary co-produced by Jed Dannenbaum and Kathleen Dowdey, Special Collections, Robert W. Woodruff Library, Emory University, Atlanta; Katherine Barnwell, "How the Vandivers Live," *Atlanta Journal-Constitution Magazine,* January 4, 1959, 46; Vandiver, OH Vandiver, 4A, pp. 17–19.

18. Vandiver, OH Vandiver 4A, pp. 4, 24, 23; Bonner, OH Vandiver 20, pp. 4–5; Samuel Ernest Vandiver Jr., interview by Hugh Cates, February 23, 1971, Richard B. Russell Oral History Collection, Russell Library, p. 1 (hereafter cited as Russell Oral History Collection); Vandiver, OH Vandiver 1A, p. 7.

19. Vandiver, OH Vandiver 1A, p. 7; Herman Eugene Talmadge, August 26, 1993, OH Vandiver 2, p. 1; *Lavonia Times,* September 16, 1932, and January 20, 1933; Vandiver, OH Vandiver 1A, p. 14; *Lavonia Times,* September 8, 1933.

20. *Lavonia Times,* September 8, 1933; Vandiver, OH Vandiver 1A, pp. 14–15; Fite,

Richard B. Russell, Jr., 137–48; Vandiver, OH Vandiver 4A, pp. 27–28; *Lavonia Times,* September 13, 1936.

21. Vandiver interview by Pyles, 11–12; *Lavonia Times,* September 16, 1938.

22. Sutton, "Talmadge Campaigns," 204; *Lavonia Times,* January 17, 1941; Vandiver, OH Vandiver 1A, p. 8; *Lavonia Times,* January 17, 1942.

23. Bonner, OH Vandiver 20, p. 10; Vandiver, OH Vandiver 4A, pp. 3, 21; Vandiver's Darlington School transcript and Ernest Vandiver Jr. to Ernest Vandiver Sr. and Vanna Vandiver, November 24, 1935, letter in possession of Vandiver.

24. Vandiver, OH Vandiver 4A, p. 22; Ernest Vandiver Jr. to Ernest Vandiver Sr. and Vanna Vandiver, October 18, 1935, letter in possession of Vandiver; *Jabberwolk 1936* (Darlington School annual), 38; Vandiver, OH Vandiver 4G, p. 40; Vandiver's Darlington School transcript.

25. Vandiver, OH Vandiver 4A, pp. 28–29; typed biographical information provided to author by Vandiver; copy of goals provided to author by Vandiver; Vandiver, OH Vandiver 4A, p. 29.

26. James Coleman Owen Jr., March 16, 1994, OH Vandiver 21, p. 2; Robert Claude Norman, June 9, 1994, OH Vandiver 25, pp. 3, 5; James Anderson Dunlap, March 18, 1994, OH Vandiver 17, pp. 4–5.

27. Vandiver, OH Vandiver 4A, pp. 31–34.

28. Ibid., *Lavonia Times,* January 11, 1946, October 26 and December 14, 1945, and February 1, 1946; Vandiver, OH Vandiver 4A, pp. 36–37; Vandiver, OH Vandiver 1A, pp. 17–18.

29. Vandiver, OH Vandiver 4A, p. 35; *Lavonia Times,* January 10, 1947; U.S. Bureau of the Census, *Census of Population: 1950, 2, Characteristics of the Population, Part 11, Georgia,* 11, 14 (hereafter cited as *Census of the Population: 1950, 2, Part 11*).

30. Vandiver, OH Vandiver 4A, p. 38; Fite, *Richard B. Russell, Jr.,* 37–121; Samuel Ernest Vandiver Jr., September 14, 1993, OH Vandiver 4B, pp. 24–25.

31. Fite, "Richard Brevard Russell," 2:859–60; *Census of Population: 1950, 2, Part 11,* 11.

32. Typed biographical information provided to author by Vandiver; Betty Vandiver, OH Vandiver 13A, pp. 2–9.

33. Betty Vandiver, OH Vandiver 13A, pp. 34–36, 11, 13–14.

34. Ibid., pp. 6–8, 14–15; typed biographical information provided to author by Betty Vandiver.

35. Betty Vandiver, OH Vandiver 13A, pp. 23–26, 28.

36. Ibid., pp. 17–19, 21.

37. Ibid., pp. 18, 21–22.

38. Ibid., p. 26; Virginia W. Russell to Betty Vandiver, June 26, 1947, Richard B. Russell Jr. to Betty Vandiver, June 23, 1947, Henry E. Russell to Betty Vandiver, June 19, 1947, Ernest Vandiver Sr. to Robert L. and Sybil N. Russell, August (n.d.) 1947, letters in possession of Betty Vandiver.

39. *Winder News* article on the marriage reprinted in *Lavonia Times,* September 19, 1947.

TWO. Georgia at Midcentury

1. U.S. Bureau of the Census, *Census of Population: 1950, 1, Number of Inhabitants*, 14, 21.

2. *Census of Population: 1950, 2, Part 11*, 35, 37–38, 35, 6; U.S. Bureau of the Census, *Census of Population: 1960, 1, Characteristics of the Population, Part 12, Georgia*, 13.

3. U.S. Bureau of the Census, *Census of Population: 1950, Characteristics of the Population, 2, United States Summary, Part 1*, 106; *Census of Population: 1950, 2, Part 11*, 39, 56, 54.

4. Joiner, general ed., *History of Public Education in Georgia*, 73; Saye, *Constitutional History of Georgia*, 288; Wynes, "Education, Life, and Culture," 247–49; Bartley, "Race Relations," 361.

5. Bureau of Business Research, College of Business Administration, University of Georgia, *Georgia Statistical Abstract, 1955*, 148, 155; Meadows, *Modern Georgia*, 281, 257; *Georgia Statistical Abstract, 1955*, 54, 149; *Census of Population: 1950, 2, Part 11*, 54.

6. *Census of Population: 1950, 2, Part 11*, 54; Meadows, *Modern Georgia*, 281, 285; *Census of Population: 1950, 2, Part 11*, 50, 54; Meadows, *Modern Georgia*, 281.

7. U.S. Bureau of the Census, *Statistical Abstract of the United States, 1952*, 258; U.S. Bureau of the Census, *Statistical Abstract of the United States, 1953*, 117, 110, 121.

8. Bartley, *From Thurmond to Wallace*, 13–33, 45–46, 2–3.

9. Department of Archives and History, Mrs. J. E. Hays, comp., *Georgia's Official Register, 1945–1950*, 75–201; *Census of Population: 1950, 2, Part 11*, 37–38.

10. Saye, *Constitutional History of Georgia*, 364; *Census of Population: 1950, 2, Part 11*, 37–38; Rigdon, *Georgia's County Unit System*, 40.

11. Boney, "Politics of Expansion and Secession," 36–48; Clark and Kirwan, *South since Appomattox*, 52; Key, with Heard, *Southern Politics in State and Nation*, 9.

12. Williamson, "Contemporary Tendencies," 21; Kenneth Coleman, general ed., *History of Georgia*, app. A, 411–12; Williamson, "Contemporary Tendencies," 52–55; Bass and DeVries, *Transformation of Southern Politics*, 34–35.

13. U.S. Bureau of the Census, *Historical Statistics of the United States: Colonial Times to 1970, Part 2*, 1075–76; Seagull, *Southern Republicanism*, 41; Shadgett, *Republican Party in Georgia*, vii.

14. Woodward, *Origins of the New South*, 81, 105–6, 248–63; Arnett, *Populist Movement in Georgia*, 153–55; Woodward, *Tom Watson*, 64–69, 107–8.

15. Key, with Heard, *Southern Politics in State and Nation*, 106–7; Anderson, *Wild Man from Sugar Creek*, xiv; Key, with Heard, *Southern Politics in State and Nation*, 107; Bernd, "Study of Primary Elections," 23.

16. Key, with Heard, *Southern Politics in State and Nation*, 106: Pyles, "Race and Ruralism in Georgia Elections," 4; Saye, *Constitutional History of Georgia*, 356–59, 364; Rigdon, *Georgia's County Unit System*, 40.

17. Key, with Heard, *Southern Politics in State and Nation*, 122; Bernd, *Grass Roots Politics in Georgia*, 6; Anderson, *Wild Man from Sugar Creek*, 200, 229–30, 237–38;

Herman Eugene Talmadge, interview by author, March 24, 1986, Harold Paulk Henderson Sr. Oral History Collection, Russell Library (hereafter cited as Henderson Oral History Collection).

18. Lemmon, "Ideology of Eugene Talmadge," 226–28; Lemmon, "Public Career of Eugene Talmadge," 156–244; Key, with Heard, *Southern Politics in State and Nation,* 117; Bartley, *From Thurmond to Wallace,* 24.

19. Bernd, *Grass Roots Politics in Georgia,* 21, 26–27; Herndon, "Eurith Dickenson Rivers," 132–34; Harold P. Henderson, *Politics of Change in Georgia,* 33–50, 243–45; Henderson, "1946 Gubernatorial Election in Georgia," 63.

20. Henderson, *Ellis Arnall,* 171–88.

21. Ibid., 212; Pajari, "Talmadge and the Politics of Power," 79–80; Talmadge with Winchell, *Talmadge,* 134–39; Brooks, *Georgia in 1950,* 1, 5, 28, 7.

22. Bernd, "Study of Primary Elections," 158–62; Talmadge with Winchell, *Talmadge,* 107.

23. Bernd, "Georgia: Static and Dynamic," 320–21; Talmadge with Winchell, *Talmadge,* 108; Gosnell and Anderson, *Government and Administration of Georgia,* 109.

24. Cook, *Governors of Georgia,* 267–68; Herman Eugene Talmadge, interview by author, June 26 and July 17, 1987, pp. 43–44, 47–49, Georgia Government Documentation Project, Special Collections, Pullen Library; Pajari, "Talmadge and the Politics of Power," 82–84.

25. Talmadge with Winchell, *Talmadge,* 154–58; Bernd, "White Supremacy," 492–513; Bass and DeVeries, *Transformation of Southern Politics,* 187; Pajari, "Talmadge and the Politics of Power," 91; Bartley, *Creation of Modern Georgia,* 191; Cook, *Governors of Georgia,* 267–68.

26. Thompson, *Reconstruction in Georgia,* 22; Kousser, *Shaping of Southern Politics,* 209–22.

27. Woodward, *Origins of the New South,* 235–63; Arnett, *Populist Movement in Georgia,* 185–211; Bacote, "Negro in Georgia Politics," 499–500; Grantham, "Georgia Politics," 20–21; Kousser, *Shaping of Southern Politics,* 223; Owen, "Rise of Negro Voting," 11.

28. Owen, "Rise of Negro Voting," 3; *Nixon v. Herdon,* 273 U.S. 536 (1927); *Nixon v. Condon,* 286 U.S. 73 (1932); *Grovey v. Townsend,* 295 U.S. 45 (1935); *Smith v. Allwright,* 321 U.S. 649 (1944); *King v. Chapman, et al.,* 62 Fed. Supp. 639 (1945); *Chapman v. King,* 154 F. 2nd 460 (1946); Henderson, "Gubernatorial Election of 1946," 25–26.

29. Henderson, *Ellis Arnall,* 43–45; Key, with Heard, *Southern Politics in State and Nation,* 522–23.

30. Key, with Heard, *Southern Politics in State and Nation,* 126; Bernd, "Study of Primary Elections," 63; Bernd, "White Supremacy," 502–10; Bernd, *Grass Roots Politics in Georgia,* 30; Bernd, "Corruption in Georgia Primaries and Elections," 101–2; Bernd, "Study of Primary Elections," 229.

31. Henderson, "Gubernatorial Election of 1946," 260, 113–40, 126; Henderson, "M. E. Thompson," 63; Bernd, "Corruption in Georgia Primaries and Elections," 126–27, 130; Grant, *Way It Was in the South,* 368–69; Gosnell and Anderson, *Government*

and Administration of Georgia, 37; Shadgett, *Voter Registration in Georgia,* 3–4; Mathews and Prothro, *Negroes and the New Southern Politics,* 18.

THREE. Vandiver and State Politics, 1946–1955

1. Samuel Ernest Vandiver Jr., September 14, 1993, OH Vandiver 4A, pp. 8–10, 40–41; Vandiver, September 14, 1993, OH Vandiver 4B, pp. 1–4; Sybil Elizabeth "Betty" Vandiver, January 22, 1994, OH Vandiver 13A, pp. 41–42.

2. Henderson, "Gubernatorial Election of 1946," 68–71.

3. Henderson, *Politics of Change in Georgia,* 173.

4. Ibid., 173–75; Vandiver OH 4B, p. 5.

5. Henderson, *Politics of Change in Georgia,* 176–85; Vandiver, OH Vandiver 4B, pp. 5–7; Vandiver, OH Vandiver 4A, p. 33.

6. Henderson, "Gubernatorial Election of 1946," 116–25.

7. Vandiver, OH Vandiver 4B, p. 9; Ernest Vandiver Sr. to Ernest Vandiver Jr., February 2, 1948, letter in possession of Vandiver; Vandiver, OH Vandiver 4B, p. 9; Talmadge, OH Vandiver 2, p. 3; *Lavonia Times,* July 16, 1948.

8. Vandiver, OH Vandiver 4B, p. 9; Talmadge, OH Vandiver 2, p. 4; introductions in Memorandum B (undated), Statements and Clippings, Lieutenant Governor of Georgia 1954, Campaigns, S. Ernest Vandiver Papers, Russell Library (hereafter cited as Vandiver Papers); Bernd, "Study of Primary Elections," 117–18.

9. Betty Vandiver, OH Vandiver 13A, pp. 51–52; Vandiver, OH Vandiver 4B, pp. 13–14.

10. Vandiver, OH Vandiver 4B, pp. 14–15.

11. Samuel Ernest Vandiver Jr., interview by Charles B. Pyles, April (n.d.) 1990, p. 17, Georgia Government Documentation Project, Special Collections, Pullen Library; Vandiver, OH Vandiver 4B, p. 15; *Georgia Guardsmen* (February 1953): 8; Douglas Embry, March 3, 1994, OH Vandiver 19, pp. 4–6.

12. Vandiver, OH Vandiver 4B, p. 15.

13. Ibid., pp. 18–19; biography of Vandiver folder, Subject File, U.S. Senate 1972, Campaigns, Vandiver Papers.

14. Vandiver, OH Vandiver 4B, pp. 20–22; Samuel Ernest Vandiver Jr., interview by Hugh Cates, February 23, 1971, pp. 26–27, Russell Oral History Collection.

15. Betty Vandiver, OH Vandiver 13B, p. 17; typed biographical information provided by Vandiver; Embry, OH Vandiver 19, pp. 1–2, 9–10.

16. *Atlanta Constitution,* February 10 and 27, 1954; Vandiver, OH Vandiver 4B, p. 16; *Atlanta Journal,* March 7 and June 18, 1954; Charles R. Fox to Vandiver, July 1, 1954, and Bernard M. Daviey to Vandiver, July 2, 1954, letters in 1952–58 Scrapbook, Vandiver Papers.

17. *Atlanta Constitution,* August 9 and September 6, 1954; Bernd, "Study of Primary Elections," 159; Herdon, "Eurith Dickinson Rivers," pp. 322–31.

18. *Atlanta Constitution,* August 9 and September 6, 1954.

19. *Lavonia Times,* July 16, 1954; *Macon News* editorial, March 11, 1954, Statements

and Clippings, Lieutenant Governor of Georgia 1954, Campaigns, Vandiver Papers; Vandiver, OH Vandiver 4B, pp. 26–27; Betty Vandiver, OH Vandiver 13A, pp. 59–60; Owen, OH Vandiver 21A, p. 11.

20. Betty Vandiver, OH Vandiver 13A, p. 61; Vandiver, OH Vandiver 4B, pp. 26–27; William Donaldson Ballard, July 28, 1994, OH Vandiver 30A, p. 21; Henry Getzen Neal, November 26, 1993, OH Vandiver 9, p. 28; David Campbell Jones, July 22, 1994, OH Vandiver 27, p. 39.

21. Vandiver, OH Vandiver 4B, pp. 27–28; Department of Archives and History, Mary G. Bryan, comp., *Georgia's Official Register, 1955–1956*, 324, 214; James Anderson Dunlap, March 18, 1994, OH Vandiver 17, pp. 18–19; Norman, OH Vandiver 25, p. 12.

22. Vandiver, OH Vandiver 4B, pp. 29–31; Betty Vandiver, OH Vandiver 13B, pp. 3–5; Owen, OH Vandiver 4B, p. 10.

23. Talmadge, OH Vandiver 2, p. 5; Vandiver, OH Vandiver 4B, p. 26; Betty Vandiver, OH Vandiver 13B, p. 6; William Lovel Lanier Sr., July 21, 1994, OH Vandiver 26A, p. 7.

24. Vandiver, OH Vandiver 4B, p. 16; *Atlanta Journal-Constitution*, July 25, 1954; *Griffin Daily News* editorial reprinted in *Atlanta Constitution*, September 4, 1954; *Camilla Enterprise* editorial reprinted in *Atlanta Constitution*, September 1, 1954; *Bulloch Herald* editorial reprinted in *Atlanta Constitution*, August 28, 1954; *Augusta Chronicle* editorial reprinted in *Atlanta Journal-Constitution*, August 24, 1954; *Winder News* editorial reprinted in *Atlanta Constitution*, September 6, 1954; Vandiver, OH Vandiver 4B, pp. 34–35.

25. Bernd, "Georgia: Static and Dynamic," 325–26; Bernd, "Study of Primary Elections," 261–62; Vandiver, OH Vandiver 4B, pp. 31–32.

26. Bartley, "Race Relations," 363–64; *Atlanta Constitution*, May 18, 1954.

27. *Atlanta Constitution*, July 22, 1954; *Atlanta Journal*, July 22, 1954; *Atlanta Constitution*, August 6, 1954; *Atlanta Journal*, July 27, 1954.

28. Bernd, "Static and Dynamic," 321–325; *Atlanta Constitution*, August 6, 1954.

29. Vandiver, OH Vandiver 4B, p. 33; *Atlanta Journal*, August 4, 1954; *Atlanta Constitution*, August 4, 1954; *Atlanta Journal*, June 20, 1954; Vandiver, OH Vandiver 4B, p. 29; *Atlanta Constitution*, August 5 and 21, 1954; Vandiver, OH Vandiver 4B, pp. 35, 28.

30. *Atlanta Constitution*, March 31, 1954; *Atlanta Journal*, March 31, 1954; *Atlanta Constitution*, July 21, 1954.

31. Department of Archives and History, Mary G. Bryan, comp., *Georgia's Official Register, 1953–1954*, 631–34; Vandiver, OH Vandiver 4B, pp. 35–36.

32. *Lavonia Times*, September 17, 1954.

FOUR. The Griffin Years

1. Samuel Ernest Vandiver Jr., September 14, 1993 OH Vandiver 4B, pp. 36–37; Vandiver, OH Vandiver 4C, pp. 2–3; Betty Vandiver, OH Vandiver 13B, pp. 14–16.

2. *Atlanta Constitution*, October 1, November 10, December 1, 17, 1954; *Atlanta Journal*, January 10, 1955.

3. *Atlanta Journal-Constitution,* February 20, 1955; *Atlanta Constitution,* January 11, 1955; Department of Archives and History, Mary G. Bryan, comp., *Georgia's Official Register, 1955–56,* 319; Vandiver, OH Vandiver 4C, p. 2; Samuel Ernest Vandiver Jr., interview by Hugh Cates, February 23, 1971, p. 14, Russell Oral History Collection.

4. Department of Archives and History, Mary G. Bryan, comp., *Georgia's Official Register, 1955–56,* 295–318; Gosnell and Anderson, *Government and Administration of Georgia,* 51–52; Harold Davis in *Atlanta Journal-Constitution,* December 19, 1954; Talmadge with Winchell, *Talmadge,* 102.

5. *Journal of the House of Representatives of the State of Georgia at the Regular Session Commenced at Atlanta, Monday, January 10th, 1955 and Adjourned February 18th, 1955* (Hapeville, Ga.: Longino & Porter, 1955), 34–44 (hereafter cited as *Georgia House Journal* [Regular Session, 1955]).

6. Ibid., 44–47.

7. Ibid., 164–165.

8. General Assembly, *Acts and Resolutions of the General Assembly of the State of Georgia, 1953* (Hapeville, Ga.: Longino & Porter, 1953), 151 (hereafter cited as *Acts and Resolutions,* by year); *Georgia House Journal* (Regular Session, 1955), 166–67, 380; *Journal of the Senate of the State of Georgia at the Regular Session Commenced at Atlanta, Monday, January 10th, 1955 and Adjourned February 18, 1955* (Hapeville, Ga.: Longino & Porter, 1955), 137 (hereafter cited as *Georgia Senate Journal* [Regular Session, 1955]); *Organizational Meeting of State Programs Study Committee, Held in the Senate Chamber, State Capitol Atlanta, Georgia March 4, 1955, Transcript of the Proceedings,* 19–20.

9. Department of Archives and History, Mary G. Bryan, comp., *Georgia's Official Register, 1955–56,* 212; *Macon Telegraph,* January 10, 13, 1955; Robert Alwyn Griffin, October 8, 1993, OH Vandiver 6, p. 3; Vandiver, OH Vandiver 4C, p. 4.

10. *Atlanta Journal,* January 10, 1955; *Atlanta Journal-Constitution,* January 9, 1955; *Atlanta Journal,* January 15, 1955; *Georgia House Journal* (Regular Session, 1955), 134–36.

11. *Georgia House Journal* (Regular Session, 1955), 423; *Georgia Senate Journal* (Regular Session, 1955), 237, 77; *Acts and Resolutions* (1955), 138; *Georgia House Journal* (Regular Session, 1955), 195; *Georgia Senate Journal* (Regular Session, 1955), 347; *Acts and Resolutions* (1955), 659–62, 210–17, 398–400, 174–76; *Atlanta Journal-Constitution,* February 20, 1955; *Macon Telegraph,* February 18, 1955.

12. Vandiver, OH Vandiver 4B, pp. 44–45; *Atlanta Journal,* January 31, 1955, January 9, 1956; *Macon Telegraph,* January 10, 1956.

13. *Atlanta Constitution,* February 15, January 17, 21, March 2, 1955.

14. Ibid., February 14, 15, 18, 1955.

15. Ibid., May 13, 1955; Vandiver, OH Vandiver 4C, p. 3; *State Programs Study Committee Report on the Financial Operations of the State in Compliance with Resolutions of General Assembly Adopted in Regular Session 1955* (May 25, 1955), 1, 2, 38, 5–7.

16. *Atlanta Constitution,* June 1, 1955; *Journal of the Senate of the State of Georgia at the Extraordinary Session Commenced at Atlanta June 6th, 1955 and Adjourned June 17, 1955* (Hapeville, Ga.: Longino & Porter, 1956), 6–8, 23, 19–20 (hereafter cited as *Geor-*

gia Senate Journal [Extraordinary Session, 1955]); *Atlanta Constitution,* June 6, 7, 1955. For critical editorials see *LaGrange Daily News, Macon Telegraph, Brunswick News, Gainesville Daily Times,* and *Augusta Herald* reprinted in *Atlanta Constitution,* June 8, 1955; *Atlanta Constitution,* June 10, 1955; Henry Long to editor, letter printed in *Atlanta Constitution,* June 17, 1955.

17. *Atlanta Constitution,* June 15, 18, 1955; *Georgia Senate Journal* (Extraordinary Session, 1955), 79; *Acts and Resolutions of the General Assembly of the State of Georgia, Extraordinary Session Convened by Proclamation of the Governor June 6, 1955* (Hapeville, Ga.: Longino & Porter, n.d.), 66–67.

18. *Atlanta Journal,* February 1, 2, 1955; *Atlanta Constitution,* June 28, 1955.

19. *Atlanta Constitution,* July 29, 26, 28, 1955.

20. The grand jury presentments of the 1955 July–August term of the Fulton County Superior Court and the editorial are in *Atlanta Constitution,* September 2, 1955; ibid., September 3, 1955.

21. *Atlanta Constitution,* September 17, 1955; *Atlanta Journal,* December 29, 1955; *Macon Telegraph,* January 1, 1956; *First Report, Joint Committee on Economy. Prepared for Hon. S. Marvin Griffin, Governor, Members of the General Assembly, the Public,* 64–65 (hereafter cited as *First Report, Joint Committee on Economy*).

22. *Atlanta Constitution,* October 24, December 23, November 18, 19, December 30, 31, 1955.

23. Recommendations may be found throughout the reports. See *First Report, Joint Committee on Economy* and *Second Report, Joint Committee on Economy. Prepared for Hon. S. Marvin Griffin, Governor, Members of the General Assembly, the Public* (hereafter cited as *Second Report, Joint Committee on Economy*); *First Report, Joint Committee on Economy,* 3, 6; *Second Report, Joint Committee on Economy,* 44, 15–20.

24. *Atlanta Constitution,* January 3, 1956; *Atlanta Journal,* July 15, 1955; *Atlanta Constitution,* January 9, 1956; *Macon Telegraph,* January 10, 1956.

25. *Journal of the Senate of the State of Georgia at the Regular Session Commenced at Atlanta, January 9, 1956 and Adjourned February 17th, 1956* (Hapeville, Ga.: Longino & Porter, 1956), 108 (hereafter cited as *Georgia Senate Journal* [Regular Session, 1956]); *Journal of the House of Representatives of the State of Georgia at the Regular Session Commenced at Atlanta, January 9th, 1956 and Adjourned February 17th, 1956* (Hapeville, Ga.: Longino & Porter, 1956), 880 (hereafter cited as *Georgia House Journal* [Regular Session, 1956]); *Georgia Senate Journal* (Regular Session, 1956), 805; *Atlanta Journal,* February 17, 1956.

26. *Atlanta Constitution,* February 16, 1956; *Acts and Resolutions* (1956), 1:255–56; *Macon Telegraph* editorial reprinted in *Atlanta Constitution,* February 29, 1956; *Rome News-Tribune* editorial reprinted in *Atlanta Constitution,* February 29, 1956.

27. *Georgia Senate Journal* (Regular Session, 1956), 110–12; *Acts and Resolutions* (1956), 1:6–15, 642–48, 607–9, 673–74, 685–87, 605–6; *Atlanta Journal-Constitution,* February 19, 1956.

28. *Acts and Resolutions* (1956), 1:4–6; *Atlanta Constitution,* January 25, 26, 27, February 2, 1956. For some editorials in opposition, see *Atlanta Constitution,* February 2, 1956, *Savannah Morning News,* and *Rome News-Tribune* editorials reprinted in *Atlanta*

Constitution, January 30, 1956, *Cartersville Daily Tribune News* editorial reprinted in *Atlanta Constitution,* February 1, 1956, and *Calhoun Times* editorial reprinted in *Atlanta Constitution,* February 8, 1956; *Georgia Senate Journal* (Regular Session, 1956), 278, 375; *Georgia House Journal* (1956), 562–64; Vandiver, OH Vandiver 4C, p. 7.

29. *Brantley Enterprise* editorial reprinted in *Atlanta Constitution,* March 1, 1956; *Rome News-Tribune* editorial reprinted in *Atlanta Constitution,* February 29, 1956; *Macon Telegraph,* February 18, 1956; *Waycross Journal-Herald* editorial reprinted in *Atlanta Constitution,* February 13, 1956; *Atlanta Constitution,* March 9, 10, 1956; *Atlanta Journal,* March 9, 1956.

30. *Atlanta Journal,* April 11, August 8, 1956; *Atlanta Constitution,* August 8, 17, 18, 20, 1956.

31. Melton, "1960 Presidential Election in Georgia," 20–26; Samuel Ernest Vandiver Jr., interview by John F. Stewart, May 22, 1967, pp. 1–4, John F. Kennedy Oral History Program, John Fitzgerald Kennedy Library, Boston (hereafter cited as Kennedy Library); John F. Kennedy to Vandiver, July 12, 1957, and Vandiver to John F. Kennedy, July 24, 1957, box 933, John F. Kennedy Pre-Presidential Papers, Kennedy Library.

32. *Atlanta Journal-Constitution,* January 1, 1957; *Atlanta Constitution,* January 7, 14, 15, 1957; *Atlanta Journal,* January 23, 1957; *Atlanta Constitution,* February 5, 1957; *Journal of the Senate of the State of Georgia at the Regular Session Commenced at Atlanta, Monday, January 14th, 1957 and Adjourned February 22, 1957* (Hapeville, Ga.: Longino & Porter, 1957), 75, 62, 385–86 (hereafter cited as *Georgia Senate Journal* [Regular Session, 1957]); *Journal of the House of Representatives of the State of Georgia at the Regular Session Commenced at Atlanta, Monday, January 14th, 1957 and Adjourned February 22, 1957,* (Hapeville, Ga.: Longino & Porter, 1957), 1028 (hereafter cited as *Georgia House Journal* [Regular Session, 1957]); *Augusta Chronicle* editorial reprinted in *Atlanta Journal-Constitution,* January 6, 1957.

33. *Georgia House Journal* (Regular Session, 1957), 33–43, *Atlanta Journal,* January 16, 1957; *Atlanta Constitution,* January 16, 1957.

34. *Atlanta Journal-Constitution,* February 24, 1957; *Macon Telegraph,* February 21, 1957; *Atlanta Constitution,* February 23, 1957; *Atlanta Journal-Constitution,* February 24, 1957; *Macon Telegraph,* February 21, 1957; *Atlanta Journal,* February 21, 1957.

35. *Atlanta Constitution,* May 1, 2, 3, 1957.

36. *Atlanta Journal,* May 6, 1957; *Atlanta Constitution,* May 9, 25, 1957.

37. *Atlanta Constitution,* November 1, 2, 1957.

38. "Marvin Griffin Remembers," an interview by Gene-Gabriel Moore for Georgia Public Television in Henderson and Roberts, *Georgia Governors in an Age of Change,* 138.

FIVE . The 1958 Legislative Session

1. *Augusta Courier,* November 26, 1956; *Atlanta Journal-Constitution,* January 13 and February 17, 1957; *Moultrie Observer* editorial reprinted in *Augusta Courier,* March 11,

1957. For similar editorials, see Unannounced Candidate—Editorials 1956–57 folder, News Clippings 1956–58, Governor of Georgia 1958, Campaigns, Vandiver Papers.

2. *Macon News,* August 29, 1957, in Unannounced Candidate—Editorials 1956–57 folder, News Clippings 1956–58, Governor of Georgia 1958, Campaigns, Vandiver Papers; Vandiver to Fields Whatley, April 24, 1957, Fields Whatley folder, Announcements, Platform, Speaking Schedules, U.S. Senate 1972, Campaigns, Vandiver Papers; *Atlanta Constitution* April 27 and May 13, 1957.

3. *Atlanta Constitution,* April 17, 1957; copy of speech in Fields Whatley folder, U.S. Senate 1972, Campaigns, Vandiver Papers.

4. *Atlanta Constitution,* July 10, 11, 18, 1957; *Atlanta Journal-Constitution,* July 21, 1957.

5. *Atlanta Constitution,* July 20, 23, 1957.

6. Ibid., March 29, June 15, 19, July 2, August 13, September 14, and June 22, 1957; Vandiver, OH Vandiver 4B, p. 37.

7. *Atlanta Constitution,* March 6, 1957; Department of Archives and History, Mary G. Bryan, comp., *Georgia's Official Register, 1955–1956,* 149; Vandiver, OH Vandiver 4C, p. 13; *Atlanta Constitution,* March 6, 1957.

8. *Atlanta Journal,* March 8, 1957; Vandiver's letter to the editor is in *Atlanta Journal,* March 18, 1957.

9. *Atlanta Constitution,* June 29, 1957; Department of Archives and History, Mary G. Bryan, comp., *Georgia's Official Register, 1955–1956,* 214; *Atlanta Constitution,* July 1, 1957; *Atlanta Journal,* July 1, 1957; *Augusta Courier,* July 15, 1957.

10. *Atlanta Constitution,* August 16 and December 18, 1957.

11. Ibid., September 14, 1957; Department of Archives and History, Mary G. Bryan, comp., *Georgia's Official Register, 1955–1956,* 74; *Atlanta Constitution,* January 8, 1958.

12. *Atlanta Journal,* January 6, 1958; *Acts and Resolutions* (1955), 124–48; *Atlanta Journal-Constitution,* January 6, 1958; *Atlanta Constitution,* January 13, 1958.

13. *Journal of the Senate of the State of Georgia at the Regular Session Commenced at Atlanta, Monday, January 13, 1958 and Adjourned February 21, 1958,* 19 (hereafter cited as *Georgia Senate Journal* [Regular Session, 1958]); *Atlanta Journal,* January 14, 1958; Vandiver, OH Vandiver 4B, p. 37; Talmadge, OH Vandiver 2, p. 6; Peter Zach Geer Jr., November 3, 1993, OH Vandiver 5A, p. 13; *Atlanta Constitution,* January 15, 1958.

14. *Atlanta Constitution,* January 18, 1958; letter is reprinted in *Atlanta Journal-Constitution,* January 19, 1958.

15. *Atlanta Constitution,* January 18, 20, 1958; *Austell Enterprise* editorial reprinted in *Atlanta Constitution,* January 22, 1958; *Thomaston Free Press* editorial in Editorials—January–June 1958 folder, News Clippings 1956–58, Governor of Georgia 1958, Campaigns, Vandiver Papers; *Albany Herald,* January 25, 1958; *Walker County Messenger* editorial in Rural Roads Bonds Clippings folder, Subject File, Lieutenant Governor Office Files 1955–58, Vandiver Papers; *Augusta Chronicle,* January 27, 1958.

16. *Macon News* January 24, 1958; Robert Alwyn Griffin, October 8, 1993, OH Vandiver 6, p. 6; Griffin Boyette Bell, December 8, 1993, OH Vandiver 7, p. 3; *Atlanta Constitution,* January 29, 1958; George Dekle Busbee, March 17, 1993, OH Vandiver 23, p. 2.

17. Geer, OH Vandiver 5A, p. 10; Vandiver, OH Vandiver 4C, p. 8; Griffin, OH Vandiver 6, p. 7; *Atlanta Constitution,* January 28, 1958; Geer, OH Vandiver 5A, p. 11; Jones, OH Vandiver 27, p. 12; *Macon Telegraph,* January 29, 1958; Talmadge, Vandiver OH 2, p. 6.

18. *Atlanta Constitution,* January 28, 1958; *Macon Telegraph,* January 20, 1958; *Atlanta Journal,* January 22, 1958; *Atlanta Constitution,* January 23, 1958; *Atlanta Journal,* January 22, 1958.

19. Marvin Griffin to R. A. McLendon, January 16, 1958, January 1958 folder, Marvin Griffin Papers, Library, Bainbridge College, Bainbridge, Georgia (hereafter cited as Griffin Papers); Jones, OH Vandiver 27, p. 12; Geer, OH Vandiver 5A, pp. 11–12; Griffin, OH Vandiver 6, p. 6; Jones, OH Vandiver 27, p. 6.

20. *Journal of the House of Representatives of the State of Georgia at the Regular Session Commenced at Atlanta Monday, January 13th, 1958 and Adjourned February 21, 1958,* 71 (hereafter cited as *Georgia House Journal* [Regular Session, 1958]); *Atlanta Constitution,* January 22, 23, 1958; *Georgia House Journal* (Regular Session, 1958), 164–66; *Macon Telegraph,* January 23, 1958; *Atlanta Constitution,* January 23, 1958.

21. *Macon Telegraph,* January 23, 25, 1958; copy of form letter to boards of county commissioners dated January 23, 1958, in January 1958 folder, Griffin Papers; *Atlanta Constitution,* January 29, 1958.

22. Dubay, "Marvin Griffin and the Politics of the Stump," 101; Roberts, "Traditions and Consensus," 8; Geer, OH Vandiver 5B, p. 3; Jones, OH Vandiver 27, pp. 36–37; *Atlanta Constitution,* January 28, 1958; *Atlanta Journal,* January 28, 1958.

23. *Atlanta Constitution,* January 28, 1958.

24. Ibid., January 28, 29, 1958.

25. *Georgia House Journal* (Regular Session, 1958), 238–42; *Atlanta Constitution,* January 28, 1958.

26. *Georgia House Journal* (Regular Session, 1958), 259–61; *Atlanta Constitution,* January 29, 1958; *Atlanta Journal,* January 29, 1958.

27. *Macon Telegraph and News,* February 24, 1958; *Savannah Morning News,* January 29, 1958; *Columbus Enquirer,* February 24, 1958; *Rome News-Tribune,* January 29, 1958, editorials in Rural Roads Bonds Clippings folder, Subject File, Lieutenant Governor Office Files 1955–58, Vandiver Papers; *Albany Herald,* January 29, 1958; *Atlanta Constitution,* March 19, 1958.

28. *Georgia Senate Journal* (Regular Session, 1958), 46; *Atlanta Journal,* February 21, 1958; *Macon Telegraph,* February 22, 1958; *Atlanta Journal,* February 23, 1958.

29. *Atlanta Constitution,* February 5, 1958; *Atlanta Journal,* February 11, 4, 12, 1958; *Macon Telegraph,* February 12, 4, 1958.

30. *Atlanta Journal,* February 21, 1958.

31. George Thornewell Smith, March 23, 1993, OH Vandiver 22, p. 11; Lanier, OH Vandiver 26A, p. 8; *Atlanta Constitution,* April 4, 23, 1958; *Atlanta Journal,* May 20, 1958.

32. *Atlanta Journal,* March 1, 1958; *Atlanta Journal-Constitution,* March 2, 1958; *Atlanta Constitution,* March 3, 1958.

33. *Atlanta Journal,* March 27 and April 10, 1958; *Atlanta Constitution,* May 3, 1958.

34. *Atlanta Constitution,* May 16, 19, 24, 1958.

35. Ibid., April 24, 16, 17, and June 14, 1958; *Atlanta Journal,* August 31, 1958.

36. *Atlanta Constitution,* March 13, April 19, July 9, March 14, April 4, April 5, 1958; *Atlanta Journal,* April 9, June 3, 1958.

37. *Atlanta Journal,* April 22, 23, 1958; *Atlanta Constitution,* May 13 and April 29, 1958; *Atlanta Journal-Constitution,* May 11, 1958.

38. *Atlanta Journal-Constitution,* June 1, 1958; *Atlanta Journal,* June 13, 1958.

39. *Atlanta Journal,* April 22, 23, and June 2, 1958.

40. *Atlanta Journal,* May 2, 1958; *Atlanta Constitution,* April 28, 30, 25, 1958.

41. *Atlanta Journal,* February 22, 1958; *Atlanta Constitution,* February 28, 1958; *Atlanta Journal,* March 3, 5, 1958; *Atlanta Constitution,* April 4, 1958.

42. *Atlanta Journal-Constitution,* April 13, 1958; *Atlanta Journal,* June 24, 1958; *Atlanta Constitution,* June 25, 26, 1958; *Atlanta Journal,* June 30, 1958; *Atlanta Constitution,* August 13, 15, 16, 1958; *Atlanta Journal,* August 15, 1958.

SIX. The 1958 Governor's Election

1. *Atlanta Constitution,* March 18, 1958; Samuel Ernest Vandiver, interview by Charles B. Pyles, April (n.d.) 1990, p. 27, Georgia Government Documentation Project, Special Collections, Pullen Library; Denmark Groover Jr., interview by James F. Cook, September 12, 1989, p. 12, Georgia Government Documentation Project; *Atlanta Journal,* March 25, 1958; *Atlanta Constitution,* March 26, 1958; Henderson, *Politics of Change in Georgia,* 219.

2. *Tifton Daily Gazette,* May 24, 1958; Griffin, OH Vandiver 6, p. 11; Mrs. William T. Bodenhamer to Marvin Griffin, December 1958 folder, Griffin Papers; Vandiver interview by Pyles, 27; *Atlanta Constitution,* March 7, 1958; Vandiver, OH Vandiver 4C, pp. 13–14; *Atlanta Journal,* May 6, 1957; *Atlanta Constitution,* November 1, 2, 1957.

3. Geer, OH Vandiver 5A, pp. 14–15; *Tifton Gazette,* May 24, 1958.

4. A copy of Bodenhamer's platform is in Opposition folder, Plans and Speeches, Governor of Georgia 1958, Campaigns, Vandiver Papers.

5. A copy of *Georgia Progress* is in ibid.

6. *Atlanta Constitution,* September 2, 1958; *Atlanta Journal,* August 26, 1958; Bodenhammer's advertisement in *Macon Telegraph and News,* September 7, 1958, in Opposition folder, Plans and Speeches, Governor of Georgia 1958, Campaigns, Vandiver Papers; *Atlanta Constitution,* July 24, 1958.

7. *Tifton Daily Gazette,* July 5, 1958; Vandiver, OH Vandiver 4C, pp. 14–15.

8. *Atlanta Journal-Constitution,* August 10, 1958; *Atlanta Constitution,* September 4, 1958; *Georgia Progress,* Opposition folder, Plans and Speeches, Governor of Georgia 1958, Campaigns, Vandiver Papers.

9. Vandiver interview by Pyles, 27; *Atlanta Constitution,* August 4, 5, 1958; script of Vandiver's election eve appeal in Campaign Releases # 1 folder, Speech and Press, Vandiver Papers; Sam Scheinman to Vandiver, June 17, 1958, Radio and TV Schedule folder, Publicity, Governor of Georgia 1958, Campaigns, Vandiver Papers.

10. *Atlanta Journal,* July 20, 1958; *Walton Tribune* editorial reprinted in *Atlanta Constitution,* September 10, 1958; *Atlanta Constitution,* August 8, 1958; *Atlanta Journal-Constitution,* July 13, 1958; *Atlanta Constitution,* August 8, 1958.

11. *Atlanta Journal,* August 7, 23, 1958; *Atlanta Constitution,* August 23, 1958.

12. *Atlanta Journal-Constitution,* July 13, 1958; a copy of Vandiver's Dublin Speech is in Campaign Speeches folder, Plans and Speeches, Governor of Georgia 1958, Campaigns, Vandiver Papers.

13. Vandiver, "Vandiver Takes the Middle Road," 158–159; Vandiver, OH Vandiver 1, pp. 61–62; Vandiver, OH Vandiver 4C, pp. 15–16; Vandiver interview by Pyles, 29–30. Vandiver, in an essay published in 1988, remembered the statement "Neither my child nor yours will ever attend an integrated school during my administration—no, not one" being in his Dublin speech. Copies of the Dublin speech in the Vandiver Papers, however, do not contain that statement, nor does Charles Pou's article covering the speech for the Atlanta papers. The Vandiver political newspaper that stressed Vandiver's segregationist position contains the "When I am your governor" statement in the text. Vandiver does use variations of a statement "As long as Ernest Vandiver is your governor, there will be no mixed schools or college classrooms in this State—no, not a single one!" in speeches, a press release, and an election eve television appeal for votes. However, the exact wording of the statement is not important; what is important is the pledge of no desegregation in his administration. See Vandiver, "Vandiver Takes the Middle Road," 159; copies of speeches at Dublin and Albany and the press release dated July 27, 1958, in Campaign Speeches folder, Plans and Speeches, Governor of Georgia 1958, Campaigns, Vandiver Papers; Text of Vandiver's campaign speech at Thomson, Thomson 8-16-58 folder, Speech and Press, Vandiver Papers; a script of Vandiver's election eve appeal is in Campaign Releases # 1 folder, Speech and Press, Vandiver Papers; copies of the Vandiver newspaper are filed unclassified in the Vandiver Papers; Pou's article is in *Atlanta Journal-Constitution,* July 13, 1958.

14. Vandiver, OH Vandiver 4C, p. 16; Talmadge, OH Vandiver 2, p. 7; Glenn Wilson Ellard, July 29, 1994, Vandiver OH 29, p. 10; Busbee, Vandiver OH 23, pp. 4–5; Ballard, Vandiver OH 30A, pp. 18–19; Norman, Vandiver OH 25, pp. 14–15; Dunlap, Vandiver OH 17, pp. 14–15; Lanier, Vandiver OH 26A, pp. 18–19; Sanders, Vandiver OH 3, p. 3.

15. Bartley, *Rise of Massive Resistance,* 101–2, 258.

16. Memorandum B (undated) in Statements and Clippings folder, Lieutenant Governor of Georgia 1954, Campaigns, Vandiver Papers; *Atlanta Constitution,* July 22, 1954; *Atlanta Journal,* July 27, 1954; Vandiver's Dublin speech, Campaign Speeches folder, Plans and Speeches, Governor of Georgia 1958, Campaigns, Vandiver Papers; Bartley, *Rise of Massive Resistance,* 54.

17. Vandiver's statement before the Georgia Commission on Education, July 19, 1954, Segregation—Statements Press Releases folder, Subject File, Lieutenant Governor Office Files 1955–58, Vandiver Papers; *Augusta Courier,* November 11, 1957; *Atlanta Constitution,* September 28, 1958; *Atlanta Journal,* February 21, 1957; *Atlanta Journal-Constitution,* June 16, 1957.

18. Bernd, "Georgia: Static and Dynamic," 321–25; *Atlanta Constitution,* August 6, 1954.

19. Vandiver, Vandiver OH 4C, p. 18; *Atlanta Journal-Constitution,* August 10, 1958; Campaign Release No. 1 folder, Speech and Press, Vandiver Papers.

20. Copies of the editorials of *Miller County Liberal,* August 21, 1958, *Camden County Tribune,* September 5, 1958, and *Columbus Enquirer,* September 9, 1958, may be found in Editorials—July–August 1958 folder, News Clippings 1956–58, Governor of Georgia 1958, Campaigns, Vandiver Papers; copies of the editorials of *Macon Telegraph,* September 10, 1958, *Waycross Journal-Herald,* September 6, 1958, and *Augusta Herald,* September 5, 1958, may be found in William T. Bodenheimer [*sic*] Folder 1, Subject File, Early Senate Years 1946–58, Herman E. Talmadge Collection, Russell Library (hereafter cited as Talmadge Collection); *Atlanta Journal-Constitution,* August 17, 1958; *Augusta Chronicle,* September 5, 1958; *Albany Herald,* September 3, 1958; a copy of the *Americus Times-Recorder,* September 5, 1958, editorial is in the Bodenheimer [*sic*] folder, Talmadge Collection.

21. Bell, OH Vandiver 7, p. 6; Geer, OH Vandiver 5A, pp. 18, 26; Talmadge, OH Vandiver 2, p. 6; Vandiver, OH Vandiver 4C, pp. 9–10.

22. For a list of newspapers endorsing Vandiver, see *Atlanta Journal,* September 5, 1958; copy of *Augusta Herald* editorial of May 28, 1958, in Editorials—January–June 1958 folder, News Clippings 1956–58, Governor of Georgia 1958, Campaigns, Vandiver Papers; *Atlanta Journal-Constitution,* August 31, 1958; copy of *Atlanta Daily World* editorial of September 7, 1958, in Editorials—July–August 1958 folder, News Clippings 1956–58, Governor of Georgia 1958, Campaigns, Vandiver Papers; copy of *Augusta Chronicle,* May 25, 1958, editorial and copy of *Savannah Morning News,* May 27, 1958, editorial in Editorials—January–June 1958 folder, News Clippings 1956–58, Governor of Georgia 1958, Campaigns, Vandiver Papers.

23. Vandiver, OH Vandiver 4C, p. 11 ; Geer, OH Vandiver 5A, pp. 23–24; Vandiver, OH Vandiver 4C, p. 12.

24. Betty Vandiver, OH Vandiver 13B, pp. 21–23, 27.

25. Geer, OH Vandiver 5B, pp. 2–3; Lanier, OH Vandiver 26B, p. 4; Busbee, OH Vandiver 23, p. 18; Garland Turk Byrd, December 6, 1993, OH Vandiver 11, p. 29; Griffin, OH Vandiver 6, p. 18; Smith, OH Vandiver 22, pp. 23–24; Geer, OH Vandiver 5B, p. 1; Betty Vandiver, OH Vandiver 13A, p. 20; Jane Brevard Vandiver Kidd, February 27, 1994, OH Vandiver 14, p. 1; Vanna Elizabeth "Beth" Vandiver, February 27, 1994, OH Vandiver 15, p. 1; Samuel Ernest "Chip" Vandiver III, February 27, 1994, OH Vandiver 16A, p. 1.

26. *Atlanta Journal,* July 21, 22, 23, 24, 1958; *Atlanta Constitution,* July 23, 1958; *Macon Telegraph* editorial reprinted in *Atlanta Constitution,* July 28, 1958; *Atlanta Journal,* July 23, 15, 1958.

27. *Atlanta Journal,* July 24, 25, 26, 1958; *Atlanta Constitution,* August 29, 1959.

28. Department of Archives and History, Mary G. Bryan, comp., *Georgia's Official Register, 1957–1958,* 730–33; William M. Bates in *Atlanta Constitution,* September 13, 1958; *Atlanta Journal,* September 12, 1958; *Lavonia Times,* September 19, 1958; political advertisement in *Lavonia Times,* October 3, 1958; *Atlanta Journal,* September 11, 1958.

29. Vandiver, OH Vandiver 4C, pp. 18–19.

30. A copy of Governor-elect Vandiver's acceptance speech is in State Democratic

Convention—Macon—October 14, 1958, folder, Speech and Press, Vandiver Papers; *Atlanta Journal*, October 3, 1958.

31. *Atlanta Journal*, December 1, 1958; Vandiver, OH Vandiver 4B, p. 42; Velie, "Strange Case of the County Slickers," *Reader's Digest* (April 1969): 108–9; Dubay, "Marvin Griffin and the Politics of the Stump," 108; Cook, *Carl Sanders*, 47; Robert Sherrill, *Gothic Politics in the Deep South*, 97. For a vigorous defense of the Griffin administration, see Griffin and Chalker, "S. Marvin Griffin," 113–30, in particular 125–27.

32. Vandiver, "Vandiver Takes the Middle Road," 159; Samuel Ernest Vandiver Jr., interview, name of interviewer not given, June 23, 1987, pp. 6–7, Vandiver interview transcript folder, "Dawn's Early Light: Ralph McGill and the Segregated South," 1988 documentary co-produced by Jed Dannerbaum and Kathleen Dowdey, Project Files, Special Collections, Robert W. Woodruff Library, Emory University, Atlanta; *Cooper v. Arron*, 358 U.S.1 (1958), 17; Sanders, Smith, and Vandiver, "Georgia Legends."

33. McGrath, "Great Expectations," 108–12; *Atlanta Constitution*, September 27, 1958; *Atlanta Journal*, November 14, 1958; *Atlanta Constitution*, November 19, 1958; *Atlanta Journal-Constitution*, November 16, 1958; *Atlanta Journal*, November 19, 1958; *Atlanta Journal-Constitution*, November 30, 1958; *Atlanta Journal*, November 15, 17, and December 15, 1958.

34. *Atlanta Journal*, November 23, 1958; *Atlanta Journal-Constitution*, November 30, 1958; *Atlanta Journal*, December 10, 14, 1958; *Atlanta Journal-Constitution*, December 21, 1958; *Atlanta Constitution*, December 29, 1958; *Macon Telegraph and News*, January 11, 1958.

SEVEN. Vandiver's First Year

1. *Atlanta Constitution*, January 14, 1959; *Journal of the House of Representatives of the State of Georgia at the Regular Session Commenced at Atlanta, Monday, January 12th, 1959 and Adjourned February 20, 1959* (Hapeville, Ga.: Longino & Porter, 1959), 38 and 32 (hereafter cited as *Georgia House Journal* [Regular Session, 1959]); *Macon Telegraph*, January 14, 1959; Maddox's comments are in "Pickrick Says" advertisement in *Atlanta Constitution*, February 14, 1959.

2. Neal, OH Vandiver 9, pp. 6–8; Gosnell and Anderson, *Government and Administration of Georgia*, 93; Turnbull, "Politics in the Budgetary Process," 57–77.

3. See chapter 4 for a discussion of Governor Griffin's ouster of Gillis.

4. *Atlanta Constitution*, November 11, 1958; *Georgia House Journal* (Regular Session, 1959), 103–4; *Journal of the House of Representatives of the State of Georgia at the Regular Session Commenced at Atlanta, Monday, January 11th, 1960 and Adjourned February 19, 1960* (Hapeville, Ga.: Longino & Porter, 1960), 347–49 (hereafter cited as *Georgia House Journal* [Regular Session, 1960]); *Journal of the Senate of the State of Georgia at the Regular Session Commenced at Atlanta, Monday, January 12th, 1959 and Adjourned February 20, 1959* (Hapeville, Ga.: Longino & Porter, 1959), 46 (hereafter cited as *Georgia Senate Journal* [Regular Session, 1959]); *Journal of the Senate of the State of Georgia at the Regular Session Commenced at Atlanta, Monday, January 11th,*

1960 and Adjourned February 19, 1960 (Hapeville, Ga.: Longino & Porter, 1960), 34–36 (hereafter cited as *Georgia Senate Journal* [Regular Session, 1960]); Vandiver, OH Vandiver 4C, p. 14; Department of Archives and History, Mary G. Bryan, comp., *Georgia's Official Register, 1959–1960*, 339.

5. Department of Archives and History, Mary G. Bryan, comp., *Georgia's Official Register, 1959–1960*, 274, 229, 312–13, 300–301, 308–9, 316–17, 209, 236, 260–61, 320–21, 295–99, 276–77; *Atlanta Journal*, December 14, 1958.

6. Vandiver, OH Vandiver 4B, pp. 8–9; William Redding Bowdoin, March 22, 1994, OH Vandiver 18, pp. 4–6; *Atlanta Constitution*, June 28, 1955; Department of Archives and History, Mary G. Bryan, comp., *Georgia's Official Register, 1959–1960*, 215.

7. *Atlanta Constitution*, January 13, 15, 23, 1959; *Atlanta Journal*, January 14, 1959.

8. *Atlanta Journal*, January 2, 1959; *Atlanta Journal-Constitution*, January 25, 1959; *Atlanta Constitution*, January 23, 1959; *Macon Telegraph*, January 6, 1959; *Atlanta Constitution*, January 7, 1959; *Atlanta Journal*, November 4, 1958.

9. Vandiver, OH Vandiver 4C, p. 11, *Atlanta Journal*, January 5, 1959; *Atlanta Constitution*, March 4, 9, 1959; *Atlanta Journal*, March 6, 1959.

10. Vandiver, OH Vandiver 4C, pp. 21–22; Vandiver, OH Vandiver 4D, pp. 2–5; *Georgia House Journal* (Regular Session, 1959), 15; Department of Archives and History, Mary G. Bryan, comp., *Georgia's Official Register, 1959–1960*, 371–72; Vandiver, OH Vandiver 4C, p. 21; Vandiver, OH Vandiver 4D, pp. 2–4.

11. *Georgia Senate Journal* (Regular Session, 1959), 34–45.

12. Ibid., 44–45, 65–68, 110, 223–25; *Georgia House Journal* (Regular Session, 1959), 140–42, 199, 200, 234–34, 415–16.

13. *Acts and Resolutions* (1959), 1:20; *Macon Telegraph*, January 29, 1959; *Atlanta Constitution*, January 26, 1959; *Atlanta Journal*, January 23, 28, 1959; *Georgia Senate Journal* (Regular Session, 1959), 67; *Georgia House Journal* (Regular Session, 1959), 234–35.

14. *Georgia House Journal* (Regular Session, 1959), 78, 204–5; *Georgia Senate Journal* (Regular Session, 1959), 69; *Acts and Resolutions* (1959), 1:6; *Georgia House Journal* (Regular Session, 1959), 123; *Georgia Senate Journal* (Regular Session, 1959), 89; *Acts and Resolutions* (1959), 1:9; *Georgia Senate Journal* (Regular Session, 1959), 42, 32, 52, 22, 73, 53, 58, 13.

15. *Atlanta Journal-Constitution*, February 22, 1959; *Acts and Resolutions* (1959), 1:34–44; *Georgia Senate Journal* (Regular Session, 1959), 196–97; *Georgia House Journal* (Regular Session, 1959), 368–69; *Atlanta Constitution*, January 20, 1959; *Atlanta Journal*, January 21, 27, and February 13, 1959.

16. *Atlanta Journal-Constitution*, February 22, 1959; *Atlanta Constitution*, February 20, 1959; *Waycross Journal-Herald*, February 23, 1959; *Dekalb New Era*, February 26, 1959; *Savannah Morning-News*, February 22, 1959; *Atlanta Journal*, February 21, 1959.

17. *Atlanta Journal*, March 12, 23, 24, 1959; *Atlanta Constitution*, March 24, 1959.

18. *Atlanta Journal*, April 28, March 20, April 17, 1959; *Atlanta Journal-Constitution*, April 19, 1959; *Atlanta Journal*, May 21, 1959.

19. *Atlanta Constitution*, June 1, 2, 1959; *Atlanta Journal*, June 2, 1959; *Walker*

County Messenger editorial reprinted in *Atlanta Constitution*, July 10, 1959; *Carroll County Georgian* editorial reprinted in *Atlanta Constitution*, June 19, 1959; *Atlanta Journal*, June 2, 1959.

20. *Atlanta Journal*, June 29, July 20, 1959; transcript of television address by Vandiver in Statewide TV Report—July 21, 1959, folder, Speech and Press, Vandiver Papers.

21. *Georgia Senate Journal* (Regular Session, 1959), 42; *Acts and Resolutions* (1959), 1 : 8–11; *Final Report by the Governor's Commission on Economy and Reorganization, December 28*, 1959, 1–4, 10.

22. *Atlanta Journal*, August 14, 18, 19, 1959; *Savannah Morning News* editorial reprinted in *Atlanta Constitution*, August 20, 1959.

23. *Atlanta Constitution*, March 7, 10, 1959.

24. Ibid., March 7, 10, 9, 1959; "Report to the Governor of the Medical Association of Georgia Committee Appointed by the President of the Association at the Request of the Governor to Study Milledgeville State Hospital, April 23, 1959," 13–14, 18–19.

25. Ibid., 17–21, 32–38, 41–44, 1; *Atlanta Constitution*, May 21, 1959.

26. *Atlanta Constitution*, April 25, 27, 1959; *Macon Telegraph* and *Thomaston Free Press* editorials reprinted in *Atlanta Constitution*, April 30, 1959; *Atlanta Journal*, May 20, 1959; *Georgia Medical Association Journal* editorial reprinted in *Atlanta Constitution*, June 4, 1959.

27. *Atlanta Constitution*, April 25, 28, May 8, 1959; *Atlanta Journal*, May 4, 1959; *Atlanta Constitution*, May 4, 8, 1959; *Atlanta Journal-Constitution*, June 28, 1959.

28. *Atlanta Constitution*, July 9, 1959.

29. Ibid., June 13, 23, 1959.

30. Ibid., July 3, 10, 11, 1959.

31. Ibid., July 11, 1959.

32. Ibid., November 3, 24, and June 30, 1959.

33. *Atlanta Journal-Constitution*, October 25, 1959; *Atlanta Constitution*, December 10, 1959; *Atlanta Journal-Constitution*, December 13, 1959; *Atlanta Constitution*, November 24, 1959.

34. Betty Vandiver, OH Vandiver 13B, p. 46; *Atlanta Constitution*, December 17, 1959. The Georgia Municipal Association's Christmas project continues with the gifts distributed at the state's regional mental hospitals as well as at the hospital at Milledgeville; letter from Vandiver to author, July 20, 1996.

35. *Atlanta Journal*, March 30, 31, April 13, 1959; *Atlanta Constitution*, April 10, 1959; *Atlanta Journal*, April 15, 1959.

36. *Atlanta Journal*, May 6, 12, and June 9, 1959; U.S. Congress, Senate, *Committee on the Judiciary, Constitutional Amendment Reserving State Control over Public Schools: Hearings before a Subcommittee of the Committee on the Judiciary, 86th Cong., First Sess.*, 12, 13, 14, 15, and 21, May 1959, 39, 47.

37. *Atlanta Journal*, June 10, 1959; Mertz, "Mind Changing Time," 44–45; *James v. Almond*, 170 F. Supp. 331 (1959); Wilkinson, *Harry Byrd*, 146–49.

38. *Atlanta Constitution*, June 7, 17, 1959, July 10, 19, 1959; *Atlanta Journal*, November 30 and December 1, 1959.

39. *Atlanta Journal,* December 4, 1959; *Atlanta Constitution,* December 4, 16, 19, 1959; see "The Beginning of Hope: The Story of the Struggle for Open Schools in Georgia," HOPE Papers, Southern Regional Council Records, Series 13:30, Robert W. Woodruff Library, Clark Atlanta University, Atlanta (hereafter cited as HOPE Papers, followed by series).

40. *Atlanta Constitution,* December 15, 16, 17, 1959; *Walker County Messenger* editorial reprinted in *Atlanta Constitution,* June 17, 1959.

E I G H T . A Year of Accomplishment and Stress

1. *Georgia House Journal* (Regular Session, 1960), 16–29.

2. Ibid., 19; *Macon Telegraph,* January 9, 1960; Department of Audits, *State Auditor's Report, Year Ending June 30, 1959,* 7.

3. *Georgia House Journal* (Regular Session, 1960), 18–21.

4. Ibid., 22–27.

5. *Atlanta Journal-Constitution,* January 17, 1960; *Atlanta Constitution,* January 12, 1960; *Macon Telegraph,* January 12, 1960; *Cobb County Times* editorial reprinted in *Atlanta Constitution,* February 1, 1960; *Atlanta Journal,* January 12, 1960.

6. *Atlanta Journal-Constitution,* February 21, 14, 1960; *Macon Telegraph,* February 20, 1960; *Atlanta Journal-Constitution,* February 21, 1960; *Georgia House Journal* (Regular Session, 1960), 460–61; *Georgia Senate Journal* (Regular Session, 1960), 388–89.

7. *Atlanta Journal,* January 12, 1960; *Georgia Senate Journal* (Regular Session, 1960); 13; *Atlanta Constitution,* January 12, 1960; *Atlanta Journal,* January 21, 1960; *Georgia Senate Journal* (Regular Session, 1960), 133; *Georgia House Journal* (Regular Session, 1960), 415.

8. *Atlanta Journal,* January 29, 1960; *Macon Telegraph and News,* February 7, 1960; *Atlanta Journal-Constitution,* February 7, 1960.

9. *Atlanta Constitution,* February 13, 16, 1960; *Georgia Senate Journal* (Regular Session, 1960), 536–37; *Atlanta Journal,* February 22 and March 2, 1960; *Atlanta Constitution,* March 19, 1960.

10. Vandiver, OH Vandiver 4D, p. 15; *Atlanta Constitution,* March 21, 1960; Betty Vandiver, OH Vandiver 13C, p. 27; *Atlanta Constitution,* May 3, 1960.

11. The school desegregation plan may be found in *Georgia House Journal* (Regular Session, 1960), 441–46.

12. *Atlanta Journal-Constitution,* January 10, 1960; *Macon Telegraph,* January 28, 1960; *Atlanta Constitution,* February 9, 1960; *Macon Telegraph,* January 27, 1960; *Atlanta Journal,* January 5, 1960; *Macon Telegraph,* January 1, 1960; *Atlanta Journal,* January 5, 1960; *Atlanta Constitution,* January 26, 1960.

13. *Atlanta Constitution,* February 10, 1960; *Atlanta Journal,* January 14, 1960; *Macon Telegraph,* January 18, 1960; *Atlanta Journal,* February 16, 1960; *Atlanta Constitution,* January 12, 1960.

14. Cook, *Carl Sanders,* 68; Gerald Walker, "How Women Won the Quiet Battle of Atlanta," *Good Housekeeping* (May 1962): 204 ff.

15. Statement of Mrs. Philip Hammer, chairman of the Education Committee of the League of Women Voters of Georgia, to the General Assembly Committee on Schools March 23, 1960, in League of Women Voters Collection, Georgia Records, Georgia Department of Archives and History, Atlanta; *Atlanta Constitution,* February 10, 1960; *Atlanta Journal,* January 21, 1960; *Atlanta Constitution,* January 13, 1960; *Atlanta Journal,* February 10, 1960; *Atlanta Constitution,* February 18, 1960. Mrs. Hubert Bradley's letter to Vandiver is reprinted in *Atlanta Journal,* January 19, 1960; J. M. Hines to Vandiver, January 13, 1960, and James H. Lightbourne Jr. to Vandiver, December 23, 1960, HOPE Papers, Series 12:1.

16. *Atlanta Constitution,* January 30, 1960; *Atlanta Journal,* January 4, 5, 27, 1960; *Atlanta Constitution,* January 19, 1960; *Atlanta Journal,* January 20, 23, 27, and February 4, 22, 1960; *Atlanta Constitution,* January 20 and March 19, 1960.

17. *Atlanta Journal,* February 11, 15, 1960; *Atlanta Constitution,* January 22, 1960.

18. *Atlanta Journal,* January 18, 1960.

19. *Macon Telegraph,* January 19, 26, 1960. Kidd's options were close the schools, integrate them, provide for local option, create a private school system, or provide for a pupil placement plan; *Atlanta Constitution,* February 3, 1960; *Macon Telegraph,* January 31, 1960.

20. Margaret Long in *Atlanta Journal,* January 21, 1960; Bartley, *From Thurmond to Wallace,* 13–33; Bartley, *Creation of Modern Georgia,* 191–93.

21. Vandiver, "Vandiver Takes the Middle Road," 159; Bell, OH Vandiver 7, p. 23.

22. Vandiver, OH Vandiver 4D, p. 25; Jack Patterson, "The Unruffled Mr. Sibley," *Atlanta Magazine* (February 1962): 61–63; Roche, "Reconstruction of Resistance," 139–43.

23. John A. Sibley to Jessee Draper, July 31, 1958, Governor Ernest Vandiver folder, John Adams Sibley Papers, Special Collections, Robert W. Woodruff Library, Emory University, Atlanta (hereafter cited as Sibley Papers); Vandiver to John A. Sibley, September 18, 1958, Alpha Files, Sibley Papers; John A. Sibley to Vandiver, September 11, 1958, John A. Sibley to Vandiver, August 14, 1959, Vandiver to John A. Sibley, August 12, 1959, Governor Ernest Vandiver folder, Sibley Papers; Bell, OH Vandiver 7, p. 24; Vandiver, OH Vandiver 4D, p. 26; Patterson, "Unruffled Mr. Sibley," 63.

24. Bell, OH Vandiver 7, pp. 23–24; Busbee, OH Vandiver 23, p. 11; Geer, OH Vandiver 5A, pp. 37–38; Busbee, OH Vandiver 23, p. 10; Geer, OH Vandiver 5A, pp. 37–38; Busbee, OH Vandiver 23, p. 10; Griffin B. Bell to John A. Sibley, January 5, 1984, Griffin B. Bell folder, Sibley Papers; Bell, OH Vandiver 7, pp. 30–31; Busbee, OH Vandiver 23, p. 12.

25. *Georgia House Journal* (Regular Session, 1960), 15–29; *Atlanta Journal,* January 19, 1960; *Atlanta Constitution,* January 25, 1960; *Macon Telegraph,* February 7, 1960.

26. *Atlanta Journal,* February 1, 1960; *Georgia House Journal* (Regular Session, 1960), 644–46; *Georgia Senate Journal* (Regular Session, 1960), 275–76; *Acts and Resolutions* (1960), 1:1191; *Atlanta Journal,* February 4, 1960; *Atlanta Journal-Constitution,* February 7, 1960.

27. *Acts and Resolutions* (1960), 1:1187–91; Griffin Boyette Bell, interview by Clifford M. Kuhn and William L. Bost, June 12, 1990, p. 36, Georgia Government Documentation Project, Special Collections, Pullen Library.

28. *Atlanta Constitution*, February 18, 1960; Sibley's remarks may be found in the transcript of "Meeting of the General Assembly Committee On Schools, Courtroom, Sumter County Courthouse, Americus, March 3, 1960," 7–21.

29. *The Report of the General Assembly Committee on Schools, April 28, 1960*, 3 (hereafter cited as *Report of Committee on Schools*). There are discrepancies in the numbers cited in the report. A compilation, entitled "Summary of Hearings by Districts," found in the Sibley Papers had only 1,578 witnesses testifying with 64 percent favoring closing the public schools in order to prevent desegregation. The minority report had 1,739 witnesses with 54 percent favoring closing of the schools. Jeff Roche in his thesis concluded that the committee heard 1,620 witnesses. The *Atlanta Constitution* reported that 1,620 witnesses testified with 51 percent favoring closing the schools. One committee member, Representative J. Render Hill, added an additional statement to the report that contended that "approximately 55 percent of the witnesses favored closing the schools." See Bills, Resolutions, Correspondence, Sibley Commission 1960–61 folder, Sibley Papers; *Report of Committee on Schools*, 21; Roche, "Reconstruction of Resistance," 250; *Atlanta Constitution*, April 1, 1960; *Report of Committee on Schools*, 26; Homer Meade Rankin, January 13, 1994, OH Vandiver 12, pp. 10–12; *Atlanta Journal*, March 28, 1960; Rankin, OH Vandiver 12, p.12; Robert O. Arnold to John A. Sibley, May 12, 1960, League of Women Voters of Athens resolution April 1, 1960, John J. Hurt to John A. Sibley, May 2, 1960, School Study Commission, Personal Correspondence (J. A. S.) 1960 folder, Sibley Papers.

30. John A. Sibley to Vandiver, April 28, 1960, School Study Commission Personal Correspondence (J. A. S) 1960 folder, Sibley Papers; *Report of Committee on Schools*, 19–20.

31. *Report of Committee on Schools*, 2, 4–5, 13, 15, 19–20; John A. Sibley to Howell Hollis Jr., May 13, 1960, School Study Commission Personal Correspondence (J. A. S.) 1960 folder, Sibley Papers.

32. *Report of Committee on Schools*, 22–25.

33. Roche, "Reconstruction of Resistance," 269; *Atlanta Journal*, April 28, 1960; *Augusta Herald* and *Albany Herald* editorials reprinted in *Atlanta Journal*, April 29, 1960.

34. The *Columbus Ledger, Macon Telegraph*, and *Valdosta Times* editorials are reprinted in *Atlanta Journal*, April 29, 1960; *Atlanta Constitution*, April 29, 1960; copy of *Griffin Daily News*, April 29, 1960 editorial in School Study Commission Personal Correspondence (J. A. S.) 1960 folder, Sibley Papers; *Atlanta Constitution*, April 29, 1960; Robert O. Arnold to John A. Sibley, May 12, 1960, School Study Commission Personal Correspondence 1961 (misfiled) folder, Sibley Papers; Frank A Hooper to John A. Sibley, May 18, 1960, School Study Commission Personal Correspondence 1961 (misfiled) folder, Sibley Papers.

35. *Atlanta Journal*, May 10, 1960; editor Sylvan Meyer is quoted in Mertz, "Mind Changing Time," 57.

36. Mertz, "Mind Changing Time," 58–59; Grace T. Hamilton, "A Record of Process

[*sic*]— Community Preparation for Desegregation of Public Schools in Atlanta, Georgia," p. 2, HOPE Papers, Series 13:30; John A. Sibley to Homer M. Rankin, November 28, 1960, and Rankin to Sibley, November 25, 1960, letters in possession of Homer Rankin.

37. *Atlanta Constitution,* May 27, October 4, 14, 20 and November 29, 1960; undated list in HOPE Papers, Series 12:7.

38. Sorensen, "Election of 1960," 3451–53; Melton, "1960 Presidential Election in Georgia," 22–40; John F. Kennedy to Vandiver, January 14, 1958, Kennedy to Vandiver, September 12, 1958, Vandiver to Kennedy, September 2, 1958, Vandiver to Kennedy, January 5, 1960, Vandiver to Kennedy, December 28, 1959, Kennedy to Vandiver, March 21, 1960, box 933, John F. Kennedy Pre-Presidential Papers, Kennedy Library.

39. *Atlanta Journal,* May 12, 1960; Samuel Ernest Vandiver Jr., interview by Hugh Cates, February 23, 1971, p. 35, Russell Oral History Collection; For a discussion of the Johnson-Russell relationship, see Goldsmith, *Richard B. Russell;* Talmadge with Winchell, *Talmadge,* 169–70; Vandiver, interview by Cates, p. 35.

40. *Atlanta Constitution,* June 7, July 14, 1960; Samuel Ernest Vandiver Jr., interview by Karen Kelly, August 7, 1980, p. 43, Russell Oral History Collection; For the civil rights plank in the Democratic Party's platform, see Sorensen, "Election of 1960," 3508–10; *Atlanta Journal,* July 12, 1960; *Atlanta Constitution,* July 13, 1960; Samuel Ernest Vandiver Jr., interview by Charles B. Pyles, April (n.d.) 1990, pp. 41–42, Georgia Government Documentation Project, Special Collections, Pullen Library; *Atlanta Journal,* July 18, 1960.

41. *Atlanta Journal,* July 14, 18, 19, 20, 1960; *Atlanta Constitution,* July 26, August 9, 1960; the 1952 unpledged elector law expired in 1956. It was reenacted in the 1958 session and, like its predecessor, expired four years later. *Acts and Resolutions* (1952), 1–12; *Acts and Resolutions* (1958), 1:208–13.

42. Vandiver, OH Vandiver 4D, p. 11; Samuel Ernest Vandiver Jr., interview by John F. Stewart, May 22, 1967, pp. 28–29, John F. Kennedy Oral History Program, Kennedy Library; *Atlanta Constitution,* August 23, 1960; Roy V. Harris to Vandiver, October 19, 1960, Richmond County folder, County Files, Governor's Office File 1959–62, Vandiver Papers; Department of Archives and History, Mary G. Bryan, comp., *Georgia's Official Register 1959–1960,* 867; *Atlanta Journal,* September 15, 1960.

43. Griffin Boyette Bell, interview by Clifford M. Kuhn and William L Bost, June 12, 1990, pp. 47–50, Georgia Government Documentation Project, Special Collections, Pullen Library; Bell, OH Vandiver 7, pp. 19–21.

44. *Atlanta Journal,* October 10, 1960. Lyndon B. Johnson to Vandiver, October 21, 1960, Va-Vd 1960 folder, box 190, Lyndon Johnson Senate Papers, Lyndon B. Johnson Library, Austin, Texas; texts of Vandiver's introduction of Senator Kennedy at Warm Springs, his introduction of Senator Johnson at Atlanta, his remarks at the Jefferson-Jackson dinner, and Henrico County dinner in Texts (S.E.V.) October–December 1960 folder, Speech and Press, Vandiver Papers; Henderson, *Politics of Change in Georgia,* 152–56; *Atlanta Constitution,* September 21, 1960.

45. Wofford, *Of Kennedys and Kings,* 13; William Berry Hartsfield, interview by Charles T. Morrissey, January 6, 1966, pp. 2–3, John F. Kennedy Oral History Program, Kennedy Library; Abrams, *Day Is Short,* 128.

46. Wofford, *Of Kennedys and Kings,* 15–16.

47. Vandiver, interview by Clifford M. Kuhn, January 25, 1994, pp. 19–26, Georgia Government Documentation Project, Special Collections, Pullen Library; Branch, *Parting the Waters,* 377, 301, 267. For a discussion on the history of the King arrest and release, see Kuhn, "'There's a Footnote to History!,'" 583–95.

48. Robert F. Kennedy, interview by Anthony Lewis, December 4, 1964, pp. 347–48, John F. Kennedy Oral History Program, Kennedy Library; *Atlanta Journal,* October 31, 1960; Diamond, *Guide to U.S. Elections,* 296; John A. Sibley to Robert F. Kennedy, April 4, 1961, Griffin B. Bell folder, Sibley Papers; Melton, "1960 Presidential Election," 188–90, 219–30; Wofford, *Of Kennedys and Kings,* 25–27; Vandiver to John F. Kennedy, June 13, 1963, June–July 1963 folder, Personal Correspondence, Legal Office Files 1963–66, Vandiver Papers.

49. Bartley, "Race Relations," 367; Bolster, "Civil Rights Movements in Twentieth Century Georgia," 169–73.

50. *Atlanta Journal,* March 9, 1960.

51. Ibid., March 15, 16, 1960; Allen with Hemphill, *Mayor,* 36–42; Smith, "Vandivers of Lavonia," 12; Pomerantz, *Where Peachtree Street Meets Sweet Auburn,* 324.

52. Vandiver to John F. Kennedy, June 13, 1963, Vandiver Papers.

53. U.S. Congress, House of Representatives, *Committee on the Judiciary, Miscellaneous Bills Regarding the Civil Rights of Persons within the Jurisdiction of the United States, Hearings before a Subcommittee of the Committee of the Judiciary, March 4, 5, 11, 12, 13, 18, 19; April 14, 15, 16, 17, 22, 23, 24, 29, 30; May 1, 1959,* 563–67.

54. "An Appeal for Human Rights" statement printed in the March 9, 1960, issue of the *Atlanta Constitution;* Grant, *Way It Was in the South,* 378; Bartley, "Race Relations," 363; *Eighty-eighth and Eighty-ninth Annual Reports of the Department of Education to the General Assembly of the State of Georgia for the Biennium Ending June 30, 1960,* 421.

N I N E . School Desegregation

1. *Atlanta Journal,* December 30, 1960; Vandiver to author, February 27, 1997; Vandiver, OH Vandiver 4C, p. 1; *Augusta Courier,* January 16, 1961; Samuel Ernest Vandiver Jr., interview by John F. Stewart, May 27, 1967, p. 43, John F. Kennedy Oral History Program, Kennedy Library; Vandiver, OH Vandiver 4C, p. 23; Samuel Ernest Vandiver Jr., interview by Charles B. Pyles, April (n.d.) 1990, p. 47, Georgia Government Documentation Project, Special Collections, Pullen Library.

2. *Atlanta Constitution,* January 2, 1961.

3. *Atlanta Journal,* January 3, 1961; *Augusta Courier,* January 16, 1961; *Atlanta Constitution,* January 3, 2, 1961; *Macon Telegraph,* January 4, 1961; Ralph E. McGill to Robert F. Kennedy, January 5, 1961, Robert F. Kennedy folder, Subject Series, Ralph E. McGill Papers, Special Collections, Robert W. Woodruff Library, Emory University, Atlanta (hereafter cited as McGill Papers).

4. *Atlanta Constitution,* January 4, 5, 1961.

5. Ibid., January 5, 1961; *Atlanta Journal,* January 10, 1961; *Atlanta Constitution,* January 10, 3, 1961; Ralph E. McGill to Robert F. Kennedy, January 5, 1961, McGill Papers; *Atlanta Constitution,* December 2, 1960.

6. *Atlanta Constitution,* January 6, 1961; Vandiver to author, February 27, 1997; *Atlanta Journal,* January 6, 1961; *Americus Times-Recorder,* January 6, 1961; *Waycross Journal-Herald,* January 7, 1961; *Atlanta Journal-Constitution,* January 29, 1961; Ralph E. McGill to Robert F. Kennedy, January 5, 1961, McGill Papers; *Macon News,* January 6, 1961; *Atlanta Constitution,* January 6, 1961.

7. *Holmes v. Danner,* 191 F. Supp. 394 (1961), 416–17; Grant, *Way It Was in the South,* 382. For a discussion of Ward's efforts, see Silverman, "Horace T. Ward v. Board of Regents"; *Holmes v. Danner,* 191 F. Supp. 385 (1960), 385–92. For an excellent discussion of the desegregation of the university, see Dyer, *University of Georgia,* 303–34.

8. *Acts and Resolutions* (1956), 1:762, 764–65.

9. *Atlanta Constitution,* January 7, 1961; *Atlanta Journal,* January 7, 1961; Hunter-Gault, *In My Place,* 171; *Atlanta Constitution,* January 7, 11, 1961; Vandiver, "Vandiver Takes the Middle Road," 161.

10. *Atlanta Constitution,* January 7, 1961; *Atlanta Journal,* January 9, 1961; *Macon Telegraph and News,* January 8, 1961; *Waycross Journal-Herald,* January 12, 1961; *Brunswick News,* January 9, 1961; *Savannah Morning News,* January 12, 1961; *Columbus Enquirer,* January 8, 1961; *Atlanta Constitution,* January 7, 1961; *Macon Telegraph and News,* January 8, 1961; *Atlanta Journal,* January 9, 8, 1961.

11. *Atlanta Journal-Constitution,* January 8, 1961; Hunter-Gault, *In My Place,* 172–74.

12. *Journal of the Senate of the State of Georgia at the Regular Session Commenced at Atlanta, Monday, January 9th, 1961 and Adjourned February 2, 1961 Reconvened February 20, 1961 and Adjourned March 6, 1961* (Hapeville, Ga.: Longino & Porter, 1961), 17–28 (hereafter cited as *Georgia Senate Journal* [Regular Session, 1961]).

13. *Atlanta Constitution,* January 10, 1961; *Macon Telegraph,* January 10, 1961; *Atlanta Constitution,* January 10, 1961; *Atlanta Journal,* January 10, 1961.

14. Samuel Ernest Vandiver Jr., September 14, 1993, OH Vandiver 4D, p. 29; *Atlanta Journal,* January 10, 1961.

15. Vandiver's letter to Lieutenant Governor Byrd and Speaker Smith reprinted in *Atlanta Journal,* January 10, 1961; *Atlanta Constitution,* January 10, 1961.

16. *Atlanta Journal,* January 10, 1961; *Holmes v. Danner,* 191 F. Supp 394 (1961), 412–17; *Atlanta Journal,* January 11, 1961.

17. *Danner v. Holmes,* 364 U.S. 939 (1961); *Holmes v. Danner,* 191 F. Supp. 394 (1961), 414–16.

18. House Speaker George L. Smith II appointed a special committee "to find and ascertain facts concerning the certain happenings and episodes" pertaining to the desegregation of the university. The committee's report is printed in *Journal of the House of Representatives of the State of Georgia at the Regular Session Commenced at Atlanta, Monday, January 9th, 1961 and Adjourned February 2, 1961 Reconvened February 20, 1961 and Adjourned March 6, 1961* (Hapeville, Ga.: Longino & Porter, 1961), 260–67

(hereafter cited as *Georgia House Journal* [Regular Session, 1961]); see also the statement and responses of Dr. Harmon W. Caldwell, chancellor of the university system, and Robert O. Arnold, chairman of the board of regents, to questions by members of the special committee as well as the letters of Attorney General Cook and Buck Murphy to the chairman of the special committee on whether Hunter had to be housed on campus in ibid., 267–77; *Atlanta Journal*, January 12, 13, 1961, *Atlanta Constitution*, January 12, 1961; Trillin, *Education in Georgia*, 53; Hunter-Gault, *In My Place*, 177–85; Dyer, *University of Georgia*, 332.

19. William P. Trotter to author, July 3, 1997; undated memorandum to Vandiver from Trotter in which Trotter states that he is recalling the events of "last night," referring to the disturbance, Press Releases (January–March 1961) folder, Speech and Press, Vandiver Papers.

20. *Atlanta Journal*, January 12, 1961; *Atlanta Constitution*, January 14, 1961. In the interval between the request and his authorization, Vandiver conferred with Attorney General Cook and Dr. Aderhold on the situation at the university, Press Release of January 12, 1962, Press Releases (January–March 1962) folder, Speech and Press, Vandiver Papers.

21. *Athens Banner-Herald*, January 12, 1961; *Macon News*, January 14, 1961; *Atlanta Constitution*, January 13, 1961; a copy of Jake C. Harris's telegram to Vandiver is reprinted in *Atlanta Constitution*, January 16, 1916; a copy of W. R. Brewster's letter to Vandiver is reprinted in *Atlanta Constitution*, January 18, 1961; *Macon News*, January 15, 1961; *Atlanta Constitution*, January 13, 1961; *Atlanta Journal*, January 16, 1961; *Atlanta Constitution*, January 13, 1961.

22. *Holmes v. Danner*, 191 F. Supp. 394 (1961), 416–17; *Atlanta Constitution*, January 14, 17, 1961.

23. Betty Vandiver, OH Vandiver 13C, p. 10; Talmadge, OH Vandiver 2, p. 8; Vandiver, OH Vandiver 4D, p. 31; Vandiver, OH Vandiver 1B, p. 35; Betty Vandiver, OH Vandiver 13C, p. 55.

24. *Georgia House Journal* (Regular Session, 1961), 231; Byrd, OII Vandiver 11, p. 19; Betty Vandiver, OH Vandiver 13C, p. 10; Smith, OH Vandiver 22, p. 18.

25. *Georgia House Journal* (Regular Session, 1961), 230–38.

26. *Atlanta Constitution*, January 19, 1961; *Macon Telegraph*, January 23, 1961; *Columbus Enquirer*, January 20, 1961; *Atlanta Journal*, January 19, 1961; *Atlanta Journal-Constitution*, January 22, 1961; *Marietta Daily Journal*, January 19, 1961; *DeKalb New Era*, January 26, 1961; *Carroll County Georgian*, January 26, 1961.

27. *Atlanta Constitution*, January 20, 1961; *Atlanta Journal*, January 20, 1961; *Atlanta Constitution*, January 21, 1961; O. C. Aderhold to Vandiver, January 31, 1961, in E. Vandiver Letter folder, O. C. Aderhold Papers, University of Georgia Archives, Athens.

28. *Augusta Courier*, January 30, 1961; *Atlanta Journal*, January 23, 21, 1961; Sanders, Smith, and Vandiver, "Georgia Legends."

29. *Atlanta Journal*, January 23, 1961; Vandiver, "Vandiver Takes the Middle Road," 161–62.

30. *Georgia House Journal* (Regular Session, 1961), 330–33; *Georgia Senate Journal*

(Regular Session, 1961), 198; *Acts and Resolutions* (1961), 1:31–35; *Georgia House Journal* (Regular Session, 1961), 333–35; *Georgia Senate Journal* (Regular Session, 1961), 198–200; *Acts and Resolutions* (1961), 1:595–96; *Georgia House Journal* (Regular Session, 1961), 428–30; *Georgia Senate Journal* (Regular Session, 1961), 141–43; *Acts and Resolutions* (1961), 1:35–39. At the governor's request, the legislature also passed a bill detailing procedure for appealing local board of education decisions to the state board, *Acts and Resolutions* (1961), 1:39–41; *Atlanta Constitution,* January 28, 1961; *Atlanta Journal,* January 27, 29, 1961.

31. *Georgia House Journal* (Regular Session, 1961), 181; *Georgia Senate Journal* (Regular Session, 1961), 12; *Gainesville Daily News* editorial reprinted in *Atlanta Journal-Constitution,* January 22, 1961.

32. *Atlanta Constitution,* January 10, 1961; *Bainbridge Post-Searchlight,* March 16, 1961; *Macon Telegraph,* January 12, 1961; *Atlanta Constitution,* January 12, 1961; *Georgia House Journal* (Regular Session, 1961), 132–33; *Georgia Senate Journal* (Regular Session, 1961), 63–64; *Georgia House Journal* (Regular Session, 1961), 171–73; *Georgia Senate Journal* (Regular Session, 1961), 47; *Acts and Resolutions* (1961), 1:3–24.

33. *Georgia House Journal* (Regular Session, 1961), 92, 179–180; *Atlanta Journal,* January 17, 1961.

34. Turnbull, "Politics in the Budgetary Process," 57–77; Vandiver, "Vandiver Takes the Middle Road," 165; Ballard, OH Vandiver 30A, p. 42; Geer, OH Vandiver 5A, p. 43; Turnbull, "Politics in the Budgetary Process," 73; *Augusta Courier,* March 20, 1961; George Thornwell Smith, interview by Tom Chaffin, August 19 and 20, 1992, pp. 20–21, Georgia Government Documentation Project, Special Collections, Pullen Library.

35. Vandiver, OH Vandiver 4E, p. 38; *Georgia Senate Journal* (Regular Session, 1960), 11; *Georgia House Journal* (Regular Session, 1961), 92, 27.

36. *Atlanta Journal,* January 16, 19, 25, 1961; *Atlanta Constitution,* January 17 and 26, 1961; *Atlanta Journal,* January 26, 1961; *Macon Telegraph,* January 28, 1961.

37. *Macon Telegraph,* February 3, 1961; *Atlanta Journal,* February 2, 1961; *Georgia House Journal* (Regular Session, 1961), 557–58; *Georgia Senate Journal* (Regular Session, 1961), 285; *Atlanta Journal,* February 5, 1961; Turnbull, "Politics in the Budgetary Process," 96; *Atlanta Journal,* February 10, 1961; *Atlanta Constitution,* February 22, 1961.

38. *Atlanta Journal,* February 6, 1961.

39. *Macon Telegraph,* February 7, 1961; *Atlanta Journal,* February 8, 1961; *Atlanta Constitution,* February 23, 1961.

40. *Atlanta Journal,* February 20, 1961.

41. Department of Law, *Opinions of the Attorney General, 1960–61, Eugene Cook Attorney General,* 443–44; *Atlanta Journal,* February 21, 1961.

42. *Atlanta Journal,* February 21, 1961.

43. Ibid.; *Georgia House Journal* (Regular Session, 1961), 682–701; *Atlanta Constitution,* February 22, 1961; *Macon Telegraph,* February 22, 1961; *Atlanta Journal,* February 21, 22, 1961.

44. Vandiver, OH Vandiver 4D, p. 41.

45. Byrd, OH Vandiver 11, p. 22; Neal, OH Vandiver 10, p. 5; *Augusta Courier,* March 13, 1961; *Bainbridge Post-Searchlight,* March 2, 1961; *Atlanta Journal,* February 24, 1961; Jones, OH Vandiver 27, p. 22.

46. *Atlanta Journal,* February 22, 1961; *Atlanta Constitution,* February, 23, 1961; *Macon Telegraph,* February 25,1961.

47. *Atlanta Constitution,* February 24, 1961; *Atlanta Journal,* February 29, 1961; Samuel Ernest Vandiver Jr., interview by John F. Stewart, May 27, 1967, p. 45, John F. Kennedy Oral History Program, Kennedy Library; *Atlanta Constitution,* March 1, 1961; Georgia Senate Journal (Regular Session, 1961), 570–96.

48. Vandiver, OH Vandiver 4D, p. 41; *Georgia House Journal* (Regular Session, 1961), 1130; *Atlanta Constitution,* March 3, 1961.

49. *Georgia House Journal* (Regular Session, 1961), 1130–58; *Augusta Courier,* March 20, 1961; *Atlanta Journal,* March 3, 1961; *Acts and Resolutions* (1961), 1:297–98.

50. OASIS's "Background: A Handbook for Reporters Covering the Desegregation of Atlanta Public Schools," OASIS Papers, Southern Regional Council Papers, Special Collections, Robert W. Woodruff Library, Clark Atlanta University, Atlanta; McGrath, "Great Expectations," 171–75, 204–5.

51. *Atlanta Journal,* June 5, 1961.

52. Ibid., June 10, July 11, 1961; *Atlanta Constitution,* August 9, 1961.

53. *Atlanta Journal,* August 30, 31, 1961; *Public Papers of the Presidents of the United States John F. Kennedy Containing the Public Messages, Speeches, and Statements of the President January 20 to December 31, 1961* (Washington: U.S. Government Printing Office, 1962), 572; Vandiver to John F. Kennedy, June 13, 1963, Vandiver Papers.

54. Leverett, OH Vandiver 8, p. 24.

TEN. The Final Year

1. Charles Pou in *Atlanta Journal-Constitution,* January 7, 1962; *Atlanta Journal,* January 5, 1962; *Journal of the Senate of the State of Georgia at the Regular Session Commenced at Atlanta, Monday, January 8th, 1962 and Adjourned February 16, 1962* (Hapeville, Ga.: Longino & Porter, 1962), 21, 30, 24 (hereafter cited as *Georgia Senate Journal* [Regular Session, 1962]).

2. *Georgia Senate Journal* (Regular Session, 1962), 27; the Pannel Report was printed in ibid., 62–71; ibid., 27–29.

3. *Atlanta Journal,* January 11, 1962; *Macon Telegraph,* January 11, 1962; *Atlanta Constitution,* January 11, 1962.

4. *Atlanta Constitution,* January 11, 1962; *Macon Telegraph,* January 25, 1962.

5. *Atlanta Constitution,* January 18, 1962; *Journal of the House of Representatives of the State of Georgia at the Regular Session Commenced at Atlanta, Monday, January 8th, 1962 and Adjourned February 16,1962* (Hapeville, Ga.: Longino & Porter, 1962), 272–78 (hereafter cited as *Georgia House Journal* [Regular Session, 1962]); *Georgia Senate Journal* (Regular Session, 1962), 115–19; 542–44; *Acts and Resolutions* (1962), 1:17–37.

6. *Acts and Resolutions* (1962), 1:750–55; *Georgia House Journal* (Regular Session, 1962), 1342–47; *Georgia Senate Journal* (Regular Session, 1962), 544–46; Department of Archives and History, Mary G. Bryan, comp., *Georgia's Official Register, 1961–1962*, 1522–23; *Atlanta Journal-Constitution*, February 18, 1962; *Atlanta Constitution*, February 13, 1962.

7. *Atlanta Constitution*, January 6, 1962; *Atlanta Journal*, January 6, 9, 1962; *Macon Telegraph*, January 9, 1962; *Atlanta Constitution*, January 10, 1962; *Atlanta Journal*, January 14, 1962; *Atlanta Constitution*, January 15, 1962.

8. *Atlanta Journal*, January 14, 1962; *Atlanta Constitution*, January 15, 1962.

9. *Atlanta Constitution*, January 18, 1962; *Georgia Senate Journal* (Regular Session, 1962), 121; *Atlanta Constitution*, January 25, 1962; *Atlanta Journal*, February 1 and January 24, 26, 1962; *Macon Telegraph*, February 8, 1962; *Atlanta Constitution*, February 9, 1962; *Georgia Senate Journal* (Regular Session, 1962), 12, 55–57; *Georgia House Journal* (Regular Session, 1962), 2351–55; *Georgia Senate Journal* (Regular Session, 1962), 1268.

10. *Baker v. Carr*, 369 U.S. 186 (1962); *Colegrove v. Green*, 328 U.S. 549 (1946); *Atlanta Journal*, March 27, 1962; *Atlanta Constitution*, March 27, 1962.

11. Key, with Heard, *Southern Politics in State and Nation*, 119; Bartley, *From Thurmond to Wallace*, 22–25; Saye, *Constitutional History of Georgia*, 258–59, 412–14; Rigdon, *Georgia's County Unit System*, 40; Bartley, *From Thurmond to Wallace*, 15.

12. For a collection of newspaper editorials critical and supportive of the county-unit system, see *What Georgia Thinks of the County Unit System: A Cross-section of Editorial Comment Occasioned by the Filing of a Suit in Federal Courts on March 15, 1958 by Mayor William B. Hartsfield to Void the County Unit System, Prepared and Distributed by Mayor William B. Hartsfield*, What Georgia thinks of the county unit system folder, Writings of Hartsfield, William Berry Hartsfield Papers, Special Collections, Robert W. Woodruff Library, Emory University, Atlanta; Key, with Heard, *Southern Politics in State and Nation*, 122; Bernd, *Grass Roots Politics in Georgia*, 6; Anderson, *Wild Man from Sugar Creek*, 200, 229–30, 237–38; Lemmon, "Ideology of Eugene Talmadge," 226–28, 248; Lemmon, "Public Career of Eugene Talmadge," 156–244.

13. Talmadge with Winchell, *Talmadge*, 98–112, 134–39; Pajari, "Talmadge and the Politics of Power," 81–85; Herman Eugene Talmadge, interview by author, June 26 and July 17, 1987, pp. ix–x, Georgia Government Documentation Project, Special Collections, Pullen Library; Bernd, "Georgia: Static and Dynamic," 321–24.

14. *Cook v. Fortson*, 68 F. Supp. 624 (1946); *Turman v. Duckworth*, 68 F. Supp 744 (1946); *Fortson v. Cook*, 329 U.S. 675 (1945); *Duckworth V. Turman*, 329 U.S. 675 (1945).

15. *South v. Peters*, 89 F. Supp. 672 (1950); *Peters v. South*, 339 U.S. 276 (1950); *Cox v. Peters*, 208 Ga. 498 (1951); *Methvin v. Peters*, 208 Ga. 506 (1951); *Cox v. Peters*, 342 U.S. 936 (1952); *Hartsfield v. Sloan*, 357 U.S. 916 (1958).

16. *Atlanta Journal*, April 2, 1962.

17. Ibid., April 3, 1962; *Atlanta Constitution*, April 2, 1962; *Atlanta Journal*, April 2, 1962; *Georgia County Government Magazine* (April 1962): 20–21.

18. *Atlanta Constitution*, April 3, 1962; Vandiver, OH Vandiver 4E, p. 2; *Atlanta Constitution*, April 5, 1962.

19. *Journal of the House of Representatives of the State of Georgia at the Extraordinary Session Commenced at Atlanta, Monday, April 16th, 1962 and Adjourned Friday, April 27th, 1962* (Hapeville, Ga.: Longino & Porter, 1962), 2373–74 (hereafter cited as *Georgia House Journal* [Extraordinary Session, April 1962]); *Atlanta Journal*, April 6, 1962; *Atlanta Constitution*, April 6, 1962.

20. *Atlanta Journal*, April 5, 6, 7, 10, 1962; *Atlanta Constitution*, April 10, 1962.

21. *Atlanta Constitution*, April 10, 1962; *Atlanta Journal*, April 10, 1962.

22. *Atlanta Constitution*, April 10, 1962; *Atlanta Journal*, April 11, 1962; *Atlanta Constitution*, April 11, 1962; *Atlanta Journal*, April 10, 1962; *Georgia House Journal* (Extraordinary Session, April 1962), 2374–75.

23. *Atlanta Journal*, April 11, 1962; *Atlanta Constitution*, April 10, 13, 14, 1962; *Atlanta Journal*, April 16, 1962.

24. *Atlanta Journal*, April 13, 16, 1962; Lefkoff, "Georgia County Unit Case," 43–44; *Atlanta Journal*, April 16, 24, 1962.

25. *Atlanta Constitution*, April 17, 1962; *Georgia House Journal* (Extraordinary Session, April 1962), 2383–88.

26. *Atlanta Constitution*, April 17, 1962; *Atlanta Journal*, April 17, 1962.

27. *Atlanta Constitution*, April 19, 1962.

28. Ibid., April 20, 1962; *Atlanta Journal*, April 20, 23, 1962.

29. *Atlanta Journal*, April 23, 1962; Byrd, OH Vandiver 11, pp. 23–24.

30. *Georgia House Journal* (Extraordinary Session, April 1962), 2414–25; *Atlanta Constitution*, April 25, 1962; *Journal of the Senate of the State of Georgia at the Extraordinary Session Commenced at Atlanta, Monday, April 16th, 1962 and Adjourned Friday, April 27th, 1962* (Hapeville, Ga.: Longino & Porter, 1962), 1368–72 (hereafter cited as *Georgia Senate Journal* [Extraordinary Session, April 1962]); *Atlanta Constitution*, April 27, 1962; *Georgia Senate Journal* (Extraordinary Session, April 1962), 1377–79; *Atlanta Constitution*, April 27, 1962; *Georgia House Journal* (Extraordinary Session, April 1962), 2457–62; *Georgia Senate Journal* (Extraordinary Session, April 1962), 1380–84; *Atlanta Constitution*, April 27, 28, 1962; *Atlanta Journal*, April 28, 1962. The law provided for twenty-seven population brackets for allocating unit votes. See *Act and Proclamations Extraordinary Session of the General Assembly of the State of Georgia 1962* in *Acts and Resolutions* (1962), 1:1217–22.

31. *Sanders v. Gray*, 203 F. Supp. 158 (1962), 170–71; Bell, OH Vandiver 7, p. 39; *Atlanta Journal-Constitution*, April 28, 1962; *Atlanta Journal*, April 29, 1962; *Atlanta Constitution*, April 30, 1962; Carter, *Turning Point*, 40.

32. *Atlanta Journal*, April 30, 1962; Dubay, "Marvin Griffin and the Politics of the Stump," 105.

33. *Toombs v. Fortson*, 205 F. Supp. 248 (1962), 251, 259; *Atlanta Journal*, May 28, 1962; *Atlanta Constitution*, June 6, 1962.

34. *Atlanta Constitution*, June 19, 1962; *Atlanta Journal*, June 27, 1962; Rigdon, *County Unit System*, 25–26.

35. *Journal of the House of Representatives of the State of Georgia at the Extraordinary Session Commenced at Atlanta on September 27, 1962 and Adjourned October 8, 1962,* (Hapeville, Ga.: Longino & Porter, 1962), 6–7; *Acts and Proclamations Extraordi-*

nary Session of the General Assembly of the State of Georgia 1962 September 27, 1962–October 8,1962 (Hapeville, Ga.: Longino & Porter, 1962), 7–52; *Atlanta Constitution,* October 6, 1962.

36. *Gray v. Sanders,* 372 U.S. 368 (1963), 381; Leverett, OH Vandiver 8, pp. 22–24.

ELEVEN. Well Done

1. Samuel Ernest Vandiver Jr., interview by Hugh Cates, February 23, 1971, p.18, Russell Oral History Collection.

2. Samuel Ernest Vandiver Jr., OH Vandiver 4E, p.7; Vandiver to author, September 25, 1997; Samuel Ernest Vandiver Jr., interview by Charles B. Pyles, April (n.d.) 1990, p. 57, Georgia Government Documentation Project, Pullen Library.

3. Department of Archives and History, Mary G. Bryan, comp., *Georgia's Official Register, 1961–62,* 64; Garland Turk Byrd, OH Vandiver 11, p.1; Cook, *Carl Sander,* 82; Samuel Ernest Vandiver Jr., interview by Charles B. Pyles, April (n.d.) 1990, p. 56, Special Collections, Pullen Library; Carl Edward Sanders, OH Vandiver 3, p. 16.

4. Carl Edward Sanders, interview by James F. Cook, August 5, 12, 1986, pp. 23–24, Georgia Government Documentation Project, Special Collections, Pullen Library.

5. Cook, *Carl Sanders,* 83; Vandiver, OH Vandiver 4E, p. 6; Vandiver to author, September 25, 1997; Samuel Ernest Vandiver Jr., interview by Karen Kelley, August 7, 1980, p. 21, Russell Oral History Collection; Sanders, telephone interview by author, October 3, 1997; Henry Gretzen Neal, OH Vandiver 10, p. 9.

6. Vandiver to author, September 25, 1997; Fite, *Richard B. Russell,* 426–31; Cook, *Carl Sanders,* 233; Sanders, telephone interview by author, October 3, 1997; Vandiver, telephone interview by author, October 26, 1997.

7. Vandiver, OH Vandiver 4E, pp. 5–6.

8. Ibid., p. 5; *Atlanta Constitution,* September 5, 1962; Department of Archives and History, Mary G. Bryan, comp., *Georgia's Official Register, 1959–1960,* 981; *Atlanta Constitution,* September 6, 8, 1962; Roswell Hair, "President's Letter," *Georgia Municipal Journal* (October 1962): 5.

9. *Atlanta Journal-Constitution,* August 12, 1962; *Atlanta Journal,* August 21, 18, 1962; *Atlanta Journal-Constitution,* August 12, 1962; *Atlanta Journal,* August 21, 18, 1962; Louis Harris and Associates, "A Survey of the Political Climate in the State of Georgia July 1962," pp. 6, 8, Survey of Georgia Politics 1950–58, Political, Herman E. Talmadge Collection, Russell Library.

10. Grimes and Barry, "Vandiver's Rendezvous with Destiny," 51; *Atlanta Journal,* September 13, 1962; *Georgia Recorder,* July 27, 1961; *Bainbridge Post-Searchlight,* June 30, November 3, 1960.

11. Robert Howell Hall, July 28, 1994, OH Vandiver 28, p. 9; The number of indictments was given in an article by Jack Nelson in *Atlanta Journal-Constitution,* August 26, 1962; *Bainbridge Post-Searchlight,* May 18, 1961; *Atlanta Constitution,* December 22, 1960.

12. *Bainbridge Post-Searchlight,* July 27, 1961; *Atlanta Journal,* August 14, 1962; *Bainbridge Post-Searchlight,* August 31, 1961.

13. *Georgia Recorder,* March 9, 1962; *Atlanta Journal,* August 31, 1962; *Atlanta Journal-Constitution,* July 22, 1962; *Georgia Recorder,* July 13, 1962.

14. *Atlanta Journal-Constitution,* July 22, 1962; *Georgia Recorder,* July 13, 1962; *Atlanta Journal-Constitution,* September 9, 1962; *Georgia Recorder,* August 17, 1962; *Atlanta Journal,* July 19, 1962.

15. *Atlanta Journal,* July 23, 1962; *Atlanta Constitution,* July 24, 17, 1962; *Atlanta Journal,* July 30, 1962; *Atlanta Constitution,* July 24, 1962.

16. *Atlanta Journal-Constitution,* September 2, 1962; *Atlanta Constitution,* September 3, 1962.

17. Department of Archives and History, Mary G. Bryan, comp., *Georgia's Official Register, 1961–1962,* 1436; *Atlanta Journal,* September 13, 1962; Cook, *Carl Sanders,* 96; Bernd, "Georgia: Static and Dynamic," 333–34.

18. *Atlanta Journal-Constitution,* April 15, 1962; Vandiver, "Vandiver Takes the Middle Road," 162; text of remarks of Vandiver at final news conference as governor, December 31, 1962, Texts—November–December 1962 folder, Speech and Press, Vandiver Papers; *Atlanta Constitution,* January 15, 1963.

19. Department of Audits, *State Auditor's Report, Year Ending June 30, 1958,* 29; Department of Audits, *State Auditor's Report, Year Ending June 30, 1962,* 33; *Georgia Senate Journal* (Regular Session, 1962), 23.

20. *Georgia House Journal* (Regular Session, 1962), 183; *A Report from S. Ernest Vandiver, of Lavonia, Seventy-third Governor of Georgia to the People of Georgia, to Their Representatives in the General Assembly, and to the Nation Covering the First Three Years of the Administration, January, 1959 to January, 1962 Published January 10, 1962,* 10–12, 41 (hereafter cited as *Report from Vandiver*); Department of Education, *Ninetieth and Ninety-first Annual Reports of the Department of Education to the General Assembly of the State of Georgia for the Biennium Ending June 30, 1962,* 77–78; *Athens Banner-Herald,* January 11, 1963; *Atlanta Journal,* June 14, 1962, and January 30, 1963.

21. Text of remarks of Vandiver, January 11, 1963, Speech Texts—January 1963, Speech and Press, Vandiver Papers; *Report from Vandiver,* 60–62.

22. *Georgia House Journal* (Regular Session, 1962), 183; *Report from Vandiver,* 54.

23. *Georgia House Journal* (Regular Session ,1962), 183; *Report from Vandiver,* 34–36, 96.

24. Bartley, *New South,* 162, 256; *Atlanta Constitution,* June 2, 1961; Vandiver, "Vandiver Takes the Middle Road," 163. The tours began in 1960, according to W. Cam Mitchell, chairman of the Industrial Development Council of the Georgia State Chamber of Commerce. Mitchell to Henry W. Troutman, April 17, 1964, Red Carpet Tours 1963, 1964, 1965 folder, General Correspondence, Legal Office Files 1963–66, Vandiver Papers; address of Vandiver welcoming participants in the Red Carpet Tour, December 5, 1960, Texts (S.E.V.)—October–December 1960 folder, Speech and Press, Vandiver Papers; Vandiver, "Vandiver Takes the Middle Road," 163.

25. Text of address given by Vandiver in San Francisco, October 11, 1962, September–October 1962 folder, Speech and Press, Vandiver Papers; text of address given by Vandiver in Atlanta, December 5, 1960, Texts (S.E.V.)—October–December 1960 folder, Speech and Press, Vandiver Papers; text of address given to a joint meeting of elected officials from Telfair and Wilcox Counties at Fitzgerald, Georgia, on January 31, 1966, Speeches—January 1966 folder, Speech and Press, Vandiver Papers.

26. *Report from Vandiver,* 40; Bartley, *Creation of Modern Georgia,* 199; *Report from Vandiver,* 40.

27. Text of remarks by Vandiver at Atlanta, November 13, 1962, Texts—November–December 1962 folder, Speech and Press, Vandiver Papers; address by Vandiver at Jekyll Island, August 21, 1961, Speeches and Releases—July–August 1961 folder, Speech and Press, Vandiver Papers; *Report from Vandiver,* 46–52.

28. *Report from Vandiver,* 46–48; *Atlanta Journal,* November 11 and December 21, 1962.

29. Pyles, "Ernest Vandiver and the Politics of Change," 152–53; Vandiver, "Vandiver Takes the Middle Road," 164–65; John A. Sibley to J. M. Cheatham, November 15, 1961, Mrs. Vandiver and Gov. Vandiver 1961–62 folder, Chapel of All Faiths, Sibley Papers; Sybil Elizabeth "Betty" Vandiver, OH Vandiver 13B, pp. 45–47; Betty Vandiver, OH Vandiver 13C, pp. 3–6.

30. Department of Audits, *Report of the State Auditor of Georgia Year Ending June 30, 1958. Supplement,* viii; *Report of the State Auditor of Georgia Year Ending June 30, 1962. Supplement,* viii; *Report from Vandiver,* 8; *Atlanta Constitution,* September 5, 1962; Department of Education, *Eighty-eighth and Eighty-ninth Annual Reports of the Department of Education to the General Assembly of the State of Georgia for the Biennium Ending June 30, 1960,* 420; *Ninety-second and Ninety-third Annual Reports of the Department of Education to the General Assembly of the State of Georgia for the Biennium Ending June 30, 1964,* 245–46. While the average salaries of teachers can readily be obtained in the report for the 1958–59 school year, the report for 1962–63 includes teachers and teaching principals in its determination of average teachers' salaries; University System of Georgia, *1959 Annual Report University System of Georgia,* 6; *1963 Annual Report University System of Georgia,* 7; text of remarks by Vandiver at his final news conference as governor, December 31, 1962, Texts—November–December 1962 folder, Vandiver Papers; *Report from Vandiver,* 110; Jack M. Forrester to Vandiver, July 2, 1962, Governor's Special File, October 1962–September 1963 folder, Personal Files, Governor's Office Files 1959–62, Vandiver Papers.

31. Vandiver, "Vandiver Takes the Middle Road," 162; *Report from Vandiver,* 9; Vandiver to Mrs. Myrtle Oxford, July 28, 1998, copy provided to author by Vandiver; Ivan Allen Jr. to Vandiver, July 11, 1961, Fulton County folder, County Files, Governor's Office Files 1959–62, Vandiver Papers; Vandiver, "Vandiver Takes the Middle Road," 165–66.

32. *Report from Vandiver,* 58, 76; Department of Archives and History, Mary G. Bryan, comp., *Georgia's Official Register, 1959–1960,* 981; "A Big Day for Georgia's Towns and Cities" speech given by the governor in Atlanta on September 6, 1962, text

reprinted in *Georgia Municipal Journal* (October 1962): 7–8; George, "Executive Director's Report," 6.

33. Pou, "Epilogue," 43; Cook, *Carl Sanders,* 124; *Columbus Ledger,* January 3, 1963; *Atlanta Journal-Constitution,* September 16, November 25, 1962; Galphin, *Riddle of Lester Maddox,* 106.

34. *Athens Banner-Herald,* January 6, 1963; *Macon Telegraph,* January 11, 1963; *Atlanta Constitution,* July 2, December 18, 1962.

35. Williams remarks reprinted in Charles Pou's article in *Atlanta Journal-Constitution,* January 6, 1963; *Savannah Morning News,* January 4, 1963; *Georgia Municipal Journal* (December 1962): 7; copy of *Georgia State AFL-CIO News,* January 1963 editorial in Administrative Policy 1962 folder, Subjects 1961–62, Governor's Office Files 1959–62, Vandiver Papers; *Atlanta Journal-Constitution,* January 6, 1963.

36. Odell Dyer to Vandiver, June 5, 1962, Richmond County folder, County Files, Governor's Office Files 1959–62, Vandiver Papers; Hudson Malone to Vandiver, January 7, 1963, Governor's Special File—October 1962–September 1963 folder, Personal Files, Governor's Office Files 1959–62, Vandiver Papers; E. M. Vereen to Vandiver, May 4, 1960, Colquitt County, County Files, Governor's Office Files 1959–62, Vandiver Papers; Mrs. H. M. Dixon to Vandiver, January 1, 1963, Vandiver Papers; J. E. Cay Jr. to Vandiver, November 12, 1962, Vandiver Papers; Guy K. Hutcherson to Vandiver, May 20, 1963, Personal Correspondence January–May 1963 folder, Personal/Political, Vandiver Papers; Buchner F. Milton to Vandiver, December 6, 1962, Vandiver Papers; "Governor Vandiver Day," a WRBL radio and television editorial by George Gingell, January 8, 1962, Governor's Special File October 1962–September 1963 folder, Personal Files, Governor's Office Files 1959–62, Vandiver Papers.

37. Text of remarks of O. C. Aderhold introducing Vandiver at Athens Appreciation Day dinner, January 11, 1963, copy in possession of the governor; P. T. McCutchen to Vandiver, January 7, 1963, Vandiver Papers; Glenn W. Ellard to Vandiver, May 16, 1962, Personal Correspondence—January–May 1963 folder, Personnal/Political, Legal Office Files 1963–66, Vandiver Papers; W. H. Duckworth to Vandiver, December 19, 1962, Vandiver Papers; text of remarks by W. Frank Branch in the House of Representatives on February 5, 1962, Personal Correspondence—February 1966 folder, Personnal/Political, Legal Office Files 1963–66, Vandiver Papers; Fielding L. Dilliard to Vandiver, June 25, 1962, incorrectly filed in July–August 1962 folder, Press Releases, Speech and Press 1954–66, Vandiver Papers.

38. Henderson, *Politics of Change in Georgia,* 158–163; Vandiver, OH Vandiver 4F, pp. 20–21; Betty Vandiver, OH Vandiver, 13C, p. 34.

39. *Report from Vandiver,* 44; Bayer, *Race and the Shaping of Twentieth Century Atlanta,* 191; Herbert, *Highways to Nowhere,* 110.

40. Ivan Allen Jr. to Vandiver, March 4, 1963, and Vandiver to Allen, March 5, 1963, Rapid Transit Committee of 100 January–June 1963 folder, General Correspondence, Legal Office Files 1963–66, Vandiver Papers; Congressman G. Elliott Hagan to Vandiver, April 20, 1964, Vandiver to Congressman James C. Davis, April 7, 1964, Congressman Charles L. Weltner to Vandiver, April 16, 1964, Rapid Transit January–June 1964

folder, General Correspondence, Legal Office Files 1963–66, Vandiver Papers; *Atlanta Journal,* March 14, 1963. A membership list of the Committee of 100 and the executive committee is in Rapid Transit Committee of 100 January–June 1963 folder, General Correspondence, Legal Office Files, 1963–66, Vandiver Papers.

41. Telegram from Vandiver to Senators Russell and Talmadge (n.d.), Rapid Transit Committee of 100 January–June 1963 folder, General Correspondence, Legal Office Files 1963–66, Vandiver Papers; Congressman Weltner to Vandiver, June 30, 1964, Rapid Transit January–June 1964 folder, General Correspondence, Legal office Files 1963–66, Vandiver Papers.

42. *Acts and Resolutions* (1964), 1:1008–11; *Atlanta Journal,* October 7, 1964: *Atlanta Constitution,* October 21, 1964.

43. Ivan Allen Jr. to Vandiver, March 4, 1963, Rapid Transit Committee of 100 January–June 1963 folder, General Correspondence, Legal Office Files, 1963–66, Vandiver Papers; Vandiver to Herbert C. McMullum, July 14, 1964, Rapid Transit July–December 1964 folder, General Correspondence, Legal Office Files 1963–66, Vandiver Papers; W. P. Corley to Vandiver, July 14, 1964, Rapid Transit July–December 1964 folder, General Correspondence, Legal Office Files 1963–66, Vandiver Papers; Vandiver to Col. Oscar Thompson, December 13, 1963, Rapid Transit Citizens Committee 1963–66 folder, General Correspondence, Legal Office Files 1963–66, Vandiver Papers; Vandiver to J. D. Gay, August 4, 1964, Rapid Transit July–December 1964, General Correspondence, Legal Office Files, 1963–66, Vandiver Papers; *Atlanta Constitution,* October 7, 1964; *Atlanta Journal,* October 7, 1964.

44. *Acts and Resolutions* (1966), 1:1283–84; *Atlanta Constitution,* November 5, 1964; Ivan Allen Jr. to Vandiver, November 18, 1964, City of Atlanta Board of Aldermen Resolution adopted November 16, 1964, Rapid Transit July–December 1964 folder, General Correspondence, Legal Office Files 1963–66, Vandiver Papers; Richard H. Rich to Vandiver, November 6, 1964, Rawson Haverty to Vandiver, November 5, 1964, Rep. Wilson Brooks to Vandiver, November 5, 1964, Rapid Transit July–December 1964 folder, General Correspondence, Legal Office Files 1963–66, Vandiver Papers; minutes of final meeting, Metropolitan Atlanta Rapid Transit Committee of 100 and form letter sent to committee of 100 members, no date given, Rapid Transit Committee of 100 January–June 1963 folder, General Correspondence, Legal Office Files 1963–66, Vandiver Papers.

45. *Atlanta Constitution,* November 5, 1964; *Atlanta Journal,* January 26, 1965; *Atlanta Constitution,* May 19, 1965; *Atlanta Journal,* June 17, 1965; Vandiver to Major General James F. Cantwell, November 12, 1963, National Guard Association of the United States folder, General Correspondence, Legal Office Files 1963–66, Vandiver Papers.

46. *Atlanta Journal,* May 24 and June 17, 1963; *Atlanta Constitution,* February 15, 1964; Vandiver to Philip H. Alston, July 21, 1964, University of Georgia folder, General Correspondence, Legal Office Files 1963–66, Vandiver Papers; Dr. John W. Ferree to Vandiver, October 8, 1964, Georgia Society for Prevention of Blindness folder, General Correspondence, Legal Office Files 1963–66, Vandiver Papers; Basil O'Connor to Vandiver, August 22, 1963, March of Dimes folder, General Correspondence, Legal Office

Files 1963–66, Vandiver Papers; William Rotterman to Vandiver, May 28, 1964, Mental Health Association folder, General Correspondence, Legal Office Files 1963–66, Vandiver Papers; T. Baldwin Martin to Vandiver, April 1, 1964, Mercer University folder, General Correspondence, Legal Office Files 1963–66, Vandiver Papers; *Atlanta Journal,* April 1, June 7, 1964; Vandiver to Philip H. Alston Jr., February 2, 1965, University of Georgia folder, General Correspondence, Legal Office Files 1963–66, Vandiver Papers.

TWELVE. Family Life

1. Vandiver, September 15, 1993, OH Vandiver 4G, pp. 13, 9; Sybil Elizabeth "Betty" Vandiver, OH Vandiver 13A, pp. 20, 2–3.
2. Jane Brevard Vandiver Kidd, OH Vandiver 14, pp. 10–11, 3.
3. Ibid., p. 25.
4. Ibid., pp. 1–2, 12.
5. Vanna Elizabeth "Beth" Vandiver, OH Vandiver 15, pp. 5, 1–2, 11.
6. Samuel Ernest "Chip" Vandiver III, OH Vandiver 16A, pp. 1–2, 4, 7–10.
7. Ibid., pp. 2–5, 10–11, 30–32.
8. Jane Kidd, OH Vandiver 14, p. 6; Beth Vandiver, OH Vandiver 15, p. 4; Chip Vandiver, OH Vandiver 16A, p. 29; Barnwell, "How the Vandivers Live," 44; Chip Vandiver, OH Vandiver 16A, p. 29.
9. Betty Vandiver, OH Vandiver 13A, p. 46.
10. Betty Vandiver, OH Vandiver 13B, pp. 16–18; William Rowe, "Vandivers Strong on Family Life," *Columbus Sunday Ledger-Enquirer Magazine* [no date given], in biographical folder, Subjects, Governor's Office Files 1959–62, Vandiver Papers.
11. Betty Vandiver, OH Vandiver 13B, pp. 19–20.
12. Cook, *Carl Sanders,* 137–38; Vandiver, OH Vandiver 4G, pp. 2–3; *Acts and Resolutions* (1961), 1:283–85; *Acts and Resolutions* (1962), 1:441–42.
13. Betty Vandiver, OH Vandiver 13B, pp. 33–34.
14. Barnwell, "How the Vandivers Live," 10, 44; Betty Vandiver, OH Vandiver 13B, pp. 34–35.
15. Vandiver, OH Vandiver 4G, pp. 3–4; Betty Vandiver, OH Vandiver 13B, pp. 39–40; Jane Kidd, OH Vandiver 14, p. 16.
16. Barnwell, "How the Vandivers Live," 44; Betty Vandiver, OH Vandiver 13B, pp. 42–43; Chip Vandiver, OH Vandiver 16A, pp. 36–37; Betty Vandiver, OH Vandiver 13B, p. 43; Jane Kidd, OH Vandiver 14, p. 7.
17. Jane Kidd, OH Vandiver 14, pp. 14–15.
18. Ibid., pp. 9, 11; Beth Vandiver, OH Vandiver 15, pp. 6–7, 11; Chip Vandiver, OH Vandiver 16A, pp, 33; Jane Kidd, OH Vandiver 14, pp. 12, 15–16.
19. Betty Vandiver, OH Vandiver 13, p. 35; Barnwell, "How the Vandivers Live," Bp. 46.
20. Betty Vandiver, OH Vandiver 13B, pp. 37–38; Jane Kidd, OH Vandiver 14, pp. 13–14; Chip Vandiver, OH Vandiver 16A, pp. 35–36; Betty Vandiver, OH Vandiver 13B, p. 38.
21. Barnwell, "How the Vandivers Live," 46; Betty Vandiver, 13B, pp. 39–40.

22. Jane Kidd, OH Vandiver 14, pp. 17–18.

23. Beth Vandiver, OH Vandiver 15, p. 8; Jane Kidd, OH Vandiver 14, pp. 16–17; Chip Vandiver, OH Vandiver 16A, p. 10; Barnwell, "How the Vandivers Live," 44.

24. Neal, OH Vandiver 9, pp. 24–25; Betty Vandiver, OH Vandiver 13B, p.41; Betty Vandiver, OH Vandiver 13C, pp. 17–18.

25. Barnwell, "How the Vandivers Live," 46; Betty Vandiver, OH Vandiver 13B, pp. 43–47.

26. Vandiver, OH Vandiver 4G, pp. 5–7; Jane Kidd, OH Vandiver 14, p. 27.

27. Barnwell, "How the Vandivers Live," 44.

THIRTEEN. Vandiver's Last Hurrahs

1. Vandiver to Lyndon B. Johnson, November 27, 1963, Personal Correspondence August–December 1963 folder, Personal/Political, Legal Office Files 1963–66, Vandiver Papers.

2. U.S. Bureau of the Census, *Historical Statistics of the United States: Colonial Times to 1970, Part 2*, 1075–76; Clark and Kirwan, *South since Appomattox*, 52; Petersen, *Statistical History of the American Presidential Elections*, 126; Bartley and Graham, *Southern Elections*, 95; Vandiver to John F. Kennedy, June 13, 1963, Vandiver Papers.

3. Cosman, *Five States for Goldwater*, 40–41, 62; Cook, *Carl Sanders*, 209–10; *Augusta Courier*, November 16, 1964; Vandiver to author, November 21, 1997.

4. Smith, "Vandivers of Lavonia," 11–12; Beschloss, *Taking Charge*, 71.

5. Bartley and Graham, *Southern Elections*, 95; *Atlanta Constitution*, November 12, 13, 1964; Vandiver, Russell Oral History # 107, pp. 33–34; Vandiver to President and Mrs. Lyndon Johnson, December 2, 1964, Personal Correspondence—September–December 1964 folder, Personal/Political, Legal Office Files 1963–65, Vandiver Papers.

6. *Atlanta Constitution*, June 15, 1965; Vandiver to Lyndon B. Johnson, June 22, 1965, Personal Correspondence—June–July 1965 folder, Personal/Political, Legal Office Files 1963–66, Vandiver Papers.

7. *Atlanta Journal-Constitution*, September 2, 1963; *Atlanta Journal-Constitution*, April 28, 1963; Beschloss, *Taking Charge*, 71; *Savannah Evening Press*, March 25, 1965, Political Clippings—1965 folder, Personal/Political, Legal Office Files 1963–66, Vandiver Papers; Zell B. Miller to Vandiver, July 31,1964, Personal Correspondence—July–August 1964 folder, Personal/Political, Legal Office Files 1963–66, Vandiver Papers; *Augusta Courier*, November 30, 1964; *Columbus Ledger*, April 8, 1965; Political Clippings—1965 folder, Personal/Political, Legal Office Files 1963–66, Vandiver Papers; transcript of letter dictated via telephone by Ralph McGill to Jack ———, February 11, 1965, Vandiver, A–E folder, White House Central Files, box 18, Lyndon Baines Johnson Papers, Lyndon B. Johnson Library, Austin, Texas.

8. Vandiver to J. Lucius Black, September 24, 1964, Congratulations to Legislators—1964 folder, Personal/Political, Legal Office Files 1963–66, Vandiver Papers; Vandiver to Curtis C. Herdon, January 13, 1964, Invitations to Legislature—1964, Personal/Political,

Legal Office Files 1963–66, Vandiver Papers; Vandiver to Robert H. Farmer, May 14, 1965, Letters to Legislators—May–July 1965 folder, Letters of Support, Governor of Georgia 1966, Campaigns, Vandiver Papers; Vandiver to Richard Kenyon, September 14, 1965, and telegram from Vandiver to Joe Hurst, September 20, 1965, General Correspondence—September 1965 folder, General Correspondence, Legal Office Files 1963–66, Vandiver Papers; Vandiver to T. E. Kennedy, July 30, 1965, Personal Correspondence—June–July 1965 folder, Personal/Political, Legal Office Files 1963–1966, Vandiver Papers; see list of Christmas cards and thank-you letters in Personal/Political, Legal Office Files 1963–65, Vandiver Papers; 1965 and 1966 Speech Schedule, Speech and Press 1954–66, Vandiver Papers.

9. *Atlanta Constitution,* May 25, 1965; Henderson, "1966 Gubernatorial Election in Georgia," 51–52.

10. *Atlanta Constitution,* May 25, 1965.

11. *Atlanta Constitution,* July 2, June 30, August 13, December 11, July 24, 1965; Herman E. Talmadge interview by author, April 21, 1981, Henderson Oral History Collection; *Atlanta Constitution,* July 24, 1965; Samuel Ernest Vandiver, interview by author, May 23, 1981, Henderson Oral History Collection.

12. *Atlanta Constitution,* July 23, 1965; Henderson, "1966 Gubernatorial Election in Georgia," 75–77; Henderson, "Ellis Arnall, " 27–28; Henderson, "1966 Gubernatorial Election," 97–98.

13. Carl Edward Sanders, interview by author, June 11, 1981, Henderson Oral History Collection; Henderson, *Ellis Arnall,* 153–58.

14. Henderson, *Ellis Arnall,* 33–50; 171–89, 206–7, 144–45, 220–21.

15. Samuel Ernest Vandiver Jr., interview, May 23, 1981, Henderson Oral History Collection; Henderson, "1966 Gubernatorial Election," 81–83.

16. Henderson, "1966 Gubernatorial Election," 83–87, 57.

17. *Atlanta Constitution,* November 18, 1965; Vandiver interview, May 23, 1981, Henderson Oral History Collection; *Atlanta Constitution,* October 6, November 18, and August 24, 1965.

18. *Atlanta Constitution,* August 24, 27, 1965; Vandiver, OH Vandiver 4B, pp. 13–14, Vandiver Papers; Vandiver to Brooks Smith, January 4, 1966, Personal Correspondence—January 1966 folder, Personal/Political, Legal Office Files 1963–66, Vandiver Papers; Ellis Arnall's letter to the editor reprinted in *Marietta Daily Journal,* February 3, 1966, News Clippings—December 1965–March 1966 folder, News Clippings, Governor of Georgia 1966, Campaigns, Vandiver Papers; Vandiver, OH Vandiver 4E, pp. 13–14.

19. *Atlanta Constitution,* November 6 and September 2, 1965; Vandiver, OH Vandiver 4E, pp. 11–13; *Atlanta Constitution,* September 2, August 24, 1965, and April 25, 1966; for background information pertaining to the routing of I-85, see Highway Department—Interstate 85 folder, Subjects, Governor's Office Files 1959–62, Vandiver Papers.

20. *Atlanta Constitution,* July 21, 1965; *A Platform for Progress for Georgia by Ernest Vandiver Presenting His Candidacy for Governor of Georgia,* Campaign Speeches 1966 folder, Speech and Press, Vandiver Papers.

21. Henderson, "1966 Gubernatorial Election," 188–90.

22. *Atlanta Constitution,* November 26, 1964, and January 26, 1965; *Atlanta Journal,* February 14, 1965; *Athens Banner-Herald,* September 4, 1965; *Atlanta Journal,* February 19, 1965; Howard Hollis Callaway, telephone interview by author, May 8, 1981, Henderson Oral History Collection.

23. Vandiver interview, May 23, 1981, Henderson Oral History Collection; Vandiver, OH Vandiver 4E, p. 8; Betty Vandiver, OH Vandiver 13C, p. 31; Carter Smith to Vandiver, May 16, 1966, Correspondence May 1–May 17, 1966 folder, Correspondence, Governor of Georgia 1966, Campaigns, Vandiver Papers.

24. Vandiver interview, May 23, 1981, Henderson Oral History Collection; Vandiver, OH Vandiver 4E, pp. 8–9; *Atlanta Constitution,* May 19, 1966.

25. Henderson, "1966 Gubernatorial Election," 61–69.

26. Ibid., 72–75; Vandiver, OH Vandiver 4E, pp. 16–17.

27. Henderson, *Ellis Arnall,* 234–35.

28. Henderson, "1966 Gubernatorial Election," 178, 181–82.

29. Ibid., 235, 248–56, 262.

30. Cook, *Carl Sanders,* 320–21; Fite, *Richard B. Russell,* 491, 489.

31. Vandiver, OH Vandiver 4F, pp. 33, 25; Sanders, OH Vandiver 3, p. 18.

32. Vandiver, OH Vandiver 4F, pp. 25–26, 32; Bell, OH Vandiver 7, pp. 51–53.

33. Vandiver, OH Vandiver 4F, pp. 32–33, 26; Jimmy Carter, interview by Kenneth J. Bindas, Melvin T. Steeley, and Kenneth W. Noe, May 4, 1993, Georgia Political Heritage Series, Special Collections, Irvin S. Ingrams Library, State University of West Georgia, Carrollton.

34. *Atlanta Journal-Constitution,* August 16, 1970; Vandiver, OH Vandiver 4F, pp. 27, 34; Morris, *Jimmy Carter,* 188; Samuel Ernest Vandiver, interview by Charles B. Pyles, April (n.d.) 1990, p. 66, Georgia Government Documentation Project, Special Collections, Pullen Library; *Atlanta Journal,* November 19, 1970.

35. Fite, *Richard B. Russell,* 491; *Atlanta Constitution,* January 22, 1971; *Atlanta Journal,* January 22, 1971; *Atlanta Constitution,* January 28, 26, 1971; Carter interview, Georgia Political Heritage Series; Tamadge interview, OH Vandiver 2, p. 13.

36. Betty Vandiver, OH Vandiver 13C, pp. 34–35, Vandiver, OH Vandiver 4F, p. 28.

37. *Atlanta Journal,* February 1, 1971; Betty Vandiver, OH Vandiver 13C, p. 36; Mellichamp, *Senators from Georgia,* 287; *Macon Telegraph and News,* July 16, 1972; Lanier, OH Vandiver 26B, p. 7; Department of Archives and History, Edna Lackey, comp., *Georgia Official and Statistical Register 1971–72,* 978; Mellichamp, *Senators from Georgia,* 287.

38. Carter interview, Political Heritage Series; *Atlanta Constitution,* February 2, 1971; *Atlanta Journal,* February 2, 1971; William R. Hamilton & Staff, *A Survey of Political Opinions in Georgia, Part 1, Prepared for: Senator David Gambrell, Job 267, July 1971,* pp. 7, 12, Survey of Georgia Politics, Politics, Herman E. Talmadge Collection, Russell Library.

39. *Atlanta Constitution,* February 3, 1971; Carter interview, Political Heritage Series; Vandiver, OH Vandiver 4F, pp. 36–37.

40. *Atlanta Journal,* November 1, 1971; Announcement Speech—February 16, 1972

folder, Announcements, Platform, Speaking Schedules, U.S. Senate 1972, Campaign, Vandiver Papers; Grimes and Barry, "Vandiver's Rendezvous with Destiny," 52; Atlanta Press Club Speech, December 7, 1971, folder, Speeches and Press Releases, U.S. Senate 1972, Campaign, Vandiver Papers.

41. Department of Archives and History, Edna Lackey, comp., *Georgia Official and Statistical Register, 1971–1972*, 1629–40; *Atlanta Constitution*, April 11, 1972; Cook, *Carl Sanders*, 342; Vandiver interview by Pyles, 67; Vandiver, OH Vandiver 4F, pp. 29–30; *Atlanta Constitution*, June 15, 1972.

42. Text of Vandiver's speech in Double-talk Speech folder, Speeches and Press Releases, U.S. Senate 1972, Campaigns, Vandiver Papers; *Atlanta Constitution*, June 30, 1972; *Atlanta Journal*, June 27, 28, 1972; statement by Vandiver on July 6, 1972, in Press Releases folder, Subject File, U.S. Senate 1972, Campaigns, Vandiver Papers.

43. *Gwinnett Daily News*, March 15, 1972; text of Vandiver's speech in E. E. O. C. Speech, May 17, 1972, folder, Speeches and Press Releases, 1972 U.S. Senate, Campaigns, Vandiver Papers; *Atlanta Journal*, July 27, 1972; Announcement Speech—February 16, 1972, folder, Vandiver Papers.

44. Announcement Speech—February 16, 1972 folder, Vandiver Papers; *Atlanta Constitution*, May 25, 1972; *Atlanta Journal*, June 28, 1972; *Statesboro Herald*, April 12, 1972; *Atlanta Constitution*, July 18, 1972; *Atlanta Journal-Constitution*, July 30, 1972.

45. Announcement Speech—February 16, 1972 folder, Vandiver Papers; *Atlanta Journal*, January 19, 1972.

46. "Ernest Vandiver Faces the Issues" newsletter in Regulation of Advertising folder, Subject File, U.S. Senate 1972, Campaigns, Vandiver Papers; "Ernest Vandiver's Position on Law and Order," Position Papers folder, Subject File, U.S. Senate 1972, Campaigns, Vandiver Papers; Atlanta Press Club Speech—December 7, 1971, folder, Speeches and Press Releases, U.S. Senate 1972, Campaigns, Vandiver Papers; Announcement Speech—February 16, 1972, folder, Vandiver Papers.

47. Announcement Speech—February 16, 1972, folder, Vandiver Papers; Atlanta Press Club Speech December 7, 1971, folder, Speeches and Press Releases, U.S. Senate 1972, Campaigns, Vandiver Papers; *Waycross Journal-Herald*, April 15, 1972; *Savannah Morning News*, November 11, 1972; Announcement Speech—February 16, 1972, folder, Vandiver Papers; *Atlanta Constitution*, July 28, 1972.

48. "Ernest Vandiver's Position on Welfare," Position Papers folder, Subject File, U.S. Senate 1972, Campaigns, Vandiver Papers; Sons of the American Revolution Speech—February 26, 1972, folder, Speeches and Press Releases, U.S. Senate 1972, Campaigns, Vandiver Papers.

49. Big Government Speech folder, Speeches and Press Releases, U.S. Senate 1972, Campaigns, Vandiver Papers; Vanwagon News folder, Announcements, Platform, Speaking Schedule, U.S. Senate 1972, Campaigns, Vandiver Papers.

50. Hire Me Speech folder, Speeches and Press Releases, U.S. Senate 1972, Campaigns, Vandiver Papers; *Gwinnett Daily News*, January 18, 1972, and November 12, 1972; *Rome News-Tribune* editorial reprinted in *Atlanta Constitution*, August 5, 1972; *Macon Telegraph and News*, June 25, 1972.

51. "Ernest Vandiver Faces the Issues" newsletter, Vandiver Papers; *Atlanta Constitution,* May 25 and July 29, 1972; Vickers Neugent to Vandiver, February 18, 1972, Atkinson County folder, Vandiver to Henry S. Bishop, February 17, 1972, Bacon County folder, Stanley N. Collins Jr. to Vandiver, February 14, 1972, Dekalb County folder, Correspondence by Counties, U.S. Senate 1972, Campaigns, Vandiver Papers; *Atlanta Journal,* August 1, 1972.

52. Department of Archives and History, Edna Lackey, comp., *Georgia's Official and Statistical Register, 1971–1972,* 1634, 1640; Vandiver, OH Vandiver 4F, p. 43; *Atlanta Constitution,* August 9, 1972; Bartley and Graham, *Southern Elections,* 115. Voters had to vote for a candidate to complete Senator Russell's unexpired term and for a candidate to serve a full six-year term. Bartley and Graham used the results of the vote for a candidate to complete Senator Russell's unexpired term in their tabulations.

53. Vandiver, OH Vandiver 4F, pp. 30–31; Vandiver interview by Pyles, 67.

54. Vandiver, OH Vandiver 4F, pp. 37, 40, 38; Geer, OH Vandiver 5A, pp. 50–52; Vandiver, OH Vandiver 4F, p. 39; Betty Vandiver, OH Vandiver 13C, pp. 41–42.

55. Vandiver, OH Vandiver 4F, p. 39; Chip Vandiver, OH Vandiver 16A, pp. 13–23.

56. Vandiver, OH Vandiver 4F, pp. 40–44; Owen, OH Vandiver 21B, pp. 15–16; Bell, OH Vandiver 7, p. 49; Chip Vandiver, OH Vandiver 16A, p. 17.

57. Vandiver, OH Vandiver 4F, pp. 41–42.

58. Ibid., pp. 42–43; Betty Vandiver, OH Vandiver 13C, p. 43; Dunlap, OH Vandiver 17, p. 30; Betty Vandiver, OH Vandiver 13C, p. 43; Vandiver, OH Vandiver 1C, p. 29; *Atlanta Constitution,* August 10, 1972; Dunlap, OH Vandiver 5A, p. 52; Neal, OH Vandiver 9, pp. 33–34; Jones, OH Vandiver 27, p. 38; William R. Hamilton and Staff, *A Survey of Public Opinion in Georgia, Prepared for Senator David Gambrell, Part 1, Job 312, July 1972,* Surveys of Georgia Politics, Politics, Herman E. Talmadge Collection, Russell Library; Talmadge, OH Vandiver 2, p. 15; Sanders, OH Vandiver 3, p. 19.

59. Vandiver interview by Pyles, 69; Vandiver, OH Vandiver 4F, pp. 30–31; Department of Archives and History, Edna Lackey, comp., *Georgia Official and Statistical Register, 1971–1972,* 1745, 1841.

60. Vandiver, OH Vandiver 4I, pp. 1–2.

61. Ibid., p. 2.

62. Ibid., 4–5.

63. Vandiver, OH Vandiver 1C, p. 29; Samuel Ernest "Chip" Vandiver III, OH Vandiver 16A, pp. 24–25.

FOURTEEN. A Solid Sort of Fellow

1. George Dekle Busbee, OH Vandiver 23, p.15; George Thornewell Smith, OH Vandiver 22, p. 20; Hyatt, *Zell,* 262.

2. William Redding Bowdoin, OH Vandiver 18, p. 19; Carl Edward Sanders, OH Vandiver 3, p. 1; Henry Getzen Neal, OH Vandiver 9, p. 20; Herman Eugene Talmadge, OH

Vandiver 2, p. 9; Robert Howell Hall, OH Vandiver 28, pp. 21–22; Homer Meade Rankin, OH Vandiver 12, p. 30; Samuel Freeman Leverett, OH Vandiver 8, p. 25; Bowdoin, *Georgia's Third Force Thoughts and Comments on the People of Georgia and Their Government,* 11.

3. Talmadge, OH Vandiver 2, p. 10; Sanders, OH Vandiver 3, p. 4; Garland Turk Byrd, OH Vandiver 11, p. 27; Robert Claude Norman, OH Vandiver 25, p. 28; James Coleman Owen Jr., OH Vandiver 21B, p. 11; Busbee, OH Vandiver 23, pp. 16–17, 19; Smith, OH Vandiver 22, p. 21.

4. Vandiver, OH Vandiver 4G, pp. 13, 16; Talmadge, OH Vandiver 2, p. 10; Sanders, OH Vandiver 3, p. 4; Peter Zack Geer Jr., OH Vandiver 5B, p. 1; Ralph E. McGill to Robert F. Kennedy, January 5, 1961, McGill Papers.

5. Pou, "Epilogue," 45; Norman, OH Vandiver 25, p. 29; DeNean Stafford Jr., OH Vandiver 24, p. 13; Busbee, OH Vandiver 23, pp. 18–19; Owen, OH Vandiver 21B, pp. 12–13; William Donaldson Ballard, OH Vandiver 30B, p. 7.

6. Smith, OH Vandiver 22, p. 23; Hall, OH Vandiver 28, p. 24; Sybil Elizabeth "Betty" Vandiver, OH Vandiver 13C, p. 24; Griffin Boyette Bell, OH Vandiver 7, p. 47; David Campbell Jones, OH Vandiver 27, p. 35; Leverett, OH Vandiver 8, p. 28.

7. Talmadge, OH Vandiver 2, p. 12; Geer, OH Vandiver 5A, p. 28; James Anderson Dunlap, OH Vandiver 17, p. 24; Glenn Wilson Ellard, OH Vandiver 29, p. 28; Byrd, OH Vandiver 11, p. 26; Bell, OH Vandiver 7, p. 44; Chip Vandiver, OH Vandiver 16A, p. 18; William Lovel Lanier Sr., OH Vandiver 26A, p. 20.

8. Leverett, OH Vandiver 8, p. 30; Talmadge, OH Vandiver 2, p. 10; Lanier, OH Vandiver 26B, pp. 4–5; Byrd, OH Vandiver 11, p. 29; Neal, OH Vandiver 9, p. 29.

9. Smith, OH Vandiver 22, pp. 23–24; Ballard, OH Vandiver 30B, pp. 5–6; Betty Vandiver, OH Vandiver 13C, pp. 45–46; Samuel Ernest "Chip" Vandiver III, OH Vandiver 16A, p. 7; Bowdoin, OH Vandiver 18, pp. 23–24; Robert Grier Stephens, OH Vandiver 31, p. 21.

10. Vandiver, OH Vandiver 4A, p. 4; Jane Brevard Vandiver Kidd, OH Vandiver 14, p. 1; Vanna Elizabeth "Beth" Vandiver, OH Vandiver 15, p. 1; Chip Vandiver, OH Vandiver 16A, p. 1; Neal, OH Vandiver 9, p. 23; Geer, OH Vandiver 5A, p. 49; Owen, OH Vandiver 21B, p. 16; Smith, OH Vandiver 22, p. 27; Lanier, OH Vandiver 26A, p. 5; Jones, OH Vandiver 27, p. 34; McGill to Robert Kennedy, January 5, 1961, McGill Papers; Cook, *Governors of Georgia,* 279.

11. Vandiver, OH Vandiver 4F, pp. 15–16.

12. Vandiver, OH Vandiver 4B, pp. 42–43; Vandiver, OH Vandiver 4C, pp. 11, 20–21; Betty Vandiver, OH Vandiver 13C, p. 21; Vandiver to Dick Mendenhall, September 18, 1963, Personal Correspondence August–September 1963 folder, Personal Correspondence, Legal Office Files 1963–66, Vandiver Papers.

13. Betty Vandiver, OH Vandiver 13B, pp. 11, 28; Betty Vandiver, OH Vandiver 13C, p. 23; Jane Kidd, OH Vandiver 14, p. 3; Smith, OH Vandiver 22, p. 21; Vandiver, OH Vandiver 4G, p. 15.

14. Lemmon, "Ideology of Eugene Talmadge," 226–28, 248: Lemmon, "Public Ca-

reer of Eugene Talmadge," 156–244; Anderson, *Wild Man from Sugar Creek,* 200, 229–30, 237–38; Herdon, "Eurith Dickinson Rivers," 391–93, 252–89, 399–404; Henderson, *Politics of Change in Georgia,* 97–115.

15. Pajari, "Talmadge and the Politics of Power," 81–84; Dubay, "Marvin Griffin and the Politics of the Stump," 107–8.

16. Cook, *Carl Sanders,* 96, 159–160.

17. Bartley, *From Thurmond to Wallace,* 24; Herdon, "Eurith Dickinson Rivers," 390–91; Henderson, *Ellis Arnall,* 49, 249–51; Vandiver, OH Vandiver 4I, p. 5.

18. Martin, *Ralph McGill, Reporter,* 151–54.

19. Bartley, *New South,* 226–30; Pou, "Epilogue," 45; *Atlanta Journal,* June 10, 1959; Mertz, "Mind Changing Time," 44–45; Bartley, *Rise of Massive Resistance,* 320–27.

20. Bartley, *Rise of Massive Resistance,* 332; Bartley, *New South,* 251–53.

21. Bass and DeVries, *Transformation of Southern Politics,* 199–202; Woodward, *Strange Career of Jim Crow,* 175.

22. Carter, *Politics of Rage,* 105, 148–51.

23. Pierce, *Deep South States of America,* 393–94.

24. Vandiver, OH Vandiver 4G, p. 14; biographical information provided by Vandiver; Cook, *Governors of Georgia,* 282.

BIBLIOGRAPHY

INTERVIEWS

By the author in the Samuel Ernest Vandiver, Jr. Oral History Collection at the Richard B. Russell Library for Political Research and Studies, University of Georgia Libraries, Athens

Akin, Louise Dixon. September 15, 1993.
Ballard, William Donaldson. July 28, 1994.
Bell, Griffin Boyette. December 8, 1993.
Bonner, William Hubert. March 19, 1994.
Bowdoin, William Redding. February 22, 1994.
Busbee, George Dekle. March 17, 1994.
Byrd, Garland Turk. December 6, 1993.
Dunlap, James Anderson. March 18, 1994.
Ellard, Glenn Wilson. July 29, 1994.
Embry, Douglas. March 16, 1994.
Geer, Peter Zack, Jr. November 3, 1994.
Griffin, Robert Alwyn. October 8, 1993.
Hall, Robert Howell. July 28, 1994.
Jones, David Campbell. July 22, 1994.
Kidd, Jane Brevard. February 27, 1994.
Lanier, William Lovel, Sr. July 21, 1994.
Leverett, Ernest Freeman. December 3, 1993.
Neal, Henry Getzen. November 23, 1993, and January 7, 1994.
Norman, Robert Claude. June 9, 1994.
Owen, James Coleman, Jr. March 16, 1994.

Rankin, Homer Meade. January 13, 1994.
Sanders, Carl Edward. September 3, 1993.
Smith, George Thornewell. March 23, 1994.
Stafford, DeNean, Jr. June 15, 1994.
Stephens, Robert Grier. July 29, 1994.
Talmadge, Herman Eugene. August 26, 1993.
Vandiver, Samuel Ernest, Jr. September 14, 15, 1993, and July 18, 1998.
Vandiver, Samuel Ernest, III. February 27, 1994.
Vandiver, Sybil Elizabeth. January 22, 1994.
Vandiver, Vanna Elizabeth. February 27, 1994.

By the author in the Harold Paulk Henderson, Sr. Oral History Collection at the Richard B. Russell Library for Political Research and Studies, University of Georgia Libraries, Athens

Arnall, Ellis Gibbs. May 6, 1981.
Callaway, Howard Hollis. Telephone interview, May 8, 1981.
Sanders, Carl Edward. June 11, 1981.
Vandiver, Samuel Ernest, Jr. May 23, 1981.

Other interviews by the author

Sanders, Carl Edward. Telephone interview, October 3, 1997.
Talmadge, Herman Eugene, June 26 and July 17, 1987. Georgia Government Documentation Project, Special Collections, William R. Pullen Library, Georgia State University, Atlanta.
Vandiver, Samuel Ernest, Jr. Telephone interview, October 26, 1997.

Other interviews

Bell, Griffin Boyette. Interview by Clifford M. Kuhn and William L. Bost, June 12, 1990. Georgia Government Documentation Project, Special Collections, William R. Pullen Library, Georgia State University, Atlanta.
Carter, James Earl, Jr. Interview by Kenneth J. Bindas, Melvin T. Steeley, and Kenneth W. Noe, May 4, 1993. Georgia Political Heritage Series, Special Collections, Irvin S. Ingrams Library, State University of West Georgia, Carrollton.
Groover, Denmark, Jr. Interview by James F. Cook, September 12, 1989. Georgia Government Documentation Project, Special Collections, William R. Pullen Library, Georgia State University, Atlanta.
Hartsfield, William Berry. Interview by Charles T. Morrissey, January 6, 1966, John F. Kennedy Oral History Program, John Fitzgerald Kennedy Library, Boston.
Kennedy, Robert Francis. Interview by Anthony Lewis, December 4, 1964, John F. Kennedy Oral History Program, John Fitzgerald Kennedy Library, Boston.
"Marvin Griffin Remembers." Interview by Gene-Gabriel Moore, June (n.d.) 1976. In

Georgia Governors in an Age of Change: From Ellis Arnall to George Busbee, edited by Harold P. Henderson and Gary L. Roberts, 131–39. Athens: University of Georgia Press, 1988.

Sanders, Carl Edward. Interview by James F. Cook, August 5, 12, 1986, Georgia Government Documentation Project, Special Collections, William R. Pullen Library, Georgia State University, Atlanta.

Smith, George Thornewell. Interview by Tom Chaffin, August 19, 20, 1992. Georgia Government Documentation Project, Special Collections, William R. Pullen Library, Georgia State University, Atlanta.

Vandiver, Samuel Ernest, Jr. Interview by Charles B. Pyles, April (n.d.) 1990. Georgia Government Documentation Project, Special Collections, William R. Pullen Library, Georgia State University, Atlanta.

———. Interview by Clifford M. Kuhn, January 25, 1994. Georgia Government Documentation Project, Special Collections, William R. Pullen Library, Georgia State University, Atlanta.

———. Interview by Hugh Cates, February 23, 1971. Richard B. Russell Oral History Collection, Richard B. Russell Library for Political Research and Studies, University of Georgia Libraries, Athens.

———. Interview by interviewer not given, June 23, 1987, "Dawn's Early Light: Ralph McGill and the Segregated South" Project Files, Ralph E. McGill Papers, Special Collections, Robert W. Woodruff Library, Emory University, Atlanta.

———. Interview by John F. Stewart, May 27, 1967. John F. Kennedy Oral History Program, John Fitzgerald Kennedy Library, Boston.

———. Interview by Karen Kelly, August 7, 1980. Russell Oral History Collection, Richard B. Russell Library for Political Research and Studies, University of Georgia Libraries, Athens.

———. Interview by Melvin T. Steeley and Theodore B. Fitz-Simmons, June 25, 1985. Georgia Political Heritage Series, Special Collections, Irvin S. Ingrams Library, State University of West Georgia, Carrollton.

SPECIAL COLLECTIONS

Griffin, S. Marvin. Papers. Bainbridge College Library, Bainbridge College, Bainbridge, Georgia.

Hartsfield, William B. Papers. Special Collections. Robert W. Woodruff Library, Emory University, Atlanta.

HOPE Papers. Southern Regional Council Records. Robert W. Woodruff Library, Clark Atlanta University, Atlanta.

Johnson, Lyndon Baines. Papers. Lyndon B. Johnson Library, Austin, Texas.

Kennedy, John Fitzgerald. Papers. John Fitzgerald Kennedy Library, Boston.

League of Women Voters Collection, Georgia Records, Georgia Department of Archives and History, Atlanta.

McGill, Ralph E. Papers. Special Collections. Robert W. Woodruff Library, Emory University, Atlanta.

OASIS Papers. Southern Regional Council Records. Clark Atlanta University.

Russell, Richard B., Jr. Collection. Richard B. Russell Library for Political Research and Studies, University of Georgia Libraries, Athens.

Sibley, John Adams. Papers. Special Collections. Robert W. Woodruff Library, Emory University, Atlanta.

Talmadge, Herman E. Collection. Richard B. Russell Library for Political Research and Studies Library, University of Georgia Libraries, Athens.

Vandiver, S. Ernest. Papers. Richard B. Russell Library for Political Research and Studies, University of Georgia Libraries, Athens.

OTHER SOURCES

Abrams, Morris B. *The Day Is Short: An Autobiograhy.* New York: Harcourt Brace Jovanovich, 1982.

Allen, Ivan, Jr., with Paul Hemphill. *Mayor: Notes on the Sixties.* New York: Simon and Schuster, 1971.

Anderson, William. *The Wild Man from Sugar Creek: The Political Career of Eugene Talmadge.* Baton Rogue: Louisiana State University, 1975.

Arnett, Alex M. *The Populist Movement in Georgia: A View of the "Agrarian Crusade" in the Light of Solid South Politics.* New York: Columbia University Press, 1922. Reprint, New York: AMS Press, 1967.

Bacote, Clarence A. "The Negro in Georgia Politics, 1880–1908." Ph.D. diss., University of Chicago, 1955.

Barnwell, Katherine. "How the Vandivers Live." *Atlanta Journal-Constitution Magazine,* January 4, 1959, 10 ff.

Bartley, Numan V. *The Creation of Modern Georgia.* Athens: University of Georgia Press, 1983.

———. *From Thurmond to Wallace: Political Tendencies in Georgia, 1948–1968.* Baltimore: Johns Hopkins University Press, 1970.

———. *The New South, 1945–1980.* Baton Rouge: Louisiana State University Press, 1995.

———. "Race Relations and the Quest for Equality." In *A History of Georgia,* general editor, Kenneth Coleman, 361–74. Athens: University of Georgia Press, 1977.

———. *The Rise of Massive Resistance: Race and Politics in the South in the 1950s.* Baton Rogue: Louisiana State University Press, 1969.

Bartley, Numan V., and Hugh D. Graham. *Southern Elections: County and Precinct Data, 1950–1972.* Baton Rouge: Louisiana State University Press, 1978.

Bass, Jack, and Walter DeVries. *The Transformation of Southern Politics: Social Changes and Political Consequences since 1945.* New York: Basic Books, 1976.

Bayer, Ronald H. *Race and the Shaping of Twentieth Century Atlanta.* Chapel Hill: University of North Carolina, 1996.

Bernd, Joseph L. "Corruption in Georgia Primaries and Elections, 1938–1950." Master's thesis, Boston University, 1953.

———. "Georgia: Static and Dynamic." In *The Changing Politics of the South,* edited by William C. Havard, 294–365. Baton Rouge: Louisiana State University Press, 1972.

——— *Grass Roots Politics in Georgia: The County Unit System and the Importance of the Individual Voting Community in Bifactional Elections, 1942–1954.* Atlanta: Emory University Research Committee, 1960.

———. "A Study of Primary Elections in Georgia, 1946–1954." Ph.D. diss., Duke University, 1957.

———. "White Supremacy and the Disfranchisement of Blacks in Georgia, 1946." *Georgia Historical Quarterly* 66 (Winter 1982): 492–513.

Beschloss, Michael R., ed. *Taking Charge: The Johnson White House Tapes, 1963–1964.* New York: Simon and Schuster, 1997.

Bolster, Paul. "Civil Rights Movements in Twentieth Century Georgia." Ph.D. diss., University of Georgia, 1972.

Boney, F. N. "The Politics of Expansion and Secession, 1820–1861." In *A History of Georgia,* general editor, Kenneth Coleman, 129–52. Athens: University of Georgia, 1977.

Bowdoin, William R. *Georgia's Third Force Thoughts and Comments on the People of Georgia and Their Government.* N.p.: Foote and Davies, Div. of McCalls, n.d.

Branch, Taylor. *Parting the Waters: America in the King Years, 1954–1963.* New York: Simon and Schuster, 1988.

Brooks, Robert P. *Georgia in 1950: A Survey of Financial and Economic Conditions.* Atlanta: Tax Revision Committee, n.d.

Bureau of Business Research, College of Business Administration, University of Georgia. *Georgia Statistical Abstract, 1955.* Athens: University of Georgia Press, 1955.

Carter, Dan T. *The Politics of Rage: George Wallace, the Origins of the New Conservatism, and the Transformation of American Politics.* New York: Simon and Schuster, 1995.

Carter, Jimmy. *Turning Point: A Candidate, a State, and a Nation Come of Age.* New York: Times Books, 1992.

Clark, Thomas D., and Albert D. Kirwan. *The South since Appomattox: A Century of Regional Change.* New York: Oxford University Press, 1967.

Coleman, Kenneth, general ed. *A History of Georgia.* Athens: University of Georgia, 1977.

Cook, James F. *Carl Sanders: Spokesman of the New South.* Macon, Ga.: Mercer University Press, 1993.

———. *Governors of Georgia.* Huntsville, Ala.: Strode Publishers, 1979.

Cosman, Berand. *Five States for Goldwater: Continuity and Change in Southern Presidential Voting Patterns.* University: University of Alabama Press, 1966.

Department of Archives and History. Edna Lackey, comp. *Georgia's Official and Statistical Register, 1971–1972.* Atlanta: HLM & P, n.d.

———. Mary G. Bryan, comp. *Georgia's Official Register, 1953–1954.* Hapeville, Ga.: Longino & Porter, n.d.

———. Mary G. Bryan, comp. *Georgia's Official Register, 1955–1956.* Hapeville, Ga.: Longino & Porter, n.d.

———. Mary G. Bryan, comp. *Georgia's Official Register, 1957–1958.* Hapeville, Ga.: Longino & Porter, n.d.

———. Mary G. Bryan, comp. *Georgia's Official Register, 1959–1960.* Hapeville, Ga.: Longino & Porter, n.d.

———. Mary G. Bryan, comp. *Georgia's Official Register, 1961–1962.* Hapeville, Ga.: Longino & Porter, n.d.

———. Mrs. J. E. Hayes, comp. *Georgia's Official Register, 1945–1950.* Hapeville, Ga.: Longino & Porter, n.d.

Department of Audits. *Report of the State Auditor of Georgia Year Ending June 30, 1958. Supplement.*

———. *Report of the State Auditor of Georgia Year Ending June 30, 1962. Supplement.*

———. *State Auditor's Report, Year Ending June 30,1958.*

———. *State Auditor's Report, Year Ending June 30, 1959.*

———. *State Auditor's Report, Year Ending June 30, 1962.*

Department of Education. *Eighty-eighth and Eighty-ninth Annual Reports of the Department of Education to the General Assembly of the State of Georgia for the Biennium Ending June 30, 1960.*

———. *Ninetieth and Ninety-first Annual Reports of the Department of Education to the General Assembly of the State of Georgia for the Biennium Ending June 30, 1962.*

———. *Ninety-second and Ninety-third Annual Reports of the Department of Education to the General Assembly of the State of Georgia for the Biennium Ending June 30, 1964.*

Department of Law. *Opinions of the Attorney General, 1960–61.* Complied by Benjamin F. Johnson and P. T. McCutchen Jr. Hapeville, Ga.: Longino & Porter, 1962.

Diamond, Robert A., ed. *Guide to U.S. Elections.* Washington: Congressional Quarterly, 1975.

Dubay, Robert W. "Marvin Griffin and the Politics of the Stump." In *Georgia Governors in an Age of Change: From Ellis Arnall to George Busbee,* edited by Harold P. Henderson and Gary L. Roberts, 101–12. Athens: University of Georgia Press, 1988.

Dyer, Thomas G. *The University of Georgia: A Bicentennial History, 1785–1985.* Athens: University of Georgia Press, 1985.

Executive Department. *A Report from S. Ernest Vandiver, of Lavonia, Seventy-third Governor of Georgia, to the People of Georgia, to Their Representatives in the General Assembly, and to the Nation Covering the First Three Years of the Administration, January, 1959 to January, 1962 Published January 10, 1962.*

Final Report by the Governor's Commission on Economy and Reorganization, December 28, 1959.

First Report, Joint Committee on Economy. Prepared for the Hon. S. Marvin Griffin, Governor, Members of the General Assembly, the Public.

Fite, Gilbert C. *Richard B. Russell, Jr., Senator from Georgia.* Chapel Hill: University of North Carolina Press, 1991.

————. "Richard Brevard Russell." *Dictionary of Georgia Biography,* edited by Kenneth Coleman and Charles S. Gurr, 2:859–60. Athens: University of Georgia Press, 1983.

Franklin County Historical Society. *History of Franklin County.* Roswell, Ga.: W. H. Woffe Associates, 1986.

Galphin, Bruce. *The Riddle of Lester Maddox.* Atlanta: Camelot Publishing Co., 1968.

General Assembly. *Acts and Resolutions of the General Assembly of the State of Georgia, 1955–1963.*

————. *Journals of the House of Representatives of the State of Georgia, 1955–1963.*

————. *Journals of the Senate of the State of Georgia, 1955–1963.*

————. "Meeting of the General Assembly Committee on Schools, Courtroom, Sumter County Courthouse, Americus, March 3, 1960." Sibley Papers.

————. *The Report of the General Assembly Committee on Schools, April 28, 1960.*

George, W. Elmer. "Executive Director's Report." *Georgia Municipal Magazine* (October 1962): 6.

Goldsmith, John A. *Richard B. Russell and His Apprentice, Lyndon B. Johnson.* Washington: Seven Locks Press, 1993.

Gosnell, Cullen B., and C. David Anderson. *The Government and Administration of Georgia.* New York: Thomas Y. Crowell Co., 1956.

Grant, Donald L. *The Way It Was in the South: The Black Experience in Georgia.* Edited by Jonathan Grant. New York: Carroll Publishing Group, 1993.

Grantham, Dewey W., Jr. "Georgia Politics and the Disfranchisement of the Negro." *Georgia Historical Quarterly* (March 1948): 1–21.

Griffin, Samuel M., Jr., and Roy F. Chalker, Sr. "S. Marvin Griffin: Georgia's 72nd Governor." In *Georgia Governors in an Age of Change: From Ellis Arnall to George Busbee,* edited by Harold P. Henderson and Gary L. Roberts, 113–30. Athens: University of Georgia, 1988.

Grimes, Millard, and Tom Barry. "Vandiver's Rendezvous with Destiny." *Georgia Trend* (October 1992): 48–52.

Henderson, Harold P. "Ellis Arnall and the Politics of Progress." In *Georgia Governors in an Age of Change: From Ellis Arnall to George Busbee,* edited by Harold P. Henderson and Gary L. Roberts, 25–39. Athens: University of Georgia Press, 1988.

————. "M. E. Thompson and the Politics of Succession." In *Georgia Governors in an Age of Change: From Ellis Arnall to George Busbee,* edited by Harold P. Henderson and Gary L. Roberts, 49–65. Athens: University of Georgia Press, 1988.

————. "The 1946 Gubernatorial Election in Georgia." Master's thesis, Georgia Southern University, 1967.

————. "The 1966 Gubernatorial Election in Georgia." Ph.D. diss., University of Southern Mississippi, 1982.

————. *The Politics of Change in Georgia: A Political Biography of Ellis Arnall.* Athens: University of Georgia Press, 1991.

Henderson, Harold P., and Gary L. Roberts, eds. *Georgia Governors in an Age of Change: From Ellis Arnall to George Busbee.* Athens: University of Georgia Press, 1988.

Herbert, Richard. *Highways to Nowhere: The Politics of City Transportation.* Indianapolis: Bobbs-Merrill Co., 1972.

Herdon, Jane W. "Eurith Dickenson Rivers: A Political Biography." Ph.D. diss., University of Georgia, 1974.

Hunter-Gault, Charlayne. *In My Place.* New York: Farrar Giroux, 1992.

Hyatt, Richard. *Zell: The Governor Who Gave Georgia HOPE.* Macon, Ga.: Mercer University Press, 1977.

Joiner, Oscar H., general ed. *A History of Public Education in Georgia, 1734–1976.* Columbia, S.C.: R. L. Bryan Co., 1979.

Key, V. O., Jr., with Alexander Heard. *Southern Politics in State and Nation.* New York: Alfred A. Knopf, 1949.

Kousser, J. Morgan. *The Shaping of Southern Politics: Suffrage Restriction and the Establishment of the One-Party South.* New Haven: Yale University Press, 1974.

Kuhn, Clifford M. "'There's a Footnote to History!': Memory and the History of Martin Luther King's October 1960 Arrest and Its Aftermath." *Journal of American History* 84 (September 1997): 583–95.

Lefkoff, Merle. "The Georgia County Unit Case: One Man—One Vote." Master's thesis, Emory University, 1965.

Lemmon, Sara M. "The Ideology of Eugene Talmadge." *Georgia Historical Quarterly* 38 (September 1954): 226–48.

————. "The Public Career of Eugene Talmadge, 1926–1946." Ph.D. diss., University of North Carolina, 1952.

Martin, Harold H. *Ralph McGill, Reporter.* Boston: Little, Brown, 1973.

Mathews, Donald R., and James W. Prothro. *Negroes and the New Southern Politics.* New York: Harcourt, Brace, and World, 1966.

McGrath, Susan M. "Great Expectations: The History of School Desegregation in Atlanta and Boston, 1954–1990." Ph.D. diss., Emory University, 1992.

Meadows, John C. *Modern Georgia.* Athens: University of Georgia Press, 1951.

Mellichamp, Josephine. *Senators from Georgia.* Huntsville, Ala.: Strode Publishers, 1976.

Melton, Thomas R. "The 1960 Presidential Election in Georgia." Ph.D. diss., University of Mississippi, 1985.

Mertz, Paul E. "Mind Changing Time All over Georgia: HOPE, Inc., and School Desegregation, 1958–1961." *Georgia Historical Quarterly* 77 (Spring 1983): 41–61.

Morris, Kenneth E. *Jimmy Carter: American Moralist.* Athens: University of Georgia Press, 1996.

Owen, Hugh C. "The Rise of Negro Voting in Georgia, 1944–1950." Master's thesis, Emory University, 1951.

Pajari, Roger N. "Herman E. Talmadge and the Politics of Power." In *Georgia Governors in an Age of Change: From Ellis Arnall to George Busbee,* edited by Harold P. Henderson and Gary L. Roberts, 75–92. Athens: University of Georgia, 1988.

Petersen, Svend. *A Statistical History of the American Presidential Elections.* New York: Frederick Unger Publishing Co., 1963.

Pierce, Neal R. *The Deep South States of America: People, Politics, and Power in the Seven Deep South States.* New York: W. W. Norton, 1974.

Pomerantz, Gary M. *Where Peachtree Street Meets Sweet Auburn: The Saga of Two Families and the Making of Atlanta.* New York: Scribner, 1996.

Pou, Charles. "Epilogue: The Vandiver Years." *Atlanta Magazine* (December 1962): 43 ff.

Public Papers of the Presidents of the United States John F. Kennedy Containing the Public Messages, Speeches, and Statements of the President, January 20 to December 31, 1961. Washington: U.S. Government Printing Office, 1962.

Pyles, Charles B. "Ernest Vandiver and the Politics of Change." In *Georgia Governors in an Age of Change: From Ellis Arnall to George Busbee,* edited by Harold P. Henderson and Gary L. Roberts. Athens: University of Georgia Press, 1988.

———. "Race and Ruralism in Georgia Elections, 1948–1966." Ph.D. diss., University of Georgia, 1967.

"Report to the Governor of the Medical Association of Georgia Committee Appointed by the President of the Association at the Request of the Governor to Study Milledgeville State Hospital, April 23, 1959." Milledgeville Hospital folder, Subjects, Governor's Office Files, 1959–62, Vandiver Papers.

Rigdon, Louis T., II. *Georgia's County Unit System.* Decatur, Ga.: Selective Books, 1961.

Roberts, Gary L. "Traditions and Consensus: An Introduction to Gubernatorial Leadership in Georgia, 1943–1983." In *Georgia Governors in an Age of Change: From Ellis Arnall to George Busbee,* edited by Harold P. Henderson and Gary L. Roberts, 1–21. Athens: University of Georgia, 1988.

Roche, Jeff. "A Reconstruction of Resistance: The Sibley Commission and the Politics of Desegregation in Georgia." Master's thesis, Georgia State University, 1995.

Sanders, Carl Edward, George Thornewell Smith, and Samuel Ernest Vandiver Jr. Bill Shipp, moderator. "Georgia Legends." Video Program #2, n.d. Georgia Public Policy Foundation, Atlanta.

Saye, Albert B. *A Constitutional History of Georgia, 1732–1968.* Rev. ed. Athens: University of Georgia Press, 1970.

Second Report, Joint Committee on Economy. Prepared for Hon. S. Marvin Griffin, Governor, Members of the General Assembly, the Public.

Seagull, Louis M. *Southern Republicanism.* New York: John Wiley and Sons, 1975.

Shadgett, Olive H. *The Republican Party in Georgia: From Reconstruction through 1900.* Athens: University of Georgia Press, 1964.

———. *Voter Registration in Georgia: A Study of Its Administration.* Athens: Bureau of Public Administration, University of Georgia, 1955.

Sherrill, Robert. *Gothic Politics in the Deep South: Stars of the New Confederacy.* New York: Ballantine Books, 1969.

Silverman, Peter H. "Horace T. Ward v. Board of Regents of the University System of Georgia: A Study in Segregation and Desegregation." Master's thesis, Emory University, 1970.

Smith, Charlotte H. "The Vandivers of Lavonia." *Atlanta Journal-Constitution Magazine*, August 23, 1964, 10–13.

Sorensen, Theodore C. "Election of 1960." In *History of American Presidential Elections, 1789–1968*, edited by Arthur M. Schlesinger Jr. New York: McGraw-Hill, 1971.

Sutton, William A., Jr. "The Talmadge Campaigns: A Sociological Analysis of Political Power." Ph.D. diss., University of North Carolina, 1952.

Talmadge, Herman E., with Mark R. Winchell. *Talmadge: A Political Legacy, a Politician's Life, a Memoir.* Atlanta: Peachtree Publishers, 1987.

Thompson, C. Mildred. *Reconstruction in Georgia: Economic, Social, and Political.* New York: Columbia University Press, 1915. Reprint, Savannah: Beehive Press, 1972.

Trillin, Calvin. *An Education in Georgia: Charlyne Hunter, Hamilton Holmes, and the Integration of the University of Georgia.* Athens: University of Georgia Press, 1991.

Turnbull, Augustus B., III. "Politics in the Budgetary Process: The Case of Georgia." Ph.D. diss., University of Georgia, 1967.

University System of Georgia. *1959 Annual Report University System of Georgia.*

———. *1963 Annual Report University System of Georgia.*

U.S. Bureau of the Census. *Census of Population: 1950, 1, Number of Inhabitants.* Washington: U.S. Government Printing Office, 1952.

———. *Census of Population: 1950, 2, Characteristics of the Population, Part 11, Georgia.* Washington: U.S. Government Printing Office, 1953.

———. *Census of Population: 1950, Characteristics of the Population, 2, United States Summary, Part 1.* Washington: U.S. Government Printing Office, 1953.

———. *Census of Population: 1960, 1, Characteristics of the Population, Part 12, Georgia.* Washington: U.S. Government Printing Office, 1963.

———. *Fifteenth Census of the United States, 1930, Population, 3, Part 1, Alabama-Missouri.* U.S. Government Printing Office, 1932.

———. *Historical Statistics of the United States: Colonial Times to 1970, Part 2.* Bicentennial ed. Washington: U.S. Government Printing Office, 1975.

———. *Statistical Abstract of the United States, 1952.* Washington: U.S. Government Printing Office, 1952.

———. *Statistical Abstract of the United States, 1953.* Washington: U.S. Government Printing Office, 1953.

———. *Tenth Census of the United States, 1880: Statistics of the Population of the United States.* U.S. Government Printing Office, 1883. Reprint, New York: Norman Ross Publishers, 1991.

U.S. Congress. House of Representatives. *Committee on the Judiciary, Miscellaneous Bills regarding the Civil Rights of Persons within the Jurisdiction of the United States: Hearings before a Subcommittee of the Committee of the Judiciary March 4, 5, 11, 12, 13, 18, 19; April 14, 15,16, 17, 22, 23, 24, 29, 30; May 1, 1959.*

————. Senate. *Committee on the Judiciary, Constitutional Amendment Reserving State Control over Public Schools: Hearings before a Subcommittee of the Committee on the Judiciary, 86th Cong., 1st Sess., 12, 13, 14, 15, and 21 May 1959.*

Vandiver, Ernest, Jr. "A Big Day for Towns and Cities." *Georgia Municipal Journal* (October 1962): 7–8.

Vandiver, Samuel Ernest, Jr. "Vandiver Takes the Middle Road." In *Georgia Governors in an Age of Change: From Ellis Arnall to George Busbee,* edited by Harold P. Henderson and Gary L. Roberts, 157–66. Athens: University of Georgia Press, 1988.

Velie, Lester. "Strange Case of the County Slickers vs. the City Rubes." *Reader's Digest* (April 1960): 108–12.

Williams, Marie H. *Lavonia, Gem of the Piedmont.* Hartwell, Ga.: Hurley Printing Co., 1977.

Wilkinson, J. Harvie, III. *Harry Byrd and the Changing Face of Virginia Politics, 1945–1966.* Charlottesville: University Press of Virginia, 1968.

Williamson, Matt W. "Contemporary Tendencies towards a Two-Party System in Georgia." Ph.D. diss., University of Virginia, 1969.

Wofford, Harris. *Of Kennedys and Kings: Making Sense out of the Sixties.* Pittsburgh: University of Pittsburgh Press, 1980.

Woodward, C. Vann. *Origins of the New South, 1877–1913.* Baton Rouge: Louisiana State University Press, 1951.

————. *The Strange Career of Jim Crow.* 3d rev. ed. New York: Oxford University Press, 1974.

————. *Tom Watson: Agrarian Rebel.* New York: Macmilliam, 1938. Reprint, New York: Oxford University Press, 1963.

Wynes, Charles E. "Education, Life, and Culture." In *A History of Georgia,* general editor, Kenneth Coleman, 238–54. Athens: University of Georgia, 1977.

INDEX